FOR THE COMMON GOOD

A volume in the series
American Institutions and Society
Edited by Brian Balogh and Jonathan Zimmerman

A full list of titles in the series is available at www.cornellpress.cornell.edu.

FOR THE COMMON GOOD

A New History of Higher
Education in America

Charles Dorn

CORNELL UNIVERSITY PRESS ITHACA AND LONDON

First published 2017 by Cornell University Press
Printed in the United States of America

Library of Congress Cataloging-in-Publication Data

Names: Dorn, Charles, author.
Title: For the common good : a new history of higher education in America / Charles Dorn.
Description: Ithaca : Cornell University Press, 2017. | Includes bibliographical references and index.
Identifiers: LCCN 2016052777 (print) | LCCN 2016054349 (ebook) | ISBN 9780801452345 (cloth : alk. paper) | ISBN 9781501712609 (epub/mobi) | ISBN 9781501712616 (pdf)
Subjects: LCSH: Education, Higher—United States—History. | Universities and colleges—United States—History.
Classification: LCC LA226 .D67 2017 (print) | LCC LA226 (ebook) | DDC 378.73—dc23
LC record available at https://lccn.loc.gov/2016052777

Cornell University Press strives to use environmentally responsible suppliers and materials to the fullest extent possible in the publishing of its books. Such materials include vegetable-based, low-VOC inks and acid-free papers that are recycled, totally chlorine-free, or partly composed of nonwood fibers. For further information, visit our website at www.cornellpress.cornell.edu.

For Niles

**We are compelled to readjust our viewpoint—
to learn how to work together for common ends
and for the common good.**

—Stanford University President Ray Lyman Wilbur, 1916

Contents

Acknowledgments

I am extremely grateful to many friends, family members, students, and colleagues who supported me throughout the time I worked on this project. Although its faults are my own, the book would not exist had it not been for their contributions. I am also thankful for the very generous research travel and sabbatical support that Bowdoin College and the Spencer Foundation have provided over the past several years.

Many Bowdoin College students participated in the book's development. I especially appreciate the helpful comments I received on drafts of the manuscript from students in my history of higher education courses. In addition, Kate Berkley, Georgia Nowers, Molly Porcher, Erin St. Peter, Serena Taj, Anna Williams, and particularly Ryan Szantyr assisted in tracking down citations, proofing text, editing footnotes, and making multiple trips to the library. I thank them for their diligence and patience.

My research benefited overwhelmingly from the assistance of a talented group of college and university librarians and archivists. Listed according to the order in which their respective institutions appear in the book's chapters, they are: Ginny Hopcroft, Caroline Moseley, Guy Saldanha, Graham Duncan, Patrick Scott, Elizabeth West, Lynn Conway, Ann Galloway, Ed Busch, Cynthia Ghering, Rebecca Kohn, Danelle Moon, Daniel Hartwig, Maggie Kimball, Karen Kukil, Nanci Young, Teddy Abebe, Clifford Muse, Andy Huse, John Collins, Briana Fiandt, and Robin Potter.

Fellow scholars, particularly members of the History of Education Society, kindly agreed to read early versions of chapters and provide critical input. Many also gave of their time to discuss the project as it developed. Special thanks to Barbara Beatty, Connie Chiang, Linda Eisenmann, Scott Gelber, Nancy Jennings, Peter Kallaway, Matt Klingle, Kathy Luckett, Maggie Nash, Chris Ogren, Dan Perlstein, Julie Reuben, Doris Santoro, Rob Siebörger, Kim Tolley, and Wayne Urban. A smaller group of colleagues not only encouraged me at crucial moments when the project felt as if it were grinding to a halt, but also read the entire manuscript (some, more than once) and offered thoughtful suggestions. Thank you David Hecht, Chris Loss, Hilary Moss, Brian Purnell, and Rob Sobak.

As series coeditor, Jonathan Zimmerman shepherded this book through multiple revisions, reading each chapter many times and providing constructive feedback combined with detailed recommendations. When I hit the wall at mile twenty, he was the person who kept the project moving. Jon, I am deeply indebted to you.

I am blessed to have many friends who have been sources of support, advice, and inspiration over the years. My heartfelt thanks to all of them, especially Jim Adolf, Michele LaForge, Jen Scanlon, Michael Arthur, Sarah and Peter Chingos, Karen Topp, Thomas Baumgarte, Hadley and Fred Horch, Janice Jaffe, Jim Higginbotham, Doris Santoro, Kent Koth, Ling Yeh, Melanie and Peter Rand, Alec Morrison, Jayne Oh, Randy Curren, and Brianne and Drew Weaver.

I am especially grateful to my family for their unwavering love—my parents, Mary Ann and LeRoy; my wife, Susie; and her parents, Kay and Charlie. Thanks also to Richard, Carol, Bruce, and Sandy for their kind generosity. I dedicated my dissertation to Susie and my first book to my parents and in-laws. This book, I have been working on for a full half of my son's life. Although I'm delighted for it to be in print, I can't help but regret the many hours that research and writing took away from my being with him. Be that as it may, time marches on and he has become a compassionate, respectful, and thoughtful young man. Niles, I dedicate this book to you.

FOR THE COMMON GOOD

Prologue

Higher education in America is against the ropes. Almost weekly, a new book is published, a report released, an address delivered, or a documentary premiered declaring colleges and universities to be in a state of crisis. To some critics, these institutions are no better than playgrounds, coddling students for four, five, even six years before sending them into the real world, adrift with few skills or job prospects.[1] To others, these same colleges and universities have bent too far in a different direction—they have become too modern, too accommodating, so enamored of emerging thought as to follow each academic fad. They forgo the classics in favor of lightweight and trendy subjects, leaving graduates wanting for the fundamentals of a liberal education. Still other critics believe that the problem with these institutions is not what they teach but whom they enroll: poor and middle-class students are being squeezed out of higher education, they assert, leaving colleges with an ever-shrinking educated elite who enjoy exclusive access to some of the world's best professional and cultural opportunities. And while these divergent opinions come from across the political spectrum, all seem to agree that American higher education has simply become unaffordable, as colleges and universities cling to an inefficient and unsustainable financial model. From the editorial boardroom to the kitchen table, Americans are asking: How has a college education become so expensive and yet so deficient?

Are the critics right? Have colleges and universities become frivolous, inaccessible, ineffective, and overpriced? Is higher education no longer worth the investment? Might college, as one critic has recently asserted, be coming to an end?[2]

The answers depend, in large part, on what we compare contemporary higher education to. Before observers can justly accuse colleges and universities of having become unresponsive to the demands of their stakeholders, they should know to what extent these institutions have responded over time to the inclinations of students, parents, trustees, government officials, corporations, donors, and a range of other interested groups. Likewise, they cannot legitimately criticize them for being inaccessible without understanding who has—and has not—gained entry to the wide variety of higher-education institutions established in the United States over the past two centuries. In short, we can't know why higher education functions as it does in the present without fully comprehending what it was in the past.

This book resolves that problem.

For the Common Good examines more than two hundred years of American higher education, beginning with the late eighteenth century and ending with the turn of the twenty-first. Providing a comprehensive historical analysis through which to assess higher education's current strengths and shortcomings, the book also engages a fundamental question with which colleges and universities have been grappling since the nation's founding: How does higher education contribute to the common good?

Over time, as Americans established colleges and universities across the nation, they stridently declared these institutions' commitment to advancing the public good. At the beginning of the nineteenth century, for instance, South Carolina's governor announced the establishment of a state-supported college in the capital city, Columbia, in order to foster "the good order and the harmony of the whole community."[3] Just months later and over a thousand miles north, in the town of Brunswick in the present-day state of Maine, Bowdoin College's first president proclaimed that "literary institutions" were "founded and endowed for the common good, and not for the private advantage of those who resort to them for education."[4] Meanwhile, the clergy who founded the United States' first Roman Catholic college—Georgetown—and located it near the nation's future capital, maintained that the purpose of their institution was "to promote more effectually the grand interests of society."[5]

And so it continued. Decade after decade, as a wide range of institutions opened their doors to an array of students, they proclaimed promoting the common good as a principal aim. Yet as distinguishing an institutional mission as this has been, we know surprisingly little about how colleges and universities have achieved it over time, if at all.[6]

This book takes a new approach to informing our understanding of American higher education. It investigates the founding decades of eleven very different colleges and universities and explains how these institutions' characteristics both reflected and responded to changes in American society. In doing so, it answers key questions such as: Why did colleges and universities extol promoting the public good as a central purpose? How did higher-education leaders articulate this objective? What forces influenced its adoption? How did policies and curricula evolve to help schools achieve it? How did students respond, if at all, to assertions that they were obliged to use higher learning for the benefit of the public good? And, perhaps most importantly, what challenges have colleges and universities confronted in maintaining this commitment?

For the Common Good illustrates the ways in which four socially widespread preferences and attitudes—civic-mindedness, practicality, commercialism, and affluence—proved influential in shaping US colleges and universities between the late eighteenth and early twenty-first centuries, especially their dedication to the common good.[7] Present in American society from early in the nation's history, each ethos came to predominate over the others during one of the four chronological periods examined here, informing the character of institutional debates and telling the definitive story of its time. This book, then, serves as a historical compass, distinguishing changes in higher education's orientation toward the nation's prevailing social ethos over the course of two centuries.

This book begins during the early national period, when widespread attitudes rewarding civic virtue and a dedication to the public good fostered an ethos of civic-mindedness.[8] "No phrase except 'liberty,'" historian Gordon S. Wood writes, "was invoked more often by the revolutionaries than the 'public good.' It expressed the colonists' deepest hatreds of the old order and their most visionary hopes for the new day."[9] Forged in the fire of revolution and imbued with reformed-Protestant social and moral norms, the common good "enjoyed preeminence over the immediate interests of individuals," according to political scientist Barry Shain. "Local communities catered little to the particular wants of individuals and the autonomous self was thought to be at the core of human sinfulness.... The priority of the public good was a value that eighteenth-century Americans did not question."[10]

As dominant as an ethos of civic-mindedness was during the early national period, the rise of an urban, industrial, class-stratified society soon began transforming the United States. Over the next two centuries, with citizens increasingly seeking private advantage in a more aggressively competitive environment, the individual slowly became preeminent. Consequently, social institutions' authority to influence human behavior weakened over time. As this occurred, many realigned their goals to parallel a growing societal disposition toward personal gain. This transformation involved the nation's social ethos reorienting away from civic-mindedness and toward practicality during the antebellum and Civil War eras, commercialism in the period from Reconstruction through the Second

World War, and affluence during the postwar era. In response, entirely new forms of higher education and, correspondingly, new institutional types arose in the United States. Beginning with the all-male denominational college, higher education expanded to include agricultural and "normal" schools, women's colleges and Historically Black institutions, and research universities and junior colleges. Indeed, what we conveniently call "higher education" today is in actuality a composite of institutional types that developed over the course of two hundred years.

Yet throughout this time, amidst dramatic institutional reform and adaptation, American higher education remained committed to the public good. The form this commitment took surely changed over the years and college and university officials undoubtedly employed the rhetoric of the public interest while simultaneously advancing policies and practices that did little to advance it. Nevertheless, the archival record informing this study reveals a broad array of higher-education institutions demonstrating a continuing dedication to the common good even while broader social, political, and economic forces undermined, if not directly opposed, that aim.

In the Shadow of Laurence Veysey

In 2015, education writer Kevin Carey published a biographical essay in *The Chronicle of Higher Education* under the title "Meet the Man Who Wrote the Greatest Book about American Higher Ed."[11] The man was the late Laurence Veysey, a long-time professor at the University of California, Santa Cruz. Although Carey surprised some readers with his depiction of an elderly Veysey living out his years as a tattooed nudist in Hawaii, the essay underlined something quite remarkable in the annals of American scholarship: that the volume that continues to assert the greatest interpretive influence in the field of higher-education history was published over fifty years ago.

In *The Emergence of the American University*, Veysey offered a broad interpretation of what he claimed were revolutionary changes that transformed higher education between the years 1865 and 1910.[12] Published in 1965, the book compelled scholars to reconceptualize college and university history by offering competing purposes for American higher education in the decades following the Civil War: "discipline and piety" (which Veysey ascribed to the classical colleges) and "utility," "research," and "culture" (which he associated with the university). This landmark work effectively moved the field of higher-education history away from its parochial origins. Prior to Veysey, much scholarship on colleges and universities took the form of celebratory studies that were descriptive rather than analytical and asserted close alignment among institutional mission, administrative efforts, and curricular and cocurricular programming. Most of these accounts were written about single institutions; some were called "house histories" because an employee of the featured college or university authored the work. Laurence Veysey turned that model of scholarship on its head, comparing and contrasting institutions in ways that demonstrated higher education as incorporating multiple and sometimes conflicting ambitions. The book became required reading on college and university syllabi as well as a standard entry on graduate student oral examination lists, leading future scholars to adopt it as a touchstone in their own intellectual development. Furthermore, *The Emergence of the American University* inhibited potential scholars from writing on the subject, at least in part because Veysey's work dominated the field for decades. As historian Julie Reuben has observed, only somewhat facetiously, "Why write when Veysey has already said anything that could be possibly said?"[13]

As with much higher-education scholarship published over the last fifty years, *For the Common Good* owes Laurence Veysey a debt of gratitude. Yet a half-century following the appearance of *The Emergence of the American University*, the book you now hold—the first comprehensive historical analysis of higher education published since Veysey's that is both thesis-driven and grounded in original archival research—also seeks to bring the field of higher education out from under his shadow.

Although Veysey's work was authentically groundbreaking, scholars increasingly concur that it was limited in fundamental ways, both interpretively and methodologically. Reuben, for instance, notes that the three categories making up Veysey's conceptual framework for the university's growth were anachronistic. "In the late nineteenth century," she writes, "no university reformer thought of seeking one rather than another. Only from the perspective of the twentieth-century rejection of the ideal of unity do these seem to be three separate goals of education."[14] Moreover, Veysey's focus on relatively elite universities during the period from Reconstruction through the Progressive Era resulted in his slighting, if not completely disregarding, entire segments of American higher education. He wrote little about women's colleges and Historically Black universities, for instance, although his period of analysis was one of significant growth for both. He also characterized the "old-time" liberal-arts college as fixed and inert. Borrowing a well-established interpretation anchored in university-boosters' claims, Veysey used the collegiate ideal as a kind of historical straw man against which to compare the spirited birth of the university. As a number of scholars have since demonstrated, however, classical colleges were capable of significant institutional adaptation, with many modifying courses of study and expanding extracurricular programs in ways that rivaled the emerging universities.[15]

Equally important, because Veysey wrote during the early 1960s about an era that had ended fifty years earlier, *The Emergence of the American University* is silent on higher education's transformation in the decades following World War II. From the standpoint of the twenty-first century, this period, characterized as it was by skyrocketing student enrollments, massive increases in expenditures, the remaking of the curriculum, and an unprecedented expansion of public colleges and universities, probably eclipses the so-called revolution Veysey described. A case in point: at the time he completed his manuscript, two-year junior and community college enrollments were growing faster than any segment of American higher education—ever.[16] In fact, student demand was so high that over the next four years, more than one new community college campus opened every week.[17]

Most significantly for the field of higher-education history, Veysey greatly underestimated the dynamic and pliable nature of American higher education. Although describing the university during its emergence as having a generous capacity for innovation and modernization, he characterized higher-education institutions prior to 1865 as static, if not torpid, and claimed that the university's evolution came to an end as early as the first decade of the following century. "By 1910," he wrote, "the structure of the American university had assumed its stable twentieth-century form," adding provocatively, "Few new ideas have been advanced on the purpose of higher education since 1900, and there have been few deviations in its basic pattern of organization."[18]

In dramatic contrast, *For the Common Good* offers a new historical interpretation, one that reveals American higher education both prior to and following the university's establishment engaged in a continual process of institutional modification, revision, and renewal. With the prevailing social ethos reflecting the political, economic, and social changes that prompted transformation among existing colleges and universities—as well as the establishment of entirely new kinds of institutions—higher education in the United States was refashioned over time in essential and often vibrant ways.

This book investigates a wide range of institutional types, including public, private, parochial, single-sex, coeducational, racially segregated, racially integrated, and two- as well as four-year colleges and universities. It focuses on eleven institutions established over the course of two centuries and represents the major regions of the mainland United States. Of course, none of these colleges and universities are representative of all higher-education institutions at any moment in time; they are illustrative only. Yet thoughtfully chosen cases can inform our understanding of decisive periods in the history of higher education. To that end, this volume offers instructive insight into the ways that changes in the nation's prevailing social ethos fostered new visions of what higher education could, and should, accomplish. This process continues today as a dominant ethos of affluence compels colleges and universities to again reconsider their aims and methods.

Higher Education and the Common Good

In the modern day, according to economist Henry Levin, the term "common good" has become closely associated with seventeenth-century British philosopher John Locke, who devoted his *Second Treatise* on government to the concept and its implications. Locke argued that by entering into a social contract, people sacrifice some liberties to acquire the protection of a broader set of rights and freedoms. A society comprising individuals united by a shared or common good, Locke observed, guarantees rights that would not exist in a "pre-social" setting.[19] Accordingly, the notion of the common good has often been applied to the development of educational systems and institutions. Beyond the private advantages one may reap by acquiring an education, including knowledge and understanding, as well as increased social status and income, Levin notes that society benefits from "the forging of a population with a common language, civic behavior, economic participation, means of resolving disputes, participation in legal and political institutions, and so on."[20] In other words, as individuals gain from becoming educated, so does the broader society in which they live.

During the early national period, a social ethos of civic-mindedness informed higher education's dedication to the common good. Bowdoin, South Carolina, and Georgetown Colleges, for instance, derived their central aims from civic-mindedness while simultaneously seeking to cultivate it among students. Adopting a classical curriculum, pedagogical methods such as memorization and recitation, and codes of conduct designed to severely regulate student behavior, the three colleges sought to inculcate mental discipline and integrity. College officials expected that students would, consequently, become virtuous members of the liberal professions and contribute to the stability and maintenance of the new republic.

While sharing overarching similarities, the three colleges also differed in important ways. Bowdoin, although affiliated with the Congregational Church, struggled to obtain the resources necessary to become financially secure during its first decade. Chartered in 1794 by the General Court of Massachusetts, it did not open its doors to students until eight years later. Alternatively, South Carolina College (the present-day University of South Carolina) was the first state-sponsored higher-education institution in the United States to receive ample political and financial support. With Governor John Drayton championing the college's founding and the state's General Assembly providing a generous appropriation, the institution opened in less than half the time it took Bowdoin.

The founding of Georgetown College (present-day Georgetown University) in 1788 predated that of both Bowdoin and South Carolina Colleges. Yet the Roman Catholic priests who established it as their first higher-education institution in America failed to obtain any legislative approval to operate until the US Congress granted it the nation's first federal charter in 1815.

Ultimately all three colleges prospered. Yet no sooner had they become firmly established than changes to America's political economy began reorienting its social ethos away from civic-mindedness and toward practicality. With the growth of economic development in industry and commerce "reshaping American culture," as historian Jack Lane describes, "winds of cultural change . . . brought challenges to the traditional concept of liberal education."[21] During the antebellum and Civil War eras, a social ethos of practicality was institutionalized through the creation of colleges and universities devoted to the study of agriculture, mechanics, mining, and the military (later abbreviated as "A&M"), as well as teacher training.

Established in 1855 as the first four-year college in America to teach "scientific agriculture," the Agricultural College of the State of Michigan (present-day Michigan State University) provided a prototype for what became the nation's land-grant universities. Although the state had founded a university as early as 1817, it established its "agricultural school" in the decade prior to the Civil War to generate increased agricultural productivity through experimental research as well as to provide greater access to higher learning for the sons of farmers. When US Representative Justin Morrill sought a model on which to base the land-grant act that would bear his name, he looked to Michigan. Practicality also catalyzed the creation of "normal schools" dedicated to teacher training. In 1862, the California legislature founded the California State Normal School (present-day San José State University) as the first public higher-education institution on the West Coast. Women students especially benefited by gaining access to a form of postsecondary education they would not otherwise have had. The same social ethos of practicality that led to the democratic expansion of higher education also privileged the nation's economic growth over its political and social development, effectively diminishing the obligation that colleges had earlier ascribed to students to advance the public good through their life pursuits. Consequently, the tension between students' use of higher education as a mechanism for personal advancement and as a means to foster the common good intensified. The field of teacher education provided a vivid example. Women who hoped to become teachers through normal-school training prized the salary—and the promise of independence—such work provided, yet they also believed they might better society by educating the rising generations.

Even as practicality achieved preeminence, the transformation of society resulting from political, economic, and social upheaval accompanying the Civil

War began reorienting higher education toward a social ethos of commercialism. From Reconstruction through the Second World War, commercialism reflected what historian Alan Trachtenberg calls the "influence of corporate life" on America. "Any account of that influence," he explains, "must include subtle shifts in the meaning of prevalent ideas, ideas regarding the identity of the individual, the relation between public and private realms, and the character of the nation."[22] That is to say, although commercialism continued to emphasize the nation's economic growth, it also promoted private advantage as a deserved and rightful goal. In keeping with this ethos, colleges and universities began to embrace students' personal success as an institutional priority.

When Leland and Jane Stanford, who personified the rise of commercialism through their remarkable accumulation of wealth, established a university in northern California in their son's memory (and granted it the largest endowment of any higher-education institution at that time), they distinguished between their university's purpose, which they stated was "to promote the public welfare," and its object, "to qualify students for personal success."[23] Believing that a university degree provided an advantage in obtaining employment in an increasingly competitive marketplace, Stanford students responded enthusiastically to the emphasis that commercialism placed on professional status and personal advancement.

While further reorienting higher education away from its dedication to the common good, commercialism nevertheless did not extinguish it. As Stanford's two-part mission suggests, colleges and universities established during the late nineteenth and early twentieth centuries maintained a commitment to the public good even as commercialism moved the nation in an opposing direction. The founders of Smith College, for instance, drew on an ethos of civic-mindedness to justify their institution's unique commitment to women's higher education. Similarly, Howard University, established during Reconstruction and dedicated to the higher education of emancipated people, harnessed the civic-minded ideal when it implemented a course of study modeled on the collegiate programs of institutions such as Bowdoin College. Both Smith and Howard further contributed to higher education's democratization by expanding access to higher learning to previously marginalized groups. Yet, as at Stanford, both Smith and Howard students found commercialism's emphasis on professional status and personal advancement enticing: it firmly influenced their reasons for enrolling as well as their postgraduate life trajectories.

As the twentieth century ushered in a period of economic expansion, collapse, and war, America's social ethos underwent a final reorientation, the one that continues to tell the definitive story of *our* time. As economist John Kenneth Galbraith described in his 1958 work *The Affluent Society*, US postwar prosperity, rather than satisfying Americans' needs and wants, had the paradoxical effect of creating an ever-greater consumer impulse. "Because the society sets great store by ability to produce a high living standard," Galbraith observed, "it evaluates people by the products they possess. The urge to consume is fathered by the value system, which emphasizes the ability of the society to produce. The more that is produced, the more that must be owned in order to maintain the appropriate prestige."[24]

A social ethos of affluence had profound consequences for higher education. With increasing numbers of Americans viewing a college degree as a ticket to the good life and the federal government providing the financing to enroll (through the GI Bill, Pell Grants, and subsidized student loans), higher-education participation exploded. Students increasingly sought a diploma for the occupational and financial benefits it promised, while colleges and universities, no less influenced by an ethos of affluence than the students they enrolled, sought institutional wealth and status in an increasingly competitive "higher-education marketplace."[25] Consequently, the final decades of the twentieth century witnessed a dramatic escalation in the tension between civic-mindedness as manifested in the ideal of a liberal education and students' increasing vocational orientation.

Scholars have dubbed the years between 1945 and 1970 a "golden age" in American higher education because of the massive institutional growth and dramatic enrollment increases that occurred during the period. The University of South Florida (USF) provides a useful example. When the university first opened in 1960, it had an annual budget of $2.4 million, ten buildings, 341 employees (including 109 full-time faculty), and fewer than two thousand students. A decade later, USF's budget was $38.4 million per year and it had 73 buildings, over 1,700 employees (834 full-time faculty), almost eighteen thousand students, and a branch campus in St. Petersburg.[26] Initially, growth of this kind combined with increasing state appropriations to attenuate the rift between liberal education and vocationalism by creating the capacity for colleges and universities to satisfy both aims. Following 1970, however, the nation's retrenchment, accelerated by the recession that began three years later, sent institutions scrambling for resources and students for job security, giving rise to what the *Chronicle of Higher Education* termed "the new vocationalism." Nowhere was this transformation more visible than in junior and community colleges. Established to serve "nontraditional" and first-generation students, these institutions came to prioritize occupational training programs that provided students with opportunities to achieve vocational ambitions and acquire wealth, ultimately resulting in some adopting slogans such as "Career Dreams Begin Here" and "Learn More. Earn More." Accordingly, although the term "affluent" has rarely been used to describe public higher education, especially colleges and universities that have for decades confronted the challenge of declining state support, the current study demonstrates that a social ethos of affluence has had a powerful effect on these institutions.

At the beginning of the twenty-first century American higher education maintained its commitment to advancing the common good despite pressures resulting from an ethos that prioritizes individual gain. Why? As this book illustrates, although the United States borrowed extensively from European models of higher education—including British residential colleges, Prussian agricultural institutes, French teacher-training schools, and German research universities—the best way to understand American higher education's historic commitment to the public good is to contrast it with its European predecessors. Although English universities emphasized the production of gentlemen and German research universities the production of scholars, US colleges and universities sustained at their institutional core a fundamental obligation to educate students for active lives of service.[27] Reaching back to the early national period, this commitment—informed as it was by an ethos of civic-mindedness—established such a powerful precedent that even today, as some for-profit enterprises have recently learned, colleges and universities that dismiss it as outmoded do so at their own risk.

From research that benefits the public welfare to the active recruitment of students from marginalized populations to sustained efforts to cultivate civic competence, colleges and universities continue to advance the common good in the twenty-first century. As has been the case for over two hundred years, however, civic-mindedness, practicality, commercialism, and affluence remain in tension on campuses across the nation. A heightened awareness of this tension—ever-present and fully embedded in higher education's historical development—as well as its implications for colleges and universities today, is essential if we are to assess with any degree of accuracy the characteristics of the so-called crisis many Americans believe higher education currently confronts. Achieving that awareness is this book's primary aim.

THE EARLY NATIONAL PERIOD

"LITERARY INSTITUTIONS ARE FOUNDED AND ENDOWED FOR THE COMMON GOOD"

The Liberal Professions in New England

Late in the summer of 1802, residents of Brunswick, a town in a noncontiguous part of the Commonwealth of Massachusetts known as the District of Maine, gathered to witness a rare event in the history of their young nation—the opening of an institution of higher education. Bowdoin College would, within just twenty-five years, become alma mater to future US president Franklin Pierce, acclaimed poet Henry Wadsworth Longfellow, celebrated novelist Nathaniel Hawthorne, and John Brown Russwurm—the third African-American to receive a college degree and cofounder of the country's first black newspaper, *Freedom's Journal.*[1] At the end of the eighteenth century, however, Bowdoin's success was far from assured. Although town boosters throughout New England aspired to establish colleges for primarily economic reasons and zealous congregations sought to construct them as centers of religious training, Bowdoin was not a result of either effort.[2] Instead, its founding resembled what historian David Potts has termed "localism" in nineteenth-century higher education. That is to say, although Bowdoin was indeed a Congregationalist undertaking, its establishment was characterized more by municipal support than by denominational backing.[3]

Bowdoin College was supported by ambitious district elites who, beginning in 1794, worked to erect a regional center of higher learning to which they could send their sons rather than incur the cost of dispatching them south to Dartmouth or Harvard Colleges.[4] With James Bowdoin III providing modest financial support, the college's founders named the institution after the late Massachusetts governor James Bowdoin II, received a charter from the General

Court of Massachusetts, and slowly raised the additional funds necessary to appoint a president, hire a faculty member, and erect a single brick building, Massachusetts Hall.

On the morning of September second, a stately procession of college trustees, overseers, and assorted dignitaries celebrated Bowdoin's opening. Officials introduced John Abbot as the institution's sole professor (of ancient languages) and installed Dartmouth College graduate and former Beverly, Massachusetts pastor Joseph McKeen as president.[5] McKeen's inaugural address assured the college's proponents that they would benefit greatly by having established a "literary institution" in their region. "The page of inspiration teaches that for the soul to be without knowledge, it is not good," McKeen proclaimed. "Without the knowledge of the duties of his station in life, no man can act his part with honor to himself, or advantage to the community."[6]

Forging a link between the learning students would undertake while enrolled at the college and their capacity to contribute to society, McKeen then pronounced Bowdoin's primary mission: "That the inhabitants of this district may have of their own sons to fill the liberal professions among them, and particularly to instruct them in the principles and practice of our holy religion, is doubtless the object of this institution."[7]

McKeen's proclamation highlighted his interpretation of the institution's primary objective: preparing students to become ministers. Yet as he made clear, the ministry was only one of the "liberal professions" graduates might pursue. The others (which, like ministerial work, were characterized by specialized noncommercial, nonartisanal activities) included medicine, teaching, law, and statecraft.[8] Somewhat paradoxically, however, McKeen's primary interest was not in students' occupational advancement. As Bowdoin's first president was certainly aware, practicing the liberal professions did not require a college degree. Ordination into the ministry typically required theological study leading to a divinity degree, while most physicians and lawyers received their training through apprenticeships. Schoolteachers, for the most part, needed only some secondary education, while statesmen, especially those who served in elected offices, frequently came to positions of influence after establishing themselves in other occupations.

What, then, did McKeen mean precisely when he described "the object of this institution" as he did?

Believing that higher learning provided the moral, ethical, and cognitive training necessary to fulfill the social obligations students incurred upon receiving a higher education, he declared:

> It ought always to be remembered that literary institutions are founded and endowed for the common good, and not for the private advantage

of those who resort to them for education. It is not that they may be enabled to pass through life in an easy or reputable manner, but that their mental powers may be cultivated and improved for the benefit of society. If it be true, that no man should live to himself, we may safely assert, that every man who has been aided by a public institution to acquire an education and to qualify himself for usefulness, is under peculiar obligations to exert his talents for the public good.[9]

This claim that, rather than using higher education for personal benefit, Bowdoin students were "under peculiar obligations" to promote the common good hardly proposed a new role for the American college.[10] Numerous scholars have noted how revolutionary leaders assigned educational institutions responsibility for advancing the public good and ensuring the republic's survival. Thomas Jefferson, for instance, serving in his first term as US president at the time of McKeen's inauguration, believed that grammar schools and colleges would produce "a virtuous citizenry, actively engaged in public affairs and willing to place the common good ahead of self interest."[11] Indeed, the Bowdoin president's conception of higher education's function in American society drew heavily on a late eighteenth- and early nineteenth-century social ethos of civic-mindedness that assigned priority to social responsibility over individuals' self indulgence.

How did this ethos influence higher education during the early national period? Characterized by the practice of civic virtue and a commitment to the public good, civic-mindedness provided social institutions, including those dedicated to higher learning, a source from which to derive their central aims. Predating contemporary distinctions between public and private colleges and universities, McKeen's identification of Bowdoin as a "public institution" suggested the degree to which he believed the college existed to serve society by producing intellectually enlightened and morally disciplined graduates. Many elites during the era shared his view, including John Witherspoon, who in 1772 insisted that graduates of the College of New Jersey (present-day Princeton University) "apply their talents to the service of the public and the good of mankind."[12] Similarly, the authors of the landmark Yale Report of 1828 reaffirmed civic-mindedness when they warned against the growing presence of a social ethos of commercialism and its influence on American higher education. According to historian Jurgen Herbst, the Yale College faculty members who authored the report "believed it their duty to inoculate their graduates against the insidious influences of a creeping commercialism, a reckless individualism, and a rampant desire for self-promotion and aggrandizement." Herbst continues, "For the country's future professional leadership to succumb to the drive for exploitation of America's riches, and, in such materialistic abandon, to forget all thought of commonwealth and nation appeared to Yale's faculty an abandonment of duty. It was the college's task to prevent such treason."[13]

McKeen offered more than a rhetorical flourish, however, when he declared that Bowdoin College would advance the common good by educating students to become virtuous practitioners of liberal professions. Aware that students might obtain social stature through their occupational achievements, college officials nevertheless expected graduates to subordinate personal desires in order to make tangible contributions to the republic—the essence of the civic-minded ideal.[14] In a sermon preached in 1814, the Reverend Jesse Appleton, the college's second president, used the example of seeking public office to convey the importance that citizens attached to the public good: "To enjoy the confidence of a wise people, there must be a consistency of character, a uniform regard to moral principle and the public good. They will clearly perceive, that the civil interests of millions cannot be secure in the hands of men, who, in the more confined circle of common intercourse, are selfish, rapacious, or aspiring."[15]

How did McKeen, Appleton, and other faculty intend to cultivate students' embrace of these "peculiar obligations"? Most believed that the college's course of study fostered students' "mental powers," while its residential program inculcated proper behavior—a two-pronged approach to nurturing virtue that higher-education institutions throughout New England employed during the early national period. Following John Abbot's appointment as Bowdoin's first faculty member, for instance, he and McKeen visited the College of Rhode Island (present-day Brown University) and Yale, Harvard, and Williams Colleges in search of models for Bowdoin's collegiate program. The journey resulted in McKeen's insisting on adopting the same admissions requirements for Bowdoin as existed at Harvard, including facility in Latin and Greek, demonstrated proficiency in reading *Select Orations of Cicero* and Virgil's *Aeneid*, and an acquaintance with mathematics "as far as the rule of three."[16]

Bowdoin's requirements aligned well with the classical course of study offered at many colleges at the time, both within and outside of New England. With McKeen and Abbot dividing instruction between the former's expertise in mathematical sciences and moral philosophy (ethics) and the latter's mastery of languages, students in all classes studied Latin, Greek, and the classics (including Horace, Juvenal, and Cicero). Freshmen also studied geography, sophomores logic, and juniors political philosophy, including John Locke's *Essay Concerning Human Understanding*. Senior study included William Paley's *Evidences of Christianity*, Joseph Butler's *The Analogy of Religion*, and Dugald Stewart's *Elements of the Philosophy of the Human Mind*. All classes learned rhetoric and elocution through the recitation method, requiring that students memorize and recite passages from assigned texts.[17]

In 1802, with the president's residence still under construction, McKeen and his family, Abbot, and the college's first eight students all lived, studied, and prayed together in Massachusetts Hall. By the 1830s, in contrast, Bowdoin's enrollment had quadrupled, residence halls and a chapel had been constructed, the academic program had been organized into departments, and faculty had adopted additional courses of study. Recitation, however, remained the primary pedagogy, along with students attending lectures and writing themes, or short essays. In just one year, seniors participated in seventy-four recitations in astronomy and spherical trigonometry during their first term, seventy-four in chemistry during their second, and forty-nine in natural history during their third. In addition, they attended forty-one lectures on mineralogy and geology and another thirty-three on natural philosophy. Essay writing was even more intensive: in the Department of Rhetoric, Oratory, and Political Economy, seniors wrote one hundred themes during their first term and one hundred and twenty more during their second.[18]

Bowdoin's curriculum did not depart in any substantial way from the academic program in place at many American colleges.[19] As historian Caroline Winterer has observed, a "culture of classicism" prevailed in these institutions, with the "complex liturgy of classical language acquisition" providing the focus of most colleges' academic programs.[20] As with many higher-education leaders, Bowdoin officials agreed with the authors of the 1828 Yale Report, who claimed that the mind was "a receptacle and a muscle capable of being strengthened through proper mental exercise."[21] For educators in the early nineteenth century, the classics, especially the study of Latin and Greek, provided the subject matter with which to fill this receptacle, while recitation provided the method through which to exercise the muscle.

Support for the classics, however, did not prevent colleges from engaging in curricular reform, particularly in the direction of practicality.[22] Over time, Bowdoin began offering exercises in subjects such as mechanics, surveying, and navigation as well as electricity, magnetism, and optics. Consequently, while the college maintained its traditional academic program, faculty appended elements of specialized training and applied learning that characterized higher education's reorientation toward a social ethos of practicality during the antebellum and Civil War eras.

The work of Bowdoin's Parker Cleaveland, professor of mathematics and natural and experimental philosophy, illustrates how the college integrated practical studies into its curriculum beginning even during the early national period. Born in Rowley, Massachusetts, in 1780, Cleaveland enrolled at Harvard

College at the age of fifteen. Following graduation, he taught school for four years before becoming a tutor in mathematics and natural philosophy at his alma mater. Accepting the Bowdoin professorship two years later, Cleaveland quickly became popular among students for his engaging lectures. During this time, he also underwent a scholarly transformation. Developing an interest in the variety of minerals in the rocky New England landscape, Cleaveland began self-education in chemistry and the fledgling field of mineralogy. (He would later claim to have graduated from Harvard believing there was only one kind of rock in the world.[23])

Cleaveland offered his first lectures in chemistry and mineralogy at Bowdoin in 1808. Eight years later, he published *An Elementary Treatise on Mineralogy and Geology*, the field's first major American work. With French and German texts on the subject not yet having been translated into English, and with those works providing little to no information on rocks and minerals in the United States, Cleaveland's book became popular both in his home country and abroad.[24] He developed international renown, turned down positions at the University of Pennsylvania, Dartmouth College, and Harvard, was celebrated by the German poet Goethe (who was also a scientist), and was eulogized following his death by former student Henry Wadsworth Longfellow.[25] Perhaps most importantly for Bowdoin's academic program, Cleaveland infused the institution's curriculum with practical studies such as mineralogy and chemistry, subjects that became standard offerings at the college during and after his remarkable fifty-two-year career.

If academic study aimed to discipline students' minds, Bowdoin officials believed that a routinized and highly regulated daily schedule would discipline their character. Beginning with the ringing of the chapel bell at 6:00 a.m., the president led morning prayers before students proceeded to their first recitation. They then ate breakfast and had free time until summoned to return to their rooms at 9:00 to study. Two hours later, the college held the day's second recitation, after which students were permitted free time and could visit the college library. They then took their midday meal and were again free until 2:00 p.m., when they returned to their rooms to study. Following the afternoon recitation, they attended evening prayers, after which they had no formal exercises until 8:00. At that time, students returned to their rooms for the night. This schedule was regularly followed Monday through Friday. On Saturdays, faculty excused students following a morning recitation.[26]

Cyrus Hamlin, an 1834 graduate, missionary, and founder of Istanbul's Robert College, recalled the regularity of Bowdoin's instructional schedule. "I immediately found college study quite different from my fitting course," Hamlin observed in his memoir, comparing Bowdoin to his secondary education. "Not that I studied harder, but everything was regular and measured. Three recitations a day, with some stated variations; and then we must go thoroughly into a thing. Our professors were men of power. Shallow, surface work was their abomination."[27] Another student, Alpheus S. Packard, who would later serve as Bowdoin College professor of ancient language and classical literature, similarly described his professor and college president, the Reverend Jesse Appleton, as exacting. "The students well knew that ignorance or sloth could not escape the severe scrutiny they were obliged to undergo," Packard recalled. "Close attention and a vigorous exercise of their powers could alone stand the test, and the attentive pupil never left the recitation room without new topics for reflection, suggested both by the searching nature of the examination through which he had just passed, and by the remarks of the President."[28]

Although Bowdoin faculty sought to cultivate students' civic virtue by combining mental discipline with a regimented daily schedule, the latter were not always willing participants. Indeed, resistance to college authorities has been a hallmark of American higher education, with students creating "an elaborate world of their own within and alongside the official world of the College," according to historian John Thelin. "For many undergraduates, compliance with the formal curriculum was merely the price of admission into 'college life.'"[29]

This elaborate world did not necessarily contradict colleges' civic-minded goals. Sometimes, in fact, students opposed college policies because they found them lacking, if not irrelevant, in preparing them to be good citizens. At Bowdoin, this collegiate world included student-initiated cocurricular opportunities such as the Theological Society, a bible-study group called the Praying Circle, and the Society of Inquiry, an organization dedicated specifically to supporting missionary work (an undertaking that many students believed directly benefited the common good).[30] It also involved student high jinks, which over the years included hazing freshmen (usually by dragging a student outside to the pump and dousing his head in cold water), the burning of the "Temple" (the college outhouse), and the mock funeral sophomores held each year during which they cremated "Anna Lytics" (their analytical geometry textbooks) and interred the remains on the campus grounds.[31]

For some students, collegiate life involved frequently violating college "laws" (figure 1). Among other things, Bowdoin students could be penalized for "negligence in study," "ignorance of Euclid," "leaning head on seat in front at prayers," "playing cards for money," and "making bon fire in yard." Punishments for minor offenses often involved a fine. In August 1823, college authorities fined Nathaniel Hawthorne twenty cents for "absence from college for one night," fifty cents for "neglect of declamation," and twenty cents for "absence from public worship."[32] (A term's tuition, by comparison, was eight dollars.)

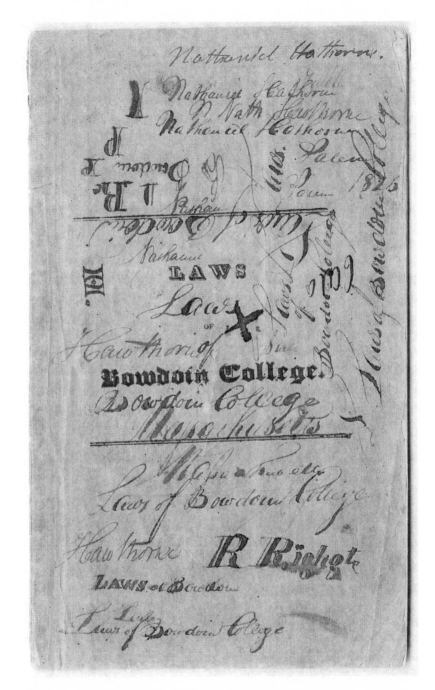

FIGURE 1. Front cover of Nathaniel Hawthorne's copy of the *Laws of Bowdoin College, in the State of Maine*, 1824. Courtesy of the George J. Mitchell Department of Special Collections & Archives, Bowdoin College Library, Brunswick, Maine.

More serious violations usually resulted in "public admonitions," which entailed singling out perpetrators during chapel services, lecturing them, and then imposing a penalty, all in the company of their classmates. In 1805, for example, McKeen admonished two students, whose parents he had already contacted due to a previous incident, for fighting, saying: "It is with pain that we find ourselves under a necessity of calling you forward in the presence of your fellow-students to be reproved and admonished for repeated acts of violence into which you have suffered yourselves to be hurried by ungoverned passion."[33] As repeat offenders, these students not only received the public admonition but risked rustication, a punishment requiring them to depart the college for a specified period and take up residence with a member of the clergy who exercised absolute authority over their daily lives. Alternatively, the students might have been suspended. Considered an extreme penalty for misbehavior, suspension lasted from six to twelve months and sometimes resulted in students not returning to campus. Of the sixteen Bowdoin students suspended between 1807 and 1819, six permanently departed the college.[34]

Perhaps more than any other element of the elaborate worlds students constructed, literary societies prepared them to fulfill civic and, for some, professional obligations following graduation. Providing members with opportunities to discuss great literary works, debate lofty theoretical questions, and engage the most pressing political, social, and economic issues of the day, literary societies served as forums for democratic deliberation and disputation. Describing higher education's role, and especially that of college literary societies, during the early national period, historian Joseph Kett writes:

> In the context of eighteenth century assumptions, colleges could best serve the public by turning callow youth into leaders of public life. Yet the effect of colleges on public life was by no means restricted to offices held, discoveries made, sermons preached, causes pleaded, or patients cured by their graduates, for collegians absorbed from their student years, and especially from the student literary societies, a culture of self-education and mutual improvement that they projected into their later lives and habitats. In the eighteenth century the ideal of liberal education was bound intimately to that of self-education, both in the general sense that a liberal education included the acquisition of qualities of character, for example, the habit of placing civic duty above self-interest, and also of many subjects—history, the law of nations, modern polemics, and modern poetry—that rarely formed part of the collegiate curriculum.[35]

The history of Bowdoin's literary societies confirms Kett's central claim. Even prior to the college's first commencement, students joined together to form an organization for the purpose of promoting "literature and friendship" and attaining "habits of discussion and elocution."[36] Writing a constitution and agreeing to a one-dollar-per-term "tax" on each member (as well as a fine of twelve cents for each missed meeting), the society quickly expanded. Choosing a name appropriate to their locale, students borrowed from the Greek term for "pine-covered," named their organization the Peucinian Society, and established an elaborate initiation ceremony that involved holding pine branches over the heads of new members while reciting the organization's oath.[37]

Peucinian Society members met once every two weeks in the fall and spring, with most meeting times dedicated to students' developing eloquence through debate. Questions included "Whether the District of Maine becoming a separate State would be to the advantage of the inhabitants?," "Whether the fear of shame or the love of honor be the greater inducement to virtue?," "Whether the practice of Dueling be justifiable or not?," "Whether eloquence be advantageous to a commonwealth?," and "Whether the crimes resulting from barbarism or the vices allied to refinement be most pernicious to society?"[38] Although membership in the Peucinians continued to rise during its first three years, disgruntled members formed a competing society in 1808. Given the initial club's popularity, however, the Athenaeans struggled to gain a footing. The new organization dissolved in 1811, was revived two years later, dissolved again in 1816, and was restored the next year. Finally, the Athenaean Society attracted enough paying members to become firmly established. From that point forward, fierce competition erupted between the two student groups, with the Peucinians claiming future luminaries such as Henry Wadsworth Longfellow and the Athenaeans counting Nathaniel Hawthorne and Franklin Pierce among their members.[39]

The societies also sponsored their own libraries, relieving the college of the expense of acquiring volumes for its collection. Beginning with the Athenaeans and adopted in rivalry by the Peucinians, members built up the libraries' holdings by contributing either personal volumes or cash, with one alumnus recalling that "the loyalty of each student" to his society "was measured by his gifts to the library."[40] As a result, the Peucinian library reached hundreds of volumes by 1830, with the Athenaean collection close behind. Unfortunately, the rivalry also resulted in an excessive duplication of acquisitions, so much so that the following year the college's governing boards proposed that the societies merge their libraries. The students, according to Bowdoin alumnus and historian Louis C. Hatch, rejected the proposal "with indignation."[41]

In addition to sponsoring libraries, literary societies also hosted lectures, such as the one delivered by Nehemiah Cleaveland in September 1821 to celebrate the thirteenth anniversary of the Peucinian Society's founding. Cleaveland, who had served as a college tutor between 1817 and 1820, used the address to recognize the role of grammar, history, and poetry in contributing "very materially to the charms of perfection of eloquence."[42] Drawing on a social ethos of civic-mindedness, Cleaveland asserted that the study of these subjects was beneficial only to the degree that they were "not merely interesting" but "useful to the community." Taking the opportunity to demonstrate his own elocutionary powers, Cleaveland urged students to use the occasion of the society's anniversary to reflect on the college as an arena for fellowship as well as a source of virtue: "With such a sentiment and such feelings, often as we shall visit, whether at frequent or at distant intervals, this abode of learning, we shall find in its halls, its walks, and groves, the mementos, not of former enjoyments only, but of obligations also, which we have yet to discharge."[43] Echoing McKeen's inaugural claim, Cleaveland asserted that when graduates returned to campus in future years they would recall the joys of their college days as well as be reminded of the peculiar obligations they had incurred to promote the common good when they acquired a higher education.

How did Bowdoin College students respond to expectations such as Cleaveland's and McKeen's that they were obliged to use their higher educations to promote the public good? Assembling detailed, career-line studies of Bowdoin's early graduates is difficult. Substantial documentary evidence exists, however, to suggest that a large majority of the undergraduates enrolled during Bowdoin's first decades indeed met these expectations. Of the class of 1810's twelve graduates, for instance, five became ministers (three after having served as schoolteachers), four became lawyers (one after having taught school and another who later served as a Maine state legislator), one became a physician, one a soldier (and later editor, civil servant, and philanthropist), and one worked in his family's mercantile business.[44] Similarly, of the five members of the class of 1813, one became a school principal, one a merchant, and three lawyers (one eventually serving as Maine state attorney general and another as a Maine state senator, US congressman, US attorney for the district of Maine, and mayor of the city of Portland).[45] Indeed, in the decade between 1820 and 1830, by one scholar's accounting, Bowdoin College "helped prepare for their life-work":

> thirty-eight doctors of medicine, of whom three had been teachers in important medical schools; fifty-one preachers of the Gospel, of whom two had been important foreign missionaries; thirty-two teachers, including one college president and nine college professors; one hundred and thirteen lawyers, including, if you will believe it,

thirty-three State Representatives; four of whom had been speakers of the House; seventeen State Senators; six judges of State Supreme Courts; four judges of District Courts; three State Attorneys General; two governors of States; eight members of the National House of Representatives; six members of the United States Senate; one United States Comptroller of the Currency; two Secretaries of the United States Treasury; and one President of the United States; and perhaps more importantly and more significantly than all else, the authors of at least three hundred and thirty-eight books, several of which had been translated into four or five other languages and republished in foreign lands; and, to crown all, among those authors the most widely-read and best-loved poet of America, and also the man who, even to this day, is considered by many the greatest romance writer of the New World.[46]

Did these alumni, however, willingly embrace the civic obligations their alma mater ascribed to them, or did they simply fulfill social responsibilities en route to personal success? That is to say, did civic-mindedness dictate graduates' occupational trajectories or did a competing social ethos, such as commercialism and its correlates of individual success and professional status, have greater influence on their career choices? There is good reason to believe that Bowdoin College students eagerly pursued increased social status. As historian David Allmendinger has demonstrated, many students attending New England colleges in the first half of the nineteenth century were poor, relying on charity and employment to pay for their tuition, room, and board. As younger sons of farmers who typically practiced primogeniture, many college students rightly believed that higher education, although not a prerequisite for individual success, provided an advantage in establishing themselves in a career. It is important to note, of course, that none of the liberal professions promised significant financial gain. Through occupational mobility, however, graduates of limited means could escape their potential future as landless hired hands, city laborers, or clerks and achieve a degree of fiscal stability and social stature otherwise unattainable.[47]

Students attending Bowdoin College in 1829 offer a convincing example of Allmendinger's findings. Of the 114 students enrolled at Bowdoin in that year, more than half were poor. Of the sixty-four who relied on financial support from sources other than their families or benefactors, forty-three acquired grants from the college after providing documentation of their indigence, and six received financial support from the American Education Society, an organization providing scholarships to young men interested in the ministry.

Forty-five of them supported themselves by "keeping school" during the winter; in other words, they taught at rural grammar schools over winter break, occasionally taking leaves of absence during the academic term to continue their work.[48] Indeed, so many Bowdoin students taught school to support their studies that in 1834 they formed the "Teachers' Association of Bowdoin College," the purpose of which they stated as "the mutual improvement of the members in their vocation, as teachers."[49] Further evidence of student indigence had appeared ten years earlier, when Bowdoin College undergraduates formed one of New England's first college "boarding clubs" in an effort to lower the cost associated with meals.[50]

Undoubtedly, a significant proportion of Bowdoin students believed that higher education afforded greater access to occupational success than they would otherwise have had. It would be a mistake, however, to assume that this belief was incompatible with their acceptance of the civic obligations the college ascribed to them. Rather, documentary evidence produced by Bowdoin students suggests that many were extremely concerned that they live out the civic-minded ideal by becoming "useful" citizens and serving the public good through their life pursuits.

While at college, Class of 1837 graduate George F. Talbot consistently wrote of his plans to make a meaningful contribution to society. On his birthday in 1836, he reflected on the worldly distractions competing for his attention while emphasizing this desire: "Amidst the din of contending passions and the outbreakings of unsatisfied desires, consciousness lifts up his voice and calls us to forsake the pursuits which cannot give real happiness . . . and pursue some real good, some lasting substantial record."[51] Especially as graduation approached, Talbot continued to ponder his life's pursuits as well as the responsibilities he incurred by obtaining a college education. "I began a boy at home, a home from which I had never been absent," he wrote toward the middle of his senior year, "[and] since then I have passed into a somewhat higher situation and have experienced all the joys and sorrows, pleasures and responsibilities of college life, and at its close I find myself almost ready to leave these scenes, and enter upon the still more active duties of busy life. Increase of knowledge brings increase of responsibilities, and the higher we rise the more is expected of us the more we expect of ourselves."[52] As with many of his classmates, Talbot eventually met McKeen's expectation that he "exert his talents for the public good." Becoming a lawyer in Maine's Washington County, Talbot served as US district attorney for the state of Maine and US solicitor of the treasury.[53]

Student reflections such as Talbot's on the obligations that acquiring a higher education incurred typically aligned with Bowdoin College's institutional mission to promote the common good. A product of the prevailing social ethos of civic-mindedness, this alignment was perhaps most complete for students who planned to enter the ministry—a vocation that afforded minimal opportunity for acquiring material wealth but relatively high social stature. As diaries suggest, students made little distinction between serving God and serving society; most considered the role of minister, by definition, to be one of social value and usefulness. Bowdoin College, however, did not grant divinity degrees. Why, then, would students who hoped to enter the ministry enroll?

John Marsh Mitchell provides a revealing example. An impoverished student from Norway, Maine, Mitchell began his studies at Bowdoin in 1839. Although he taught school in nearby Freeport, received scholarships from the American Education Society, and was employed sawing wood for the college, a lack of financial resources consistently threatened his enrollment. Yet Bowdoin offered Mitchell an extraordinary opportunity to prepare for usefulness, one that he acknowledged upon his arrival in Brunswick. Rooming with an equally impoverished "chum" in college housing, Mitchell observed at the end of his first day at Bowdoin,

> After supper we engaged in studying until about nine o'clock, and after a short time was spent in reading and in conversation we retired to rest for the first time as members of college within these consecrated walls; and I was about to say, would that it might be the last time, but no, rather let me be content to remain and endeavour by the grace of God to prepare myself for usefulness, and so to improve the talents entrusted to me that I may at the last great day hear the welcome sentence pronounced to me 'come ye blessed of my father, enter into the kingdom prepared for you from the foundation of the world.[54]

Having begun a successful teaching career while still enrolled, Mitchell moved to Alabama following his graduation in 1843 and taught for another six years. Eventually receiving a divinity degree from the College of William and Mary, he spent almost twenty-five years as a minister in Alabama and Georgia before finally returning to Maine.[55]

Students engaged in higher learning during the early national period were frequently predisposed toward self-improvement and acquiring the capacity to contribute to the common good. Acknowledging their desire for occupational advancement, they sought social status not as an end in itself but as a result of their civic service and usefulness to society. That institutions of higher education such as Bowdoin College promoted this behavior as the ideal for their graduates is hardly surprising, for it fit well with the prevailing social ethos. Nevertheless, in its town meeting–style politics, religious fervor, and diverse economic base consisting of shipbuilding, fishing, and small-scale agriculture, Maine's social, political, and economic development differed quite extensively from the nation's other regions, especially the South. South Carolina, in particular, provides a revealing example of a state confronting the challenges of rapidly changing demographics and regional contestation, factors that would, in part, lead to the founding of South Carolina College.

2

"THE GOOD ORDER AND THE HARMONY OF THE WHOLE COMMUNITY"

Public Higher Learning in the South

As the residents of Brunswick, Maine, prepared to celebrate the opening of Bowdoin College in 1802, legislators in the South Carolina General Assembly, one thousand miles to the south, gathered to cast their votes to establish a state-supported, state-controlled college in the capital city of Columbia. The act was unusually bipartisan in a season of rancorous party politics. Having been guided through the American Revolution and the Constitutional Convention by Federalist leaders such as John Rutledge and Thomas Pinckney, South Carolina voters helped elect Democratic-Republican Thomas Jefferson to the presidency in 1800. Simultaneously, they turned the state legislature over to members of Jefferson's party, resulting in the selection of John Drayton as governor.[1]

Like Jefferson, Drayton advocated expanding educational opportunities in his home state, including a publicly funded school system. South Carolinians opposed to a school tax, however, greeted his efforts with the same resistance that led Jefferson's "Bill for the More General Diffusion of Knowledge" to fail in Virginia.[2] Yet, unlike Jefferson's initial efforts to found the University of Virginia, Drayton's "Act to Establish a College at Columbia" was warmly received. Introducing legislation into the General Assembly in November 1801, Drayton offered two related justifications for a state-supported higher-education institution. Reflecting the influence of a social ethos of civic-mindedness, Drayton first claimed, "The establishment of a College in a central part of the State, where all its youth may be educated, will highly promote the instruction, the good order, and the harmony of the whole community." He then spoke directly to critics who believed higher education should be a private endeavor rather than a state-supported one. "The proper education of youth contributes greatly to the prosperity of society," the governor asserted, "and ought always to be an object of legislative attention."[3] The legislature agreed and Drayton signed the bill into law in less than a month.

The speed with which South Carolina College's chartering legislation sailed through the General Assembly during a politically contentious era urges the question of how legislators found political common ground on this issue when developing consensus in other areas of political life proved so elusive. There were three primary reasons. First, although legislators differed in their opinions on the usefulness of a public system of grammar schools for white children throughout South Carolina, most agreed that providing a higher education for the state's future leaders contributed greatly to the prosperity of society—a central manifestation of civic-mindedness during the early national period. As Maximilian LaBorde, South Carolina College faculty member and author of the institution's first history, observed, the college's supporters "saw plainly, that to preserve our rights we must understand them; that ignorance was incompatible with liberty; and that the only security for its perpetuation was to be found in the education of the people."[4] As with representatives of the District of Maine, South Carolina legislators believed that education provided the means through which the vices associated with freedom and liberty would be tamed and the republic sustained.

Second, and again similar to Maine residents who supported establishing Bowdoin College, many wealthy South Carolinians resented sending their sons away from home for a higher education, in the latter case to Northern institutions such as Yale University or even to Europe. As Drayton reminded legislators in his proposal to establish the college, where Northern states such as Massachusetts, Connecticut, and New Jersey had succeeded in providing educational opportunities to prepare future leaders, South Carolina had failed. Even worse, he noted, the failure was not for lack of interest, but effort. "Were a person to look over the laws of the State," Drayton claimed, "he would find that five Colleges are incorporated therein; and, did his inquiries proceed no further, he would naturally imagine we had already arrived at an enviable excellence in literature." Of those five, however, he observed that one had been closed for financial reasons, two were more "respectable" grammar schools than colleges, and two were "as yet scarcely known but in the land which incorporated them."[5] For this reason, Drayton declared—and a large majority of legislators concurred—South Carolina needed a state-supported, state-controlled institution of higher education.

Third, and most compellingly for the state's wealthy planter class, the college's founding provided a means through which to attenuate the extreme sectionalism developing *within* South Carolina. During the late eighteenth and early nineteenth centuries, few "Americans" defined themselves as such. Rather, home states, and even regions within states, informed individuals' primary political identities. In some cases, however, regional differences within states fostered rivalry over a range of political and economic issues. Such was the case in South Carolina, where by 1800 the antagonism between the less-populated but wealthier, Federalist-oriented low-country (or tidewater) section and its more populous but poorer, Democratic-Republican-oriented up-country (or piedmont) section had become severe. As early as 1786, up-country demands had received a hearing when state officials moved the capital both north and west from Charleston to Columbia. Yet the piedmont's increasing numbers (111,534 white residents in 1790 compared to 28,644 tidewater residents) led to its seeking greater political power. On the other hand, low-country residents paid a far greater share of taxes and were reluctant to surrender their control of the State House, where they maintained influence partly due to property-based voting qualifications.[6]

The Democratic-Republican victory in the election of 1800 signaled a political shift away from low-country Federalism toward up-country Populism, one that Charlestonians and the aristocratic planter class of the tidewater ignored at their own peril. As a result, a majority of the state's legislators became convinced that a college in Columbia would bring future leaders from both sections of the state together where they would establish cordial relations, thus promoting the common good. (As Drayton wrote of the college's purpose, "The friendships of young men would thence be promoted and strengthened throughout the State, and our political union advanced thereby."[7]) Moreover, the college would provide its students a thorough political education, the principles of which were frequently dictated by the tidewater. Years after participating as a legislator in founding South Carolina College, Henry W. DeSaussure recalled in frank terms, "We of the lower country knew that the power of the State was thence forward to be in the upper country and we desired our future rulers to be educated men."[8]

During its first fifty years, South Carolina College fulfilled many of its founders' intentions. Drawing students from the tidewater and piedmont sections, it acculturated them through a common educational experience and, as its graduates came to dominate political offices, assisted in maintaining the state's unity. With college officials seeking to foster civic-mindedness through an educational program similar to that in Northern institutions such as Bowdoin, South Carolina College students studied the classics and pursued practical courses such as civil engineering while also debating controversial issues through cocurricular literary societies. Yet, to an even greater degree than at Bowdoin, students at South Carolina openly resisted the regulated and routinized daily schedule that officials imposed, including the ban on settling disputes through dueling. Perhaps the greatest difference between Bowdoin and South Carolina Colleges, however, was the latter institution's advocacy of states' rights, nullification, and, especially, slavery. With many Southerners considering slavery central to the preservation of the republic, the college defined the common good in terms that both tolerated human bondage and maintained it as a fundamental republican principle. Consequently, as the antebellum era ushered in contentious political conflicts between Northern and Southern states over the federal government's authority, many South Carolina College faculty and administrators infused the defense of slavery into the college's curriculum, stimulating student radicalism and, eventually, secession.

When the legislators founded South Carolina College, they were unusually generous in their support. The bill establishing the institution included a $50,000 appropriation for the construction of student living quarters and educational facilities as well as an authorization for the annual transfer of $6,000 from the state treasury to pay faculty salaries.[9] Such financial commitments were exceptional at the time. Georgia's state legislature chartered the University of Georgia (the first state university in the nation) in 1785, yet the institution received no financial support until legislators granted it $5,000 in 1802, a year after it enrolled its first students. Similarly, in 1795 the University of North Carolina (the first state university in the nation to enroll students) received a $10,000 loan from the state government with no promise of future appropriations. Although their respective state legislatures granted land to both institutions, those grants were rarely converted quickly into income.[10]

South Carolina's munificence may be explained, in part, by the authoritative role the college's chartering legislation assigned the state's General Assembly. Legislators maintained, among other powers, authority to appoint the college's first board of trustees as well as nominate new board members every four years. Consequently, South Carolina College's first thirteen-member board was chaired by Governor Drayton and included the state's lieutenant governor, the president of the state senate, and the presiding officer of the state's House of Representatives. Moreover, the judges of the Court of Equity (an early form of the state's Court of Appeals) were assigned the role of ex-officio members of the board.[11]

Although such a close relationship with the state government eventually posed challenges for college administrators, it proved tremendously beneficial to the fledgling institution. Whereas colleges such as Bowdoin waited eight years or more between being chartered and enrolling students, South Carolina College opened on January 10, 1805, just over three years after being chartered (on

December 19, 1801). Once Drayton signed the legislation establishing the institution, board members wasted no time in erecting the college. By the end of May 1802, they had planned for the construction of a forty-eight-room residence for approximately one hundred students and three professors, a chapel, two lecture rooms, and a library. (During this time, officials constructed a functional space for the college's collection of books and documents; thirty-eight years later it erected the first freestanding college library in America.) The board chose a building site within view of the State House, symbolically representing the close relationship between the institution and the state.[12]

Arguably the trustees' most important decision involved selecting the college's president and faculty. By offering the presidency to Jonathan Maxcy, a native of Massachusetts who had graduated from Brown University and (beginning at the young age of twenty-four) served as its president for ten years, the board guaranteed that South Carolina College would operate, for at least its first several years, in the image of a New England college.[13]

For his part, Maxcy was undoubtedly pleased to receive the offer. Along with the provision of a residence, he received a salary of $2,500 a year, an exceptional sum compared to that received by Bowdoin College's Joseph McKeen ($1,000), Princeton's Samuel Smith ($1,600), and the University of North Carolina's David Lowry Swain (who in 1855 still received $250 a year less than Maxcy had fifty years earlier).[14] Moreover, Maxcy's membership in the Baptist Church, a possible point of contention for the board's predominantly Episcopalian and Presbyterian members, caused little stir. Indeed, the absence of controversy reveals the general toleration of religious belief in South Carolina in the decades prior to the spread of evangelical fervor throughout the state.[15]

With Maxcy installed as president and Yale graduate Enoch Hanford appointed as its first faculty member, the all-white, all-male South Carolina College opened in January 1805 with nine students, two of whom the institution admitted as sophomores and the remaining seven as freshmen. Commencing classes in January, the college's academic year paralleled the calendar year, with the first session being held from midwinter through spring and the second in the fall. (The threat of disease, especially malaria, prevented its holding classes during the summer months.) The college held commencement on the first Monday in December, a schedule that permitted legislators, present in Columbia at that time each year, to attend graduation.[16]

With the state's strong support, South Carolina College grew rapidly, enrolling 237 students by 1849.[17] Scholars have noted the high rate at which sons of the Southern planter elite attended college. Of the 440 South Carolinian planters historian Chalmers Davidson has investigated, for instance, two-thirds were college-educated, with almost a quarter of those graduating from

FIGURE 2. South Carolina College, c. 1850. Courtesy of the South Caroliniana
Library, University of South Carolina, Columbia, SC.

South Carolina College.[18] The causes for such high rates of college attendance are
complex, although a central reason Southern parents sent their sons to college
was their belief that higher education provided the knowledge and dispositions
necessary to achieve status as honorable gentleman and, ultimately, positions
of political influence.[19] They were correct: so many South Carolina College
graduates pursued political careers at both the state and national levels that it
is impractical to list them here. One revealing indicator of alumni's domina-
tion of South Carolina political offices was the extent to which this consistently
provoked complaints from those who had not graduated from the institution.[20]
This is not to say that South Carolina College graduates did not also fulfill their
responsibility to advance the common good by becoming attorneys, teachers,
physicians, and ministers; some did. Unlike in the North, however, agriculture
remained a lucrative enterprise throughout much of South Carolina, especially
following the invention of the cotton gin. Consequently, many South Carolina
College graduates entered into public service without first spending years establishing themselves in a liberal profession.

  As at Northern colleges such as Bowdoin, a social ethos of civic-mindedness
influenced South Carolina College's residential program. Seeking to cultivate
virtuous behavior, members of the college's board of trustees adopted a series
of rules regulating student conduct, beginning with an academic schedule that
remained in place for almost half a century. Students rose early for prayers in the
college chapel before proceeding to recitations or lectures or returning to their
rooms to study. Later in the morning, they came together in the dining common

for breakfast before returning to their rooms at 9:00 a.m., where they studied unless summoned to recitation, which frequently occurred one-on-one with a faculty member. At noon, the students ate dinner (the largest meal of the day) and were then free until 2:00 p.m., when they again returned to their rooms and waited to be summoned. At 5:00, their day ended as it began, with prayers in the college chapel, before they proceeded to supper. They returned to their rooms at 7:00 and studied until 9:30, at which point they were required to remain in their rooms until sunrise. On Saturdays, faculty excused students following the morning recitation.[21]

Whether attending college in the North or the South, students rarely greeted such regimes with enthusiasm. Significant differences in social norms between the two regions, however, resulted in students experiencing restrictions on residential life in significantly different ways. At Bowdoin, the sparseness of official college life aligned, at least to some degree, with the piety of New England culture. At South Carolina, the institution's exhaustive list of prohibitions conflicted almost completely with regional behavioral expectations, consistently challenging faculty and administrators in their efforts to cultivate civic virtue among the college's students.

As scholars of the American South have observed, planters' sons underwent an intensive socialization process beginning in childhood.[22] Historian Bertram Wyatt-Brown writes that parents "insisted upon early signs of aggressiveness" in their sons, which they believed was "demanded by notions of white masterhood." He continues, "The male child was under special obligation to prove early virility, an obligation in which shame and honor played a crucial, if not exclusive, role."[23] This upbringing continued into adolescence, when "entry into young manhood" took "more social forms" in the South than in the North.[24] "By age fourteen or so," according to Wyatt-Brown, "many of them had learned to drink, swear, gamble at cards, fight and wrestle, and imitate the mannerisms of older brothers and fathers," which also included visiting brothels and engaging in sexual relations with enslaved women.[25]

It is hardly surprising, then, that the rules regulating student life at South Carolina College included restrictions on "blasphemy," "robbery," "fornication," "forgery," using "profane or obscene language," and appearing "in indecent dress."[26] Moreover, trustees' efforts to govern student conduct were formally encoded in the "Laws on Misdemeanors and Criminal Offenses at South Carolina College." These included: (1) "Students are not only required to abstain from all vicious, immoral or irregular conduct, but they are, on every occasion, to conduct themselves with propriety and decorum, and in all their intercourse with the officers of the College, with each other, and the public generally, it is expected of them to preserve that high toned feeling and courtesy which ever distinguish the gentleman" and (2) "No student shall presume to come into the chapel, or any apartment for recitation, without being fully dressed, nor shall they lounge or sit in an indecorous position, nor talk, nor in any manner offend against the rules of propriety common among gentlemen assembled for grave purposes."[27]

That both laws upheld the behavior of "gentlemen" as the standard to which students should aspire is hardly a coincidence. As historian John Reesman writes, "A gentleman lived according to a specific moral and ethical code. The code had to be integral to one's personality to be real, and it was part of the College's larger purpose to teach young men to be 'real' gentleman. As such, to be a gentleman had an almost transcendant [sic] importance for both faculty and the students."[28] Moreover, Reesman notes, although one attained a "high place" in one's community as a result of becoming a gentleman, such an elevated status "was not a license for unrestrained self-interest."[29] Accordingly, the social and political responsibilities that South Carolina College officials ascribed to the "gentleman" graduates of their institution closely paralleled the obligations that Bowdoin College officials, such as Joseph McKeen, ascribed to their students. This was the social ethos of civic-mindedness, Southern style.

Requiring that students behave as gentlemen through published rules and successfully enforcing those rules were two very different tasks. When planters' sons moved out from under their fathers' authoritative roofs to attend college, they often took advantage of their newfound freedoms in far more aggressive and boisterous ways than their Northern counterparts. William J. Grayson, for instance, an 1809 graduate who went on to serve in the South Carolina General Assembly and US Senate, observed in his autobiography, "Collegiate provisions for imparting or preserving good morals" were completely inadequate in Southern colleges, especially his alma mater. "The raw freshman," he wrote, "is subjected to the influence of companions a little older than himself. He is ambitious to emulate the high spirited example of his senior. He makes rapid advances in smoking, chewing, playing billiards, concocting sherry cobblers, gin slings, and mint juleps . . . and takes degrees in arts and sciences about which his diploma is altogether silent."[30]

According to historian Daniel Walker Hollis, the problem with South Carolina College student discipline lay less with the institution's regulations and more with the way they conflicted with "the prevailing *mores* of South Carolina society" [emphasis in the original]. "The puritanical code" in place at the college, he writes, "clashed with the hedonistic spirit of South Carolina in the early 1800's. The State society during the first generation of the nineteenth century was not a religious one—the great triumph of evangelical religion and with it, a more moralistic outlook on life, did not come for three or four more decades."[31] As South

Carolinian John C. Calhoun observed while attending Yale University in 1803, his Northern classmates were "certainly more penurious, more contracted to their sentiments, and less social, than the Carolinians." However, Calhoun conceded, "as to morality we must yield."[32]

Faculty and administrators at South Carolina College, guided by an ethos of civic-mindedness and intent on promoting gentlemanliness and virtue, nevertheless regularly enforced institutional prohibitions. Many students reacted by opposing their efforts with equal regularity. In November 1813, for instance, the faculty recommended expelling junior John Gaillard "for insulting language and conduct" toward mathematics and natural philosophy professor George Blackburn (a stern disciplinarian who was unpopular among students). Having been called before the faculty to answer the charges against him, an unbowed Gaillard reportedly "treated the Faculty in the most rude & indecent manner, accusing them of injustice & oppression & declaring his determination not to subscribe to them."[33] Yet infractions of this sort rarely resulted in serious punishment. According to the author of South Carolina College's first published history, faculty were quick to "pass sentence" but members of the board of trustees frequently rejected their proposed sanctions, further revealing the tensions that existed between college policy and prevailing social norms. In Gaillard's case, the trustees convinced Blackburn to accept an apology from the offender along with a promise of improved behavior.[34]

Depending on the severity of the misbehavior, however, repeat offenders might be directed to depart the college. Reserving expulsion for the most egregious violations, college officials occasionally imposed three-to-six-month suspensions. In February 1806, faculty members called sophomore William Davis before them to explain his misbehavior during the previous evening's chapel service. Although the faculty did not record Davis's offense in detail, they noted that his conduct had been "designed to show disrespect" and recommended a three-month suspension, "Then to be restored on the condition of producing, from a reputable instructor, a certificate of his good moral conduct and diligent attention to study, during that period."[35] In another instance, faculty members accused a student of "making a festive entertainment at the house of an infamous mulatto woman" and brandishing a pistol "with which he intended to defend property not his own." In an interesting comparison with William Davis, this student's conduct, combined with a "peculiar obstinacy" demonstrated in the "presence of the Faculty," earned the student the same three-month suspension.[36]

With trustees typically undermining faculty authority, it was only a matter of time before infractions such as Gaillard's and Davis's, as well as mischievous but popular exploits such as stealing turkeys from local residents' yards, developed into more serious disruptions. Such an event occurred in February 1814, when faculty, including Professor Blackburn, apprehended three students for trying to steal the college bell (with the intent of preventing the day's exercises from beginning). When faculty members recommended the three be suspended, and the trustees uncharacteristically agreed to the punishment, students rose up in revolt. Following the 7:00 p.m. ringing of the bell, a group of students who had been drinking and were in disguise burned Blackburn in effigy, marched to the building that housed the bell, broke down its main door, and destroyed the bell. The students proceeded to hurl bricks at the windows of a college tutor who had helped to foil the original bell heist. From there, they attacked Blackburn's house and engaged in random acts of vandalism. Reports suggest that chaos ensued. Unable to calm the rioters, faculty contacted the trustees, who called out the town militia. When the latter arrived, the revolt came to an end. As a security measure, however, the militia posted guards at the homes of faculty members for the rest of the night.[37]

Following the riot, the trustees swiftly expelled its leaders and the college schedule resumed. Perhaps not surprisingly, faculty eventually added the follow-ing rule to the institution's bylaws: "All combinations amongst the students to oppose the authority of the Faculty, or impede the operation of the laws, are strictly forbidden."[38] Nevertheless, students continued to openly flout college regulations. In an 1846 letter addressed to the board of trustees, then-President William C. Preston, who had himself graduated from South Carolina College in 1812, reported student Alexander D. Sparkes for expulsion, having convicted him "of riotous & disorderly conduct in the campus, firing frequently a pistol loaded with ball & of utilizing very abusive language to Professors." Preston noted in the letter that three other students were being recommended for suspension as a result of their engaging in "black riding," an offense "of longstanding and of frequent occurrence," which involved students blackening their faces, donning long coats, carrying torches, and riding horses through campus at night to the cheers of their classmates.[39]

It is difficult to square the extent of student misbehavior at South Carolina College with John Reesman's claim that being a gentleman had an almost tran-scendent importance for students. The work of Robert F. Pace and Christopher A. Bjornsen, however, helps makes sense of the apparent conflict.[40] Southern social norms dictated that a central element of being a gentleman involved subscribing to a code of honor.[41] In regional terms, only those who adopted the Southern code could responsibly promote "the good order and the harmony of the whole community"—the very purpose for which South Carolina College was estab-lished. Yet, as Pace and Bjornsen explain, "The concept of honor that governed Old South society was, at times, a difficult and confusing code. Southern honor consisted of a set of rules that advanced the *appearance* of duty, pride, power, and self-esteem, and conformity to these rules was required if one was to be considered an honorable member of society" [emphasis in the original].[42] They go on to describe the particular challenges that teenage college students confronted in their attempts to learn and practice this code: "Adolescence is not a sturdy, straight bridge between childhood and adulthood, but a transition fraught with conflicts and struggles. One of the major struggles was the drive to become an adult while retaining childhood desires and behaviors. . . . A second critical struggle . . . was the need to become a part of the culture of their authority figures, while also creating an 'adult' culture of their own that focused on their peer group and involved a peer-designed code of honor."[43]

South Carolina College regulations were in obvious conflict with conduct many students deemed acceptable. College officials, however, seemed aware of the developmental stages to which Pace and Bjornsen allude, establishing rules that provided disincentives for students to engage in childish pranks and unfettered rivalry, yet also occasionally revising regulations to respect their peer-designed code of honor. The college's first set of bylaws, for instance, dictated, "If any student shall refuse to give evidence respecting the violation of any of the laws of the College, when required by the Faculty, he shall be admonished or suspended." Students, however, considered it dishonorable to snitch on their classmates.[44] Over time, therefore, administrators modified the regulation to read, "The Faculty shall not, for mere College misdemeanors, call on one student to give information against another, unless when riotous or disorderly conduct shall take place in the room of any student, in which case he shall be bound to designate the true offender, if he was present at the time, or be considered as taking the guilt of the offence on himself, and shall be punished accordingly."[45]

Still, college officials were inflexible regarding one practice associated with Southern social norms: dueling. Imposing punishments on both the "principal" (the dueler) and the "second" (his assistant), the college's bylaws dictated simply, "Any student who shall be guilty of any infamous or atrocious offence, or shall fight a duel, or give or accept a challenge to fight a duel, or act as a second to those who shall give or accept a challenge, shall be forthwith suspended from the College and reported for expulsion."[46]

Scholars have conducted numerous examinations of the role of dueling in Southern society, especially in South Carolina, where it was more common than in other states.[47] As Steven Stowe has written, until recently historians have "tended to summon the duel for its drama and for its sense of a world now lost, making it a colorful window-dressing for more central considerations of politics or law." However, he continues, "the duel was not so peripheral to the planter class, nor was it sufficient to itself. It was only the most visible part of the affair of honor, a masculine ritual that went deeply into the reaches of authority and manhood in the planter elite."[48] In fact, many Southern leaders—the very men South Carolina College students hoped to emulate—embraced the duel, thereby providing young men with role models that South Carolina society respected and celebrated. In 1838, for instance, John Lynde Wilson, who served as the state's governor between 1822 and 1824, published *The Code of Honor*, in which he detailed "rules for the government of principals and seconds in duelling." The text became, as one scholar describes, "the standard guide for southern duelists."[49]

South Carolina College student Preston Smith Brooks provides a particularly compelling case in the way that honor and dueling were integrated into the lives of many white Southern men. By the time he was elected to the US Congress from South Carolina, Brooks had already publicly defended his honor multiple times. While a college student, Brooks accused classmate Lewis Simons of being a "falsifier" for campaigning against him for an elected position in one of the college's debating clubs after promising not to. When Simons heard the accusation, he challenged Brooks to a duel. Brooks responded that college regulations prohibited dueling but that he would give Simons a "boy's satisfaction" through a fistfight. The next day, when several people informed him that Simons had acquired a pair of pistols and was waiting for him in the steward's hall, Brooks took a friend's gun to defend himself. When the group arrived at the dining hall, Simons was waiting. Again he issued a challenge. When Brooks refused, Simons pulled out a horsewhip and began beating him. Brooks then produced the gun. Declaring himself unarmed, Simons threw down the whip. Brooks responded by doing the same with the gun and the two young men settled the dispute with their fists.[50]

Several years later, at the age of twenty-two, Brooks again came into conflict, this time with Louis Wigfall, who was also a graduate of South Carolina College. Both men were politically active and had exchanged a series of insults over their support for opposing candidates in the 1840 South Carolina gubernatorial election. After efforts by intermediaries to resolve the conflict failed, Brooks and Wigfall agreed to a duel. Confronting each other in November of that year, the men's first shots missed. Brooks's second bullet hit Wigfall in the thigh and Wigfall's became lodged in Brooks's hip. Both men survived, but Brooks's wound resulted in his using a walking cane for the rest of his life.[51]

That cane would go on to become one the most famous in American history when in May 1856, Brooks, who by that time was serving in the US House of Representatives, took personal offense at Massachusetts Senator Charles Sumner's "Crime against Kansas" speech. Sumner had directed part of the speech at Andrew Butler—a US senator from South Carolina, South Carolina College alumnus, and cousin of Preston Smith Brooks—attacking both Butler and his home state. Butler was not present during the speech, however, and Brooks considered it his duty to defend his family's and state's honor. Intending to challenge Sumner to a duel, Brooks consulted his friend and House colleague, South Carolina College graduate Laurence M. Keitt. Reminding Brooks that the code of honor dictated that only gentlemen of equal social stature duel, Keitt argued that Sumner was not Brooks's equal. Two days following Sumner's speech, therefore, Brooks entered the Senate chamber and approached Sumner, who was seated at his desk. After chastising him verbally, Brooks repeatedly beat Sumner with his cane, stopping the assault only when the cane broke in two.[52] It took Sumner three years to recover from the attack.

In the midst of the controversy following the assault, Brooks resigned from Congress. Yet, Southerners celebrated him and his constituents quickly reelected him to office. Only eight months later, however, Brooks died unexpectedly from croup in a Washington, DC hotel. Conspiracy theories quickly spread. When Brooks's body was returned to South Carolina in February 1857, thousands of Columbia residents, including South Carolina College students, turned out to memorialize him. On that day, college President William C. Preston observed in a letter to a friend, "The corpse of poor Preston Brooks is to be in Columbia today and I go in spite of the cold to be present in the mournful cortege. It is really a very mournful ceremony to me and I am shocked and stunned at the occasion. My acquaintances on the street suspect *poison*—and I do not indicate my doubts lest I should be charged with abolitionism. Such is the frightful state of public opinion."[53]

For a college seeking to foster civic virtue among young men so that they might contribute to the good order and harmony of the whole community, dueling posed a particularly thorny problem. It clearly conflicted with college officials' assumption of authority over student behavior and, of course, it put students' lives at risk. As Steven Stowe writes, however, dueling was only the most visible part of the affair of honor. In that regard, it was only one element (although undoubtedly the most lethal) of a broader set of practices that college officials desired to regulate in order to accomplish their institutional goal.

The second primary method South Carolina officials used to foster civic virtue among students was cultivating mental discipline through the study of the classics. The college's admissions requirements, which were similar to those at many other higher-education institutions at the time, included the ability to: (1) "render from Latin into English" the works of Roman biographer Cornelius Nepos and Roman historian Gaius Sallustius Crispus (known as "Sallust"), Caesar's *Commentaries*, and Virgil's *Aeneid*, (2) translate into English any passage from St. John in the Greek Testament, (3) provide a "grammatical analysis of the words of, and have a general knowledge of the English Grammar," (4) write in a "good, legible hand," and (5) "spell correctly" as well as being "well acquainted" with mathematics "as far as the Rule of Proportion."[54]

Once admitted, students studied a curriculum in the freshman year that included works by Livy and Horace, Xenophon's *Anabasis*, and Homer's *Iliad*, as well as Latin composition, algebra, ancient history, and English.[55] Maintaining a primarily classical orientation, the sophomore curriculum also included the history of the Middle Ages and elocution. The classics continued to hold a central place in the junior year, including Cicero's *Rhetorical Work*, Horace's *Art of Poetry*, and the satires of Juvenal; yet juniors also took courses in modern history, moral and political philosophy, and physiology. Finally, during their senior year, students studied Cicero's *Ethical Works*, political economy, and philosophy of the mind.[56]

South Carolina College fully embraced the classical curriculum. Over time, however, and especially beginning in the 1830s, the rise of a social ethos of practicality led college officials to regularly incorporate practical course offerings into the academic program. Upperclassmen studied surveying, electromagnetism, mineralogy, and agricultural chemistry, the last of which characterized the agricultural colleges established in the United States during the antebellum and Civil War eras. Moreover, in 1836 South Carolina College trustees accepted a proposal made by Professor of Mathematics Thomas Twiss to add civil engineering to the curriculum.[57] Twiss's interest in practical studies resulted from his having been educated at the United States Military Academy, an institution that, although established in 1802, began orienting its academic program around engineering and mechanics in 1817. Writing to the board, Twiss avowed, "Being desirous & anxious to see our College placed on a respectable footing, & equal, if not superior, to any other in the United States, in possessing the advantage & means of giving to the young men of the State, a sound, practical, & thorough Education, in all of the branches of Science & useful knowledge, without being compelled to go abroad to obtain it, I have bestowed such care and attention upon this subject, & the result of my reflections are respectfully submitted for the consideration."[58] Accepting Twiss's proposal, board members added civil engineering to the college's academic program.

Perhaps the most striking characteristic of the curriculum at South Carolina College prior to the Civil War, however, was one that cannot be discerned by simply examining a list of courses taken and subjects studied. Faculty lectures, student notebooks, and especially administrator addresses reveal the extent to which college officials inculcated the Southern position on states' rights, nullification, and slavery in the context of a primarily classical curriculum.[59] Among these men, Thomas Cooper was perhaps the best known and most controversial.[60]

Born in London in 1759, Cooper attended University College, Oxford, and became a barrister while also developing a reputation as a scientist and philosopher. Taking part in radical politics, he opposed the slave trade (but not slavery), advocated the expansion of suffrage, and defended the idea of natural rights. A member of the Manchester Constitutional Society, he was sent to France in 1792 to observe and report on the revolution. During four months in Paris, he delivered an address to the Society of Friends of the Constitution at the Paris Jacobin Club, yet seemed to have come into open conflict with Robespierre. He fled the country less than a month following his address and returned to England.[61]

With the suppression of radicalism intensifying in England, Cooper immigrated to Pennsylvania in 1794, became a US citizen, and quickly joined the Jeffersonian crusade against the Federalists. After publishing an attack on President John Adams, Cooper was tried for libel under the Alien and Sedition Acts, fined, and imprisoned for six months.[62] Developing a reputation as a Populist, Cooper was elected district judge in Northumberland, Pennsylvania, but left the bench to serve, first, as professor of natural philosophy and chemistry at Dickinson College, then professor of applied chemistry and mineralogy at the University of Pennsylvania. Having befriended Thomas Jefferson, Cooper hoped to obtain a position at the University of Virginia when it was chartered in 1819. Jefferson's university did not open for another six years, however, so Cooper accepted the offer of the newly created professorship in chemistry at South Carolina College. When President Jonathan Maxcy died only six months later, the trustees elected Cooper to serve as president pro tempore. The following year, they offered him the presidency.[63]

Over the next thirteen years, many South Carolinians grappled with the conflict between their admiration of Cooper's political orientation and their opposition to his religious belief. During the time that he served as president, religious fervor began to increase throughout the state. Yet Cooper was, if not an atheist, a deist who denied the existence of the soul and Christ's resurrection. Eventually, his attacks on Calvinism and Presbyterianism contributed to his resignation. Throughout his time in office, however, Cooper amassed a following as a vocal proponent of decentralization, states' rights, and laissez-faire as well as an ardent defender of nullification and slavery.

In 1823, a majority of South Carolina politicians supported nationalism and the maintenance of the Union.[64] Cooper, however, had by this time become a proponent of the doctrine of states' rights. Seeking converts among South Carolina's future leaders, he used his 1824 commencement address to propose a college course on political economy. With the trustees' approval, he taught the course to seniors the following year. It was so well received that Cooper's lectures were published in 1826 and again in 1828 and were eventually developed into *A Manual of Political Economy*, published in 1834. These works provide a detailed record of Cooper's political positions.[65] Among these, he included such "Definitions and Elementary Truths" as "I shall be justified in ranking a good government limited and restrained by a constitution adapted to secure responsibility, as among the sources, and preservatives of national wealth; and a government of opposite character, as among the most efficient causes of national poverty."[66]

No stranger to political controversy, Cooper participated in a series of public meetings held in the 1820s to protest proposed increases in tariff rates, at one point publishing his protestations in *A Tract on the Proposed Alteration in the Tariff*, which he distributed to South Carolina's congressmen in 1824.[67] Given his position on the role of the federal government, it is hardly surprising that Cooper publicly opposed the American System, a set of federal policies that protected industry through tariffs, established a national bank, and supported federal subsidies for internal improvements such as roads and canals. Accordingly, Cooper attended a protest meeting in Columbia in 1827 during which he called the American System one of "fraud, robbery, and usurpation" and urged his audience to consider the material and political costs associated with complying with protective tariffs. He then proclaimed, "I have said, that we shall, ere long, be compelled to calculate the value of our union; and to enquire of what use to us is this most unequal alliance? By which the South has always been the loser, and the North always the gainer? The question, however, is fast approaching to the alternative, of submission or separation."[68]

Cooper's comment caused an immediate uproar. Although by the eve of the Civil War South Carolinians regularly discussed secession, few Southern leaders in 1827 had publicly proposed such a radical stance. Consequently, Cooper's name became known throughout much of the nation. Three years later, during the celebrated Webster-Hayne debate over the tariff issue, US Senator Daniel Webster referred directly to Cooper, remarking, "I know that there are some persons in the part of the country from which the honorable member comes, who habitually speak of the Union in terms of indifference, or even of disparagement. The honorable member himself is not, I trust, and can never be, one of these. They significantly declare, that it is time to calculate the value of the Union; and their aim seems to be to enumerate, and to magnify all the evils, real and imaginary, which the Government under the Union produces."[69]

As Webster's remarks suggest, Cooper contributed to the South's understanding of its relationship to the federal government and the US Constitution. As for his impact on the political and economic positions of the young men enrolled at South Carolina College, Cooper was only one of many members of the faculty and administration who influenced their thinking on the central political, economic, and social issues of the time. In 1834, two years following the South Carolina General Assembly's passage of the Ordinance of Nullification (through which South Carolina claimed the federal tariffs of 1828 and 1832 unconstitutional and, therefore, null and void), student John Creighton McMaster recorded in his notebook questions and answers "adapted to four lectures" delivered by faculty member and future college president Robert Henry. They included:

Q: *What are the great objects of government?*
A: Internal harmony & external security.

Q: *Which is the more important of the objects just mentioned?*
A: Internal harmony.

Q: *With regard to these points (internal harmony & external security), what difference exists between our government and other governments?*
A: In most countries the care of both is committed to the same constitution—but in our Govt one is under the jurisdiction of the States—the other under the jurisdiction of the Genl. Govt. . . .

Q: *Are its [the General Government's] functions indispensible?*
A: Yes—though not the most important that a Govt can exercise; it rather expels evils than confers benefits. . . .

Q: *Has the State sovereignty been surrendered?*
A: No, as may be clearly seen from the preamble to the Constitution, and we have previously shown that such a surrender would have been injurious—

Q: *How far has the State sovereignty been modified?*
A: Only so far as would enable the States to cooperate harmoniously with the General Government for the common security.

Q: *By whom was the Constitution framed?*
A: By a convention of deputies from all the States.

Q: *What difference do you observe between the power of the States and the power of the Genl Govt?*

A: The power of the States is made up by limitation—That of the Genl Govt by specific grants.[70]

As McMaster's notes reveal, Henry's lectures sought to impress upon students a limited role for the "general" or federal government, one restricted to maintaining external security rather than "internal harmony" (through, for example, the imposition of tariffs to regulate the economy), as well as emphasizing state over federal sovereignty. In addition to McMaster's notes, notebooks in which Henry recorded the lectures he delivered have also survived. In one for a course on moral philosophy, Henry documented his teachings relating to William Paley's 1794 work *Evidences of Christianity* by recording,

> Our slaves are as well treated in this country as the working class in other countries. Those in manufacturing countries cannot be called free as they are dependent on their labor for their daily food and are obliged to take whatever the capitalist thinks proper to give them which is never more than sufficient for their actual wants. . . . The slave possesses this superiority. He always gets the same remuneration for his labor and has no care on his mind concerning his children whilst the ways of the manufacturer are constantly varying & sometimes subjecting himself to almost starvation.[71]

Paley's *Evidences of Christianity* was a text read by college students throughout the United States, including those enrolled at Bowdoin College. Unfortunately, an equivalent Bowdoin faculty lecture book on Paley does not exist; such a comparison would be extremely useful. Henry's notes, however, indicate that he used Paley's work to promote a justification of slavery in the United States that contrasted the evils of "wage slavery" with human bondage (a defense that George Fitzhugh, in his classic work *Cannibals All!*, would popularize in the years leading up to the Civil War).

The influence of Henry's, Cooper's and other faculty members' teachings in defense of slavery and states' rights was reflected in student literary societies. As in the North, South Carolina College students formed these organizations almost immediately upon the institution's opening in 1805, providing a social as well as educational space.[72] Yet at South Carolina College, students emphasized the opportunity that the Clariosophic and Euphradian Societies afforded to develop and practice oratory, a skill they diligently pursued because of the extremely high regard with which eloquence was held in Southern society. Euphradian Society members acknowledged as much in their organization's constitution when they wrote that the society's purpose was "to better to obtain a knowledge of Science in general but more particularly to improve in Oratory."[73] Moreover, as historian Lorri Glover writes, "genteel masculinity" required "the mastery of ora-torical skills. Confidence in public speaking (a prime indicator of refinement) and preparation for political office (the traditional path to power for southern gentry) demanded excellent oration of young men."[74] To accomplish this goal, one student typically delivered an oration at each meeting followed by a debate between four students—two in favor and two opposed—on a previously identi-fied question. Students took their participation seriously, frequently expressing a good deal of anxiety when their time to speak arrived. As one student noted in his journal on the morning of his oration, "This evening I have to speak in the Society. Can I do it? God help me."[75]

Society members judged the debates on the quality of the participants' argu-ments as well as their delivery, although the issues debated also undoubtedly influenced their judgments. The questions students chose to debate reveal a great deal about their interests and concerns, as well as how they changed over time. In 1820, two questions that students posed included, "Would it be good policy to banish the free negroes from the States?" and "Should the slaves of this State receive an education?" (The former was decided in the affirmative and the latter, by a vote of thirty-four to six, in the negative.) Three years later, students debated whether the clergy should "participate in the administration of republics" (they decided against it), whether women should "possess the Liberty of having a voice in the administration of *our* Government" (against), whether "imprisonment for debt" should "be abolished in this state" (against), and whether "a representative" should "be guided by his own judgment or that of his constituents" (students decided in favor of "his own judgment").[76]

By the 1830s, students had moved from debating somewhat broad social, political, and economic questions to those involving more specific economic and political controversies. Some of these questions, and the dates on which they were argued, included:

October 28, 1831: Whether or not South Carolina should nullify the present tariff laws, would the general government be justified in attempting to enforce the same? [students decided against]

November 5, 1831: Is nullification the rightful remedy for our suffering? [students decided in favor]

January 4, 1832: Should the Legislature of this state permit a branch of the national bank to be established in this place? [students decided against]

March 3, 1832: Should the legislature prohibit individuals from emancipat-ing their slaves? [students decided in favor]

March 10, 1832: Would a disunion of the United States, and forming them into separate governments, prove beneficial to them? [students decided against]

March 17, 1832: Which would be most politick in S Carolina to nullify the
tariff law or secede? [students chose nullification]

May 12, 1832: Has commerce or agriculture been most beneficial to mankind?
[students chose agriculture]

November 17, 1832: Should death by dueling be considered as murder?
[students decided against]

Such questions, as well as the consistency of the debates' outcomes, suggest that many students embraced the political, economic, and social views espoused by many of their professors. This is perhaps not surprising given that many white South Carolinians during the antebellum era championed these views, a creed superbly illustrated by the 1852 South Carolina College graduation of a student and future Confederate general by the name of "States Rights Gist."[77]

As growing hostility between the North and South further exacerbated sectionalism in the United States, South Carolina College became an intellectual center for the defense of states' rights, nullification, and slavery. Having established the institution in part to avoid sending their sons north to receive a higher education, white South Carolinians benefited from having a center of higher learning that inculcated local and regional positions on the important political, economic, and social issues of the day. Accordingly, as the state's politics became increasingly radicalized, student proclamations followed suit. By the 1850s, South Carolina College students issued manifestos such as the one junior John Ward Hopkins recorded in his journal and intended for publication in a local newspaper. "The students of South Carolina College," Hopkins wrote, "repudiate old [Henry] Clay and all his principles. Federalism and Abolitionism cannot flourish on the soil irradiated by the genius of [John] Calhoun. We all bow with reverence, and offer up our humble devotion at the foot of the 'great-Southern cross', the operation of the spirit there inculcated the independence of the Southern States, and foster allegiance to South Carolina; and should she secede, her College claims a 'place in the picture, near the flashing of the guns.'"[78]

Hopkins's prediction was quite accurate. One month following Abraham Lincoln's election in 1860, South Carolina led seven states in seceding from the United States, sparking a civil war that eventually drew enough young men into the Confederate forces that South Carolina College was depleted of students and transformed into a hospital.[79] By that time, a social ethos of civic-mindedness had long been eclipsed by practicality as the predominant force in American higher education. Early in the century, however, it was indeed civic-mindedness that inspired a politically fractured South Carolina General Assembly to agree to establish the college, near the state's geographic center, in order to foster what its members considered the good order and the harmony of the whole community.

Seeking to cultivate gentlemanliness and civic virtue, its faculty, administrators, and trustees implemented a collegiate program quite similar to the one in place in many Northern colleges. Distinct regional differences, however, led South Carolina students to resist college regulations to a far greater degree than did their peers at institutions such as Bowdoin. To conclude this examination of higher education during the early national period, then, we turn to Georgetown University, an institution that served both Northerners and Southerners while also implementing its own distinctive commitment to fostering the common good.

3

"TO PROMOTE MORE EFFECTUALLY THE GRAND INTERESTS OF SOCIETY"

Catholic Higher Education in the Mid-Atlantic

At first glance, Georgetown College's founding seems characterized by a collection of inconsistencies.[1] Unlike Bowdoin and South Carolina Colleges, which were established by their respective state legislatures on identifiable days, Georgetown has no corresponding date. Officials initially used 1788—the year construction began on the institution's first building—to mark its founding. In 1851, however, the college catalogue misidentified "Old South's" construction date as 1789. Consequently, Georgetown's centennial celebration occurred in 1889, and the institution has celebrated 1789 ever since. Its founders, moreover, never applied for a state charter.[2] Establishing the college without one, officials eventually received the nation's first federal higher-education charter from Congress in 1815, providing the institution the authority to confer "any degree in the faculties, arts, sciences, and liberal professions, to which persons are usually admitted in other Colleges or Universities in the United States."[3] Additionally, although it actually began as an academy, with the age for student enrollment set at between eight and fourteen, it opened under the name Georgetown College.[4]

The most intriguing incongruity associated with Georgetown's establishment, however, is that although the Jesuit order of the Roman Catholic Church founded the institution to educate young men to enter religious life—in essence, to prepare them for seminary—the college practiced religious tolerance and admitted students from a variety of Christian denominations.[5] Consequently, few graduates entered the priesthood. As for the institution's educational purpose, the first prospectus declared a dedication to advancing the common good, reading: "The directors of this Institution openly profess that they have nothing so much at heart as to implant virtue and destroy in their pupils the seeds of vice—Happy in the attainment of this sublime object, they would consider their success in this alone, as an ample reward for their incessant endeavours. To answer so desirable a purpose, and to promote more effectually the grand interests of society, no trouble is spared in the cultivation of susceptible and tender minds, and enriching them with every thing useful or ornamental in the several branches of literature."[6]

The prospectus is revealing for what it both does and does not state. No mention is made of the college's goal to educate future clergy. Rather, it expresses officials' aspirations to "implant virtue" in students while educating their "susceptible and tender minds." Undoubtedly, college officials understood that, combined with their declaration of religious tolerance, a broad-based or "catholic" approach to education rather than a denominationally specific "Catholic" approach would produce higher enrollments and thus greater revenues, making it more likely that the fledgling institution would survive. Accordingly, Georgetown acted much the same as Bowdoin College by opening its doors to young men—some members of their respective institutions' founding denominations and some not—with the hope that a satisfactory number of graduates would become ministers of the faith.

Perhaps the most compelling aspect of Georgetown's prospectus is the way that it asserted the institution's commitment to advancing the public good through promoting "the grand interests of society." Manifesting the same social ethos of civic-mindedness as Bowdoin and South Carolina Colleges, its officials aimed to educate graduates who would better society through their life pursuits. Yet, Georgetown College also differed in important ways from its peer institutions. Although Georgetown students studied a classical curriculum, they did so in the context of a centuries-old Jesuit scholarly tradition. Additionally, the college developed a distinctly international character during the early national period, enrolling many students from abroad and employing immigrant priests and seminarians. Finally, as an institution located in the Mid-Atlantic, the college drew students from both Northern and Southern states, leading to contentious and sometimes polarizing campus debates in the years leading up to the Civil War.

Many of the puzzling aspects of Georgetown's early history can be explained through the biography of its leading founder, Bishop John Carroll.[7] Born in 1735 into a prosperous family in Maryland, Carroll received his early education through tutoring by a local Jesuit priest. When Carroll turned thirteen, his parents followed a custom common to many of the colony's prominent

Catholic families: they enrolled him in St. Omers, an English Jesuit college in French Flanders. After completing preparatory studies for the priesthood, Carroll entered a nearby English Jesuit novitiate and, in 1757, began philosophical and theological studies at the Jesuit college in Liège, Belgium. Following his ordination in 1761, he taught at the college in Liège as well as the Jesuit college in Bruges.[8]

In 1773, Carroll and his fellow Jesuits received word that the Vatican had suppressed his religious order—the Society of Jesus.[9] The order, established by Saint Ignatius of Loyola in the sixteenth century, had come under increasing political attack in many European countries by the 1750s. Seeking to placate the leaders of nations such as Spain, France, and Austria, Pope Clement XIV issued a decree of suppression, extinguishing all Jesuit institutions. The decree also effectively dissolved society members' religious obligations. When Carroll and his fellow Jesuits were forced at bayonet-point to abandon the college in Bruges, they were also suddenly and unexpectedly freed from the directives of their superiors. Carroll used his newfound liberty to return home.

Arriving in Maryland, Carroll served as priest to family members in the Potomac Valley. With the outbreak of the American Revolution, however, he joined three members of the Continental Congress and future signers of the Declaration of Independence—Samuel Chase, Benjamin Franklin, and his cousin Charles Carroll—on a diplomatic mission to draw French-Canadians into the war against the British. Although the mission failed, the experience profoundly influenced Carroll. He became a strong advocate of republican government and espoused a firm commitment to religious toleration. Indeed, as early as 1779 Carroll noted the opportunities that religious tolerance provided Catholics in revolutionary America. In a letter to his friend, lifelong correspondent, and fellow Jesuit, Charles Plowden, Carroll observed, "The fullest & largest system of toleration is adopted in almost all the American states: publick protection & encouragement are extended alike to all denominations & R.C. [Roman Catholics] are members of Congress, assemblies, & hold civil & military posts as well as others."[10]

Hoping to seize the missionary opportunities he believed America's independence from England would bring, Carroll developed a plan to use Jesuit priests to minister to the already westward-looking nation. With the order suppressed, however, Carroll could not rely on an influx of newly ordained Jesuits from Europe. A central element of his plan, therefore, included establishing an educational institution that would serve as both an academy and seminary. As Carroll wrote in the final year of the American Revolution, "An immense field is opend to the zeal of apostolical men. Universal toleration throughout this immense country, and innumerable R. Cats [Romans Catholics] going & ready to go into

the new regions bordering on the Mississippi, perhaps the finest in the world &
impatiently clamorous for Clergymen to attend them. The object nearest my
heart is to establish a college on this continent for the education of youth, which
might at the same time be a Seminary for future Clergymen. But," Carroll added,
alluding to the challenge that raising funds to support such an institution posed,
"at present I see no prospect of success."[11]

The Vatican ultimately rewarded Carroll for organizing missionary activity in
the new nation (without actually reorganizing the Jesuit order), appointing him
"head of the missions in the provinces of the new Republic of the United States
of America."[12] Yet, as Carroll predicted, his preliminary efforts at fundraising to
establish an academy failed, leading him to temporarily lower his expectations.
At the end of the American Revolution, with the Maryland State Legislature chartering St. John's College (Annapolis) and Washington College (Chestertown),
Carroll wondered whether these institutions might provide a small number of
graduates interested in pursuing studies in a Roman Catholic seminary. Writing
Plowden in February 1785, he professed,

> I hope that as we R.C. are unable to raise or support one [a college] by
> private contribution and public endowment ourselves, providence had
> ordained these as a resource for the exigencies of religion. For in these
> colleges, I trust there will amongst the catholic youth trained in them
> be some from time to time inclined to an Ecclesiastical state. For these
> we propose, what I hope our abilities will enable us to execute, a small
> seminary, where they may be formed to the virtues of that state, and
> receive a Theological education. Such is the plan now in my mind.[13]

By year's end, however, Carroll had regained his commitment to establishing an academy. Although it is unclear why he changed his mind, he probably
returned to his previous belief that without a school dedicated to educating students for the seminary, the Roman Catholic establishment would simply not produce enough priests to serve the new nation.[14] Accordingly, in 1783 and again in
1790 Carroll referred to the academy as "our main sheet anchor for Religion" (a
sheet anchor being a ship's second or emergency anchor) while maintaining his
intention to found a seminary.[15] "The object nearest my heart now," he wrote in
December 1785, "& the only one, that can give consistency to our religious views
in this country, is the establishment of a school, & afterwards of a seminary for
young clergymen."[16]

Over the next few years, Carroll led the effort among the Jesuits in America to
establish an academy. Acquiring a site overlooking the Potomac River in "George-
Town," Maryland, he issued a set of proposals to solicit contributions, emphasizing that the institution would be open to students of all denominations and

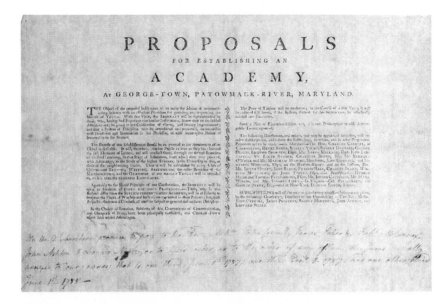

FIGURE 3.   John Carroll's *Proposals for Establishing an Academy at George-Town*, 1787. Courtesy of the Georgetown University Archives.

would allow non–Roman Catholic students to worship in their own churches (figure 3). "The Object of the proposed Institution," it read, "is to unite the Means of communicating Science with an effectual Provision for guarding and improving the Morals of Youth." It continued, "Agreeably to the liberal Principle of our Constitution, the Seminary will be open to Students of Every Religious Profession. They, who in this Respect differ from the Superintendents of the Academy, will be at Liberty to frequent the Places of Worship and Instruction appointed by their Parents."[17]

Yet even with the academy's embrace of religious tolerance as inscribed in the US Constitution, raising funds to construct a building for the school posed a continual problem. To overcome this daunting financial obstacle, Carroll tapped into the one substantial source of revenue to which he had access: proceeds from Jesuit plantations in Maryland. The order maintained significant landholdings in the state, including over twelve thousand acres divided into seven prosperous plantations. Although the leaders of many European nations had seized Jesuit properties immediately following the order's suppression, Maryland's colonial government had not. It was on these plantations that the Jesuits kept almost three hundred enslaved people.[18]

The histories of American higher education and slavery are inherently intertwined. Steven Wilder, in his award-winning work *Ebony & Ivy: Race, Slavery, and the Troubled History of America's Universities*, provides a rich and detailed accounting of this relationship.[19] At some colleges, such as Harvard, presidents owned slaves. At others, such as South Carolina, faculty and administrators mounted an intellectual defense of slavery as the nation's "peculiar institution." Enslaved people literally built some campuses, such as Georgia's Emory College (present-day Emory University), while institutions such as Virginia's College of William and Mary owned slaves outright. For many colleges and universities, more than one of the above held true.

Today, a Georgetown University working group is studying the institution's historical association with slavery. What is already clear, however, is that income from the Jesuits' landholdings, especially the plantations worked by enslaved people, underwrote the college's founding and operations. As Adam Rothman, a member of the working group, asserts, "The university itself owes its existence to this history."[20] Indeed, in 1838, with Georgetown consistently operating at a loss and plantation income failing to fully subsidize it, Jesuit leaders agreed to sell 272 enslaved men, women, and children and use part of the proceeds to underwrite the college's debt. Forced onto ships in Washington, DC, these people were transported first to New Orleans and then to plantations west and south of Baton Rouge.[21]

Georgetown University faculty and administrators are currently grappling with the legacy of this act, as well as ways to make amends, with President John J. DeGioia announcing in 2016 that the university would, among other measures, offer a formal apology, establish an institute for the study of slavery, and award preferential admission status to the descendants of the enslaved.[22] The university is the first to take such appreciable steps to rectify its past. As Wilder observed in response to DeGioia's pronouncement, "Georgetown has made a decision to recognize the humanity of the problem they're dealing with, to treat it as more than a public relations problem."[23] Whether other colleges and universities will follow Georgetown's lead in acknowledging the ways that their institutions benefited from human bondage and the slave trade while also offering substantive forms of redress remains to be seen.

The financial support that Carroll drew from the Jesuit plantations in Maryland permitted him to do what, until April 1788, he had been unable to: order construction to commence on the institution's first building, Old South. Four years later, when Georgetown opened, the term "college" had replaced "academy" in its name, the Vatican had appointed John Carroll as Bishop of Baltimore, and Georgetown officials had appointed Robert Plunkett, a thirty-nine-year-old Jesuit recently immigrated to the United States, as college president. For its academic program, the institution developed a curriculum based on centuries-old Jesuit tradition.[24] This plan, developed at the end of the sixteenth century and known as the *Ratio Studorium*, also provided the framework for the course of study that Carroll and his classmates had experienced at St. Omers. Consisting of a five- or six-year course, this "Physical, Moral, and Literary education" emphasized Latin and Greek but also included vernacular languages as well as mathematics and natural science.[25] "When the students are advanced in their scholastic career," college officials explained, "and qualify themselves for the study of higher sciences, such as history, moral and natural philosophy, the College will furnish able teachers in the several branches."[26]

By 1835, enough students had advanced in their scholastic careers for George-town to implement a seven-year academic program, with the first three years constituting preparatory studies.[27] Years four, five, and six, which comprised the collegiate curriculum, were divided into "First Humanities," "Poetry," and "Rhetoric." Students in these years studied Latin and Greek grammar, Virgil's *Aeneid*, and—like their counterparts at South Carolina College—the works of Roman historian Gaius Sallustius Crispus, or "Sallust," as well as English grammar and "Precepts of Rhetoric and Poetry." In the final year, labeled "Philosophy," students studied logic, metaphysics, ethics, and natural philosophy. The college also offered practical studies such as mensuration (measuring) and surveying.[28]

Once students completed the seven-year program, they could apply to undertake an advanced course of study. College officials designed this course, which they entitled "Natural Right," primarily for students who did not plan on entering the seminary (which was, indeed, most of the college's graduates). According to the faculty, the course prepared students to pursue the liberal professions by instructing them in "the fundamental principles of civil, political and international right and a critical history of Philosophy." As the college catalogue described it, "Whosoever is not a stranger to the ... extended course of Philosophy, will not hesitate to consider it essential to a scientific education, the object of which is to prepare the student's mind for any literary profession, that he may afterwards embrace."[29]

The college's description of Natural Right did not stop there. After acknowledging the occupational advantages of the course, Georgetown officials, informed by a social ethos of civic-mindedness and dedicated to fostering civic virtue among students, observed, "For not to speak of students of law, which evidently demands a knowledge of Natural Right, there is no station of public life, which does not require a knowledge of one's rights and duties, as a citizen. And although such a study would convey no immediate individual advantages, we cannot call into question its utility under a social point of view. The increase of our national happiness must depend greatly on the civil and political education of our youth."[30]

Descriptions such as this expressed higher education's commitment to the common good in language that echoed Joseph McKeen's proclamation that college graduates assumed a peculiar obligation to improve society rather than reap private advantages through their life pursuits. Indeed, officials such as Bernard Maguire, who taught at Georgetown in the 1840s and eventually served as the college's president from 1852–1858 and again from 1866–1870, frequently expressed hope that students would advance the public good following graduation. As early as his own graduation from St. John's College in Maryland, where he delivered the commencement address, Maguire reflected on the purpose of higher learning. "For what have we been sent hither, my young companions?" he asked his classmates. "That our tender minds be cultivated, that useful knowledge be treasured up, that we should imbibe at the fountain of science & literature. . . . Not only my dear friends do our relations . . . expect this but your Country expects it, the Republic expects it."[31]

In issuing this declaration, Maguire drew on an ethos of civic-mindedness that prioritized national happiness over students' individual advantages and perceived education as a mechanism for advancing the common good. Yet, the academic program was only one way through which Carroll and Maguire expected to educate students. As at Bowdoin and South Carolina Colleges, Georgetown officials believed that regulating student behavior was a necessary element of higher learning. Georgetown's code of student conduct, however, was modeled on those at Jesuit boarding schools such as St. Omers, and was more prohibitive than either Bowdoin's or South Carolina's. This extensive set of regulations included not leaving the college grounds without an escort, visits by parents being restricted to one day per month, the college president opening all student letters "not known to be from parents," and a prohibition on students visiting "any person" except their parents or legal guardians when not on campus. (This rule applied especially to the "day scholars" who did not board at the college.)[32] College officials also required pupils to wear a uniform that distinguished them as Georgetown students both on and off campus.[33]

Unlike at South Carolina College, where student apologies frequently resulted in forgiveness for rule violations, Georgetown officials enforced their code of conduct consistently and thoroughly, quickly expelling students for misbehavior. Between 1825 and 1840, the college rid itself of almost sixty students for reasons that included "idleness," "ran away," "violation of discipline, out nights," "disobedient," and "insubordination," as well as the far more belligerent "striking a prefect" and "stabbing a fellow student in the eye with a pen knife."[34]

Like their Northern and Southern peers, Georgetown students occasionally staged revolts in response to the severity of college rules. In 1850, for instance, after a prefect rejected students' request to hold a literary society meeting on a Sunday night, they held the meeting anyway.[35] Consequently, the prefect suspended the organization's meetings for a month. When college officials rejected a petition requesting a reprieve from this punishment, the students began a riot, breaking windows and cutting up beds. The protest culminated in what amounted to a walkout, with about sixty students taking up residence in a local hotel and an additional seventy student sympathizers simply departing campus. Partly because of the negative coverage the college received in local papers, and also because of the financial threat the walkout posed to the institution, college officials negotiated an agreement that permitted all students involved to return to campus in exchange for a public apology.[36]

Faculty and administrators' methods of nurturing civic virtue, especially onerous restrictions on students' freedom of movement and association, frequently clashed with students' expectations of the proper character of collegiate life. As Georgetown University historian Robert Curran has written, however, John Carroll did not intend to impose a "monastic regime upon students who were being educated for life in a republic."[37] Faculty provided students with frequent opportunities to observe the nation's governing bodies in session, outings that became so popular the college began promoting them in its prospectus. "The distance between the College and the Capitol being only an ordinary walk," it read, "the students of the Rhetoric class have an opportunity of being occasionally present at the debates of Congress and pleadings of the Supreme Court (always, however, attended by their prefect)."[38] Class of 1854 valedictorian Robert Ray remembered these trips a bit differently. Although noting that it was "custom" for students to walk to the nation's capitol and listen to members of Congress, including Henry Clay, John C. Calhoun, and Daniel Webster, Ray also recalled that neither he nor his classmates, nor their escort, always followed college rules during these outings. "We generally went by classes," he recalled, "and Father Force was our prefect, and he used to go with us and we often brought him home in an intoxicating condition and some of us no better, and put him to bed without anybody knowing it."[39] As at colleges such as Bowdoin and South Carolina, there was a significant difference between establishing a set of rules and procedures to govern student behavior and obliging those students (and in the alleged case of Father Force, even the institution's employees) to abide by them.

To teach classes and serve as escorts, Georgetown employed a combination of priests, seminarians, tutors, and lay faculty, with officials intentionally hiring candidates for the priesthood because they could be paid less than laymen. When anticlerical elements of the French Revolution drove a number of priests and seminarians of the Sulpician order (members of the Society of Saint-Sulpice) out of France in 1791, the college quickly capitalized on the opportunity their arrival to America presented by inducing them to teach at Georgetown.[40] Partly as a result of this kind of immigration, the institution's faculty developed a highly international character.[41]

By most accounts, faculty members took their duties seriously and demanded a great deal from students, seeking to cultivate mental discipline through memorization and recitation. J. Fairfax McLaughlin, who would eventually become editor of the Roman Catholic newspapers the *Catholic Mirror* and *The Boston Pilot*, later recalled the "absolute thoroughness" with which his teacher, a Mr. Prendergast, conducted his examination. "Five or six lines of Greek were all he required," McLaughlin remembered. "This we thought a trifling, easy task, as we could translate that little bit in a few minutes. But when 'Old Prendy' uttered the inevitable 'χαι and,' and we began and rattled off the translation, then the real trouble began. . . . We soon found that those five or six little lines of Xenophon or Lucian had many knotty intricacies in them that we hadn't dreamed of when we began to translate them so glibly at the start."[42]

Georgetown's examination reports also document faculty expectations for student performance. These reports, which recorded comments instructors made to students immediately following exams, reveal how faculty members conceived of academic achievement and personal behavior as intrinsically linked. In one entry from 1827, an instructor noted his satisfaction with students' "uniform good conduct during the past term" before advising, "To accustom one's self to behave with propriety and decorum through life, it is highly necessary to begin when young to habituate the mind to the restraint of discipline. By uniting regularity of conduct with due apriority in your literary pursuits, you will infallibly accomplish the end for which you are now in this Institution, and will prepare yourselves to occupy hereafter that Station in Society which is always allotted to integrity of character united with literary acquirements."[43] Emphasizing the importance of acquiring mental discipline at a young age as a prerequisite for developing character traits such as integrity, the instructor expressed concisely the pedagogical logic in place at Georgetown College as well as at many other higher-education institutions during the early national period.

Not all examination reports were so positive, however. In one particularly blunt example, a faculty member singled out a student for consistently failing to improve his poor performance. "Francis Ward!" his report began,

> What shall be said of Francis Ward? Misfortunes surround him on all sides; yet he laughed as cheerfully as ever. Misfortunes in Demosthenes, History and Catechism,—and total ruin in Homer; yet with all the

composure of the just man of whom Horace speaks, Francis Ward was undismayed. . . . Francis Ward has studied Horace & Homer now for a year and a half and yet we are told that he does not appear to understand either of them; yet Francis Ward constantly assures us that he studies;—what must be our inference? Shall we doubt his veracity or his capacity?[44]

For Georgetown faculty, Ward's performance bespoke not only academic failure but a character flaw that would ultimately prevent him from fulfilling his obligation to advance the common good following graduation.

Compared to their peers at Bowdoin and South Carolina Colleges, Georgetown students were ethnically diverse and, to some extent, shared the international character of the institution's faculty. Between 1792 and 1805, it educated 277 students. Of the 253 for whom data on national origin exist, 206 were from the United States, forty from Central America, six from Europe, and one from the Louisiana Territory. Of the total, approximately half were English, 20 percent French, 16 percent Scots and Scotch-Irish, 13 percent Irish, and 1 percent each Hispanic, Italian, Scandinavian, and Welsh. Of these students with known religious affiliations, about 80 percent were Roman Catholic and 20 percent practiced various Protestant denominations. Only sixteen of them, or 6 percent of the 277 total students, entered the seminary.[45]

Student enrollments rose significantly over time, from sixty-nine students in 1792 to 119 in 1816 to 333 by the late 1850s. The rise resulted partly from Georgetown's location in the Mid-Atlantic region, which tended to attract students from an increasingly expansive geographic area. By the 1830s, US students arrived on campus from as far west as Missouri, as far north as Maine, and as far south as Florida. In addition, the college became closely tied to the seat of American government, so that numerous politicians arranged for their sons, as well as the sons of family members, to enroll. George Washington's two grandnephews attended. So did Thomas Jefferson's grandson, although he sought to transfer within months of arriving due to the strict disciplinary code. Presidents Andrew Jackson, Martin Van Buren, John Tyler, and Andrew Johnson all sent sons to study at Georgetown, as did numerous congressmen and military officers. Indeed, for a time it was customary for the US president to present diplomas at commencement to the college's graduates.[46] In almost all of these cases, Georgetown's location as well as its professed denominational tolerance trumped concerns that non–Roman Catholics might have had regarding the college's religious affiliation. Moreover, international events influenced student enrollment. As early as the college's first decade, when the Haitian Revolution led many Roman Catholics to immigrate to the United

States, both private citizens and clergy found Georgetown a valuable educational and employment resource.

In many ways, however, Georgetown's students during the early national period shared an experience quite similar to that of their peers at Bowdoin and South Carolina Colleges. As one graduate recalled of college life in the 1820s, students' daily regimen included waking early (5:00 a.m. in warmer months and 5:30 in the winter), washing "at the nozzle of the pump," attending morning mass and breakfast, and then beginning classes. Recreation at 11:30 led to "dinner" at noon followed by a "short visit to the chapel" and further recreation for ninety minutes. Afternoon classes then began, ending with "rosary and evening studies, then supper of bread and tea."[47] This routine was followed throughout the week, with a half-day of class on Saturday and regular attendance at mass on Sunday. (Non-Catholics were required to attend a denominational service at a local church.) The academic year ran from September to July and included three exams, one before Christmas, one before Easter, and one before summer vacation.

Many Georgetown students also shared with their peers at other higher-education institutions the experience of literary society membership. Establishing the Philodemic Society in 1830, students took the organization's name (meaning a fondness for or love of the people) to signify their admiration for America's republican form of government. "In the first place," as an early student leader of the organization described it, "we endeavored to adapt it [the society] to the peculiar institutions of our country. We went back to the source of all power—to the foundation stone of the republic—the people."[48]

Several years after the Philodemic's establishment, students formed two additional societies, the Philonomosian and the Philistorian (the latter for younger, preparatory students).[49] As with the Philodemic's, the Philonomosian's constitution declared the organization's importance in preparing students to fulfill civic duties when it stated, "Though anxious and resolved to reap all the benefits, which it is the peculiar property of Debating Societies to confer, yet our more immediate aim, will be to promote eloquence, and acquire an accurate knowledge of history—These acquisitions we deem useful for all men, but believe them indispensible for us, considering the peculiar form of government under which we live, and the independent character of the nation, to which it is our good fortune to belong."[50]

Students valued the opportunity these organizations provided to develop rhetorical and debating skills, claiming that such skills permitted more effective participation in civil society. In his 1831 address to the Philodemic Society, for instance, alumnus Daniel J. Desmond congratulated his audience members for having established their association both because it afforded opportunities to develop eloquence and because such eloquence was central to republican government. "Permit me to say," Desmond pronounced, "that you are entitled to signal honour for creating within the bosom of a great and distinguished Literary Institution, a Society to disseminate a love of the people, and to cultivate the practice of eloquence, the best weapon to defend their rights. Our liberties depend on their just appreciation by the people. They will be the more highly valued and resolutely defended by the diffusion of knowledge, patriotism, and virtue."[51]

Similarly, lectures delivered at literary society meetings frequently echoed a social ethos of civic-mindedness by urging students to consider their obligation to serve society following graduation. In 1856, South Carolinian and Georgetown graduate Alexander A. Allemong delivered a commencement address to members of the Philodemic Society during which he declared, "To-day you close your college life. Hitherto you have been preparing; henceforth you must act. With minds well stored, I trust, with the classic lore of antiquity, enlightened by the sciences of modern times, and firmly balanced by the sage precepts of a philosophy that can never grow old, your country has a just claim to expect something from your services."[52]

As with literary societies at other institutions, Georgetown's organizations maintained libraries and provided frequent opportunities for students to debate issues of interest.[53] Although Washington, DC has historically been considered a Southern city, comparing the topics that Georgetown and South Carolina society members chose to debate reveals regional similarities as well as differences between the political, economic, and social orientations of students at the two institutions. On the central issue of slavery, for instance, members of Georgetown's Philonomosian society in the 1840s debated (1) "Whether slavery is consistent with a Republican Government," (2) "Whether slavery should be abolished or not in the United States," and (3) Whether slaves are "advantageous to the South or not." In all three cases, the students decided overwhelmingly that slavery was consistent with republican principles, was of benefit, and should be maintained.[54] About other issues of national importance, however, Georgetown students seemed far less concerned than those at South Carolina College. At a general meeting in October 1831, as the federal tariff was quickly becoming the central cause of sectional conflict in the United States, Philodemic Society members deliberated over choosing one debate question from a number of possibilities, including "Is the Tariff beneficial to the US?" Not selecting this question, they instead chose, "Which makes the most impression upon man, Fear or Joy?"[55] Later that month, as South Carolina College students debated "Whether or not South Carolina should nullify the present tariff laws, would the general government be justified in attempting to enforce the same?"

Georgetown's Philodemic Society members took up "Did Alexander deserve death for the murder of his friend and subject—Clytus?"[56] And in early January 1832, as South Carolina College students discussed "Should the Legislature of this state permit a branch of the national bank to be established in this place?" Georgetown students chose to debate the question, "Who was the greater man, Archimedes or Newton?"[57]

It is possible that early in the antebellum period Philonomosian and Philodemic Society members avoided engaging genuinely contentious issues because, unlike Bowdoin's and South Carolina's, Georgetown's student body included both Northerners and Southerners. By the eve of the Civil War, however, literary society members had become sharply divided. After a contentious debate in 1860, Philodemic members failed to come to a decision in response to the question "Ought the Southern States to oppose the coercion of any States of this Union, should any secede in the event of the election of a Black Republican President?" Moreover, just three months prior to the firing on Fort Sumter, they again struggled to respond to "Are the Southern States justifiable in seizing upon the property of the Federal Government?"[58] Finally, tempers erupted following debate on the question "Should the South now secede?" Although members maintained decorum during the actual proceedings, one student later recalled that afterward "a scene followed not unlike some of those then frequently occurring in Congress—a free fight. Bill Hodges, of Mississippi . . . sprang at the Vice-President of the Society . . . Jack Gardiner, of Maryland, rushed at me . . . Jim Dooley, of Virginia, Gus Wilson of Maryland, Jim Hoband and Pres. Sands, of Washington . . . and many other Philodemics, were mixed up in the [sic] méle."[59]

In addition to literary societies, Georgetown's primary religious organization—the Sodality—became a central part of many students' collegiate experience. Although students at other colleges in the early nineteenth century, including Bowdoin, established religious-oriented extracurricular organizations such as the Praying Circle and Society of Inquiry, Georgetown modeled its Sodality on Roman Catholic brotherhoods dating to the Middle Ages. Historically, these associations promoted piety and charitable works; as with many sodalities at the time, Georgetown students devoted theirs to the "Immaculate Conception of the Blessed Virgin Mary."[60] Predating the establishment of Georgetown's literary societies, the Sodality provided a forum for students to develop their faith, while also adopting an extensive set of rules they expected participants to follow. "All of the Members of the Sodality must studiously avoid evil companions, quarrels, contentions, murmuring, and all dangerous occasions of sin," the organization demanded. "As their Patroness is particularly honored by that ennobling title 'Queen of purity' they must strenuously endeavor, to imitate her virginal and more than Angelic purity; & always cherish an irreconcilable hatred, & aversion for the opposite degrading vice. The Sodalist must be particularly united, by the bonds of fraternal charity, ever solicitous to preserve inviolable peace & harmony among themselves, each one endeavoring to be *all to all*."[61]

College officials supported the Sodality with the hope that it would encourage members to pursue the seminary.[62] Although it is unclear to what extent the organization actually led students to make this decision, the number who became seminarians indeed correlated with the number of Sodality members.[63] For these graduates, entering religious life and advancing the common good were mutually reinforcing activities. Still, throughout the early national period and continuing into the antebellum era, most Georgetown graduates did not enter the seminary. Even following Pope Pius VII's restoration of the Society of Jesus in 1814, most Georgetown alumni graduated into one of the liberal professions rather than the priesthood.

As with its Northern and Southern peer institutions, Georgetown sought to foster among students a commitment to the public good—to the grand interests of society—and indeed a significant number of graduates became public servants of varying kinds over time. Robert Curran has assembled data demonstrating what he describes as "the extraordinary proportion" of Georgetown students who chose "a mixture of law and public service as a career" following graduation.[64] Although occupational data on graduates prior to 1830 is incomplete—of the 533 students who attended the college between its opening and 1817, information exists for only eighty-five—that for later graduates is much more reliable. Statistics for forty-eight of the sixty-four students who graduated during the 1830s reveal that approximately half became either lawyers (33 percent) or members of the clergy (18 percent), while the others became physicians (10 percent), politicians (8 percent), civil servants (4 percent), engineers/surveyors (4 percent), businessmen (4 percent), teachers, farmers, and soldiers.[65] Data on the cohort who graduated in the 1840s follow a similar trend, showing many alumni becoming lawyers and doctors, followed by clergy, farmers, and government clerks.[66] And, as Curran writes, a significant number of these graduates became public servants.

The life trajectory of Alexander Dimitry, an 1826 graduate, provides a particularly illuminating example of Curran's findings. Born in 1805 in Louisiana to a Greek immigrant father and a mother from New Orleans, Dimitry received private tutoring at home before attending the New Orleans Classical Academy and then Georgetown. Following graduation, he worked as an editor of the *New Orleans Bee*, served as a professor at Baton Rouge College, and in 1834 received an appointment to a clerkship in the US General Post Office Department.

Several years later, Dimitry returned to Louisiana, where he served as super-intendent of public schools in New Orleans and then state superintendent of public education (during which time he was credited for "organizing" and "putting into active operation" the state's public school system). Returning to Washington, DC, he was employed by the US State Department as Chief Trans-lator of Foreign Diplomatic Correspondence; upon his receiving a law degree in 1859, President James Buchanan appointed him US Minister to Costa Rica and Nicaragua. When the South seceded in 1861, Dimitry returned to Louisi-ana and assumed the position of head of the Finance Bureau of the Confederate States Post Office. Following the war, he moved to New York City before return-ing South where, in 1870, he was appointed professor of ancient languages at Christian Brothers College in Mississippi. He retired to New Orleans, where he died in 1883.[67]

Although John Carroll founded Georgetown with the primary intent of edu-cating students who would pursue the priesthood, the institution functioned much like Bowdoin and South Carolina Colleges throughout the early national period. Having been given a primarily classical education, some graduates chose the religious life but most, like Alexander Dimitry, entered a liberal profession and later became involved in civic affairs. Indeed, despite ethnoreligious con-trasts, Catholic colleges were more similar to other higher-education institutions in America than the historiography suggests. Especially in the way Georgetown manifested the prevailing social ethos in America—infused as it was by civic-mindedness and a commitment to the common good—the college assumed a broad public purpose that was almost identical to the one espoused by its peer institutions.

Georgetown's official seal, adopted in 1844, perhaps best exemplifies this characteristic. Based on a design dating back to the college's first decade, the seal eschewed most of the symbols of Roman Catholicism, instead borrowing heavily from the emblems of republican government and the Great Seal of the United States. A heraldic eagle displays at its center with a shield of stars and stripes. In one talon, the eagle clutches a cross, representing the Christian faith. In the other, it clutches a globe with calipers, representing science and knowl-edge. Stars surround the eagle, representing the original thirteen colonies (or, as they changed over time, the number of states at a particular moment in the institution's history). A lyre, representing classical culture, is positioned above the eagle's head, and in its beak it holds a banner that reads *Utraque Unum*, meaning "both are one."[68] In adopting the phrase, which echoes the American motto *E Pluribis Unum* ("out of many, one"), Georgetown officials emphasized its meaning as the joining of philosophy and religion in the Western tradition.[69]

The seal, then, provides a visual representation of the institution's commitment to integrating the Christian faith and republican government, a commitment that directly aligned with the social ethos that prevailed in America during the early national period.

Conclusion to Part I

Civic-mindedness pervaded Bowdoin, South Carolina, and Georgetown Colleges throughout the late eighteenth and early nineteenth centuries. Characterized by its commitment to the public good, this ethos led founders and officials at each of the three colleges to articulate their respective institution's purposes as advancing the "common good," fostering the "good order and harmony of the whole community," and promoting the "grand interests of society." Students often responded positively to these institutional imperatives. Frequently expressing aspirations that higher learning would result in achieving greater social status, they nevertheless declared their dedication to become useful members of society, especially by serving as leaders at the state and national levels. Graduates' career trajectories reveal that many lived out this commitment.

Regional distinctions, however, significantly influenced these institutions. Bowdoin enrolled more impoverished students than did South Carolina College, for instance. South Carolina faculty engaged students in questions of nullification and secession earlier and more often than those at Georgetown College. Georgetown enrolled students from a greater geographic area than both Bowdoin and South Carolina. Nevertheless, these distinctions existed within the framework of a broad institutional commitment to advancing the public good. Were Joseph McKeen, Jonathan Maxcy, and John Carroll to have met at a conference of college presidents during the early national period, they would have agreed that their institutions shared a central objective to advance the cause of the republic by privileging the common good over private advantage.

Even as this meeting occurred, however, the nation's social ethos would have been reorienting away from civic-mindedness and toward practicality. Some Americans would express deep concerns over this change, especially as it related to higher education. In an address delivered to Georgetown's Philodemic Society in July 1862, graduate John C. C. Hamilton both asserted the importance of the liberal arts in American education and expressed his anxiety over their decline. Given that the nation was in the midst of the Civil War, some students undoubtedly considered Hamilton's choice of topic tedious. Ultimately, however, it proved prophetic. Describing an education in liberal studies as the kind best suited to sustaining democratic government, Hamilton noted the extent to which the curriculum was becoming directed to the "practical purposes of life." He declared:

> The numerous schools and colleges scattered over the vast expanse of our country, the liberal encouragement which they receive from the public, and the munificent patronage lavished on them by the various States, amply attest to the value which the American people place on their system of general instruction. And yet, whilst the importance of the subject is recognized in this practical and substantial manner, and whilst we fully understand the great agency which the enlightenment of the citizen is to exert on the progress and final success of our peculiar form of government, it is surprising to see how great a prejudice exists against the liberal studies. The pursuit of them is regarded as a waste of time. We are told that they contribute nothing towards what are vaguely called the practical purposes of life; that they are too tedious to suit the active spirit of the American youth.[70]

He then noted what he believed was the central problem associated with higher education's reorientation away from liberal studies. "Education," he told his listeners, "is looked upon as an end rather than as a means, and courses of study are laid out very much after the fashion of our railroads—the shortest possible routes are adopted, all of which have for their terminus the busy marts of the money-making world."[71]

Hamilton's address took a chronologically expansive view of educational change. He looked to the past, when a social ethos of civic-mindedness prioritized the common good over private advantage. He looked to the present, when a social ethos of practicality emphasized applied learning and what were called the "useful arts." And he accurately envisioned the future, when a social ethos of commercialism would infuse the attributes of business enterprise into education's form and function. Yet, as the speaker was undoubtedly aware, Americans had not only begun *perceiving* of education as an end rather than a means in the years preceding the Civil War. They established entirely new kinds of higher-education institutions that took "practical purposes" as their primary concern. In the same year that Hamilton delivered his address, and just a short distance away from where he spoke, the US Congress passed the Morrill Land-Grant Act, providing federal support to institutions seeking to teach "such branches of learning as are related to agriculture and the mechanic arts . . . in order to promote the liberal and practical education of the industrial classes in the several pursuits and professions in life."[72] Although not repudiating liberal education, the Morrill Act represented the extent to which America's social ethos was being reoriented away from civic-mindedness and toward practicality. As a model for the colleges and universities this legislation would promote, advocates looked not to Bowdoin, South Carolina, or Georgetown, but rather to more recently established institutions of higher education, such as the Agricultural College of the State of Michigan.

THE ANTEBELLUM AND CIVIL WAR ERAS

4

"TO SPREAD THROUGHOUT THE LAND, AN ARMY OF PRACTICAL MEN"

Agriculture and Mechanics in the Midwest

In May 1907, US President Theodore Roosevelt traveled to East Lansing, Michigan, to celebrate the fiftieth anniversary of the opening of the Agricultural College of the State of Michigan, the first four-year college of agriculture in the United States. In an address entitled "The Man Who Works with His Hands," Roosevelt described the occasion as one of "national significance" and proclaimed to the crowd of twenty thousand, "Educational establishments should produce highly trained scholars, of course; but in a country like ours, where the educational establishments are so numerous, it is folly to think that their main purpose is to produce these highly trained scholars. . . . Book-learning is very important, but it is by no means everything; and we shall never get the right idea of education until we definitely understand that a man may be well trained in book-learning and yet, in the proper sense of the word, and for all practical purposes, be utterly uneducated."[1]

Roosevelt's presence at the golden anniversary of what was popularly known as the Michigan Agricultural College highlighted three pivotal developments in American higher education. First, it commemorated the survival of the nation's first four-year agricultural college, an outcome that had been far from assured during its early years. Second, it represented the federal government's expanding role in higher education. Referring to the financial support Congress provided states through land grants, Roosevelt declared, "The Nation is to be congratulated on the fact that the Congress at Washington has repeatedly enacted laws designed to aid the several States in establishing and maintaining agricultural and mechanical colleges. I greet all such colleges, through their representatives who have gathered here to-day, and bid them Godspeed in their work."[2] Third, Roosevelt's appearance at the celebration of an institution dedicated to the application of scientific principles to practical ends reflected the extent to which a social ethos of practicality had, by the end of the nineteenth century, become the conventional wisdom in higher education.

Fifty years earlier, practicality was not yet firmly established in colleges and universities. But throughout the antebellum era, the expansion of scientific and technical knowledge joined with the rise of political populism to lead existing institutions to add practical studies to their curricula.[3] By the beginning of the Civil War, Bowdoin, South Carolina, and Georgetown Colleges had all integrated courses such as mineralogy, civil engineering, and agricultural chemistry into their academic programs. In addition, some more traditional institutions had established separate schools (Lawrence Scientific at Harvard and what would become Sheffield Scientific at Yale) for the study of the "useful arts," including agriculture, mechanics, mining, and the military (later abbreviated "A&M").[4]

Many advocates of practical studies, however, were not satisfied with simply incorporating courses or appending schools to already-established colleges and universities.[5] They sought to break with tradition—and especially with a classical curriculum they deemed increasingly irrelevant and ineffective—by establishing a new kind of higher-education institution, one that would teach students scientific and investigative principles while also requiring the application of those principles outside of the classroom, both on the farm and in the field.[6] Of equal importance, this new institutional type would contribute to the common good by being unprecedentedly accessible and affordable to agrarian and laboring youth. By eliminating fluency in Latin and Greek as prerequisites for admission, these institutions would cease to impede the educational aspirations of students whose families could not afford the cost of preparatory academic studies. They would also provide employment to students from less-advantaged backgrounds throughout their enrollment, affording the necessary financial support for them to complete a four-year course of study leading to a bachelor's degree.

Yet, even while a rising ethos of practicality informed the critics of existing colleges, civic-mindedness remained a compelling force in higher education. Its influence guided the advocates of practical studies away from establishing proprietary or trade schools, which dated to the colonial period and offered strictly vocational preparation for work in fields such as surveying and the building trades. Instead, and in contrast with the celebratory claim Theodore Roosevelt would make fifty years later, "book-learning" remained central to the new kinds of institutions reformers envisioned. Rather than purely occupational training, the higher learning they offered would be simultaneously "liberal and practical," a phrase that both described the course of study the colleges adopted and was eventually incorporated into the Morrill Land-Grant Act.[7]

During the first half of the nineteenth century, few examples of this kind of institution existed in America. The United States Military Academy, founded in West Point, New York, in 1802, provided one such model after it began orienting its academic program around engineering in 1817. As it was sponsored by the federal government and closely tied to the army's needs, however, West Point was limited in its use as a prototype. Advocates of practicality also founded civilian schools dedicated to agricultural and mechanical studies, including Maine's Gardiner Lyceum (1823), which offered a three-year course in the application of agricultural science; New York's Rensselaer School (present-day Rensselaer Polytechnic Institute), established in 1824 "for the purpose of instructing persons, who may choose to apply themselves, in the application of science to the common purposes of life"; and Ohio's Farmer's College (1846), which offered a course of study "adapted to those who wished to qualify themselves for industrial and scientific pursuits."[8]

None of these institutions offered a bachelor's degree, however, leaving many supporters of practicality, especially agriculturalists, frustrated with the lack of attention and status ascribed to practical studies. In an 1844 report on the need for an agricultural college in their state, members of the Michigan State Senate's Committee on Agriculture claimed, "Colleges and schools have been liberally endowed and supported by the state governments, and the arts and sciences have been cherished with an honorable and enlightened zeal, but, in the meantime, agriculture, which is an art so important, a science so interesting, has been left to struggle for itself."[9] Similarly, a contributor to the periodical *Michigan Farmer* asked in 1853, "Is there any science in Agriculture? I think that it requires but a little observation to be satisfied that this is the most scientific *profession*, to which our attention can be directed. I have claimed, and still claim, that this should not only be placed *among the learned professions, but at the head of them.* There is no other profession or occupation that takes in so wide a range of science and offers so extensive a field of learning as this" [emphases in the original].[10] In these and many other cases dating from the antebellum era, supporters of practicality criticized existing colleges and universities for either completely excluding or relegating to the periphery of their institutions both practical studies and the students they believed would benefit from them.[11]

Where did reformers' commitment to practicality, especially as it concerned agriculture, originate? Although higher learning during the early national period frequently centered on classicism, interest in "useful knowledge" (derived from the reasoned investigation of nature and applied to some constructive end) was not uncommon.[12] As early as the eighteenth century, educated Americans founded organizations to foster this type of study, including the American Academy of Arts and Sciences (1780), the New York Society for the Promotion of Useful Knowledge (1785), and the Massachusetts Society for Promoting Agriculture (1792).[13] During the antebellum era, the weekly newspaper and then magazine *Scientific American*, first published in 1845, reflected the growing popular appeal of applying scientific principles to "the common purposes of life." The following year, Congress established the Smithsonian Institution with an endowment from British scientist James Smithson for the "increase and diffusion of knowledge among men." Historian Roger L. Williams concludes of the era, "Science in early nineteenth-century America still retained a decidedly deductive air, but the scientific spirit, or at least the enthusiasm for empirical investigation, enjoyed a remarkable popularity in the 1830s and 1840s."[14]

Europe played no small role in catalyzing Americans' interest in useful knowledge. Swiss and German technical academies, as well as institutions such as France's École Central des Arts et Manufactures inspired William Barton Rogers to establish the Massachusetts Institute of Technology in 1861.[15] Observing that the Parisian school offered a "broad foundation of scientific study, and building upon it practical education," Barton argued that America needed such an institution in order to prepare graduates for work in "agriculture, architecture, railroad engineering, textile manufacturing, public works, industrial chemistry, general civil engineering, machine manufacturing, metallurgy and mining, and commerce."[16] Similarly, Thomas Green Clemson, who studied mineralogy and chemistry in Paris before becoming US secretary of agriculture and eventually founding South Carolina's Clemson University (1889), noted that the absence in America of higher-education institutions dedicated to practical studies meant that students who looked to "cultivate science" were "compelled to resort to institutions maintained by the monarchial governments of Europe."[17]

European scholars also influenced the United States through research and publication. In the early nineteenth century, prosperous New England farmers looked to agricultural science to sustain crop yields and combat "worn-out soil" caused by overfarming. Forming agricultural societies and publishing agrarian periodicals, they engaged in "book farming" by applying the work of European scientists such as German chemist Justus Liebig, whose 1840 book *Organic Chemistry in Its Applications to Agriculture and Physiology* was received in America, according to historian Margaret W. Rossiter, "with tremendous enthusiasm and hope," partly because of recent widespread crop failures.[18] Counties and states established agricultural societies, too, which in turn hosted fairs dedicated to exhibiting innovative farming methods and sponsoring competitions for superior livestock. By the eve of the Civil War, the US Agricultural

Society—itself formed in 1852 through a convention called by twelve state agricultural associations—recorded over nine hundred agricultural organizations operating across the United States.[19]

Agrarian solidarity did not spring solely from farmers' anxiety over soil fertility and declining harvests, however. Political populism, which strengthened during the Jacksonian era, led farmers, mechanics, craftsmen, and skilled journeymen to demand greater governmental consideration of their interests, as well as increased access for their children to what they perceived as traditionally elitist institutions, including colleges and universities. But agrarian reformers' populism posed a dilemma. Inspired by European accomplishments, advocates of practical studies, such as Thomas Green Clemson, were nevertheless dismayed that monarchial governments rather than democratic republics were responsible for advances in agricultural science. As one contributor to the *New York Tribune* noted in 1852, "Prussia is a monarchy, with fifteen millions of people. New York is a republic with three millions. . . . Prussia has seventy-one public establishments to instruct her people in farming, the science of sciences, the art of arts. New York has not one. . . . Ought so shameful a contrast to exist between that monarchy and this republic?"[20]

To resolve this dilemma, agricultural reformers adopted the methods of European institutions and modified them to suit the prevailing US political culture.[21] Partly in response to populist demands, several states, especially those in New England and the upper Midwest, passed laws requiring the establishment of educational institutions offering instruction in practical studies. Michigan's first state constitution, for instance, directed the legislature to "encourage by all suitable means, the promotion of intellectual, scientifical, and agricultural improvements." Accordingly, legislators established the University of Michigan at Ann Arbor in 1837 to provide, in addition to preparation for the liberal professions, instruction in "practical farming and agriculture."[22] The legislature also required that the university establish branch institutions throughout the state, each of which was to include "a department of agriculture with competent instructors in the theory of the subject, including vegetable physiology and agricultural chemistry and experimental and practical farming and agriculture."[23]

Lacking the funding necessary to support a university system with multiple campuses, the institution's board of regents instead established eight preparatory schools. In a short time, however, all eight closed due to financial constraints.[24] Moreover, university officials did little to develop an agricultural program in Ann Arbor. Consequently, when state legislators established a teacher-training or "normal" school in the town of Ypsilanti in 1849, they again required instruction "in the mechanic arts, and in the art of husbandry and agricultural chemistry."[25] By this time reformers had become impatient with the state's lack of progress in providing agricultural education and began demanding that the legislature establish an independent agricultural college.[26]

Four years earlier, the *Michigan Farmer* had published US Agricultural Society member Henry Coleman's observations on "European Agriculture and Rural Economy." In this work, Coleman provided a plan for an American "agricultural institution" modeled on those in Great Britain. More than simply a school for the study of agricultural sciences, his proposal included a model farm where students would apply principles learned in the classroom, extensive gardens "for purposes of botanical instruction," and a system of labor through which students would learn to farm, earn a wage, and, in keeping with the populist spirit, be placed with their peers "in a condition of perfect equality."[27] Coleman's proposal captured the imagination of Michigan agrarian reformers who, upon founding the state's Agricultural Society, urged the legislature to establish an agricultural institution for instruction in studies "of an eminently practical kind."[28]

Meeting in executive session on December 19, 1849, the society's members drafted a legislative proposal referencing Coleman's work as a blueprint for an agricultural college and model farm in their state.[29] Reflecting a rising social ethos of practicality, society secretary John C. Holmes, a nurseryman, member of the Detroit school board, and editor of the *Horticultural Gazette*, emphasized that rather than learning for learning's sake, the society wished the college to advance the common good by engaging students in the practical application of scientific principles with a clear occupational goal in mind. "It is not a learned proficiency in the higher branches of science alone that is sought," Holmes exhorted legislators. "The great aim is, to send out into the country, to spread throughout the land, an army of practical men—young and active men, experienced in every point of the management of a farm, made hardy and handy by a practical exercise of these arts, and with minds enriched and cultivated by the studies of science and a rigid observation of nature, and ardent in the cause to which their lives and best energies are to be devoted."[30]

Michigan Agricultural Society members took advantage of a tradition of federal support for educational expansion when they convinced the state legislature to request a federal grant of 350,000 acres of land, proceeds from the sale of which would subsidize establishing the new college. Congress, however, declined the request. Undeterred, society members next convinced representatives meeting at the new state capital of Lansing in 1850 to revise the Michigan constitution to provide for an "agricultural school" as well as a state land grant to sustain the institution in its infancy.[31] With this effort, they succeeded. The provision's wording, however, left open the possibility that the school could be founded as either an independent institution or a branch of the state's university or normal school.

For the next five years, rivalry between the latter two institutions obstructed the founding of Michigan's agricultural college.[32]

During the delay, reformers considered supporting one of the two existing state institutions in their bids to host the agrarian school. By 1854, however, again convinced that only an independent institution would meet their needs, Michigan Agricultural Society members began circulating petitions in support of an agricultural college established "separate from any other institution of learning" and founded upon "an equality with the best Colleges of the State."[33] Organizing lobbying efforts and delivering petitions to state legislators, John C. Holmes spearheaded drafting a bill for the founding of the college. At his own expense, he then spent much of January 1855 successfully shepherding it through the state legislature. On February 12, Governor Kinsley S. Bingham signed the act establishing the Agricultural College of the State of Michigan.[34]

Michigan's all-male agricultural college included most of the elements that agrarian reformers had desired, including a four-year course of study, a model farm, the state land grant, free tuition for state residents, and compensated student labor. The latter characteristics, in particular, attracted the attention of young men from Michigan and other states seeking to advance their educations despite their socioeconomic backgrounds. One prospective student wrote from Philadelphia to the college's first president, Joseph R. Williams, in June 1857 to explain,

> I am a young man of very limited means but desirous of an education & take the liberty of addressing you on the subject. My means are so limited that I am compelled to give up the idea of getting an education in the east, therefore I turn to the west. . . . Do you think it is possible for a young man of sound health and industrious disposition who has a fair knowledge of farming and laboring work and with him from fifty to seventy dollars to commence with—to successfully pursue the studies & finally graduate in your University?[35]

Unfortunately for this applicant, so many Michigan residents sought to enroll in the college in its first few years that Williams was obliged to turn away those from out of state.

Reflecting the college's roots in a social ethos of practicality, the institution's founding legislation noted its "chief purpose and design" as "to improve and teach the science and practice of agriculture."[36] It would do this, according to the college's first circular, by offering a course of study that "has been arranged with direct reference to the wants and interests of the agricultural class in our State."[37] Consequently, the college's first faculty members held such titles as professor of chemistry, professor of animal and vegetable physiology and entomology, and professor of horticulture.[38] Nevertheless, although Williams assumed leadership of an institution that took practical studies as its priority, he did not reject the role of the liberal arts in preparing students—in their role as citizens of a democratic republic—to contribute to the common good following graduation. In his inaugural address, he echoed an ethos of civic-mindedness when he declared, "A farmer is a citizen, obliged to bear his portion of public burdens, amenable to the laws, and in a humbler or a wider range, may become an exponent of society. He should be able to execute, therefore, the duties of even highly responsible stations, with self-reliance and intelligence."[39]

Mindful, however, that agrarian reformers comprised the bulk of his audience—the same reformers who had demanded an independent agricultural institution—Williams added the caveat that, as necessary as it was for the new college to foster civic competence among students, this was not one of its "original and primary objects."[40] Indeed, this statement signaled a genuine shift away from civic-mindedness toward practicality. Still, the college's curriculum incorporated subjects taught at higher-education institutions such as Bowdoin, South Carolina, and Georgetown Colleges, including rhetoric, English literature, history, and moral philosophy.[41] These courses, college officials noted, were "indispensible" to students' education.[42] Over the next several years, the tension between practicality (as manifested in analytical chemistry exercises such as "preparation of artificial manures") and civic-mindedness (as manifested in English literature exercises such as memorizing passages from Chaucer) would disrupt the college's growth.[43]

In the immediate future, however, the seventy-three applicants who arrived on campus to take entrance examinations in May 1857 found a college very much under construction.[44] Having broken ground just two years earlier on a forested lot of 677 acres, three miles east of the sparsely settled state capital of Lansing, the State Board of Education had barely had time to construct three buildings. The first, College Hall, was the west wing of what officials anticipated would eventually be a centrally located building with both east and west wings. The second, which students came to call "Saints' Rest" (after a well-known Puritan devotional), was the dormitory. The third was a barn for the farm's livestock. Surrounding all three were the charred stumps of trees that students would be put to work removing as part of their daily labor (figure 4). As one student later recalled, "The College, when I first saw it May 10, 1857, consisted of a tract of mainly timber land without an acre fully cleared. A few acres had been slashed down and the logs and brush cleared. On every hand were old stubs and partially burned trees. The fire had scorched the timber next to the clearing, so that at every point of the compass to which you turned you beheld dead and blackened trees which presented a most desolate scene."[45]

FIGURE 4. Clearing land around Saint's Rest Dormitory, Agricultural College of the State of Michigan, c. 1850s. Courtesy of the Michigan State University Archives and Historical Collections.

After examining applicants in common school subjects (including arithmetic, grammar, penmanship, and spelling) rather than the classics, college officials admitted sixty-one students for the first term. By the end of the second term, 123 young men had enrolled, filling Saints' Rest to overcapacity. Most of these were in their late teens, although students as young as fourteen applied.[46] Faculty designated all as first-year students but divided them into three groups due to their varying levels of academic preparation. Over the next few years, these young men experienced both the joys and trials of enrolling at a new kind of American college, one that was state-supported yet untested. Rather than learning through farm labor, these students spent thousands of hours chopping trees and splitting wood to clear land for the college's farm.[47]

Allen B. Morse, Edward Granger, Charles A. Jewell, and their classmates discovered a rustic yet regulated student life in the college's early years. Although Michigan students did not undertake a study of the classics, many faculty members subscribed to the belief that the mind, as a muscle, needed regular exercise. In his diary, Morse recorded almost daily classroom recitations in literature, geometry, and chemistry before proceeding to the woods to chop down trees.[48] In addition, although college officials routinized students' daily schedules, they did not claim to do so as a method for cultivating civic virtue. Instead, this was more likely a logistical necessity in order for these early classes to successfully complete both the academic work and physical labor the college required. Writing in his diary one December evening, Granger noted the routinized character of student life when he described having risen that morning at 5:00 a.m., studied until chapel, had breakfast, and then studied again until his first class at 9:00. "Recited in Literature," he noted. "Recited in Geometry and Chemistry which takes till half past-twelve. Mended my old pants *beautifully*. Chopped two hours and a half. Blistered my hands some. Since supper studied."[49] Several days later, Granger again recorded his day's activities: "After breakfast did about as I usually do mornings. In fact, there is hardly any thing to disturb the monotony of School life except the periodical *'blowings'* [scoldings] Prof. gives us every morning at Chapel. Demonstrated an advanced proposition in Geometry this morning . . . Commenced working at half past one to day. Chopped three hours. . . . Studied pretty hard this evening as the lessons are pretty hard."[50]

Student experiences beyond wood-chopping reflected the frontier nature of a college that was in the process of being carved out of the Michigan woods. Morse spent time fishing for bass and picking wild strawberries to supplement the college's somewhat meager board.[51] Granger similarly described an incident that led to students having at least one meal featuring venison. Describing his roommate's absence at dinner one night, Granger recorded, "He had been out in the woods and seeing a deer in the wheat-field had come and got Prof. Tracey to shoot the deer. Although it was very dark Prof. wounded the deer pretty seriously. Perhaps we shall try to track him in the morning."[52] Successfully locating the wounded animal the following day, students killed it, dragged the carcass back to campus, and presented it to the college steward.

Although they frequently bemoaned the monotony of recitations, "demonstrating" or presenting work in mathematics to classmates, and writing compositions on topics such as "Influence of Language on Our Thoughts and Characters," many students nevertheless became enamored of the study of chemistry. In this course, Professor Lewis R. Fiske employed what in the mid-nineteenth century were innovative pedagogical approaches to college teaching: the laboratory and the experiment.[53] Accordingly, Fiske captured students' attention with chemical demonstrations. In one class, Granger reported that the professor presented "some very handsome experiments" by combining "chloride of potash and ether and sulfuric acid."[54] In another, Fiske "exploded some soap suds by charging them with a mixture of Hydrogen and Oxygen." The violent reaction "shook the room and broke the mortar in which the mixture was."[55] In yet another class, Fiske used a static-electricity generator to pass a current "between two charcoal points." (One of Granger's classmates commented, "The sun never thought of shining so brightly as that did."[56]) More than simply entertaining students, Fiske also required they engage in experimentation. "We worked in the Laboratory two hours & a half," Morse noted in May 1859. "I tested acetal of Lead and sulphate of Copper."[57] Later, Fiske assigned Morse and his classmates a task on which they would similarly undergo public examination at the end of the term: deducing which chemical substances were held in eleven unmarked bottles. "In chemistry, determined the contents of an unknown bottle to be the Oxide of Antimony," Morse noted on June 6, 1859.[58] Four days later, he completed identifying all eleven.[59]

Occasionally, innovative approaches to teaching took faculty and students out of both the classroom and the laboratory and into the field. In 1861, professors T. C. Abbott and Manly Miles led students on a geological excursion to examine rock formations along the Grand River, about fifteen miles west of the college. "The junior class, Dr. Miles and myself, headed a double wagon with provisions, camp, etc. and went to Grand Ledge," Abbott recorded in his diary. "Here the juniors now in geology have a chance to see rocks in their strata. The huge cliffs overhanging the river (Grand) are truly magnificent, and the ravine on the opposite side is beautiful and full of scenery of picturesque beauty. The stone is sandstone, the outside of which is encrusted with lime. We slept in tents, cooked our own food, and returned the next night."[60] Not only the professors but students, too, appreciated the opportunity to study geology in the field rather than simply reciting in the classroom. "Yesterday and Friday my class with two of the profs went to a famous geological locality on the Grand River," Charles A. Jewell wrote of the trip in a letter to his brother. "We were all delighted with the visit and everything connected therewith."[61]

Although a social ethos of practicality clearly informed the college's curriculum, the steady rise of commercialism in American society also began to influence the institution's course of study. As farming evolved from subsistence agriculture to a commercial occupation, for instance, the skills associated with it became increasingly complex. In addition to choosing the proper seed and fertilizer and planting in the proper soil, successfully managing a farm's many accounts became increasingly important. Consequently, the college added bookkeeping to its academic program not long after enrolling its first students. In July 1860, in addition to acquiring a copy of Shakespeare's collected works for his English literature class, Charles A. Jewell obtained a manual for his bookkeeping class. "We are getting on finely in the latter study," Jewell informed his brother. "We make our own blank books ourselves, and thus far the teacher has created the accounts, or transactions, and we have written them in proper form." Describing one exercise in further detail, Jewell wrote, "He [the professor] supposes a large or wealthy farmer takes an inventory of his property at the beginning of the year

1860, hires two men and a girl, enters into transactions with various merchants, &c. &c. for seven months, then takes another inventory, closes the books, finds he has gained $665.09 . . . that is as far as we have proceeded."[62]

At the end of the first year, President Williams pronounced the new institution a success. In his report to the State Board of Education, he noted that the "chemical and philosophical apparatus" necessary for classroom and laboratory instruction had been procured along with the tools and livestock needed to bring sixty acres of the farm under cultivation. Four homes had been constructed for the president and faculty and repairs had been made to College Hall (necessitated due to initially shoddy construction). More than two hundred applicants sought to fill the college's twenty-five vacancies for the upcoming term. Perhaps most importantly, Williams noted, the college had already become a model for other states seeking to establish similar institutions. In Wisconsin, members of the state's Agricultural Society observed that unless they established an agricultural college, "five years will not elapse before some of our sons, who would be the first in their great calling, will be crossing over to Michigan to her already promising institution."[63] "The experiment in which we are engaged," Williams concluded, "is not therefore tested for Michigan alone, but for the Agricultural population of the whole Union. The State is everywhere lauded as exhibiting a bold and comprehensive Statesmanship in the establishment of this College."[64]

Williams's optimistic appraisal masked troubling developments, however. First, the cost of establishing such an elaborate college outstripped both proceeds from the sale of the land grant as well as a two-year, forty-thousand-dollar state appropriation. With many members expecting profitable harvests from the college farm to underwrite the institution, the legislature almost immediately reduced its appropriation.[65] As students worked to clear enough land to undertake large-scale farm production, Williams observed, "If the friends of the Institution expect it to be self-supporting at this stage of its existence, they expect an impossibility."[66]

Second, critics questioned the college's commitment to practicality. When faculty members devised the four-year academic program, they emphasized the sciences, which made up about two-thirds of the course of study. Liberal arts constituted the remaining third.[67] Yet as Madison Kuhn observed in his centennial history of the institution, faculty completely omitted the word "agriculture" from the initial curriculum, frustrating even some of the school's allies. None the titles of the first five faculty members referenced agriculture, for instance; nor did the courses listed in the college's first catalogue, nor the description of the course of studies published in its first circular.[68] "Brick buildings, delicate balancing scales, and learned professors had not been assembled in a forest clearing to teach Michigan farm boys to harness a horse or wield a hoe," Kuhn concluded. "Most of the students possessed ordinary farm skills and would secure such specialized ones as the pruning of fruit trees or the laying of drain-tile in the three hour daily work assignment. The College had been founded to teach scientific agriculture, something which perhaps did not exist in 1858; it would be developed in the laboratories and experimental plots and barns of the new agricultural colleges."[69]

Confronting mounting criticism, Williams nevertheless refused to abandon his goal of inaugurating a college that successfully integrated practical studies and the liberal arts. Alternatively, he realized from the outset that additional sources of revenue would be necessary to sustain the institution over time. "The want of a permanent endowment will act as a discouragement," he provocatively asserted in his inaugural address. "In its infancy, the Institution must rely on the caprice of successive Legislatures. The adoption of a permanent [fiscal] policy, requires a stable and reliant support, that will carry it through adversity, regardless alike of the frowns or smiles of indifference, ignorance or malice."[70] Consequently, and in an effort to secure a permanent endowment, Williams became involved in an event of historic importance when he joined with US Representative Justin S. Morrill in championing a law that would ultimately provide the financial support necessary for institutions such as the Michigan Agricultural College to flourish in the decades following the Civil War.[71]

After Vermont residents elected Morrill to Congress in 1854, the junior representative wasted no time acting on an issue of particular interest to him—the establishment of agricultural colleges. Within three months of taking office, Morrill introduced a resolution encouraging the creation of "one or more national agricultural schools" through which students would "receive a scientific and practical education at public expense."[72] Although the resolution failed, the setback, according to the politician's biographer, "only stimulated Morrill's thoughts of agricultural colleges."[73]

The following year, Morrill revised his proposal to draw on the tradition of federal land grants. Beginning with the passage of the Northwest Ordinance of 1787, the federal government granted land to the states to support a variety of internal improvements, including establishing "literary institutions." Morrill's plan once again used this method, this time to support new colleges dedicated primarily to agriculture. Seeking to broaden support for the measure, however, he wrote that the financial benefits from the land sales could go toward maintaining "at least one college where the leading object shall be, without excluding other scientific or classical studies, to teach such branches of learning as are related to agriculture and the mechanic arts . . . in order to promote the liberal and practical education of the industrial classes in the several pursuits and professions of life."[74] Morrill nevertheless confronted stiff political opposition due to emotionally charged sectional politics. Southern congressmen, especially, objected to what they perceived as the measure's unconstitutionality as, they argued, it encouraged federal intrusion into states' rights.[75] "One of the most monstrous, iniquitous and dangerous measures which have ever been submitted to Congress," declared Alabama's Representative Clement Clay of Morrill's bill, while Virginia's James Mason called it an "unconstitutional robbing of the Treasury for the purpose of bribing the States."[76]

Morrill, however, had gathered a group of distinguished lobbyists to support the effort, including Michigan Agricultural College President Joseph R. Williams.[77] Providing Morrill with detailed information on the role of agricultural institutions in Europe, Williams also enlisted the help of his students in mailing thousands of supporting letters to newspaper and journal editors throughout the nation.[78] Consequently, when Morrill rose to address his colleagues from the House floor in April 1858, he held up the Michigan Agricultural College as a model land-grant institution, pronouncing, "Agricultural colleges and schools in many portions of Europe are a marked feature of the age. In our own country the general want of such places of instruction has been so manifest that States, societies, and individuals, have attempted to supply it, though necessarily in stinted measure. The 'plentiful lack' of funds has retarded their maturity and usefulness; but there are some examples, like that of Michigan, liberally supported by the State, in the full tide of successful experiment." Undoubtedly aware of the financial struggles Williams actually confronted in Michigan, he added, "Adequate means to start on a scale commensurate with the great objects in view seems an indispensible prerequisite. States have been unable to impose at once the increased taxation that would be required, and the liberality of private individuals has been unequal to the task. But if this bill shall pass, the institutions of the character required by the people, and by our native land, would spring into life, and not languish from poverty, doubt, or neglect."[79]

Over the next several months, Morrill strategized to gather the votes necessary for the bill's passage, while supporters publicly advanced the measure. In October, Williams delivered an address at the Syracuse (New York) State Fair in which he hailed the land-grant idea and Morrill's bill in particular. After reminding his audience that the federal government had repeatedly used land grants "as a sacred fund" to support expanding education in the United States, Williams urged, "Surely, if it is a legitimate use of the lands, to devote them to the promotion of Professional and Classical learning, for still more powerful reasons, justice and expediency demand a share of them for instruction of men in those Sciences and Arts which bear directly upon Industrial and especially Agricultural pursuits." Then, referring to West Point and the recently established US Naval Academy, he declared, "We support two National Schools for instruction of men in the Arts of destruction. Let something be done for the support of schools for instruction in the Arts of production."[80]

On February 7, 1859, Williams's efforts, along with those of his fellow lobbyists, came to fruition when Morrill's bill passed both houses of Congress. But just two weeks later, President James Buchanan, labeling the bill inexpedient and unconstitutional, vetoed the legislation.[81] This set back both Williams and Morrill significantly. Having anticipated using funds from the federal land grant to counter his critics and stabilize the Michigan Agricultural College financially, Williams now had nothing to show for his efforts. When the State Board of Education met the following month, members requested his resignation.[82]

Morrill, too, was surprised by Buchanan's veto, and set out to refute the president's claims.[83] Unlike Williams, however, Morrill had time on his side. Abraham Lincoln's election to the presidency in 1860 provided him with a second chance to have the bill signed into law, while the secession by Southern states in early 1861 eliminated many of his congressional opponents. Furthermore, he rewrote the legislation following the outbreak of the Civil War to add the study of military tactics to agriculture and the mechanic arts, a revision his colleagues assuredly found appealing.[84] In December 1861, Morrill introduced his revised bill—"An Act Donating Public Lands to the Several States and Territories which May Provide Colleges for the Benefit of Agriculture and the Mechanic Arts"—into Congress. Seven months later, Lincoln signed it.[85]

The Morrill Act would have far-reaching consequences. In addition to setting a precedent for federal involvement in higher education (later capitalized on through the Hatch Act of 1887, the Second Morrill Act of 1890, and the Smith-Lever Act of 1914, among others), dozens of states used its financial benefits to establish new institutions, while others designated already-existing colleges and universities recipients of land-grant support. In Michigan, the Agricultural College ultimately became the beneficiary of Morrill's legislation. Until then, however, the college confronted multiple crises.

Joseph Williams's resignation left the institution without a president or an advocate. As a vociferous defender of a four-year curriculum that integrated practical studies and the liberal arts, his departure created an opportunity for critics to demand revisions to the college's academic program. Consequently, the State Board of Education instituted sweeping changes. First, failing in its initial search for a new president, the board chose to save the cost of the executive's salary by leaving the position vacant. Although faculty members protested the decision by choosing Professor Lewis R. Fiske as acting president, Fiske lacked the authority necessary to provide the institution with the clear direction it needed.[86] Second, the board implemented draconian budget cuts, including lowering student wages for daily labor and instituting a two-cent-per-day fee for attending the college. Third, and perhaps most damaging, Superintendent of Public Instruction John M. Gregory submitted a new academic program for the board's approval that eliminated the liberal arts and decreased the college's course of study from four years to two.[87] "The Board of Education made a radical change in the character of the institution at the close of the year 1859," the college catalogue explained for the year 1860, "making the course professional in two branches, agriculture and horticulture."[88]

Students such as Edward Granger, who had previously enrolled because they desired a four-year college education rather than strictly agricultural training, responded to the radical change by withdrawing from the institution. As Professor T. C. Abbott observed regarding the scarcity of students in February 1860, "To college. About a dozen in all there—rainy—dull—discouraging."[89] The next day, Abbott again noted how few students had appeared for entrance examination: "19 students in all! Looks as though the whole thing was gone up."[90] The following day, however, Abbott and Fiske took matters into their own hands by calling together the remaining students and asking how many would prefer a return to the previous course of study. In reply, Abbott recorded in his diary, "All voted for the academic."[91]

While he agreed to a compromise, Gregory nevertheless refused a return to the previous curriculum. Members of the Michigan Agricultural Society, angered by the four-year course of study's elimination as well as the institution's precipitous decline, consequently inserted themselves into the conflict. Over the next several months, they lobbied the state legislature to establish a Board of Agriculture to supplant the Board of Education's governing role. With the college in a state of confusion, the legislature suspended the opening of the spring 1861 term while it deliberated the institution's future. Simultaneously, Joseph R. Williams, who, after resigning as college president, had returned to his home in Constantine, Michigan and been elected to the State Senate, assumed a central role in the deliberations. From his position as senate president *pro tempore*, he aggressively supported the Agricultural Society's proposal to establish a State Board of Agriculture and advocated a return to the institution's previous academic program. Writing parts of the bill that would become "An Act to Reorganize the Agricultural College of the State of Michigan, and to Establish a State Board of Agriculture," Williams ensured that the college's course of study would "embrace not less than four years," that the curriculum would combine practical studies and the liberal arts, and that the institution would have the power to grant the same degrees offered by the state university.[92] With the legislature's approval and the governor's signature, the act permitted the college, now officially called the "State Agricultural College," to reopen for classes on April 17.[93]

Just weeks after its reorganization, college enrollments increased to sixty-one students, leading many observers to believe that proponents of a four-year collegiate program combining practical studies, the liberal arts, and manual labor had finally succeeded.[94] Celebrations, however, were short-lived. Within months, Joseph R. Williams was dead of influenza at age fifty-two and the United States was plunged into civil war. In September 1861, the faculty excused the senior class to serve in the armed forces. In November, the college awarded its first bachelor of science degrees to students *in absentia*.[95]

In *Reconstructing the Campus: Higher Education and the American Civil War*, Michael Cohen demonstrates how the war severely disrupted educational institutions throughout the United States.[96] Although spared the physical destruction experienced by many Southern colleges and universities, and sustaining a small but consistent average enrollment of seventy students, Michigan's State Agricultural College was nevertheless undermined by the conflict. Throughout the war years, students such as Charles A. Jewell departed campus prior to graduation to join the Union Army. Meanwhile, college officials instituted lectures for the remaining students on military hygiene and field fortifications, as well as military drill.[97] Also during this period, the college experienced a dramatic increase in student illness. Although malaria had been a constant problem on campus due to mosquito infestations in regional swamplands, a diphtheria epidemic in 1862 took the lives of five students.[98] In addition, financial shortages continued to plague the institution. Although legislators expected Morrill Act funds to quickly replace state appropriations, proceeds from the land grant did not become available until 1869, leaving the institution consistently short of operating expenses.[99] Finally, some critics continued to assail the college for being too bookish and for training students away from the farm. Alternatively, others insisted that the institution did not do enough to spread the benefits of agricultural experimentation and discovery throughout the state.[100]

The war years, however, also marked the beginning of a period of growth for the college. With the appointment of T. C. Abbott as president in December 1862, the institution gained steady as well as consistent leadership. Abbott remained in the office for the next twenty-three years, during which a brief but fervent effort to assign Morrill Act funding to the state university rather than the agricultural college was defeated in the legislature, in large part because of Abbott's intervention. Moreover, the college grounds were finally tamed and the farm began to function as a site of agricultural experimentation rather than solely of hard labor.

Finally, the State Board of Agriculture, in conjunction with faculty, developed a statement of purpose that served to clarify the college's educational mission. Its detailed "Objects of the Institution" included to "impart a knowledge of Science, and its application to the arts of life," to "afford to its students the privilege of daily manual labor," to "prosecute experiments for the promotion of Agriculture," to "contemplate courses of instruction in the military art, and in the application of Science to the various arts of life," and to "afford the means of a general education to the farming class."[101] Although the first four objectives signaled the college's practical orientation, the fifth revealed the manner in which even an institution dedicated to practicality maintained a commitment to the common good by preparing students for competent citizenship. Study of the liberal arts, the college catalogue summarized, "help to make an intelligent and useful citizen."[102] Rather than purely occupational training, Michigan's State Agricultural College offered a higher education that was both "liberal and practical," reflecting precisely the intention of the advocates of practical studies and the Morrill Act.

By 1870, then, the college had survived multiple challenges and begun to resemble the institution that Theodore Roosevelt celebrated more than thirty years later. The stability it achieved following the Civil War also provided opportunities to expand the institution's civic-minded objectives. Although a course of study especially for women would not be offered until 1896, the college admitted its first female students in 1870.[103] Five years later, the institution made its first systematic attempt to spread knowledge of scientific and agricultural advances directly to farmers through Farmer's Institutes. Led by college faculty, held in rural communities, and sponsored by local chapters of the Michigan State Grange, the institutes became extremely popular around the state and a source of goodwill toward the college in its efforts to promote the public welfare over time.[104]

Perhaps most importantly, the college served as a land-grant model for the nation. Although states such as Pennsylvania, Maryland, and Iowa had all chartered collegiate-level agricultural institutions similar to Michigan's by the beginning of the Civil War, following the war land-grant colleges and universities began to dot the higher-education landscape nationwide.[105] As in Michigan, these institutions frequently offered courses in practical studies as well as the liberal arts. Over time, they further diversified their academic programs, while expanding their curricular reach. Changes to the institutions' names typically reflected this process. In Michigan, the State Agricultural College became the Michigan Agricultural College in 1909, the Michigan State College of Agriculture and Applied Science in 1925, the Michigan State University of Agriculture and Applied Science in 1955, and finally, in 1964, Michigan State University.[106]

Agricultural colleges were not the only kind of higher-education institution to undergo this transformation. Those dedicated to teacher education—what were called "normal schools"—also declared a commitment to the common good while being rooted in a social ethos of practicality. Federal and state governments, however, frequently excluded normal schools from becoming beneficiaries of land grants, leaving most struggling to obtain the resources necessary to train their predominantly female students to work in public elementary and secondary schools. In the western United States, the history of the California State Normal School provides a rich illustration of the way in which teacher-education institutions eventually overcame such obstacles to become a major part of American higher education.

5

"THE INSTRUCTION NECESSARY TO THE PRACTICAL DUTIES OF THE PROFESSION"

Teacher Education in the West

In the same year that Abraham Lincoln signed the Morrill Act into law, California State Superintendent of Public Instruction Andrew J. Moulder submitted a proposal to the state legislature to establish what would become California's first publicly supported higher-education institution—the California State Normal School.[1] Named after the French *école normale* and dedicated to teacher education, normal schools were initially established in the United States during the antebellum period and flourished in the decades following the Civil War. Providing women, especially, access to higher education at a time when most colleges and universities refused to admit them, normal schools manifested a commitment to the public good by welcoming poor students and offering them training to become public-school teachers. Over time, these institutions became a crucial segment of American higher education. They also underwent dramatic transformation. Unbeknownst to many of their current students, hundreds of well-known colleges and universities, including Arizona State University, James Madison University, and Kent State University (to name just a few), began as normal schools, with scores having been the first centers of higher learning in their states to receive public support.

Moulder drew his proposal from recommendations issued by educators who had the previous year attended California's first teachers' institute. A forerunner to professional associations such as the National Education Association, teachers' institutes brought classroom teachers together to share effective teaching strategies and methods of classroom discipline, receive professional guidance, and promote school reforms.[2] Meeting in San Francisco in 1861, California teachers appointed a Committee on State Normal Schools to conduct a preliminary investigation into the need for a statewide teacher-training institution.[3] Several months later, the committee issued a report that went far beyond a preliminary investigation, providing a spirited endorsement of teaching as professional work that required practical training for effective classroom instruction.

Characterizing normal schools as institutions in which "the principles of teaching are considered both as a science and an art," the report briefly described the components of a normal school program, including the study of the "powers, capacities, and laws of growth of the mind," the "moral natures of children," and the "best methods of school organization and modes of teaching." It then moved on quickly to address the need for teachers-in-training to have the opportunity to apply in the field—in a model school for elementary and secondary students— the knowledge acquired through theoretical study. "The possession of knowledge is one thing, ability to teach is another and a far different thing," the committee pronounced. "The most limited observer is aware that a very learned man may profoundly understand a subject himself, and yet fail egregiously in elucidating it to others. The profession of a teacher imperatively demands a special school for instruction in its appropriate science and methods."[4]

Distinguishing between "how to teach" and "what to teach," committee members argued that these two "classes of knowledge" were of equal importance if teachers-in-training were to learn how to effectively instruct pupils. "No one would intrust a steam engine to a man who was acquainted with that machine only through books," they claimed. "The danger and folly of thus risking life, time, and money in educating an engineer would not be questioned; universal opinion would force him to an apprenticeship under a competent master. Is there any less folly or danger in intrusting the mysterious and subtle mechanism of the mind to teachers unlearned in the practical duties of their profession? Such is the principle insisted on in all the common occupations of life." Undoubtedly drawing on the growing popularity of agricultural colleges, such as Michigan's, to provide a parallel example of the application of practical learning in the field, the committee expounded, "The gardener . . . we should all insist, must have a practical acquaintance with the nature of different soils, the habits of different plants, the best modes of cultivating and training them, and the soil and position suitable for each. In his case no amount of book knowledge would compensate for his want of such practical knowledge. So of the farmer and the mechanic; the State fosters and endows societies which reward their best practical skill."[5]

Providing vivid analogies to work in agriculture and mechanics, the committee's justification for a publicly supported normal school was important for what it emphasized and what it did not. Rather than relying primarily on an ethos of civic-mindedness to underscore the contribution that well-trained teachers would make to the common good, committee members promoted their desired institution on the grounds that practical skill was an essential element in professional preparation. Demanding a "special school" for instruction in the "science and methods" of teaching, comparing teachers' work to that of the farmer and engineer, and stressing the practical knowledge and skill necessary for teachers to effectively carry out their duties, the report drew on the prevailing ethos of practicality as its central rationale. This is not to say that the committee dismissed the civic-minded ideal; members referred to teaching in their report as "the highest social duty." Yet they assigned prominence to the practical advantages that teachers-in-training would reap, concluding their report with a financial justification for the school as a sound investment in California's future.

Alternatively, a social ethos of civic-mindedness occasionally found expression in students' claims that they sought to become teachers as a means to foster the common good. California State Normal School student Martha M. Knapp described the important contribution she believed teachers made to the public good as well as the burden that making this contribution imposed. "The profession we have chosen," she wrote, "is a noble one, but it throws upon us responsibilities which, if met successfully, will tax our energies to the utmost. We must stimulate others in the improvement of their opportunities, in the attainment of wisdom, and in their endeavors to become good citizens."[6] Similarly, one of Knapp's classmates described the great responsibility she believed teachers accepted when choosing their occupation: "Our influence will soon extend over a broad field," she wrote. "Many flexible minds will be entrusted to our training; and under our guidance many will set out upon the journey of life. The responsibilities of this great and noble profession can scarcely be over-estimated."[7]

For women in particular, however, conceiving of teaching as a civic-minded contribution to the common good was a double-edged sword. As the nation's rapidly expanding public schools increasingly employed women, Americans came to view teaching as a gendered form of public service rather than skilled professional work. Consequently, although women benefited from the financial self-sufficiency, independence, and agency teaching afforded, their labor became characterized by self-sacrifice and service to others. This conception of teaching provided communities and school districts with a rationale to undervalue and underpay women for their expertise—a problem that teacher organizations and unions would continue to confront over time.

Scholars have failed to fully excavate the relationship between the development of teacher-training institutions and the shift toward practicality in colleges and universities during the antebellum and Civil War eras. In many states, normal-school founding legislation linked teacher training with instruction in agriculture, mechanics, and the military.[8] Florida's state legislature provided for the establishment of two higher-education institutions in 1851, the purposes of which were "the instruction of persons, both male and female, in the art of teaching all the various branches that pertain to a good common school education; and next to give instruction in the mechanic arts, in husbandry, in agricultural chemistry, in the fundamental laws, and in what regards the rights and duties of citizens."[9] Similarly, Virginia state officials, not long after establishing the Virginia Military Institute (VMI) in 1839, assigned the institution a teacher-training function.[10] Requiring cadets to commit to teaching in Virginia for two years following graduation, legislators agreed to finance their board and tuition. "With this teaching requirement for its students," writes historian Bradford Wineman, "VMI became, in a sense, Virginia's first state-supported normal school."[11]

Rather than examining teacher training as a vital manifestation of practicality in higher education, many scholars have focused their attention primarily on agricultural and mechanics programs at institutions such as the Michigan Agricultural College.[12] But they are not solely to blame for the omission of normal schools from most higher-education histories: that can also be attributed to the schools themselves.[13] The low status of teaching led many to reject their institutional origins once they "matured" into state colleges and universities. Most normal schools, moreover, did not grant bachelor's degrees, an important symbol of institutional status in US higher education. Accordingly, when nineteenth-century Americans spoke of the "experiment" or "revolution" in women's higher education, they typically referred to either the expansion of coeducation or the growth of women's colleges rather than normal schools. As one alumna of Wellesley College's class of 1879 claimed, making no reference whatsoever to the higher education of women that had been taking place in normal schools for decades, "We were pioneers in the adventure—voyagers in the crusade for the higher education of women—that perilous experiment of the 1870s which all the world was breathlessly watching and which the prophets were declaring to be so inevitably fatal to the American girls."[14]

The *State* of California traces its first normal school to 1857, when San Francisco implemented what today would be considered professional development for city teachers. The *Province* of California, however, had founded its first normal school twenty-one years earlier, twelve years before the Mexican government ceded California to the United States in the Treaty of Guadalupe Hidalgo and three years prior to the founding of the first state-supported US normal school in Lexington, Massachusetts.[15] Established as part of a Mexican colonization project, the Escuela Normal de Monterey trained elementary-school teachers for work in provincial schools. José Mariano Romero, author of the first school text-book printed in California, directed the normal school, which was one of a series of Mexican educational reforms inspired by Prussia's system of state-supported teacher-training institutions. (US public-school reformers admired this model as well and advocated for similar enhanced teacher training in the 1830s and '40s.)[16]

During the early national period, America had no educational "system." Instead, most children received their schooling through an assortment of pri-vate tutors, academies, seminaries, and local district schools. Social, political, and economic changes during the antebellum and Civil War eras, however, including increases in immigration, urbanization, industrialization, and the extension of voting rights, led "common-school crusaders" such as Massachu-setts's Horace Mann and Connecticut's Henry Barnard to seek to systematize and improve public education for the primary purpose of fostering civic virtue. As historian Carl Kaestle observes, antebellum educational reformers agreed that schooling should emphasize "unity, obedience, restraint, self-sacrifice, and the careful exercise of intelligence," all of which the crusaders considered char-acteristics of the virtuous and moral citizen as well as necessary for the survival of the republic.[17]

In addition to upgrading the quality of school buildings and curricular mate-rials, reformers sought to enhance classroom instruction. Although some of the nation's mostly male schoolteachers had attended college, if not always gradu-ated, most had little or no training for their work. Through normal schools, educational reformers hoped to increase teachers' knowledge of the subjects they taught as well as augment their pedagogical methods, thus improving the quality of teaching in—and the quality of citizens produced by—public schools. As America's system of public education began to take form, however, a shortage of competent teachers threatened its development. With increas-ing and more lucrative employment options opening to men in America's expanding economy, women's advocates such as Emma Willard (founder of Troy Female Seminary) and Catharine Beecher (founder of Hartford Seminary and sister of the celebrated author Harriet Beecher Stowe) argued that women's nurturing and maternal qualities fit them perfectly to serve as schoolteach-ers.[18] In making this claim, Willard and Beecher avoided directly confronting a white middle-upper-class gender ideology that allocated the private sphere to women in their role as wives and mothers, while permitting males to dominate the public sphere through employment outside of the home. To cash-strapped local governments, however, Willard and Beecher's observation that women provided a cheaper labor source than men undoubtedly provided a compelling justification for altering employment practices.[19] With Massachusetts school boards paying women teachers an average of 60 percent less than men during the antebellum period, for instance, school districts began hiring women at an increasing rate so that by 1860 they constituted a majority of teachers in the United States.[20]

The feminization of teaching, however, posed a problem for antebellum school reformers who sought to elevate classroom teachers' educational attainment and pedagogical training. Although young white women sometimes had access to secondary schooling, their postsecondary options were extremely limited due to the belief that higher education was wasted on and potentially harmful to females. (This claim is examined more fully in chapter 7.) Many private higher-education institutions, such as Bowdoin and Georgetown Colleges, were initially closed to women, as were many publicly supported institutions, such as South Carolina College and the Michigan Agricultural College. A few colleges, such as Oberlin and Antioch, were coeducational, while the all-female institutions that did exist, such as Troy and Mount Holyoke Female Seminaries, were exceedingly small in number. Many of the colleges open to women charged tuition, which frequently made them unaffordable to families with limited means.[21]

With most young women beginning their teaching careers with little more than a smattering of secondary-level schooling, many Northeastern and Midwestern states responded positively to reformers' calls for better teacher training. Normal schools opened in Massachusetts in the 1830s, New York in the 1840s, and Connecticut, Michigan, Illinois, and Pennsylvania in the 1850s, with state legislators often tying these institutions' establishment to practical studies.[22] When Illinois officials established their state's first normal school in 1857, they gave it the name Illinois State Normal University because they expected the institution to train teachers while also providing instruction in agriculture and engineering.[23]

Legislators sometimes agreed to establish normal schools only after reformers had proven their methods effective. California provides a useful illustration. Admitted to the Union in 1850, California had opened its first public school only two years earlier in the city of San Francisco. The 1849 gold rush, however, created a population boom, increasing the number of city residents from approximately 850 in 1848 to just over thirty-six thousand four years later. Although officials opened schools and hired teachers in an attempt to keep pace with growing school enrollments, the number of students quickly outstripped municipal appropriations. By 1854, the situation in San Francisco had become dire, with the board of education describing city schools as located "in mere temporary buildings, suitable in no single respect for school purposes,—small, badly constructed, inconvenient, dilapidated, and wretched in the extreme."[24]

By contrast, the board issued a favorable report on many of the city's teachers, crediting the "Eastern Normals" some had attended with fostering the "temperaments, talents, and fitness" necessary for success in what they characterized as a "peculiar and important but too much neglected profession."[25] With the number of new hires increasing dramatically, however, board members noted the following year that teaching in a few San Francisco schools was "somewhat defective." They recommended establishing a municipal normal school in order to upgrade teachers' knowledge, skills, and qualifications as well as to discourage individuals who had neither training nor experience from applying for classroom positions. "Until the teacher's profession is understood and appreciated by the people," the board advised, "there will be a tendency to foster quackery and empiricism—to continue to place persons [in classrooms] who would make teaching an experiment or sinecure."[26]

Over the next two years, the San Francisco School Department offered weekly "normal exercises" for less-experienced teachers. Providing instruction in grammar, writing, US history, geography, and mathematics under the direction of John Swett, future state superintendent of public instruction and principal of a local school, these classes were held during a three-month term, initially on Saturday mornings from 9:00 a.m. until noon and, later, on Monday evenings from 7:30 until 10:30 p.m.[27]

With the opening of San Francisco's first high school in 1856, an opportunity arose to reorganize the exercises into a normal-school program in which both practicing teachers and secondary-school students interested in becoming teachers could enroll. Although unusual by contemporary standards, training high-school students to become teachers was hardly exceptional during the nineteenth century. As historian James Fraser has observed, most high schools combined "college preparation and 'practical' preparation (and teaching definitely fell on the practical side)." Reflecting the rise of a social ethos of commercialism in America, Fraser describes the high school as an institution that "prepared some for college" but "many more" for employment in "an increasingly industrial and commercial society." He concludes that "as one of their key components, high schools prepared teachers."[28] In keeping with this practice, San Francisco school superintendent Henry Janes proposed establishing a municipal normal school at the city high school to serve currently employed teachers as well as "scholars" (high-school students). "A Normal class," he wrote, "will be needed, and might be established during the [high school] last year's course without much additional expense. Until our State makes provision, this is the only mode of affording our own scholars the instruction necessary to the practical duties of the profession."[29]

The City Normal School, more popularly known as Minns Evening Normal School after its principal, George C. Minns, opened in 1857. During its five-year existence, the school graduated fifty-four students, all women, who completed a three-year program of study. The school's greatest contribution to California education, however, was in serving as a municipal model and catalyst for a state normal school. Less than a year following Minns' establishment, city schoolteachers met to formulate a plan for a state-supported teacher-training school. "Such an idea," they resolved, "properly carried out, cannot fail to produce beneficial results, increasing the ability of the teachers and the efficiency of the schools."[30] Two months later, Superintendent Janes proposed that the San Francisco Board of Education actively lobby the state legislature to establish a normal institution.[31]

With the number of schoolchildren in California almost doubling between 1857 and 1862 and the need for qualified teachers paralleling the rise, the state legislature passed and Governor (and future Stanford University founder) Leland Stanford signed into law an "Act to Establish and Maintain a State Normal School."[32] The legislation inaugurated a board of trustees, permitted Minns Evening School to be incorporated into the new institution, and appropriated $3,000 for its first five-month term. The act also directed that the State Normal School be located in the city of San Francisco "or at such other place as the Legislature may hereafter direct," be open to women fifteen years of age and over and men eighteen and over, and be free of charge for students who filed a written declaration of their intention to teach in the state's public schools. (Students who declined paid five dollars per term.)[33] In addition, the legislature authorized establishing a "model" primary-school class in which normal-school students would receive practical training. Alternately known as the "lab," "training," or "experimental" school, the model school provided the centerpiece of most normal-school programs. As James Fraser writes, "The heart of practical teacher preparation in the normal schools was what one historian, a century later, would call practice-oriented teaching. In the words of the normal school leaders, work in the lab or the training school was the 'center and the core of school life,' or the 'body and soul of teacher training.'"[34]

Over the next several weeks, members of the newly formed board of trustees met to plan for the State Normal School's opening. Electing Leland Stanford chairman, the board adopted a set of regulations requiring that candidates for admission pass an examination in reading, spelling, writing, grammar, geography, and music, that the school be in session five days a week, from 9:00 a.m. to 3:30 p.m., and that students complete the course of study over two years, with one five-month term making up a year of study.[35] The board also appointed Ahira Holmes, a former teacher, principal, and graduate of the State Normal School in Bridgewater, Massachusetts, principal of the new institution.[36]

On July 21, 1862, less than three months after the California Legislature established it, the State Normal School opened with a total of six students. Having capped enrollment at sixty, the trustees were undoubtedly disappointed with the turnout, especially considering that two of the initial six applicants failed the entrance exam. (They were nevertheless admitted.)[37] In addition, the legislature had declined to provide funding for a new building. Holmes described the initial facility, which occupied a vacant room in San Francisco's high school, as "exceedingly small and every way unsuited to the purposes for which it is devoted," while a student later recalled that it resembled "a hat room deprived of its racks and improvised with rickety seats."[38] The school nevertheless recovered from its less-than-auspicious beginning. By the end of the first term, it enrolled thirty-one students (twenty-eight women and three men) ranging in age from fifteen to twenty-five, and maintained a thirty-student model primary class (mainly seven-year-olds) as well as a model grammar class made up of students in grades five through eight.[39]

Although the legislature had approved normal-school funding for only one term, the board of trustees used the remainder of the initial $3,000 appropriation to reopen the school on January 2, 1863. Of the thirty-two students enrolled for the second term, twenty-two were returning from the fall. Of the ten new matriculates, several came from more distant counties, suggesting that word of the school was spreading.[40] Yet, poor facilities continued to undermine the institution. As both enrollments and the number of model classes rose over the next few years, the school moved to a variety of different locations, none of which met its needs. In October 1863, Holmes noted that the school, which had already relocated from the high school to an old music hall, had again moved, this time to San Francisco's assembly hall: "The partitions of our new building are constructed of thin boards, and therefore, sound is readily transmitted between the rooms, which proves a source of disturbance in the several class rooms while exercises are being conducted. Good deal of noise also enters the front rooms from the street, especially when the windows are thrown open."[41]

The institution would move five more times before state officials approved constructing a building for its use in the city of San José. Yet just as challenging as the problem posed by poor facilities was what Holmes described as "the haste" of pupils to graduate.[42] He wrote in May 1864, "One of the greatest obstacles to the success of the school in meeting the designs of its establishment is the disposition of the members to remain but a short time as pupils, and the want of patient and persevering effort and application on the part of many." As evidence for his concern, Holmes recorded in his journal the questions that many students asked upon being admitted to the school, including "What is the shortest possible time in which I can be 'put through' the course?," "How long will it be before I can receive my diploma?," and "Can I probably get a school [job] after I graduate?"[43]

For Holmes, students' "haste to graduate" weakened the school's efforts to elevate the status of the teaching profession. The problem's solution, he believed, was to increase admission standards so that only students seriously committed to professional training would apply.[44] In the meantime, however, he grappled with a student body who, in general, seemed intent on spending as little time as possible in attendance. In February 1865, for instance, Holmes again commented on students' inclination to abbreviate their course of study, this time writing at length and in frustration: "Many of the members enter with the expectation of being able to finish the prescribed course of study in one, or, at most, two terms, appear to appreciate the advantages of attending mainly for the reason that, as members or graduates, their chances for obtaining positions as teachers are better than they would be of graduates of other schools, and not because they can make themselves more efficient instructors by making a proper use of their time while attending upon the course."[45]

His aggravation was undoubtedly justified. As a fledgling institution, the Normal School's future was far from assured; students' rush to complete their training threatened its credibility. What Holmes failed to grasp, however, was that the practical training the school offered appealed precisely to students who did not have the luxury of remaining enrolled for long periods of time. With California's legislature still four years away from using Morrill Act funding to establish an Agricultural, Mining, and Mechanical Arts College, and six years from merging that institution with the private College of California to form the University of California (Berkeley), the state's inexpensive postsecondary educational opportunities were extremely circumscribed.[46] The Normal School, therefore, provided young men and women, often from rural areas and families with limited means, access to low-cost higher education. Martin V. Ashbrook, one of the few men who attended the State Normal School in its early years, recalled that he enrolled because it was one of the small number of institutions available to poor rural youth. "At that time," he remembered, "there were on the Pacific Coast few schools opening their portals to overgrown country louts. It was a sight to see a bearded youth carry school books. I *had* to go there or stay out of school" [emphasis in the original].[47]

What was true for coarse young men such as Ashbrook was more so for unsophisticated young women, who had even fewer higher-education options available to them. Still, although Ashbrook and many of his female classmates attended the State Normal School free of charge, they were responsible for their own room and board, which in a city such as San Francisco was not

insignificant. Students, therefore, worked while seeking to complete their studies as quickly as possible.[48] As George Minns would later claim after he succeeded Holmes as Normal School principal, the students had little choice in
the matter. "It was absolutely necessary," he wrote, "for them to do something
to support themselves."[49]

Although practicality motivated students to enroll in the State Normal
School, it existed in tension with a developing ethos of commercialism through
which they sought higher education in order to gain an edge in an increasingly
complex and competitive job market. That the institution's student body was
overwhelmingly female demonstrates the extent to which women had come
to dominate teaching by the beginning of the Civil War. However, a normal-
school diploma was not required to teach in California. Why, then, in addition
to furthering their academic preparation and receiving practical training, did
women enroll? One answer, as Holmes suggested, was that normal schools provided graduates with an advantage in obtaining teaching positions. Although
not a bachelor's degree, a normal-school diploma made an applicant for a
teaching post a more attractive candidate than someone with only a secondary
education. Many students responded to this incentive; yet for some, not even
this credential provided a weighty-enough perquisite to justify the investment.
In March 1864, five students alleged that members of the San Francisco school
department had assured them they would be appointed directly to city teaching posts following graduation. Learning this was not the case, the students
withdrew from the school.[50]

Although commercialism and civic-mindedness overlapped with a social
ethos of practicality throughout the antebellum and Civil War eras, commercialism was just beginning its ascent during the State Normal School's first decades
and civic-mindedness was receding. It was practicality, therefore, that primarily
shaped the institution in its early years, inspiring students with limited means
to acquire practical training, especially by providing women greater access to
higher learning. Accordingly, practicality fostered the common good through
the democratic expansion of higher education. Paradoxically, however, even as
these students gained access to educational opportunities previously restricted to
them, many sought to minimize the time they spent engaged in higher learning,
hoping out of necessity to acquire their diploma and obtain paid employment as
quickly as possible.[51]

Throughout its first ten years, the State Normal School underwent a series
of significant changes. Ahira Holmes served as principal until June 1865,
when George Minns briefly succeeded him. Three more men—Henry Carl-
ton, George Tait, and William Lucky—would lead the institution before the
board selected Charles Herman Allen principal in 1873. An experienced

normal-school educator, Allen provided strong leadership over the course of his sixteen-year administration, leading one historian to label his term in office the State Normal School's "golden years."[52] Also during this period, the board of trustees changed the age of admission to sixteen for both sexes, while school enrollments rose (albeit inconsistently) from fifty-nine in 1863 to 280 in 1875. Collectively, these students came from an increasingly wider geographic range. By 1873, the State Normal School enrolled students from thirty-six out of fifty California counties.[53]

Of all these changes, however, the most apparent was the normal school's relocation to San José. With enrollments rising and the destruction of many potential venues in an 1868 earthquake in San Francisco, the State Board of Education decided to move the institution to another city. Viable candidates included Sacramento, Oakland, Stockton, and San José, all in Northern California. Residents and public officials in these cities competed for the school, which they correctly believed would bring financial benefits to their communities. State Superintendent Oscar Fitzgerald and Principal William Lucky strongly supported San José: they argued that the city offered a healthy climate and that its size of approximately ten thousand residents made it small enough to shelter students from the threats and seductions of a major metropolis, yet large enough to provide suitable accommodations.[54] Lucky, in particular, preferred San José on the grounds that the city had no major state institution in its proximity, while Sacramento had the state capital, Oakland the new state university, and Stockton the state mental institution. Addressing San José residents in an effort to inspire support for the institution, Lucky urged them, with tongue in cheek, to seek to make their city "synonymous with education, as Stockton is synonymous with insanity."[55]

Ultimately, the California legislators agreed with Lucky and Fitzgerald's assessment, voting to relocate the State Normal School approximately fifty miles south of San Francisco to San José's Washington Square and legislating a statewide property tax to support a building fund. Thus in 1872, ten years following its establishment, the State Normal School opened on a twenty-six-acre campus in an elaborately constructed three-story Romanesque wooden building with Corinthian columns and a 150-foot-high tower. Providing the institutional stability that the school previously lacked, the new campus permitted the board of trustees to raise graduation requirements and lengthen the program of study to three years.[56] In doing so, the board reorganized the curricular program into four "classes": (1) Preparatory, for students who lacked the adequate academic preparation to enter directly into the Normal School, (2) Junior, for students in their first year of study, (3) Middle, for students in their second year of study, and (4) Senior, for students in their third year. Students who ended their studies after the middle class received an "elementary diploma" indicating that they had completed the elementary course of study as well as observed and taught in a model class. They also received a temporary five-year teaching certificate. Students who stayed with the program through the third year received a "full diploma," indicating that they had completed the full course of study, along with a lifetime teaching certificate.[57] The Normal School then further divided the elementary and full courses of instruction into five subject categories: Language, Mathematics, Science, Miscellaneous, and Professional. Table 1, which reproduces the junior, middle, and senior year curricular programs, indicates that students' first three terms involved academic studies only. Following the third term, students took more advanced academic courses while also observing and practice-teaching in the model, or what had become known as the "Training" School.

At first glance, the State Normal School curriculum seems to encompass a range of courses, from more basic subjects (penmanship, arithmetic, grammar) taught in elementary and secondary schools during the second half of the nineteenth century, to more advanced ones taught in colleges such as Bowdoin, South Carolina, and Georgetown, including natural philosophy, geology, and political economy. A closer examination, however, reveals that although the courses of instruction manifested this trajectory over the three-year program, they also reflected a shift from more general studies to more practical, specialized knowledge.

The category "Language," as scholar Suzanne Bordelon has observed, provides a useful illustration. Beginning with basic literacy, including "rules for spelling," "use of dictionary," and "punctuation and capitals," students progressed to writing and studying "composition as an art and as a science." By the end of the senior year, they were engaged in the study of rhetoric, literature, and literary criticism, yet did so for the express purpose of gaining "practical training in the correct and effective use of our mother tongue."[58] As Bordelon writes, "Based on the classes that [California State Normal School] students took, we can see that rhetorical education figured significantly in teacher training."[59]

Perhaps an even better example of the progression toward practical, specialized knowledge between the junior and senior years is provided by the "Professional" course of instruction. During their first two terms, students learned teaching methods by being "systematically and naturally" taught the subjects that comprised the junior-year course of instruction; that is to say, their initial teacher training involved no formal training at all. Rather, instructors expected students to learn teaching methods simply by being cognizant of how they were being taught. During the middle year, however, students engaged in more specialized learning by reading and discussing "educational works," studying

TABLE 1 California State Normal School Courses of Instruction, 1877–1878

	ELEMENTARY COURSE				FULL COURSE	
	JUNIOR YEAR		MIDDLE YEAR		SENIOR YEAR	
1—Language	Orthography English Grammar	Orthography English Grammar	Orthography English Grammar	Word Analysis Composition	Rhetoric	Criticism and English Literature
2—Mathematics	Mental and Written Arithmetic	Written Arithmetic	Arithmetic Elementary Algebra	Arithmetic Algebra	Higher Algebra	Geometry
3—Science	Geography	Elements of Natural Philosophy Physical Geography	Natural Philosophy completed Chemical Lectures	Physiology Zoology Botany	Chemistry Lectures on Astronomy and Geology	Household Science
4—Miscellaneous	Penmanship Drawing	Reading Vocal Music	US History Reading Vocal Music	School Law and Constitution	General Review of Elementary Studies	Political Economy Reading Drawing
5—Professional				Methods of Teaching Observations in the Training School	Methods of Teaching	Methods of Teaching Practice in the Training School

Source: "Course Catalogue for the California State Normal School 1877–1878" (Sacramento: State Office: F. P. Thompson, Supt. State Printing, 1878).

teaching methods in an explicit fashion, and being instructed in "classifying, grading, and managing schools." Students also gained first-hand experience in the classroom during the middle year by observing and teaching in the Training School.

By the senior year, students both studied and applied practical knowledge, including "instruction in school management and supervision," the "laws of mental growth and development," and "methods of teaching all the subjects in the public schools."[60] These students also regularly engaged in practice teaching. The challenges they expected to encounter in this final stage of their preparation typically unnerved them, as was indicated by their naming the corridor that connected the Normal School and the Training School the "Bridge of Sighs."[61] One student described the experience this way: "Each day some one is called upon to conduct a class through a five-minute exercise. Only those who have tried it can tell with what fear and trembling the poor Senior advances to face, not only a small class of children, but fifteen classmate observers and a Training School teacher besides. He who can go calmly through such an ordeal ought to be awarded a medal."[62]

In addition to furnishing greater institutional stability, the State Normal School's Washington Square campus provided space to take part in a rich collegiate life, including literary and debating societies, student publications, and a variety of extracurricular clubs and activities. Through their participation, young men and women developed leadership skills while learning to interact in a somewhat egalitarian fashion, speak and perform publicly, and compete on the athletic field. "In the process," as historian Christine Ogren writes, normal-school students "socialized themselves for participation in middle-class society through observation, emulation, and the formation of extensive webs of personal connections or social capital."[63]

Ogren's history of the US state normal school provides a detailed accounting of the ways that life at normal schools throughout the United States provided opportunities for "nontraditional" students, young women especially, to acquire self-confidence, autonomy, and a sense of professionalism, all characteristics associated with America's growing middle class. "The normal campus," she writes, "functioned as a safe space in which women could exercise their budding self-assuredness and all students could enact their new sense of middle-class social life."[64] California State Normal School student Sara Locke, in an essay entitled "Is It Worth While?," described the independence and autonomy she believed students gained as a result of enrolling at the school: "One of the grand results of the Normal system of education is self-reliance. Here are pupils, for the first time away from home, thrown more entirely upon their own resources than is possible in boarding schools or seminaries. It lies with them to decide . . . questions of right or wrong, of wise and unwise action. Whatever their decisions may be, they are obliged to recognize a moral quality in what they do, and that is something gained."[65] The extent to which at least some young women adopted the kind of self-reliance Locke describes is suggested by another student's description of the "highest type" of woman as "no longer the pale, listless individual who spends her time making fancy laces, shedding tears, and doctoring sick headaches, but rather the strong, robust Grecian type who is able to stand on both feet and look the world in the face."[66]

California State Normal School students elected a woman of the "robust Grecian type"—Harriet Quilty—as president of their first Student Association in 1898. Rather than signaling the beginning of women's active participation in student life, Quilty's election reflected its fruition. A few years earlier, she and several classmates had organized a coeducational literary organization called the Philomathian Society in which women held the positions of president, vice president, and treasurer. Meeting weekly, students performed musical pieces, read literary selections, and delivered short speeches. They also debated an eclectic mix of academic, artistic, political, and economic issues, including whether "music is a greater art than painting," protective tariffs were "more beneficial to the US than Free Trade," Emerson had "done the world more good than Holmes," and "Cuba should be annexed to the US." At one particularly lively meeting, society members debated the proposition that women were more competent teachers than men. Although the debate occurred primarily between two pairs of students, each consisting of a woman and a man, the Philomathian Society secretary recorded that "all of the young ladies" present joined in the debate, with "all but one" speaking in support of women's greater competence. When the judges, who at this meeting were all men, decided unanimously in the negative, the women in the room erupted in protest. In reaction, the secretary noted, Quilty "quelled" the disruption "by a few strokes of her new gavel."[67]

The Student Association and the Philomathian Society were only two of many organizations that students formed following the normal school's move to San José. These included a host of extracurricular clubs, including the Art Club, Shakespeare Club, and Astronomical Club (with its accompanying 3:00 a.m. "star gazings"), a number of student publications, including *The Normal Index*, the *Normal Pennant*, and the *Class Paper*, and an abundance of athletic teams, including one for the extremely popular sport of tennis (figure 5). When combined with a curriculum that provided specialized knowledge and practical training, participation in these activities and organizations nurtured the self-assuredness that Ogren describes, as well as a strong professional identity. "In their heyday," she concludes, "state normal schools enabled students to view

FIGURE 5.   San José State Normal School Tennis Club, 1893. Photo from the San Jose State University Archives Photograph Collection, published with the permission of the San Jose State University Library Special Collections and Archives.

themselves as professionals during a time when society was reluctant to grant this status to women (and people from lower social classes)."[68]

Through *The Normal Index*, in particular, a publication of attitudes and opinions on a range of topics relating to teaching, students demonstrated a budding professionalism. Issues frequently included short student-authored compositions on subjects such as the importance of parent-teacher cooperation, the role of textbooks in the classroom, the failure of corporal punishment, and the development of "progressive ideas" in education.[69] It also included longer essays in which students described the challenges they confronted in their professional preparation, such as the complicated status of women who trained for professional work while also expecting to marry.[70] Finally, students used *The Normal Index* editorial page to express their position on school-related political debates.

By 1880, the State Normal School had developed into a vibrant institution of higher education. But in February of that year it experienced a sudden and calamitous setback when a fire, beginning in a broken ash chute, burned the school's main building to the ground. With the structure declared a total loss, Principal Charles Allen joined members of the board of trustees in petitioning the state government for funding to rebuild. Just two months later, legislators appropriated $100,000 for a new building. Consequently, in May 1881 the Normal School took occupancy of a new three-story, Ionic-style building of brick construction, with over a dozen classrooms, a chemistry laboratory, a library, and an ornate bell tower.[71]

The speed with which the state provided funds for the emergency reconstruction suggests that most legislators believed the practical training the institution offered continued to benefit California residents. They further demonstrated their support for teacher training just two years later when they renamed the California State Normal School the San José State Normal School to distinguish it from a second state-supported normal school in Los Angeles. (The latter would become the University of California, Los Angeles.) Over the next three decades, California established six more normal schools: at Chico in 1889, San Diego in 1898, San Francisco in 1899, Santa Barbara in 1910, Fresno in 1911, and Arcata in 1914. This statewide expansion followed national trends. In 1869 thirty-five normal schools were in operation in the United States. By 1910, there were 170.[72] Student enrollments followed suit. During the 1879–1880 academic year, 25,700 students were enrolled in normal schools nationwide. By 1910, that number had more than quadrupled, to 111,100. At San José, enrollments increased at a similar rate, from 280 in 1875 to 675 twenty years later.[73]

By 1914, however, the initial year for Humboldt State Normal School (named for its location in Arcata, on Northern California's Humboldt Bay), two related changes had begun altering the educational landscape on which normal schools had flourished. First, universities, which had begun their own expansion, established chairs, then departments, and then schools of education. Typically emphasizing theory over practice and primarily educating students who became high-school teachers, school administrators, and normal-school faculty, these programs nevertheless competed with normal schools. Just twenty miles north of San José, for example, Stanford University established its department of History and Art of Education in 1891. One year later, the University of California, Berkeley, established a Department of Pedagogy. By 1930, more than one hundred universities nationally had opened schools or colleges of education.[74]

Second, between 1890 and 1930 high-school enrollments skyrocketed, from 202,963 to 4,399,422 students nationwide.[75] Although graduation rates did not rise to the level of enrollments, the number of students receiving high-school diplomas increased so much that normal schools, ever intent on raising academic standards, began requiring a high-school diploma for admission. Massachusetts, home to America's first normal school, did so in 1894. San José State Normal School followed in 1901, with the remainder of California's normal schools revising their admission requirements soon after.[76] Simultaneously, high-school growth demanded an increase in the number of secondary teachers trained to instruct in specific academic subjects. University schools of education offered precisely this form of higher education to students seeking certification to teach at the high-school level. Normal schools, unwilling to abandon high-school teacher training to universities, upgraded their academic offerings, including the implementation of a four-year course of study leading to the bachelor's degree. Catalyzed by organizations such as the National Education Association Department of Normal Schools and the National Council of State Normal School Presidents and Principals, this change transformed normal schools throughout the United States.[77]

California led the nation in this process of institutional transformation. A 1920 amendment to the state constitution cleared the way for the state's normal schools to offer a bachelor's degree. The following year, the legislature endorsed normal schools' transformation into colleges by passing a law renaming them "teachers' colleges."[78] Henceforth, San José State Normal School, which in 1922 began offering a four-year academic program, became known as San José State Teachers College.[79]

Over time, California continued to serve as a bellwether in transfiguring the former normal schools. In 1935, the state legislature again authorized changing the name of the state teachers' colleges to more accurately reflect the multipurpose institutions they had become. No longer requiring students to sign a declaration of their intention to teach and offering a curricular program comprising a wide range of academic disciplines, the state teachers' colleges became simply "state colleges."[80] Finally, in 1972, exactly one hundred years after the California State Normal School opened to students in Washington Square, the state legislature again transformed California's former normal schools, this time from state colleges into "state universities."[81] Today, San José State University persists as the institutional legacy of the founders of California's first publicly supported normal school.

Conclusion to Part II

In *And Sadly Teach: Teacher Education and Professionalization in American Culture*, Jurgen Herbst observes that, while state normal schools provided students from poor and rural backgrounds with a higher education they probably would not have obtained otherwise, many normal-school students did not actually become teachers.[82] He consequently concluded that normal schools were "pioneers of higher education," not for prospective teachers but "for the people."[83] Given women's disproportionate enrollment, however, Herbst might have more accurately labeled normal schools "pioneers of higher education for young women with limited means." Women made up approximately 80 percent of the student body at the California State Normal School at the time it moved from San Francisco to San José in 1872. By 1910, they accounted for about 95 percent. Although this proportion was higher than at some other normal schools at the time, women constituted a majority of students at almost all teacher-training institutions in America.[84]

Similarly, a majority of Michigan Agricultural College's mostly male graduates never went into agriculture. In 1885, only 40 percent of students who graduated from the college prior to that year were engaged in farming or fruit-growing, while approximately 17 percent had become physicians or lawyers, another 17 percent had entered into commerce, and 10 percent had become teachers. The remaining graduates were scattered among a range of occupations, including engineering, the military, and the ministry.[85]

Graduates' participation rates in teaching and farming reveal the extent to which students frequently used new forms of higher education to achieve personal and occupational goals they set for themselves rather than the ones college and university officials intended. In this regard, not just normal schools but A&M institutions dedicated to agriculture, mechanics, mining, and the military also contributed to the public good by being pioneers of higher education for the people.

Following the Civil War, people's higher education spread throughout America. In addition to the financial resources the Morrill Act provided, academic populists, as historian Scott Gelber has shown, increasingly supported colleges and universities emphasizing practical studies, further expanding access to higher learning for previously marginalized groups.[86] Practicality, however, prioritized the nation's economic growth over its political and social development. As President Joseph R. Williams reminded the promoters of the Michigan Agricultural College in 1857, fostering civic competence among students was one of the institution's educational goals but was not one of its "original and primary objects."

Even as practicality achieved dominance, the transformation of American society resulting from the political, economic, and social upheaval accompanying the Civil War slowly began reorienting higher education toward a social ethos of commercialism. Accompanied by an emphasis on individualism, personal advancement, and professional status, commercialism appealed to students at traditional colleges, A&M institutions, and normal schools as well as emerging research universities. Nowhere was this development more pronounced than in the establishment of Stanford University, an institution that embraced the objective of improving the public welfare while manifesting many of the commercial characteristics of its era, including the publicly stated goal of promoting students' personal success.

RECONSTRUCTION THROUGH THE SECOND WORLD WAR

6

"TO QUALIFY ITS STUDENTS FOR PERSONAL SUCCESS"

The Rise of the University in the West

In 1906, several years after publishing his groundbreaking *The Theory of the Leisure Class*, economist and sociologist Thorstein Veblen left the University of Chicago for northern California. While serving as associate professor at Stanford University, Veblen completed a blistering critique of American higher education entitled *The Higher Learning in America: A Memorandum on the Conduct of Universities by Business Men*. Skewering university administrators and governing boards for importing commercial practices into higher education and applying corporate principles to academic inquiry, Veblen claimed that "pecuniary values" had become predominant on college and university campuses and that "business proficiency" had replaced higher learning.[1] Higher education, according to Veblen, had abandoned its commitment to fostering civic-mindedness through a liberal education and, in its place, adopted a devotion to commercial enterprise. "It means a more or less effectual further diversion of interest and support from science and scholarship to the competitive acquisition of wealth," he wrote, "and therefore also to its competitive consumption. . . . It means an endeavor to substitute the pursuit of gain and expenditure in place of the pursuit of knowledge, as the focus of interest and the objective end in the modern intellectual life."[2]

Pecuniary values, business proficiency, and the competitive acquisition of wealth all characterized the ascendance of a commercial ethos in American society at the turn of the twentieth century. In contrast with higher-education scholars who locate the beginning of commercialism's influence in the post–World War II era, Veblen's observations indicate that higher education's adoption of these ideals—especially "the pursuit of gain and expenditure"—over civic, literary, and artistic values occurred much earlier in the century.[3] As historian Alan Trachtenberg has demonstrated, the exploitation of the American West, the role of mechanization in developing mass production, the transportation revolution, mass migration from rural to urban areas, and a dramatic increase in the stratification of national wealth produced profound political, economic, and social change in the United States in the decades following the Civil War. Yet it was the rise of commercialism that ultimately transformed US culture, resulting in what Trachtenberg has called "the incorporation of America."[4]

Veblen's criticisms of emerging universities undoubtedly resulted from his experience working at two higher-education institutions over which commercial enterprise loomed. Oil tycoon John D. Rockefeller's multi-million-dollar gift established the University of Chicago in 1892 on land donated by business magnate Marshall Field. Railroad baron and former California governor and US senator Leland Stanford and his wife Jane Lathrop Stanford founded Leland Stanford Junior University just years earlier, in 1885, as a memorial to their fifteen-year-old son. Popularly known as Stanford University, the institution was exceptional both because of the Stanfords' thirty-million-dollar endowment—the largest gift in the history of higher education up to that time—and because it represented the commercial fortune one couple could amass as a result of changes to the nation's political economy during the second half of the nineteenth century.[5] When Stanford University opened to students in 1891, it served as a conspicuous manifestation of commercialism's rise in American higher education.

Prior to founding their institution, the Stanfords consulted a number of university presidents, including Harvard University's Charles W. Eliot, Massachusetts Institute of Technology's Francis A. Walker, Johns Hopkins University's Daniel Coit Gilman, and Cornell University's Andrew White—all leaders in the emergence of the American university. Of these, White was the most influential.[6] Preaching Ezra Cornell's decree that his institution would be one "where any person could find instruction in any study," White embraced practicality, implementing an academic program that included science, engineering, agriculture, and mechanics. White also successfully lobbied the US Congress for Morrill Act funding, leading Cornell, a private institution, to become New York's land-grant university.[7]

When "The Cornell Colony at Palo Alto," as Stanford University was known, opened on the Stanfords' former horse farm thirty miles south of San Francisco, it evinced White's conception of higher education almost completely.[8] In an interview conducted less than a year before his death, Leland Stanford confirmed the importance he ascribed to practical studies at the institution. Branding graduates of Eastern colleges who sought employment from him members of a "helpless class," he remarked, "They are generally prepossessing in appearance and of good stock but when they seek employment and I ask them what they can do all they can say is 'anything.' They have no definite technical knowledge of anything. They have no specific aim, no definite purpose." Contrasting his university with that of the historic colleges from which many of these "helpless" students graduated, Stanford professed, "It is to overcome that condition, to give an education which shall not have that result, which I hope will be the aim of this University. . . . Its capacity to give a practical, not a theoretical, education ought to be accordingly foremost."[9]

As Stanford's remarks denote, practicality had become a recognized feature of American higher education by the end of the nineteenth century. Not just university founders and administrators but students, too, praised practicality in higher learning. One early Stanford student, for instance, celebrated the rise of applied knowledge by criticizing what he perceived as the irrelevance of the studies of the past. "It is an evil if the old college curriculum has survived in the popular mind in some sections of the country," he wrote, "but it is an evil in the popular mind which the modern university is fast rooting out. The university of the present time is a reaction against learning for learning's sake. We specialize with a preparation for the world in mind, whether we wish to write stories or survey land. Leland Stanford Junior University is founded with the idea of usefulness to the world uppermost in the minds of its benefactors."[10]

Yet as the University's first president, David Starr Jordan, observed, times had changed since the founding of the "old colleges" such as Bowdoin, South Carolina, and Georgetown. While scientific and technological advances increased the number of professions from which students could choose, the industrial age accelerated the growth of a commercial society. Stanford University's founding grant reflected the rise of a social ethos of commercialism in higher education when it stated that the institution's central "object" was "to qualify its students for personal success."[11] The Stanfords also stated that the university's "purpose" was to "promote the public welfare," while Jordan asserted that in receiving a higher education graduates incurred a civic-minded responsibility to advance the common good through their life pursuits.[12] "The higher education means the higher sacrifice," Jordan declared in his 1896 Stanford commencement address. "That you are taught to know is simply that you may do. . . . You shall seek your place to work, as your basis for helpfulness."[13]

According to biographer Edward McNall Burns, Jordan's educational philosophy revolved around the conception of a democratic republic as one in which

FIGURE 6.   Jane and Leland Stanford lay the cornerstone of the Leland Stanford Junior University on May 14, 1887. Courtesy of the Stanford University Archives.

"the government was guided by and responsive to an intelligent public opinion." Of the president's beliefs, he continues, "A people would have as good a government as their intelligence and civic-mindedness deserved, and no better. . . . To create the intelligent public opinion, which alone would make genuine democracy possible, Jordan believed was the peculiar mission of the universities."[14] As Jordan himself frequently pointed out, however, Stanford University's modernized academic program, which included technical training, professional education, pure research, and applied science, contrasted dramatically with the classical curriculum offered at early nineteenth-century colleges. Yet for the supporters of practicality, this was a difference in means rather than ends. Stanford University existed to "fit the graduate for some useful purpose," as the institution's founders had dictated, and Jordan argued that this goal could be accomplished through the study of philosophy as well as engineering, literature as well as ichthyology (his own field of expertise).[15] "Those who have called a college education unpractical," Jordan wrote in *The Sequoia* (a student publication that was part editorial page, part literary journal), "have in mind the college education of twenty to fifty years ago, the traditional course of study which we have inherited from Oxford and Cambridge." He continued, "These English schools were avowedly for the training of clergymen and gentlemen, and our American colleges were patterned after them. For many years all other vocations of life were outside the scope of what was called Higher Education. Now this condition is rapidly changing. It is the business of the American university to give the best possible training in any direction of intellectual effort. There is no honorable calling in life that cannot be made a learned profession."[16]

Believing that a higher education obliged graduates to contribute to society regardless of the course of study they pursued, Jordan envisioned political scientists using their academic training to eliminate corruption in city government, physicians to improve public health, engineers to enhance the quality of life in municipalities, and public-school teachers to educate students for competent citizenship.[17] Many higher-education administrators in the years following Reconstruction shared Jordan's conviction that universities should serve the public good. One element of a broader Progressive movement in America, higher education's civic responsibility became known as the Wisconsin Idea, in part because of University of Wisconsin President Charles Van Hise's pronouncement that he would "never be content until the beneficent influence of the university reaches every family in the state."[18] Van Hise, however, issued his proclamation to the Wisconsin Press Association in February 1905, by which time college and university administrators across the country had already made similar claims.[19] Three years earlier, Nicholas Murray Butler had used his inaugural address as Columbia University's twelfth president to emphasize that it was "not for scholarship alone" that institutions such as his existed. "The university is both for scholarship and service," Butler declared, "and herein lies that ethical quality which makes the university a real person, bound by its very nature to the service of others. . . . A university's capacity for service is the rightful measure of its importunity."[20]

Administrators throughout Southern states, too, proclaimed higher education's civic responsibility. University of Virginia President Edwin Alderman, University of South Carolina President Samuel C. Mitchell, and University of Georgia Chancellor Walter Barnard Hill all sought to use their institutions to contribute to the public good by developing the "new South" following Reconstruction.[21] In the West, according to historian John Aubrey Douglass, the Wisconsin Idea took the form of the California Idea, leading to the establishment of a statewide system of higher education designed to address California's specific political, economic, and social needs. In that context, Douglass writes, Stanford University featured as a "private university with a public mission."[22]

Less than a year prior to America's entry into World War I, Stanford University's third president, Ray Lyman Wilbur, offered a sweeping example of his institution's civic mission when he both reaffirmed and further extended higher education's commitment to the public good.[23] In "The University and Social Service," Wilbur argued that Americans had reached a moment in their nation's history when citizens were compelled to work together "for common ends and for the common good." "To accomplish this end," Wilbur declared, "we must have knowledge—education. We and our fellow citizens must be educated, not necessarily in Greek history or Roman mythology, or the Wars of the Roses, or how to understand arithmetical progression, but in how to live and how to help others live."[24] It was the university's obligation, according to Wilbur, to provide this form of civic-minded learning. "In California," he claimed, "only one in every 4,000 inhabitants gets into one or the other of our two large universities [Stanford and the University of California, Berkeley]. These favored ones here or elsewhere owe a great deal to their less fortunate neighbors. Their ideals should be high and the their desire for service strong. The training given them should develop a margin—and often a very wide one—of capacity to care for others, to help great causes, to advance civilization."[25]

Like Wilbur and Jordan, Stanford faculty members drew on a civic-minded ethos when they asserted that higher education's primary aim was to serve the common good. Professor John M. Stillman, for instance, in his commencement address to Stanford's "pioneer" Class of 1895, proclaimed to the gathered students, "Only when a large number of men and women are educated to a position of intelligent appreciation of the needs of society, and to an unselfish aspiration for the common welfare, can the wisest leaders of thought and action exert their due influence."[26] Similarly, Stanford Physiology Department Chairman Oliver P. Jenkins declared that all institutions of higher learning should have the "fundamental aim" of preparing students for service. He asserted, "So with the college graduate who has received the true degree, he must face the fact that the degree carries with it the greatest of responsibilities. He is a coward and worthy of scorn if, on hearing the cry for help from his fellow men, he ignores it and takes his equipment to some pleasant nook and uses his training and powers lone for the gratification of his own cultivated tastes. He does worse still if he makes use of the revelation the university gives him simply to further on his private ambition and gains."[27]

While claiming that their institution sought to promote the public welfare, Leland and Jane Stanford nevertheless embraced an ethos of commercialism by emphasizing the competitive advantage students would reap from the occupational preparation it provided. The university's early graduates similarly professed a belief in higher education's capacity to offer a significant advantage in an increasingly commercial society. Student-authored publications as well as diaries, journals, and letters home reveal that achieving personal success in their chosen field of employment was a primary reason students enrolled at the university. This is hardly surprising given that the Stanfords adopted policies resulting in a wider socioeconomic range of students having access to a four-year undergraduate education than had previously been the case at many universities. In its early decades, Stanford was coeducational and tuition-free; it frequently enrolled students who had not attended prestigious college preparatory schools.[28] Consequently, many of its students intended to use their educations to advance themselves occupationally. As the editors of the student newspaper, the *Daily Palo Alto*, wrote of less-privileged classmates in 1893, "It should be the earnest desire of every student in the University to encourage and to aid fellow students who by their own efforts are paying their way through college. All of us are students together, with one general aim—to better our present condition in life by acquiring the best education from the liberal opportunities within our reach."[29]

During the late nineteenth and early twentieth centuries, as historian Roger Geiger has described, an increasing number of families from America's "middle ranks" sought to use higher education to better their children's occupational prospects. Having the wealth necessary to forfeit their sons' and daughters' labor, these families endeavored to "buttress their social position" against what became a historic influx of immigrants into the United States. Higher education, according to Geiger, "met the needs of this group by offering its members the possibility of proximate social mobility: students could now forgo the arcane rites of the ancient languages, study practical subjects, and prepare for definite careers."[30] Validating Geiger's claim, *The Sequoia*'s student editors described the increasingly important commercial benefits they believed Stanford students received from obtaining a university degree, observing in 1895, "Higher education is becoming less and less of a luxury. Competition in professional life of every kind, whether it be school-teaching or medicine, is driving professional men and women farther each year toward adequate preparation. A college education to-day gives a teacher a better choice of positions than she would have without it. To-morrow it may be a necessary qualification without which she could get no position."[31]

Coupled with the institutional adoption of business principles against which Thorstein Veblen railed, students' expectation that a university degree provided an advantage in securing employment in a competitive job market signaled the ascendance of commercialism in higher education. As Frederick Jewel Perry of the Class of 1900 demonstrated in a letter he wrote to his mother three months prior to his graduation, "You must not pitch your hopes too high in expecting me to command a $75 a month position at the first rattle out of the box. This is not an age of miracles. Remember—though I am (or shall be then) a college graduate—with all that means—I shall be an inexperienced greenhorn and full of University theory. But time will tell, though. And someday I'll be drawing down a salary that will compensate for all the expense incurred in securing what few enjoy and none can take away—a university education."[32]

Perry's disposition toward higher learning illuminates the extent to which a social ethos of commercialism had begun exerting a significant influence on higher education by the turn of the twentieth century. Indeed, so many Stanford students during the period began explicitly asking whether a university education was a reliable financial investment that David Starr Jordan responded directly in an 1892 lecture entitled "The Value of Higher Education."[33] Acknowledging that a university degree provided a long-term financial benefit but resisting the implication that higher education was nothing more than an investment, Jordan observed, "You may ask me this question: Will a college education pay, considered solely as a financial investment? I must answer yes, but the scholar is seldom disposed to look upon his power as a financial investment. In the work of the rank and file of life, it is true that the educated man gets the best salaries. Brain work is harder than hand work, and it is worth more in any market and it will always be so."[34]

Not only students questioned "the value of higher education," however. By the turn of the century, although relatively few Americans had ever attended college, the issue of higher education's worth was a topic of popular debate. In 1900, *The Saturday Evening Post* joined in with a cover story that posed the question, "Does a College Education Pay?" In response, former US President Grover Cleveland—not a college graduate himself—authored the *Post's* first reply. (David Starr Jordan contributed the second.) Cleveland characterized the debate over higher education's value as a battle, though one about which colleges and universities need not be concerned. "It is not difficult to classify the various forces engaged in these attacks," Cleveland wrote, "and if we examine their positions and offensive operations, we shall be entirely satisfied that the high point of vantage occupied by our universities and colleges is, or at least ought to be, absolutely impregnable."[35]

Acknowledging that some college and university graduates indeed failed to accomplish their career goals, Cleveland nevertheless criticized the "peculiar logic" employed by "certain self-made men" who, because they had achieved success in the past without the benefits of higher education, believed it was wasted on everyone in the present. "They seem to be strangely slow in comprehending how fast the world moves," Cleveland observed regarding the rise of commercial organization in America. "It certainly should not escape their notice that the methods profitably employed in every enterprise and occupation have so changed within the last fifty years that a necessity has arisen for an advanced grade of intelligence and education in the use of these methods; and that as this necessity has been supplied, a new competition has been created which easily distances the young man who is no better equipped for the race than our self-satisfied, self-made man."[36]

This new competition was the same as the one Stanford student editors had earlier referred to as "driving professional men and women farther each year toward adequate preparation." Universities responded to the demand for this preparation by establishing a wide range of graduate and professional schools.[37] Accordingly, as historian Frederick Rudolph described, "The American university, in one if its characteristic manifestations, thus became a collection of postgraduate professional schools, schools which replaced the apprentice system in law, put responsibility into the study of medicine, tended to relegate theology into a separate corner, created education as an advanced field of study, and responded—in one institution or another—to the felt necessities of the time or the region, thus spawning appropriate schools at appropriate times, whether they were schools of business administration, forestry, journalism, veterinary medicine, social work, or Russian studies."[38]

At Stanford, the establishment of professional schools of law (1908), medicine (1908), education (1917), nursing (1922), and especially business (1925) signaled a surge of student interest in professional preparation.[39] The law school began in 1893 as a small department made up primarily of undergraduate majors. Leland Stanford, however, had convinced US President Benjamin Harrison to serve as one of its first professors following his failed reelection campaign in 1892. Harrison's presence at Stanford helped establish the university's reputation for legal studies, allowing the department to flourish over time.[40] By 1905, it enrolled 308 students, nearly 20 percent of the university's total student body.[41] Three years later, with the number of graduate students studying law on the rise and having instituted a Juris Doctor degree, the university renamed the department the Stanford Law School. In 1926, it began requiring a bachelor's degree for admission, leading Stanford Law to become formally established as a graduate professional school.[42]

The Stanford Business School, by contrast, functioned as a full-fledged graduate professional school from its inception. Established in 1925 at the urging of Stanford alumnus, trustee, and future US president Herbert Hoover, this was one of the first graduate schools of business in the country. Hoover, then serving as US Secretary of Commerce, proposed that business needed to be taught as a profession "upon a parity" with others such as law and medicine; his opinion was that California was "losing many good brains" to the East Coast because of its lack of university-based business programs, and that such a school needed to "conduct, as a part of instruction itself, definite research problems of business trends, of markets and distribution of the Pacific Coast, for the benefit of the commercial community and in cooperation with it."[43] Stanford administrators immediately adopted Hoover's proposal. Consequently, as Registrar J. Pearce Mitchell noted in 1958, Stanford's Business School brought "prestige and funds to the University," with faculty serving as consultants for large corporations and "leading businessmen" becoming consulting professors while "stimulating the students with their advice and practical information."[44]

Professional schools such as Stanford's both fostered and benefited from a growing "culture of aspiration" in America, as historian David Levine has observed, including the desire for status among an "emerging white-collar, consumption oriented middle class."[45] As much as the rise of commercialism (with its increasing demand for specialized, technical knowledge and training to manage more complex corporate organizations) created the conditions for the development of professionalism, it also drove status-conscious families to enroll their children in higher education at unprecedented rates, especially following World War I. As Levine concludes, "This unprecedented interest in education had little to do with any appreciation of learning. Rather, it depended on businessmen's and the public's perception of both the technical and the social legitimacy of the college experience. In the 1920s more and more businessmen and parents became convinced that the colleges promoted the efficiency of American business and the happiness of individual students in their careers and social lives."[46] As Thorstein Veblen had noted decades earlier, the establishment of university "schools of commerce," such as Stanford's business school, perhaps best characterized this development by replacing learning with what he described as "worldly wisdom" and scholarship with "facility in competitive business." Veblen concluded of the increasing popularity of business schools, "The ruling interest of Christendom, in this view, is pecuniary gain. And training for commercial management stands to this ruling interest of the modern community in a relation analogous to that in which theology and homiletics stood to the ruling interest in those earlier times when the salvation of men's souls was the prime object of solicitude."[47]

Although the culture of aspiration influenced higher education in a variety of ways between Reconstruction and World War II, its greatest effect was perhaps in leading colleges and universities—institutions previously attended by an extremely small proportion of Americans—to become exceptionally popular.[48] As with the attention that *The Saturday Evening Post* brought to the topic of higher education's value, mass magazines such as *Munsey's*, *Cosmopolitan*, and *Collier's Weekly* became "infatuated with college life," according to Daniel A. Clarke. Crediting the "magazine revolution" with transforming cultural perceptions of the collegiate experience in the United States, Clarke argues, "college was remade in the pages of these periodicals to conform to transforming economic and cultural demands, reconfigured in alignment with the emerging identity of a new white-collar, managerial middle class."[49] Central to this process of transformation, he writes, was the development of a new form of collegiate life. Characterized as it was by the "college spirit," this new life was best illustrated by the growing popularity of collegiate sports.

In September 1892, a Stanford student described the period in which he was enrolled as "an era of athletics in the American universities." Referring to the central place that literary societies had once held in college life, the student observed, "Formerly the leading diversion outside of the regular university work was the literary society. This latter fact can not be said to be true to-day. Athletics occupies the first place in the heart of the average American student."[50] During the late nineteenth and early twentieth centuries, student interest in athletic events, both as participants and spectators, soared.[51] By the mid-1920s, Stanford University fielded teams that included baseball, basketball, boxing, golf, soccer, swimming, tennis, track, field hockey, and archery.[52] As at many colleges and universities, however, football provided the greatest attraction, with no competition garnering more attention than the Big Game with local rival University of California, Berkeley.[53] First played in San Francisco in March 1892, just months following Stanford University's opening and with Herbert Hoover serving as team manager, the game initiated an annual tradition celebrated with bonfires and theatrical performances. Reflecting the romance with intercollegiate sports that developed during the era, one student went so far as to describe Stanford football as infused with an ethos of civic-mindedness. "If one has been observant," he wrote, "he will have noticed that in all things of common interest a tie peculiar to this year has bound us together. The spirit of common interest has asserted itself over individual interest. The individual has throughout the year sacrificed personal advantage to the common good. Nowhere was this seen to better advantage than in the spirited competition for places on the foot-ball team."[54]

This student was not alone in celebrating the virtues of college football, especially the Big Game. With athletics animating ever-greater alumni support, Stanford administrators constructed a stadium that, when completed in 1925, held an astounding seventy-three thousand spectators.[55] Indeed, although students had typically initiated collegiate sports competitions on a small scale for their own enjoyment, a social ethos of commercialism significantly influenced their development. With the formation of athletic associations, control over campus sports shifted from students to university administrators who, in turn, frequently employed entrepreneurial athletic officers and coaches.[56] As intercollegiate athletics began generating revenue and publicity for universities, they became, in historian John Thelin's words, "inextricably linked with commercialism."[57]

The experience of intercollegiate athletics reflected the influence of commercialism on higher education more broadly. As universities became increasingly complex bureaucratic institutions in both size and scope, they began to adopt the managerial practices of their corporate counterparts.[58] "The result," one scholar observes, "was a hierarchical arrangement long familiar in business though new to academia."[59] To direct these new organizations, boards of trustees, increasingly staffed by members of the commercial class, began to break with the tradition of choosing respected clerics or academics to lead higher-education institutions.[60] In 1860, almost 90 percent of college presidents had trained for the ministry, a rate that plummeted to only 12 percent by 1933.[61] In their place, boards selected individuals whom Thorstein Veblen satirically labeled "captains of erudition," men who were said to combine an acute intellect and intimate understanding of academia with the business sense of a financier.[62]

As commercialism infused the attributes of business enterprise into universities' form and function, and as administrators came to resemble heads of major corporations, students slowly began to adopt the role of consumer, while some faculty begrudgingly characterized themselves as hired hands. In an essay for *Scribner's Magazine* in 1907, one college professor compared his position to that of a member of a ship's crew: "There is set up within the university an 'administration' to which I am held closely accountable. They steer the vessel, and I am one of the crew. I am not allowed on the bridge except when summoned; and the councils in which I participate uniformly begin at the point at which policy is already determined. I am not part *of* the 'administration,' but am used *by* the 'administration'.... In authority, in dignity, in salary, the 'administration' are over me and I am under them."[63]

Paradoxically, just as commercialism took firm root in emerging universities, a seeming counterforce arose characterized by the antithesis of commercial studies—disinterested scholarly research.[64] Noting the institutional tension resulting from this divergence, John Marshall Barker observed in his 1894 work *Colleges in America*, "On the one hand, there is a demand that the work of our colleges should become higher and more theoretical and scholarly, and, on the other hand, the utilitarian opinion and ideal of the function of a college is that the work should be more progressive and practical. One class emphasizes the importance of true culture and of making ardent, methodical, and independent search after truth, irrespective of its application; the other believes that practice should go along with theory, and that the college should introduce the student into the practical methods of actual life."[65]

Higher-education reformers referred to the effort to conduct an "independent search after truth, irrespective of its application" as the Germanic Ideal.[66] Drawing on their experiences as students or observers at research universities in cities such as Heidelberg and Berlin, leading US educators returned home convinced that pure research unrestrained by political, social, and economic considerations provided a superior basis for the development of the American university.[67] Institutionalized in 1876 with the founding of Johns Hopkins University, the Germanic Ideal profoundly influenced American higher education, leading to the establishment of advanced studies and graduate schools, disciplinary specialization, and an increase in the number of US doctoral degrees conferred annually, from just forty-four in 1876 to more than five hundred by 1918.[68]

Stanford University's adoption of the phrase *Die Luft der Freiheit weht* (The Wind of Freedom Blows) as its motto reflected the Germanic Ideal's influence.[69] Referring to the intellectual freedom necessary for scholars to pursue pure research, the motto was introduced by David Starr Jordan, who personified the importance that universities came to ascribe to scholarship. As science journalist Edwin E. Slosson described in 1910, Jordan was "an earnest advocate of the importance of original research" and remained an active scholar even while serving as president. "No other university president of those considered here," Slosson wrote in *Great American Universities*, "has, I believe, done as much scientific investigation while in office. It is by this test that he would have a university judged."[70] Indeed, almost twenty years earlier in his Stanford inaugural address, Jordan had provocatively declared, "A professor to whom original investigation is unknown should have no place in the university."[71] By the time Slosson published his book, Jordan had begun printing a list of faculty publications in his annual presidential reports, indicating the value the institution had come to attach to original research.[72]

Faculty members' adoption of research as central to their work ultimately resulted in the development of a coherent and professionalized professoriate. As historian Bruce Kimball has described, science—loosely defined as the use of objective methods to investigate particular phenomena—emerged in the United States as a "fundamental source of cultural inspiration and legitimacy" in the decades following the Civil War.[73] Both because the scientific pursuit of knowledge required specialization, according to Kimball, and because higher education served as "the institutional locus for the cultural ideal of science," university faculty became experts in particular disciplines, with expertise increasingly designated by the acquisition of a PhD.[74] Dividing into ever-more-specialized departments, fields, and subfields, faculty members proceeded to form disciplinary organizations, such as the American Historical Association and the American

Psychological Association, which sponsored national conferences and published scholarly journals. Organizing its members into a hierarchy of rank and status (assistant professor, associate professor, full professor) and implementing tenure as a way to regulate promotion, the professoriate began to acquire a professional identity.[75]

As scholars began to identify as much with colleagues who shared their disciplinary and research interests across institutions as they did with those at their home college or university, faculty began acting in the collective interest of their profession. In 1915, joint meetings of the American Economic Association, the American Sociological Society, and the American Political Science Association led to the formation of the American Association of University Professors (AAUP), which concerned itself with a range of professional issues, including salary scales, rules governing temporary and permanent appointments, and working conditions conducive to research and teaching.[76] Perhaps the most controversial issue with which it became involved, however, was the establishment and expansion of academic freedom.[77]

For decades prior to the AAUP's establishment, faculty members were fired for publicly expressing political, economic, or social views that clashed with those held by administrators, trustees, and, at times, the general public. In two renowned cases, University of Wisconsin economist Richard T. Ely lost his position for speaking out in favor of strikes and boycotts during a period of significant labor unrest, while fellow economist Edward W. Bemis suffered the same fate at the University of Chicago for issuing a public attack on the railroads during the Pullman strike.[78] Following Darwin's publication of *The Origin of Species* in 1859, Vanderbilt University's Alexander Winchell and Cornell University's Felix Adler, among others, ran afoul of their institutions' authorities and lost their positions by espousing antiorthodox religious beliefs.[79] In many of these cases, university administrators and board members conducted hearings that resulted in either dismissal or a decision not to reappoint, leading faculty terminations to at least seem to be the product of investigation and deliberation. The case of Stanford University's Edward Ross, however, revealed the extent to which faculty members frequently served at the whim of university founders, donors, or powerful members of the board.[80]

David Starr Jordan first met Ross at Indiana University in 1891, where Jordan served as president and Ross as an economics professor. After Ross left Indiana to serve for one year as secretary of the American Economic Association (AEA) and another on the faculty at Cornell, Jordan recruited him to Stanford. Ross later claimed that during his time with the AEA he had come to understand the challenges that many scholars encountered when publicly expressing their political beliefs and resolved to "test" the extent of academic freedom in American higher education. He wrote in his autobiography, "I had gained an inside view of the growing pressure on economists and resolved that I for one would be no party to this fooling of the public. I would test this boasted 'academic freedom'; if nothing happened to me others would speak out and economists would again really count for something in the shaping of public opinion. If I got cashiered, as I thought would be the case, the hollowness of our role of 'independent scholar' would be visible to all."[81]

During his first few years at Stanford, Ross had little difficulty. Jordan considered him a talented teacher and capable scholar and Ross seemed respected by his colleagues.[82] During the US presidential campaign of 1896, however, Ross actively supported the Democratic ticket. Undoubtedly out of respect for her deceased husband, who had served as a Republican US Senator from California until his death in 1893, Jane Stanford ordered the prohibition of faculty participation in political activity.[83] Undeterred, Ross continued his political involvement, publicly supporting socialist and labor organizer Eugene V. Debs and speaking openly in favor of restricting Asian immigration (a position the Stanfords had fervently opposed because of immigrant Chinese labor's role in constructing the railroads). Jane Stanford, in turn, denounced Ross as "associating himself with the political demagogues of this city [San Francisco], exciting their evil passions" and playing "into the hands of the lowest and vilest elements of socialism."[84]

The university president and board of trustees would typically have intervened in a conflict of this kind, as David Starr Jordan attempted to do on a number of occasions. However, Jane Stanford had assumed control of the university following her husband's death, with the board serving in a primarily advisory role. Consequently, she had the institutional authority to call for Ross's dismissal. Aware of the increasing publicity academic freedom cases were receiving in the press, Jordan urged Ross to restrain himself and Stanford to reconsider. Neither effort succeeded and the president was cast in the unenviable position of having to either refuse the founder's order, which most likely would have forced his own resignation, or demanding Ross's. He chose the latter.[85]

In a press statement that described his dismissal as a direct attack on academic freedom, Ross declared, "I cannot with self-respect decline to speak on topics to which I have given years of investigation. It is my duty as an economist to impart, on occasion, to sober people, and in a scientific spirit, my conclusions on subjects with which I am expert. . . . It is plain, therefore, that this is no place for me."[86] As Jordan feared, Ross's case received widespread attention, with sensationalist articles published in newspapers throughout the country, including the *San Francisco Chronicle* and the *New York Evening Post*.[87] Publicity over the case might have ended there had Stanford historian and sociologist George E. Howard—one of the university's founding professors—not incited further controversy through a defense of Ross's actions. In his own statement to the press, Howard claimed, "the summary dismissal of Dr. Ross for daring in a frank but thoroughly scientific spirit to speak the simple truth on social questions is . . . a blow aimed directly at academic freedom, and it is, therefore, a deep humiliation to Stanford University and the cause of American education." Rather than holding Jane Stanford solely responsible, however, Howard placed blame for the altercation partly on an ethos of commercialism, which, he argued, undermined the university's role as a civic institution. "The blow does not come directly from the founder," he asserted. "It really proceeds from the sinister spirit of social bigotry and commercial intolerance which is just now the deadliest foe of American democracy."[88]

Not content to allow the controversy to subside, Jane Stanford demanded that Jordan dismiss Howard, a task that Jordan dutifully carried out. The resulting protests led to seven additional resignations from the university, sparking an additional round of publicity. In response, members of the American Economic Association conducted an investigation into the Ross case, the first professional inquiry into an alleged violation of academic freedom at a university in the United States.[89]

The Ross case is notable because it illustrates an important moment in higher-education history when academic freedom was still in a formative stage—not clearly defined and haltingly defended—yet emerging as a potentially vital protection. In addition, although the accusations against Ross centered on faculty political activity, academic freedom cases during this era often revealed the challenge that science posed to established religious orthodoxy. Ross and Howard's use of the phrase "scientific spirit" to legitimize Ross's behavior, for instance, upholds Bruce Kimball's finding that science, which began its rise in America as early as the late eighteenth century, emerged in the decades following the Civil War as a fundamental source of cultural inspiration and legitimacy.[90] The process that led to this "intellectual transformation," writes historian Julie Reuben, had important consequences for higher education and its relationship to religious belief during the twentieth century. Yet as she also argues, higher education's eventual secularization resulted not from a battle between science and religion but from liberal Protestant reformers' failure to "modernize religion to make it compatible with their conception of science" while simultaneously rejecting theological doctrine.[91]

Stanford University epitomized this intellectual transformation. By all accounts devout Christians, Leland and Jane Stanford required that students learn of "the immortality of the soul" and "the existence of an all-wise and benevolent Creator" and that obedience to God's laws was "the highest duty of man." They also, however, prohibited sectarian instruction and declared student chapel attendance optional.[92] Similarly, after Jane Stanford ordered the construction of a church building on university grounds in memory of her deceased husband, the institution's first chaplain dedicated it in 1903 by declaring, "We begin anew today no less an experiment than this: to test whether a non-sectarian church can minister to the spiritual needs of a great university. It has been built in love; not to teach a theological system, not to develop a sectarian principle, but to minister to the higher life."[93] Stanford University also never established a divinity school and, in its first year, had only one academic offering that included any examination of religious belief—an ethics class in the Philosophy Department.[94] Finally, the Stanfords hired as their first president David Starr Jordan, a man whom, as Julie Reuben notes, "supported liberal religious causes" yet embraced the theory of evolution and had "little reverence for traditional Christian practices and doctrines."[95]

Over time, although some faculty members would continue to seek ways to reconcile religious belief with the scientific spirit, higher education's opposition to theological doctrine developed into what George M. Marsden has labeled "ideological secularization."[96] As colleges and universities became primarily secular institutions, the academy began abandoning its civic-minded commitment to fostering virtue among students. Yet, most continued to affirm higher education's responsibility to promote the public good. As a number of prominent historians in the field, including Laurence Veysey, Frederick Rudolph, and Christopher Lucas, have noted, the genius of the American university ultimately rested neither solely in its stated commitment to the common good nor in the worth it assigned scholarship nor exclusively in the commercial advantage students gained from occupational preparation. Instead, the capacity to sustain multiple commitments concurrently enabled these institutions to meet the demands of a variety of constituents, thereby gaining the support necessary to flourish in the decades following the Civil War.

As commercialism assumed increasing influence in the post-Reconstruction period, some Americans nevertheless harkened back to an earlier era in order to generate support for new types of higher-education institutions. Less than a decade after the Civil War, the founders of Smith College harnessed the influence that a social ethos of civic-mindedness continued to have in American society when they explicitly opposed both commercialism and practicality in establishing an all-women's college. Seeking to provide women with a higher education equal to that offered to men, Smith College officials replicated the admission requirements and academic programs in place during the early national period at colleges such as Bowdoin, South Carolina, and Georgetown. Unlike the early nineteenth century, however, a different dominant ethos surrounded Smith's earliest attendees. How those students navigated the tensions that existed between the civic-mindedness that infused their college's founding and the commercialism that infused higher education and American society more broadly is the question to which we now turn.

7

"THIS IS TO BE OUR PROFESSION—TO SERVE THE WORLD"

Women's Higher Education in New England

On November 1, 1881, Smith College student Esther "Daisy" Brooks penned an enthusiastic letter home regarding a young woman she had met on campus for the first time that day. "Doubtless, you will be pleased to know," she wrote her mother, "that I had a pleasure, this evening, in the shape of a talk with a girl who is almost in the same circumstances that I am." Describing her classmate as "one of the best, nicest girls in all the world," Brooks went on to elaborate the circumstances she shared with her newfound friend. "*She* is determined to be a doctor as well as *I*; *her* parents are also opposed, and talk in the same style that mine employ, such as 'she'll outgrow it'; she also has had the idea for even a longer time than I have, and, altogether, although we do not need anything to strengthen our determinations, we are both resolved that we should do it sometime in our life no matter how long it takes."[1]

Brooks's letter, one of many she wrote home from Smith, reflects the challenges that a college-educated woman aspiring to an occupation other than teaching confronted in the decades following the Civil War. Intending to pursue a medical degree, Brooks had to convince her parents that she was capable of becoming a physician and, perhaps even more importantly, that she was serious about it. "I think if you know how very much in earnest I am in this," she wrote, "how much more earnest I grow with every year of my life, you would not laugh as you probably will when you read this."[2] Yet Brooks's letters, while revealing the difficulties she faced in dictating her own future, also illuminate a central question in the history of women's higher education during this period. Why, if not to prepare for some form of work outside the home, did young women attend college?

This question, and its myriad of answers, significantly influenced the lives of students such as Esther Brooks and her newfound friend Maria Vinton, while also dominating the composition, form, and method of women's higher education for well over a century. Advocates of women's colleges such as Smith sought to enlarge educational opportunities for women. Yet, they typically spurned an ethos of commercialism and its accompanying drive toward occupational preparation. They also often resisted the practical orientation that infused many teacher-training institutions, including the California State Normal School. Moreover, they frequently avoided confronting contemporary social conventions regarding women's "proper," and thus restricted, place in society.[3] Instead, supporters of women's higher education relied on a social ethos of civic-mindedness to justify their advocacy, arguing that higher learning enhanced women's capacity to contribute to the common good as wives, mothers, virtuous citizens and, they added occasionally, teachers.

For many students at women's colleges, however, practical preparation for work outside the home, paid or not, offered a primary justification for attending college. Consequently, some graduates used their higher educations to become involved in social and political causes, including settlement work and woman suffrage, while others, such as Brooks and Vinton, pursued advanced degrees. Yet others aspired to one of a slowly but consistently increasing number of employment opportunities outside of the schoolhouse. As one Smith student declared at the beginning of the twentieth century, "We are in an unusual period of transition and the future of civilization depends to no slight extent on the educated men and women that are taking their places in the world today. It is a wonderful age and we may be a vital dynamic part of it, if we will."[4]

Of the many all-women's seminaries and colleges established following the Civil War, Smith College exemplifies the ways in which supporters of women's higher education abided by social conventions as they expanded educational opportunities.[5] One of a group of all-female institutions of higher learning that came to be known as the Seven Sisters (including Barnard, Bryn Mawr, Mount Holyoke, Radcliffe, Vassar, and Wellesley Colleges), Smith was founded in 1871 in Northampton, Massachusetts, through the bequest of Sophia Smith.[6] A single woman and devout Christian, Smith sought to use the fortune she unexpectedly inherited from her brother in 1861 in a manner that would both benefit society and please God. "I have a great work to accomplish," she wrote in her journal regarding the inheritance, "I want wisdom from above to direct me in my course. Oh God, wilt Thou grant me wisdom and strength to do this wisely and well and to Thy glory?"[7]

Closely advised by her pastor, the Reverend John M. Greene, in endowing the establishment of a women's college, Smith modeled her institution partly on female seminaries such as Mount Holyoke. Located just several miles across the Connecticut River from Northampton, Mount Holyoke took as its "earnest job," according to historian Helen Lefkowitz Horowitz, the "training of women for teaching and for Republican motherhood."[8] For decades, however, seminaries such as this had maintained lower admission standards than all-male New England colleges. Sophia Smith broke with this practice, insisting that her institution provide an education "equal to those which are afforded now in our Colleges to young men."[9]

Smith's observations on why she believed women should receive such an education tightly align with historian Paula Baker's interpretation of the "domestication of politics" in the United States during the late nineteenth and early twentieth centuries.[10] Smith never advocated woman suffrage and there is good reason to believe that she supported the gendered social, political, and economic spheres ascribed to men and women throughout her lifetime. Nevertheless, regarding higher education she claimed, "It is my opinion that by the higher and more thorough Christian education of women, what are called their 'wrongs' will be redressed, their wages adjusted, their weight of influence in reforming the evils of society will be greatly increased, as teachers, as writers, as mothers, as members of society, their power for good will be incalculably enlarged."[11] As Baker suggests, there was little, if any, contradiction here. Many women in the decades following the Civil War sustained a separate-spheres ideology because the private, domestic sphere they inhabited permitted them to claim the mantle of "civic virtue and a concern for the public good."[12] Over time, women then succeeded in expanding the domestic sphere into politics. "Together with the social separation of the sexes and women's informal methods of influencing politics," Baker writes, "political domesticity provided the basis for a distinct nineteenth-century women's political culture."[13] This culture, and its respect for civic-minded virtue, was central to Smith College's institutional identity in its early decades.

Similarly, Sophia Smith's explicit reference to a "Christian education" and the important role she believed religious faith played in women's higher learning was also not unusual. "Sensible of what the Christian Religion has done for my sex," she expounded, "and believing that all education should be done for the glory of God, and the good of man, I direct that the Holy Scriptures should be daily and systematically read and studied in said College, and without giving preference to any sect or denomination, all the education and all the discipline shall be pervaded by the Spirit of Evangelical Christian Religion."[14] Although prescriptive, Smith's formulation for inculcating Christian belief and practice at her college was thoroughly conventional. Throughout much of the nineteenth century, the "Christian Spirit" permeated New England colleges, requiring that students attend chapel daily, respect the Sabbath, and, as part of their academic program, study texts such as William Paley's *Evidences of Christianity*.

Consciously replicating these customs, Smith College required its students to begin each day with a devotional service before proceeding to regular classwork, which indeed included studying Paley's text. Smith's founders did not adopt these practices simply out of tradition. Instead, they sought for Smith College to achieve precisely what colleges such as Bowdoin and Amherst (the latter located only eight miles from Smith) had claimed to affect for decades: the civic-minded development of virtuous citizens through the rigorous training of students' mental faculties. As Smith College's first president, former Amherst faculty member Reverend L. Clark Seelye, declared in his inaugural address, "Virtue is ever the crown of humanity. Only through a loyal recognition of its superior claim can the highest education be secured and perpetuated. 'To virtue, knowledge' is the sentiment upon our College seal. May the time never come when the spirit of this institution shall reverse the order of these words and make knowledge first and virtue secondary."[15]

That Sophia Smith desired for women to receive a higher education equal to men's, however, does not explain why she sought to establish an all-women's, rather than a coeducational, college. With coeducational institutions becoming more common throughout the United States, Smith might have established in Northampton what the Amherst College Board of Trustees refused to: an institution dedicated to the equitable education of young men and women. In her last will and testament, however, Smith revealed that her interest in an all-women's college arose from a desire to provide an education specifically "suited" to women's "mental and physical wants." "It is not my design to render my sex any less feminine," Smith wrote, "but to develop as fully as may be the powers of womanhood, and furnish women with the means of usefulness, happiness and honor, now withheld from them."[16]

Smith's claim reflected the complex state of women's higher education in the United States following the Civil War. A number of developments catalyzed the expansion of women's higher learning in this era. First, the growth of common schools in the Northern and Western states during the antebellum era, and throughout the South during and after Reconstruction, resulted in an increasing number of girls' receiving the elementary and secondary schooling necessary for admission to many seminaries, normal schools, colleges, and universities. Second, the related need for a greater number of schoolteachers, as well as labor shortages resulting from the war deaths of approximately three-quarters of a million Americans, led an increasing number of women to seek higher learning.[17] Finally, the effort to expand women's formal higher education among middle-class Americans had, by the 1870s, taken on the characteristics of a social movement: in historian Patricia Palmieri's words, "What the abolitionist debate was before it and the suffrage debate after it."[18]

On the other hand, strong opposition to expanding women's formal higher education arose during the same period, when resilient Victorian social norms reasserted dominance in American society.[19] This opposition took the form of three typically intertwined arguments and significantly influenced popular thought about women's higher education. First, opponents claimed that advanced learning was wasted on women who, after four years of college, would marry, have children, and fulfill their proper roles as wives and mothers. It was in the common schools, they argued, that women received the education necessary for civic virtue and republican motherhood, not colleges and universities. Second, medical experts, most famously Harvard University's Dr. Edward Clarke, insisted that biology was destiny and, more controversially, that too much book learning exposed young women to a variety of health problems.[20] In *Sex in Education, or a Fair Chance for the Girls,* Clarke claimed that academic study led the female body to draw blood from the ovaries to the brain and produced, among other ailments, "neuralgia, uterine disease, hysteria, and other derangements of the nervous system."[21] Only by avoiding strenuous academic activity, he argued, could women protect their reproductive health. Finally, as surveys began to reveal that college-educated women indeed married later and in lower numbers than non–college educated women, some prominent individuals, most notably US President Theodore Roosevelt, claimed that "old stock Americans" were committing "race suicide" through low marriage and birth rates.[22]

Although proponents of women's advanced learning disputed these assertions, especially Clarke's, the claims nevertheless influenced the development of higher-education institutions in the United States. As President Seelye noted regarding Clarke's book, "In consequence of the publication, about that time, of *Sex in Education,* by a noted Boston physician, there was much discussion concerning the physical dangers attending the higher education of women, and unusual care was taken that the mode of life and the buildings of the college should conform to the requirements of the most advanced sanitary science."[23]

The "mode of life and the buildings" to which Seelye referred made up what today would be called a system of residential life at Smith. Exchanging dozens of letters in which they debated a variety of living arrangements, the college's founders sought to develop a system that would sustain young women's physical and emotional health during the four years they were enrolled. In April 1869, John M. Greene wrote to Sophia Smith urging her to adopt a plan for the college that would differ from Mount Holyoke in two specific ways. First, he wrote, "It should not put the pupils into one large building as they do there. Mrs. Greene [a Mount Holyoke alumna] says very emphatically that the going up and down stairs is very injurious to the health of the Mount Holyoke pupils. Instead of one large building there should be several small ones. . . . This will save much of the up & down stairs which is so ruinous to the health of young women."[24]

Responding to popular belief as well as his wife's admonition that excess and improper physical exertion damaged young women's health, Greene proposed what became known as the "cottage system" at Smith. Rather than large, multi-storied dormitories, the college constructed "cottages" surrounding a main academic building. Housing between thirty and fifty students each, these structures appeared more like large homes than cottages (figure 7). Indeed, the campus' first cottage, Dewey House, had been a private residence prior to the college acquiring it.[25]

Conceiving of these structures as homes to families of students, college officials employed adult matrons to reside in each cottage along with female faculty members. Together, these women acted in loco parentis, supervising, advising, and protecting the students under their care, as their parents would have had they been present.[26]

Greene's second recommendation involved encouraging students to participate in "the social life of the town" rather than being sequestered on campus. "Thus," according to Greene, "the young ladies will not in their education lose their sympathy with real, practical life. They will be free from the affected, unsocial, visionary notions which fill the minds of some who graduate at our girls'

FIGURE 7.   Houses in the "cottage system" at Smith College, 1887. Smith College Archives, Smith College.

schools."[27] Again reacting to popular criticism—in this case that the "cloistral, abnormal, and morbid" student culture at all-female seminaries produced graduates who had lost touch with the "real duties and perplexities of life"—Greene convinced Smith and others to construct neither a chapel nor a library on campus so that students would be compelled to leave the college and interact with Northampton residents.[28]

Similarly, and in an effort to have a "home-like atmosphere pervade the whole college," Smith officials rejected the typical female seminary practice of strictly regulating students' daily schedules.[29] Other than requiring a morning devotional, recitation three times a day, and a stringent ten o'clock bedtime, college officials trusted students to use their time wisely. "Most of the students come from refined families and have been well bred in their homes," Seeyle explained in his first presidential report. "They have been granted the liberty common to such families and they have not abused it. They have been free to walk and ride whenever and wherever young women can safely do so without escort, and there is no reason to believe they have conducted themselves improperly."[30]

Seeyle's reference to students' "refined families" reveals the demographic background of many of Smith's early graduates. Members of middle- and upper-class families with means whose parents were able to pay the rather substantial $300 cost of tuition, room, and board, a majority of Smith's inaugural class had fathers who were either professionals, merchants, or business owners; only two of the fourteen members were raised on farms.[31] Geographically, most of these students were from Massachusetts, with the rest coming from Maine, Vermont, Connecticut, New York, and Delaware.[32] Ranging in age from sixteen to twenty-one (with an average age of eighteen), most of the young women were Protestants.[33] All were white.[34] This demographic distribution established a pattern that was, for the most part, replicated in each of Smith's entering classes over the next ten years. Concerned that the expense of attending Smith would limit academically capable students' access, however, Seeyle recommended to the board of trustees the year following the college's opening that the tuition of "indigent but deserving" students be remitted.[35] Consequently, a significant number of young women whose fathers were deceased began attending Smith.[36]

In addition to limiting exposure to staircases, fostering a homelike atmosphere in cottages, and encouraging interaction with local residents, college officials ensured students' well-being by adopting a range of policies they believed were appropriate to women's "mental and physical wants." By replacing the terms "Freshman" and "Sophomore" with "First Class" and "Second Class," college officials hoped that "the corresponding classes might be freed from some unpleasant masculine associations with those names."[37] Also, and in contrast to Wellesley College, which opened in the same year as Smith and hired only women instructors, Smith adopted a policy of employing both male and female faculty.[38] "It was the idea of Miss Smith," according to Greene, "that to give young women the most complete mental discipline, they need both men and women as their teachers. The school can have no better model than the family, where father and mother are the educators of the children."[39] Finally, college officials required that all students participate in "light gymnastics" four times a week in order to properly strengthen their physical health as well as compel them to abandon their studies for at least some time each day.[40] Daisy Brooks noted in 1880 that one of her professors scolded her class for not exercising "in the fresh air enough" before demanding that they inform him if they felt their "lessons were too long."[41] A few days later, according to Brooks, this same professor urged her class to pass their college lives "in a happy, healthful way" while insisting that it was their duty to "enjoy all the fun there was."[42]

College officials directed all of these exhortations toward fostering in students a kind of civic virtue they deemed particular to young women's needs. And although some students undoubtedly welcomed them, others chose to pursue their studies fervently, with at least one young woman hoping to stave off unnecessary distractions by posting a sign on her door that read, "*Engaged in Literary Pursuits*; Please do *not* annoy for any *trivial* or *frivolous* purpose."[43] Students had good reason to disregard faculty members' injunctions that they enjoy leisure time. Where Smith's founders hoped to create an innovative system of residential life, they sought just the opposite for the institution's academic program, beginning with admissions standards. Stating in the college's first circular, "The requirements for admission will be substantially the same as at Harvard, Yale, Brown, Amherst, and other New-England Colleges," officials took the unusual step of refusing to admit to the college "preparatory students" who did not meet these requirements.[44]

Seelye later described Smith's admissions policy as having developed in response to the challenges that Vassar and Wellesley Colleges confronted when they opened in 1865 and 1875, respectively. Having built enormous main buildings and living quarters for hundreds of students and faculty members, these institutions were financially obligated to fill them regardless of applicants' academic qualifications, thus admitting a large number of students who were not prepared to sit for admission exams. By contrast, Smith practiced a policy of "rigid economy" in building construction, allowing it to remain selective in admissions. "We see no other way to secure a higher education which is not a sham except by requiring enough preliminary work to make that education feasible," Seelye insisted. "Let the requirements for admission be determined, not by the number of students desired, but by the demands of the highest intellectual culture."[45] Consequently, in addition to admitting only fourteen students to

Smith's inaugural class in 1875, college officials permitted the institution to grow by only one class per year during its first four years.[46]

As Seelye suggested, students' academic preparation needed to be extremely thorough in order to qualify for admission. Two years prior to her matriculation, Daisy Brooks, who was tutored at home rather than attending a public or private secondary school, described a typical study day this way: "Today, got up 6.5. [6:30 a.m.]; studied Greek; went to breakfast; L. [Latin] Teacher came; studied Algebra; Latin; Italian; read ½ hour; wrote Phonog [Phonography; a form of shorthand]; read French; English; transl. [translated] Italian to Mamma; wrote Phonog; went to dinner; practiced ½ hour zither; wrote Phonog; studied Latin; read ½ hour; went to see Miss Hersey; wrote in here; going to write in other journal; go to tea; write Latin; go to bed."[47] Although seemingly excessive, such preparation was necessary given both the admission standards and course of study that Brooks encountered at college.

Smith required candidates for admission to demonstrate competence in a variety of subjects and texts, including "Geography; the construction of the English language . . . general outlines of History; the Latin and Greek Grammars; the Catiline of Sallust; seven Orations of Cicero; the first six books of Virgil's *Aeneid*; three books of Xenophon's *Anabasis*; two books of Homer's *Iliad*; Arithmetic; Algebra to Quadratic Equations; and two books of Geometry."[48] Basing these standards on those in place at New England colleges such as Amherst, Smith also adopted much of those institutions' academic programs. Yet the college did not directly replicate Amherst's curriculum, choosing instead to adopt a modified version of the elective system, a curricular reform that permitted students to choose or "elect" the courses in which they enrolled. Smith officials implemented the system, which was popular at universities such as Harvard, in a more constrained fashion. Beginning with the same regimen of courses during their first year, Smith students were subsequently permitted to choose one of three courses of study: (1) Classical, which the college described as "distinguished from the others by the greater attention given to Greek and Latin," (2) Literary, which gave greater attention to the modern languages, and (3) Scientific, which gave greater attention to Mathematics and Natural Science.[49] Even after designating one of these courses, however, students pursued a large majority of their studies with classmates in the other two. As the college's description of its curricular program noted, "Enough . . . of the characteristic studies of a collegiate course will be required of all the students to secure a culture as thorough and complete as that acquired in our best New England colleges."[50]

As with the classical curricula at the schools that inspired it, Smith College's academic program was dedicated strictly to mental discipline and the civic-minded ideal of forming virtuous citizens. Consequently, its founders rejected the rise of commercialism and professional training as a justification for advanced learning and claimed in the institution's 1874 circular, "The College is not intended to fit woman for any particular sphere or profession, but to develop by the most carefully devised means all her intellectual capacities, so that she may be a more perfect woman in any position."[51] Similarly, college officials eschewed the practicality infusing the nation's normal schools and land grant institutions (including the Massachusetts Agricultural College, established in nearby Amherst in 1863). Justifying the inclusion of mathematics in the Smith curriculum, for instance, Seelye claimed in his inaugural address, "It would, indeed, be easy enough to show the increasing importance of mathematics in practical life; the assistance it gives the sailor and the engineer; our indebtedness to it for the most highly-prized comforts of our civilization. But it is not for its practical utility that I advocate its place in higher education; that utility indeed, is due to the study which had no thought of practical results."[52]

Smith students occasionally joined Seelye in countering the influence of practicality and commercialism by espousing claims that a college education was meant primarily to foster mental discipline. Writing in *The Alpha Quarterly* (the Smith student literary society publication) in 1892, Florence E. May provided a spirited defense of the classics by describing the conflict that existed between practicality, commercialism, and what she believed was higher education's proper role:

> Entering the domain of education, the utilitarian says to the colleges and universities: "You are following behind in the march of progress. Your methods are theoretical and not practical, stationary and not progressive. You stand gazing into the past to no purpose, while we are looking to you to furnish us tools of present profit. We need men who can grapple with the practical problems of life.... Why will you spend so much time on Latin and Greek, of no practical benefit to anyone? Why not give it instead to French and German, living useful languages, or to science, the clue to measureless further advance?"[53]

May invoked Seeley to answer these questions, asserting that the "end" of education was "the development of each mental faculty through careful, patient training and exercise." She then identified the specific function she believed the classics played in higher learning, writing, "It is in their relation to the main purpose of education that the chief importance of the classics lies. In the training and discipline of mental power, they can be replaced by no other study."[54]

Two years following Smith College's opening, *Scribner's Monthly*, a nationally subscribed literary magazine, lauded the institution's academic approach to women's higher education as well as its innovative system of residential life. In a nine-page illustrated essay, *Scribner's* highlighted the living arrangements as especially beneficial to "the health and manners of the students," with the essay's author concluding, "The nervous tensions and excitement, which must necessarily arise where great numbers [of young women] are gathered together, and regulations multiplied, are avoided, and the quiet and freedom of a smaller family are secured."[55] What the essay did not explicitly state, but was nevertheless of central concern to educators during this time, was what *Scribner's* editor J. G. Holland had four years earlier described as the "vices of body and imagination" that arose in institutional settings in which large numbers of young women resided together "as weeds are forced in hot-beds."[56] That is to say, in addition to their concern over students' physical and emotional health, proponents of women's higher education worried about the development of sexual relations between female college students.

Holland was Seelye's cousin by marriage and the two men were close friends.[57] It is hardly surprising, then, that in the same 1873 editorial in which Holland described the "mischiefs that are bred by circumstances" at institutions such as Mount Holyoke and Vassar, he wrote that Smith College would "do a great thing for America and women if it can furnish a college education and avoid the college perils."[58] With Smith less than two years away from opening, Holland went on to recommend many elements of the collegiate program that Seelye intended to introduce, including the cottage system. Holland's greatest concern, however, was the one that propriety did not allow him to name but that he nevertheless described in Victorian fashion. "We are free to say," he wrote, "that no consideration would induce us to place a young woman—daughter or ward—in a college which would shut her away from all family life for a period of four years. The system is unnatural, and not one young woman in ten can be subjected to it without injury. It is not necessary to go into particulars, but every observing physician or physiologist knows what we mean when we say that such a system is fearfully unsafe. The facts which substantiate their opinion would fill the public mind with horror if they were publicly known."[59]

Whether Smith College or any other all-female institution of higher education actually served as "hot-beds" for the development of queer relationships, as Holland insinuated, is doubtful. Certainly women's colleges provided opportunities for young women to befriend peers they would not otherwise have met. It is impossible to determine if those friendships developed into intimate relationships at higher rates than they did at coeducational institutions. What is clear, however, is that students at colleges such as Smith developed attachments of a variety of forms to other women, while college officials, viewing these relationships as directly opposing the institution's goal of fostering civic virtue, strenuously acted to prevent them.[60]

While a Smith student, Charlotte Cheever kept a journal in which she chronicled a variety of experiences, including the quality of the essays her classmates read aloud in English class, the addresses that Seelye occasionally delivered to students, her classmates' burial of their Algebra textbooks following the end of the term (as at Bowdoin College, an annual celebration), and the entertainment provided at meetings of the college's literary association, the Alpha Society. She also described the many friendships she made at Smith, including one with a "Miss B" who, unlike other students she identified in the journal, Cheever never fully named. Relishing college life (she would eventually become president of the college's Alumnae Association and serve as a trustee from 1889 to 1895), Cheever enjoyed the company of many classmates but especially Miss B. In one journal entry, she recorded having a leisurely day and then spending the evening in Miss B's room. A week later, Cheever described spending another evening with Miss B. "The first half of the time," she wrote, "Lucy and Sally were in here and I was darning my stockings. After they went, I asked Miss B to tell me a story, and she began to give a fairy story, and I began to interrupt and contradict her and try to finish it another way. We had quite a jolly time."[61] More than a simple friendship, the young women's relationship became increasingly intimate. Returning from church one Sunday evening, Cheever entered Miss B's room to "bid her good-night." When she leaned down to kiss her on her forehead, Miss B "kissed a return on the mouth." Cheever continued, "I asked her why she did so when she did not like to kiss people on the mouth. She said she never kissed when she did not want to, also that she always had an irresistible desire to kiss me, she did not know why."[62]

In her acclaimed work *In the Company of Educated Women*, historian Barbara Solomon describes students at women's colleges in the late nineteenth and early twentieth centuries as occasionally participating in "intensified versions" of "romantic friendships."[63] Occurring often enough on some campuses to be popularly labeled as a "smash," these romances typically consisted of one young woman aggressively courting another. As Solomon writes, "Women's campuses facilitated 'smashing,' with its rituals of courting a special friend; flowers, poems, gifts, and missives accompanied declarations of affection and love of the kind usually associated with male-female relations."[64] A variation on the schoolgirl "crush," smashing typically maintained an innocent quality, posing more of a distraction for students than triggering emotional crises. On the other hand, some young women maintained relationships on campus that, at times, suggested the kind of attachments they would develop over the course of their lifetimes.

As a junior at Smith College, Mary H. Askew Mather, a member of the Class of 1883, developed a close relationship with her classmate Frona Brooks, a younger sister of Daisy Brooks. Mather, a popular student, avid tennis player, and first president of her class, kept a journal in which she documented her relationship with Brooks, occasionally employing dotted lines to substitute for behavior she deemed too sensitive to put into words. Writing about Brooks for the first time at the beginning of her junior year, for instance, Mather recorded, "Frona and I have just had a most exciting talk. We began with Psychology and ended - - - - - She said that she wanted something of me and I told her that I wished a certain thing from her, and it was altogether psychological, and - - - - - she had what she desired."[65]

Over time, Mather described her relationship with Brooks in increasing detail, using the phrase "over the stone wall" to signify falling in love with a woman. One morning, for instance, Mather recorded of the previous night, "Did not get to sleep exactly at ten. The result," she noted, "of coming over the 'stone wall. . . .'"[66] The following day, Mather recorded that she played tennis before studying and visiting with Frona. "Studied Psych. [Psychology] . . . ," she wrote, "and then skipped over to Frona's. . . . I stayed till almost ten—Said to Frona 'I think that I have gone over the wall'—'I thought you had when you came in'. . . . Q. [a classmate] came in at ten minutes of ten and we left together. She stopped and I kissed Frona good-night and *I* left without it—but came back to her for a moment afterwards. . . . I couldn't get to sleep for a long time."[67] Throughout the next several weeks, Mather continued documenting her relationship with Brooks, recording entries such as "Read . . . and then went over to Frona's. I am always going to stop for her now and I am always going to say goodnight to her and write in her room from 9–9:30 and I am always going to—and it's blissful, blissful, blissful!"[68]

Although the young women's romance ended prior to their graduation, the experience signaled for Mather the form of relationship she would seek in her adult life. Moving to Wilmington, Delaware, after finishing at Smith, Mather became involved in a variety of "civic, educational, and philanthropic interests," including establishing traveling libraries to serve rural residents, participating in the state's temperance movement, providing English instruction to adult immigrants, and establishing the Delaware branch of the American Association of University Women.[69] During this time, Mather also met her lifelong companion, Alice P. Smyth. Together, the two women contributed significantly to the establishment of a coordinate women's college at the all-male Delaware College. They also attended Mather's Smith College reunion in 1923 where, Smyth having been declared a member of the Class of 1883 "by adoption," they unveiled a sundial presented to the college by the alumnae. Just two years later, upon Mather's death, Smyth honored her companion by establishing the Mary H. Askew Mather Fund to finance a rural book service in New Castle County, Delaware.[70]

Mather's personal experience, both while at college and following graduation, was hardly unusual. As Barbara Solomon notes, intimate long-term relationships between women occurred frequently enough in New England during the late nineteenth and early twentieth centuries to receive the title "Boston marriages."[71] The attributes of many of these relationships are difficult to determine; the homophobia that arose in America beginning in the 1920s and enveloped the nation in the 1950s led many women to destroy the journals and letters that might otherwise offer insight into the nature of these relationships.[72] Nevertheless, attachments developing among young women on campus demonstrates the extent to which many students pursued what they believed were appropriate and meaningful personal relations regardless of the residential systems and structures that college officials put in place to prevent them.

Mather's later commitment to civic causes was also not unusual for the early graduates of women's colleges. Although Smith officials remained relatively silent on the topic of graduate activism, many alumnae used college as a staging ground for later participation in a range of reform movements, including (and in addition to the causes Mather championed) consumer protection, improvement of factory working conditions, and the development of public parks and playgrounds.[73] They also participated in the campaign for woman suffrage and the settlement-house movement. Providing food, shelter, education and social services to the poor, these centers in major American cities served dramatically expanding immigrant populations, with Jane Addams and Ellen Gates Starr's Hull House (founded in Chicago in 1889) becoming the best-known. Inspired by the movement, many Smith graduates joined in settlement work, including Vida Dutton Scudder, who studied at Oxford after receiving her degree from Smith in 1884 and went on to teach English literature at Wellesley College. In 1893, she helped found and then directed the Denison Settlement House in Boston. One year later, Scudder delivered an address at Smith that roused further student interest.[74] "Miss Scudder was a rare inspiration," one student observed afterward, "and gave to many a new purpose and life in college work."[75]

That a student described Scudder as giving a "new" purpose to higher education in the last decade of the nineteenth century reflects the difficulty women continued to confront in identifying tangible reasons for going to college. Doing so became even more challenging as tensions increased between the civic-minded ethos that infused the higher education women received, the continuing value Americans placed on practicality, and the rising influence of commercialism on college and university campuses. One Smith student, attempting to attenuate these tensions, redefined involvement in social, political, and economic reform as a new kind of professional undertaking that college-educated women might pursue, as men did law and commerce. In an essay to the *Smith College Weekly*, the college's student newspaper, she wrote, "The world is coming to recognize the fact that economic independence should be attained by a woman in the home as well as in the business world. . . . But we must pause before the thought that we are to take definite places in society . . . we feel that whatever we are to do must be in the way of service to society; that we are first of all members of the state or community, the social and political order, and secondarily only, individuals. This is to be our profession—to serve the world."[76]

Ada Louise Comstock, who graduated from Smith in 1897 and later served as its acting president before becoming the first full-time president of Radcliffe College, similarly addressed the tension between civic-mindedness, practicality, and commercialism in women's higher education. While serving as Smith's first dean of the college, Comstock rejected the influence of practicality and commercialism while reaffirming Sophia Smith's founding commitment to provide a broad liberal education for the purpose of developing civic virtue. "If we begin to talk of vocations with children in high schools or even with the lower classes in college," she observed, "are we not incurring the danger of leading them to look upon education from a purely commercial point of view? Is there not a possibility that the ideal of a broad and general culture will give way to desire to direct all education toward preparation for gaining a livelihood?" Comstock claimed that there was only one way to avert such peril. "And that," she said, echoing the proponents of mental discipline, was by "constant enforcement of the idea that the discipline and cultivation of the mind are the first essentials for success in any vocation." Then, referring directly to commercialism's influence on women's higher education, Comstock asked rhetorically, "Will the social changes we are bringing about by encouraging girls to go into remunerative employments demanding training and offering advancement be for the better?" Asserting her own civic-mindedness, she claimed, "Education is dangerous if it aims only at individual gain, whether cultural or pecuniary. Its abiding ideal should be citizenship."[77]

Yet, as the First World War dramatically expanded employment opportunities for women, and Smith students assailed Comstock for advice on how best to put their college educations to use, even she was compelled to come to terms with commercialism. Publishing a list of vocations she described as "open to college women," Comstock stated that she assumed women would continue to pursue work in professions such as law and medicine as well as in businesses such as real estate and insurance. To this list, Comstock advised adding "institutional management," "municipal research," "work in newspaper offices," and "probation work." She also proposed that women seek employment in such "utilitarian" endeavors as advertising, publishing, and industrial chemistry. "Success in these lines of work," she concluded, was ultimately dependent on women bringing "energy and cleverness" to their efforts.[78]

Mabel Newcomer, in her oft-cited *A Century of Higher Education for American Women*, examined trends in careers, marriage, and family size for college-educated women between Reconstruction and the Second World War. In one analysis, Newcomer used data on Mount Holyoke and Vassar graduates to confirm that the so-called first generation of college educated women (those who attended college during the 1860s, '70s, and'80s) indeed married at lower rates than non-college educated women. She also demonstrated that the members of these classes who did marry tended to do so later in life and bore fewer children than women without college educations.[79] In a second analysis, this time of the proportion of women who attained advanced degrees, Newcomer found that women's colleges as a whole graduated more than twice as many women who became scholars as would be expected from their enrollments, and that the Seven Sisters, in particular, graduated "several times their share."[80]

The life trajectories of the Smith College Class of 1882 correlate with Newcomer's findings. Almost thirty years following graduation, only thirteen of the class's thirty-seven members had married. Of these, eleven had become mothers. Eighteen members of the class acquired master's degrees, one a PhD, and five, including Daisy Brooks and her friend Maria Vinton, earned advanced degrees in medicine—Brooks at the University of Michigan and Vinton at the New York Medical College and Hospital for Women. A large proportion of the members of this class became teachers and college faculty and, in addition to participating in a range of reform movements, many pursued careers as physicians, missionaries, librarians, painters, photographers, and writers.[81]

In their later years, some members of this first generation of women's-college graduates identified what they believed were important differences between their collegiate and postgraduate lives and those of the members of the second generation. Critics claimed that the first generation generally approached college, occupations, and service work with a seriousness of purpose, while the second generation seemed more interested in participating in campus activities and having fun.[82] Alice Katharine Fallows, a Smith graduate who wrote for popular magazines such as *Scribner's Monthly*, *Harper's Bazar*, and *Good Housekeeping*, published an essay in 1898 that seemed to confirm this impression.[83] Reporting on her alma mater's turn-of-the-century campus environment, Fallows described a collegiate world that was quite different from the one Sophia Smith, John Greene, and L. Clark Seelye had devised. Rather than a small community of students whose physical health was closely supervised, Smith enrolled over eleven hundred students from thirty states and four foreign nations, making it the largest women's college in the United States. More than fifty faculty members served as instructors.[84] With the cottage system breaking under the strain of increasing enrollments, only half of the college's students resided on campus. The rest, Fallows noted, "distribute themselves as best they may among the boarding-houses in town."[85]

Most pronounced in Fallows's description, however, was the vibrant social life that Smith students had developed.[86] Dances, dramatics, and athletics were wildly popular on campus. Students especially favored basketball, which Smith had the distinction of being the first women's college to introduce and which Fallows described as "the great joy of the athletic girl."[87] In addition, dozens of clubs flourished among the undergraduates; some were anchored in academics (such as the Biological Society and the French Club) but most were organized around extracurricular activities (such as the Walking, Skating, and Glee Clubs).[88]

A recent graduate of the Class of 1897, Fallows was aware of the criticism that second-generation college women (herself included) had begun to receive for their "flippancy," "superficiality," and interest in social life over academic study. Editorials in Smith publications reveal that such criticisms were a topic of frequent discussion among students. Rather than simply rejecting the criticism, however, Fallows offered an alternative explanation. "The pioneer days of a girls' college are over," she wrote. "It was the duty of the first classes to set out stakes along the outskirts of knowledge and to overcome much prejudice. The girl student of that time was looked upon as an experiment, and felt the responsibility of her conduct strong upon her. Self-consciousness was thrust at her . . . but something of the sweet graciousness of college experience, which she made possible for later generations, was denied her. To many a girl now, the four college years come as naturally as the finishing-school a quarter of a century ago."[89]

Observing that the second generation of women's college graduates had greater opportunity to enjoy the social aspects of college life precisely because the pioneer alumnae had blazed a trail for them, Fallows rejected the claim that her generation was less interested than the first in leading meaningful, relevant lives. They were, she argued, simply in a better position to simultaneously prepare for their chosen fields of work while participating in a campus lifestyle that was becoming, at Smith as well as colleges and universities across the nation, more entertaining. Accordingly, and as historian Lynn Gordon insightfully observed, many members of the second generation of college-educated women shared "the intellectual and political goals of their predecessors," while they "gradually shifted" their vocational concerns from "service and social reform to individual achievement."[90] As one Smith student, signaling the ascendance of commercialism in women's higher education in 1911, claimed, "Men in the business world have come to realize that there are certain positions for which women are as well, if not better, suited than men. Women have awakened to the fact that there are opportunities open to them in ever-widening fields where they may chose a profession or a special branch of work for which they are really adapted and into which they can put the interest and enthusiasm necessary for success."[91]

Between Reconstruction and World War II, this reorientation or "shift" between the first and second generations of college graduates also occurred among other previously marginalized groups, such as African Americans. Howard University, for instance, provided a model of cooperation between the federal government and newly instated black citizens and their allies in founding one of the many institutions that would come to be known collectively as "Historically Black Colleges and Universities." Yet as at Smith, generational conflict erupted at Howard as commercialism reoriented students' ambitions and goals further in the direction of professional preparation and individual achievement than it had ever been.

8

"THE BURDEN OF HIS AMBITION IS TO ACHIEVE A DISTINGUISHED CAREER"

African American Higher Education in the Mid-Atlantic

In 1930, the Howard University Board of Trustees bestowed an honorary degree on acclaimed African American scholar W.E.B. DuBois. Accepting the distinction, DuBois also accepted the trustees' invitation to deliver that year's commencement address. In a talk entitled "Education and Work," he used the occasion to assess the types of education that had for decades sought to improve African Americans' economic, political, and social lives.[1] DuBois's observations on both the "Negro college" and its graduates, however, undoubtedly surprised his audience. Having previously advocated the higher education of a cadre of African Americans who would lead a movement of racial uplift, DuBois now voiced his frustration with that effort's outcome. Criticizing institutions such as Howard for neither fully understanding the impact of a social ethos of commercialism on American society nor providing a collegiate program that properly prepared young black men and women to confront the changes it wrought, he claimed, "there cannot be the slightest doubt but that the Negro college, its teachers, students and graduates, have not yet comprehended the age in which they live: the tremendous organization of industry, commerce, capital, and credit which today forms a super-organization dominating and ruling the universe, subordinating to its ends government, democracy, religion, education and social philosophy."[2]

As sharp as his judgment was of the Negro college, DuBois reserved his harshest criticism for the graduates seated before him. Frustrated with what he perceived as black students' zeal to use higher education to benefit themselves by entering "into a few well-paid professions," he observed,

> A disproportionate number of our college-trained students are crowd-ing into teaching and medicine and beginning to swarm into other professions, and to form at the threshold of these better-paid jobs a white collar proletariat. . . . Moreover, and perhaps for this very reason, the ideals of colored college-bred men have not in the last thirty years been raised an iota. Rather in the main, they have been lowered. . . . The greatest meetings of the Negro college year like those of the white college year have become vulgar exhibitions of liquor, extravagance, and fur coats. We have in our college a growing mass of stupidity and indifference.[3]

As severe as DuBois was, he was not alone in condemning African American college and university graduates for lacking both a seriousness of purpose and a commitment to improving the lives of all black Americans. Howard University alumnus, faculty member, and dean Kelly Miller similarly scolded students for adopting what he called "the mercenary motive" in seeking a higher education solely for the purpose of achieving personal success. In contrast with alumni who fulfilled their obligations to serve others in the decades following the Civil War, according to Miller, black college graduates in the early twentieth century were seduced by commercialism. In the past, he asserted, "every student was prepar-ing to reclaim and uplift his race. Now, the burden of his ambition is to achieve a distinguished career. Then the objective of his ambition was social, now it is selfish."[4] Sociologist E. Franklin Frazier, who graduated from Howard in 1916 before returning to serve as one of its most esteemed faculty members, held a comparable view. Many students, he claimed in 1924, were adopting "a narrow and selfish individualism" while "preparing themselves for the professions as a means to wealth and enjoyment, and not as a means for deeper and more respon-sible participation in our civilization."[5]

Scholars have attributed the perceived shift in African American college stu-dent aspirations partly to changes resulting from the influence of Northern phi-lanthropists on black higher-education institutions.[6] Yet the opprobrium that DuBois, Miller, Frazier, and others leveled at black college and university gradu-ates echoed the criticisms that the first generation of women's college alumna leveled at later generations of their graduates. The similarity seems to have had relatively little to do with donations to colleges and universities by organiza-tions such as the General Education Board and the Phelps-Stokes Fund. Instead, these criticisms correlated with the increasing rise of commercialism in higher education, and in American society more broadly. Indeed, what Lynn Gordon wrote of the second generation of women's college graduates—that they shared "the intellectual and political goals of their predecessors" while gradually shifting their vocational concerns from "service and social reform to individual achievement"—accurately describes early twentieth-century developments at many of the institutions that would become known as Historically Black Colleges and Universities (HBCUs).[7]

It is hardly surprising that when DuBois criticized Howard's graduating class, he took greatest issue with the corruption of student character. When established in 1867, Howard University was—as with Smith and the historic colleges of the early national period—intended primarily to contribute to the common good by developing student character and fostering civic virtue.[8] The institution was both named for and strongly influenced by US Freedmen's Bureau Commissioner Oliver Otis Howard, a celebrated Civil War general who believed that environmental factors such as slavery, rather than biological deficiencies, had prevented African Americans from developing the character traits necessary for full and equal participation in American society. It was primarily through education, Howard believed, that emancipated people and their children would acquire the virtues necessary to prosper as citizens.

Although Howard was only one of many individuals responsible for the University's founding, he served as its third president (from 1869 until 1874) and his position in the bureau permitted him to direct federal funds to the new institution. Consequently, his view of race relations and his conception of the role of higher education in addressing the needs of millions of black Americans immediately following emancipation strongly influenced the university's early development.

Born in Leeds, Maine, in 1830, Howard entered Bowdoin College at the age of sixteen, where he received a primarily classical education.[9] He later observed that his collegiate experiences had a greater effect on his personal development than on his intellectual growth, writing that "the great gain" of attending college was "the impression made upon the character of a young man."[10] Although he planned to pursue a law career following graduation, Howard's uncle, who was serving in the US House of Representatives, offered him an appointment to the US Military Academy at West Point. Upon graduating four years later, he accepted his army commission and served in Florida during the United States' continuing conflict with the Seminoles.[11] It was also during that period that Howard underwent a conversion experience. "It was the night of the last day of May, 1857," he described in his autobiography, "when I had the feeling of sudden relief from the depression that had been long upon me. I had a small office building near those of the arsenal, which I fitted up for use and made my sleeping room. In that little office, with my Bible and Vicars's Life [author Hedley Vicars's volume entitled *Diary Notes*] in my hands, I found my way into a very vivid awakening and change, which were so remarkable that I have always set down this period as that of my conversion."[12]

Howard's spiritual experience led him to reconsider his military career and contemplate entering the ministry.[13] The beginning of the Civil War, however, permanently postponed those plans as he took command of the Third Maine regiment. He would go on to lead Union forces in battles including First and Second Bull Run, Antietam, Chancellorsville, and Gettysburg. Howard received the appellation "the Christian soldier" for his piousness throughout the war.[14] He also later received the Congressional Medal of Honor for leadership at the Battle of Fair Oaks, during which he had his horse shot out from under him and, after being shot twice in the right arm, had the limb amputated.

In 1865, General Ulysses S. Grant ordered Howard to the nation's capital to receive a new assignment: leadership of a federal bureau established to address the challenges posed by the sudden emancipation of approximately four million people. Howard was unaware that the Bureau of Freedmen, Refugees, and Abandoned Lands had already become a point of political contention in Washington. As with the passage of the Morrill Land Grant Act three years earlier, Congressional approval of the bureau indicated a shifting role in American life for the federal government, from one of limited responsibility during the early national and antebellum periods to what Williamjames Hull Hoffer has described as a "second state" during and following the Civil War. The Freedmen's Bureau, he writes, extended its authority even further, adding "overt, comprehensive, and extensive supervision to its administrative agenda."[15] Consequently, some members of Congress registered their disapproval of the new bureau both during its inception and throughout its seven-year existence, consistently complicating and politicizing Howard's efforts.

In many ways the Freedmen's Bureau served as a catchall agency, tasked with responsibilities ranging from providing emancipated people with emergency medical assistance and provisions (including food and clothing), to administering confiscated Confederate lands, to instituting a system of free labor in the South. To these many obligations, Howard added educational provision. "The educational and moral condition of these people was never forgotten," Howard later recalled, and he claimed to have insisted, that the bureau's officers "should afford the utmost facility to benevolent and religious organizations, and to State authorities, where they exist, in the maintenance of good schools. Do everything possible, was my constant cry, to keep schools on foot till free schools shall be established by reorganized local governments."[16]

Given Howard's reputation and position in the bureau, the leaders of the newly formed First Congregational Church of Washington, DC, invited him to join them in late 1866 in establishing a school to educate African American ministers to serve freed men, women, and children. With tens of thousands of ex-slaves abandoning Southern plantations and moving north, especially to the nation's capital (the city many venerated as responsible for emancipation), church leaders agreed that educating freed men and women was an appropriate ministry for their congregation. Accordingly, a group of men—all white and all affiliated with Congregationalism—met in the home of Deacon Henry A. Brewster on November 20 to discuss plans to found a school. Agreeing to establish "an institution for training preachers (colored) with a view to service among the freedmen," the group adopted a proposal to name their new institution the "Howard Theological Seminary" in honor of the Freedmen's Bureau commissioner.[17] Howard protested the move, claiming that he could do more for the school through his position were he not so prominently named. The assembly insisted, however, and Howard committed the bureau to providing the institution with a "suitable building"—the same provision he had allotted other educational associations serving freed people following the war.[18]

The effort to establish a university to serve African Americans was not unprecedented in 1866. By the end of the Civil War, black higher education had developed in a variety of forms in the United States, although it was still severely limited in capacity due to racial exclusion. During the 1820s, predominantly white, all-male, New England colleges, including Middlebury, Amherst, Bowdoin, and Dartmouth, graduated the first African Americans to receive college degrees in the United States. The following decade, Ohio's Oberlin College began enrolling students, black and white, male and female. As additional historically white colleges and universities opened their doors to small numbers of African Americans, advocates began establishing institutions dedicated primarily to black higher education, such as Pennsylvania's Avery College (1849) and Ohio's Wilberforce University (1856).[19] Many of these latter colleges and universities were higher-education institutions in name only. There is no record of their granting bachelor's degrees prior to the Civil War.[20]

In addition to racial exclusion, the scarcity of higher-education opportunities for African Americans in the north and west prior to 1865 resulted from a dearth of accessible grammar and secondary schools providing the necessary academic preparation for college attendance. Following the Civil War, however, the Freedmen's Bureau gave a significant boost to free schooling for blacks. Collaborating with a variety of denominational organizations, especially the American Missionary Association, the bureau invested five million federal dollars in support of education. By 1870, it claimed to have established or assisted in establishing over four thousand schools employing almost nine thousand teachers and serving well over two hundred thousand pupils.[21] Local black congregations in the South, moreover, often led the development of schools to serve African American communities, with the African Methodist Episcopal Church, the African Methodist Episcopal Zion Church, and the Colored Methodist Episcopal Church contributing both organizational skill and financial resources.[22]

In addition to founding grammar schools during Reconstruction, Protestant church congregations, missionary associations, and freedmen's aid societies established more than one hundred secondary schools, colleges, and universities dedicated to educating African Americans.[23] At the turn of the twentieth century, W.E.B. DuBois recalled this undertaking as the "crusade of the sixties" as well as the "finest thing in American history, and one of the few things untainted by sordid greed and cheap vainglory."[24] Howard University—the higher-education institution some would eventually describe as the "capstone of Negro education"—was somewhat exceptional among this group. Although founded by members of Washington's First Congregational Church, it was established as a nondenominational institution operated by an independent board of trustees.[25] O. O. Howard's direct involvement, moreover, provided it a degree of financial stability in the early years, without which many other HBCUs struggled.

Historian James Anderson has described the "ends and means" of black higher education between Reconstruction and the Second World War as reflecting the values and purposes of three primary groups: missionary philanthropists, Negro philanthropists, and industrial philanthropists.[26] Although the first two groups' positions on education increasingly diverged following the turn of the century, prior to that time both endorsed liberal education as a means through which African Americans might achieve civil and political equality.[27] Industrial philanthropists, on the other hand, argued that what freed blacks needed most was to learn the values associated with manual labor and "the boundaries of their 'natural environment.'"[28] These values, they believed, could be obtained through a higher education that required routinized agricultural and industrial training rather than collegiate studies.

Howard University's founders drew upon all three of these approaches to higher education, as well as others already established at colleges and universities throughout the United States. O. O. Howard looked to his alma mater, Bowdoin College, as a model for the institution that would bear his name. Guided by a civic-minded ethos in its early decades, Bowdoin had aimed to cultivate mental discipline and civic virtue among its graduates through a classical course of study and strictly regulated student life. Prior to the Civil War, however, a social ethos of practicality had begun to both reshape collegiate programs such as Bowdoin's and inspire entirely new kinds of higher-education institutions, including those dedicated to teacher training, agriculture, mining, and mechanics. In addition, commercialism had begun its ascent in American society as well as on college and university campuses. Rather than choose a single archetype on which to base their new university, then, Howard's founders incorporated a wide range of attributes into the institution. The description of the university, as announced in its 1869 catalogue, vividly describes the multiplicity of purposes the Howard Board of Trustees adopted for it. "The scope of this University is broad," it claimed, "and its aims must meet the approval and co-operation of the liberal minded everywhere. It aims to provide for students the training necessary for commencing any legitimate business, to fit them for teaching others in the schools and in the professions, or to fill with credit any position which duty, necessity, or inclination may lead them to undertake."[29]

Perhaps the best example of this multiplicity of institutional attributes is reflected in the revisions that the Howard Theological Seminary underwent before it opened to students. Between the first trustees' meeting on November 20, 1866, and the second meeting just two weeks later, board members concluded that in addition to ministers, teachers would be needed by the freed men, women, and children who had been denied education under slavery. Changing the institution's name to the Howard Normal and Theological Institute for the Education of Teachers and Preachers, the board incorporated a teacher-training program such as the one in place at the California State Normal School.[30] But just one month later, as the trustees began drafting a bill to submit to the US Congress to incorporate "a college for the instruction of youth in the liberal arts and sciences," they again revised its purpose. Forming committees to plan for the provision of professional training in medicine and law, board members agreed to name the institution Howard University.[31] One week later, they expanded the institution's practical orientation, agreeing to form an Agricultural Department similar to those developing at the nation's land grant colleges and universities, such as Michigan Agricultural College.[32] Accordingly, Howard University's charter included all five of these departments as well as one more—a "collegiate" department offering the predominantly classical course of study that O. O. Howard had undertaken at Bowdoin College.[33]

The most remarkable element of Howard University's founding was the speed with which the institution went from being simply an idea to enrolling its first students.[34] Conceived of in November 1866 and chartered in March 1867, the university's Normal Department opened just two months later. Housed in a building leased for it by the Freedman's Bureau near the northern city limits and financially supported by the American Missionary Association, the department employed the Reverend Edward F. Williams as principal. It was open to both black and white students, male as well as female.[35] Indeed, the department's first pupils were the white daughters of two board members; only over time would

FIGURE 8.   Howard University students in front of "The Main Building," 1870. Courtesy of the Moorland-Spingarn Research Center, Howard University Archives, Washington, DC.

Howard become a university serving primarily African Americans.[36] Applicants were required to successfully pass a six-month probationary period before formally enrolling, and tuition, which was reduced for indigent students, was set at three dollars per term.[37] The department's three-year curriculum was similar to that offered at other normal schools and included: First Year—arithmetic, algebra, English grammar, physical geography, and Roman history; Second Year—natural philosophy, geometry, English literature, Constitution of the United States, rhetoric, botany, and physiology; Third Year—logic, chemistry, astronomy, natural theology, mineralogy and geology, modern history, political economy, and theory and practice of teaching. A reflection of the moral development in which university administrators expected students to engage, Bible lessons were held weekly throughout the term.[38]

Given the lack of educational opportunity for African Americans prior to the Civil War, it undoubtedly came as little surprise to Howard officials that few black students were academically prepared to enroll in the university. Consequently, the Board of Trustees established a Preparatory program within the Normal

Department to provide the equivalent of a secondary-school education. Its curriculum, consisting of Latin and Greek, history, geography, and mathematics, was the course of study required for admission to many of the nation's historic colleges.[39] Even so, applicants ranging in age from thirteen to thirty, with wildly different levels of academic preparation, inundated the university. Refraining from rejecting younger candidates who demonstrated academic potential, Howard officials decided to further differentiate the Normal and Preparatory programs by establishing a Model School. With the minimum age for admission set at twelve, the school served as an observation and training school for the Normal students. Accordingly, the Normal School's Preparatory Department set the low end of its admission age at fourteen.[40]

At the end of the first term, Williams resigned as principal of the Normal and Preparatory Department and the board employed John H. Combs to serve through the end of 1868 academic year. In the meantime, O. O. Howard sought to recruit fellow army officer Samuel C. Armstrong to permanently assume the principalship.[41] Raised in Hawaii by missionary parents, Armstrong graduated from Williams College and commanded the 8th US Colored Troop regiment during the Civil War. Following the war's end, Howard appointed him to the Freedmen's Bureau. With responsibility for Virginia's ninth district, Armstrong was in the process of establishing an American Missionary Association–supported school for freed people in the city of Hampton when the Howard University board invited him to attend a meeting in January 1868. When Howard offered him the principal's position for the upcoming academic year, Armstrong politely declined, claiming that he was "morally bound to the enterprise" he had initiated in Hampton.[42] Indeed, Armstrong's school—the Hampton Normal and Industrial Institute (present-day Hampton University)—would go on to be nationally recognized both because of the manual and industrial training approach it implemented and because one of its most famous graduates, Booker T. Washington, replicated the Hampton model when founding the Tuskegee Institute in 1881.

There is little evidence to suggest that Armstrong's pedagogical practices influenced developments at Howard or that what he witnessed in the nation's capital informed his plans for Hampton. What is certain, however, is that Howard University's founders envisioned engaging at least some students in the kinds of manual and industrial work for which Armstrong's Hampton Institute eventually became both renowned and reviled. Howard's Agricultural Department, for example, provided students the opportunity to earn the cost of tuition, room, and board by employing them to drain swampland and beautify the campus. It also hired students to work on the university farm, which grew cabbages, tomatoes, corn, and beans. Board members intended the department to be self-supporting, with crop sales from the farm financing its work.[43] Ultimately, the university's agricultural output was neither plentiful nor profitable enough to be sustained. Nevertheless, at the end of the institution's second year, O. O. Howard identified a clear distinction between students pursuing an academic course of study and those engaged in the kinds of manual labor for which the Hampton Institute became known. "The boys employed have been taught to *work*, as in the other departments of the University they have been shown how to study," Howard wrote in his annual report. "They have reaped the advantages which result from manual labor in open and pure air, to those who are pursuing a severe course of study, and many have at the same time, in this way, earned money without which they could not have continued their attendance at the University."[44]

Influenced as it was by a rising ethos of commercialism, the university also developed elaborate commercial enterprises in which to employ students. In the same month that the Normal and Preparatory Departments opened, for instance, the Board of Trustees approved O. O. Howard's request to establish a building-block company on campus.[45] Three months later, the company leased an acre of university land on which to construct a factory and, in March 1868, the trustees loaned it fifteen hundred dollars to finance its operations.[46] As with university agricultural work, board members intended for the factory to benefit students through manual training and employment.[47] The building-block company failed, however, largely because defects in the bricks led a wing of the Freedmen's Hospital (newly constructed as part of the university's medical complex) to collapse.[48] The failure was nevertheless followed by other commercial ventures. In March 1870, the university financial agent reported to the trustees that within the past month the institution had "opened a blacksmith shop, carpenter shop, and shoe shop, all of which were in successful operation by students of the University."[49] Two years later, the university briefly opened a sewing business to serve female students.[50] In June 1872, however, Howard noted in his annual report to the trustees that these enterprises had failed to cohere into a "well organized and well-endowed department."[51] Less than a year later, the Panic of 1873 triggered an economic depression in the United States that led to the closure of both the businesses and the department. The university would not attempt to establish Industrial or Agricultural Departments again until the 1880s.

Meanwhile, as the Normal and Preparatory Departments and Model School continued expanding (enrolling over three hundred students by the end of the 1871 academic year), the university opened its Medical, Law, Collegiate, and Theological Departments.[52] In their appointment of African American faculty to staff these departments, Howard's founders contributed to the public good by challenging historic forms of racial discrimination in US higher education while also meeting the needs of the growing African American community in and around Washington, DC.

On October 12, 1868, the board elected Oberlin College graduate, attorney, and Freedmen's Bureau Inspector General John Mercer Langston as founding member of the Howard University Law Department.[53] Langston would later serve as the first president of the Virginia Normal and Collegiate Institute (present-day Virginia State University), become the first African American to represent Virginia in the US Congress (and the last until 1972), and be appointed by President Rutherford B. Hayes to serve as Minister to Haiti. Prior to assuming these roles, however, Langston spent seven years at Howard developing the first university-based law department dedicated to training African American attorneys.

In his autobiography, Langston described how he and the department's part-time faculty—all accomplished white male lawyers—designed a program that offered courses in the evenings so that students could work during the day to earn the cost of tuition and living expenses.[54] Langston noted that with President Ulysses S. Grant's approval he was able to secure for Howard students what today would be considered paid internships with the federal government, helping to both advance their legal training and pay for school.[55] He later recalled that he had "as many as a hundred persons, male and female, colored and white, thus located, while pursuing their studies as his law students."[56] Accordingly, the department's first graduating class of ten students included Charlotte E. Ray, a former Normal and Preparatory Department teacher who is credited with being the first African American woman to graduate from a law school in the United States, pass a bar exam, and practice law.[57]

The Medical Department, too, employed African Americans and occasionally women, as well.[58] Dr. Alexander T. Augusta (who in his role as director of the Freedmen's Hospital had the distinction of being the first black hospital administrator in the United States) and Dr. Charles Purvis, a graduate of Cleveland's Western Reserve Medical College, were two of the department's founding faculty. Isabell C. Barrows, a white graduate of New York City's Woman's Medical College and specialist in ophthalmology, was the university's first female faculty member.[59] As with the Law Department, these part-time instructors taught a diverse group of students; the Medical Department's first graduating class consisted of three white and two African American students.[60] Similarly, Dr. Daniel S. Lamb, who served on the Howard Medical Department faculty from 1873 until 1928, observed in 1887 (after the Department had established pharmaceutical and dental programs), that "the valedictory address of the medical class was delivered by a Negro, that of the dental class by a white gentleman, and that of the class in pharmacy by a white lady."[61]

Yet there were also areas in which the university failed to fulfill the ideals that the institution articulated in its early decades. The first was in assigning women, both black and white, to positions of authority.[62] Although officials hired women such as Isabell C. Barrows to teach, their employment was relatively rare. Those who were hired frequently served as instructors in the Normal and Preparatory Department and Model School and, later, in the university's Home Economics Department. Moreover, a woman did not hold a position on the Board of Trustees until 1924.[63] The second failure was a sixty-year delay in not appointing an African American to serve as the institution's president. Black men were indeed among the university's initial faculty and administrative hires. In addition to Langston, Augusta, and Purvis, John B. Reeve served as founding dean of the Theological Department.[64] The Board of Trustees, too, although beginning as an all-white body, quickly added African Americans to its ranks. Within two years of the university's founding, the trustees elected five black men to the board, including the celebrated abolitionist and author Frederick Douglass, out of a total of twenty-one members.[65] Yet in 1875, when the opportunity arose to promote Law School Dean and, by then, Acting President John Mercer Langston to the university presidency, the board declined.

Langston's failure to be promoted occurred during a long and challenging administrative quagmire at the university. After the board elected O. O. Howard president in 1869, the institution continued to reap the benefits of his leadership of the Freedmen's Bureau, receiving over half a million federal dollars before the bureau dissolved in 1872.[66] Yet, Howard's work for the bureau frequently drew his attention away from the university. In addition, his public prominence as both bureau head and university president posed problems when, in 1870, Howard came under Congressional scrutiny in response to accusations that he had mismanaged bureau funds. His involvement with several failed business ventures at the university, such as the building-block company, further called into question his competence, if not his integrity.[67]

Although Congress acquitted Howard of financial wrongdoing in March 1871, his reputation was nevertheless tarnished.[68] Soon after, during the Freedmen's Bureau's final months of operation, President Grant assigned Howard to serve as peace commissioner to Native American tribes in Arizona and New Mexico.[69] To fulfill this duty, Howard requested and the Board of Trustees granted him a leave of absence beginning in June 1872.[70] From that point until his formal resignation from the presidency two and a half years later, he remained involved in university operations but did not effectively lead the institution. Consequently, the board appointed Amzi L. Barber acting president, a poor choice given that Barber soon took his own leave of absence to join his father-in-law in real-estate speculation.[71] Without firm leadership, and with the closing of the Freedmen's Bureau and the Panic of 1873 upending the university's primary sources of support, the institution drifted into financial trouble. Between 1872, when the bureau was dissolved, and 1880, when Congress issued its first appropriation to the university, the institution received no federal funds. By 1875, it was one hundred thousand dollars in debt.[72] Partly for that reason and partly because Howard confronted a second round of accusations of corruption (of which he would again be acquitted), the Board of Trustees created the position of university vice president and, in December 1873, appointed John Mercer Langston to the post.[73]

One year later, on Christmas Day 1874, Howard resigned as university president.[74] At the trustees' meeting the following week, board members voted to postpone electing a new president until the end of the academic year and agreed instead to appoint a new acting president. On January 12, John Mercer Langston accepted the position. Over the next six months, Langston's service positioned him as the obvious candidate for the presidency. Yet when the board met to elect a new president the following June, they selected a white man—American Missionary Association secretary and Howard University board member the Reverend George Whipple—revealing the racial boundaries that even as progressive an institution as Howard University was unwilling to surpass.[75]

Langston resigned weeks later. He eventually claimed that "every colored trustee" had voted for him while "every white one voted for Mr. Whipple."[76] The board, however, did not record individual trustees' votes in its meeting minutes and Langston did not report from where he obtained his information. Consequently, as Rayford W. Logan concludes in his history of the university, "The evidence concerning the racial factor in the election of Whipple for the presidency is plausible but not convincing."[77] Nevertheless, press reports of Whipple's election to succeed O. O. Howard as president, rather than a highly qualified African American, stoked controversy. New York's *Evening Post* followed the story throughout late June and July and the ensuing friction led Whipple to decline the position.[78] Not until April 1877, when the board elected another white man to the presidency—the Reverend William W. Patton—did the university again benefit from consistent leadership.

Despite the "anarchy" that historian Walter Dyson describes as having consumed the Howard University administration throughout these years, the institution continued to mature during the late nineteenth and early twentieth centuries (in large part because, according to Dyson, departmental deans controlled the institution's day-to-day operations).[79] Indeed, historian Zachery R.

Williams has observed that "the stellar Howard University intellectual community that blossomed in the 1930s" laid its foundation between 1890 and 1926.[80] During this period, Alexander Crummel served as a Howard faculty member before establishing the American Negro Academy in 1897, while Carter G. Woodson taught briefly at the university soon after founding the Association for the Study of Negro Life and History and the *Journal of Negro History*. Philosopher Alain Locke, who would be credited with giving a name to the New Negro Movement of the 1920s, served as a faculty member for decades.[81] And in 1926, the University Board of Trustees finally elected an African American to the presidency.[82] Mordecai Johnson would serve in the office until 1960, playing a significant role in shaping the university both prior to following World War II.[83]

Many of these men, as well as other distinguished male Howard faculty and graduates, including Law School dean Charles Hamilton Houston, Supreme Court Justice Thurgood Marshall, Nobel Prize recipient Ralph Bunche, and historian and Presidential Medal of Freedom winner John Hope Franklin, have received significant historical attention.[84] Less well known but equally accomplished Howard luminaries include African American women such as Dr. Sara W. Brown. A graduate of Howard's Medical Department, Brown pioneered health education for women and girls, returning to the university to lecture on gynecology between 1908 and 1911. During these years she also joined with Mary Church Terrell, Fairfax Brown, and Mary Cromwell to establish what would become the National Association of University Women. In 1924, the Howard University Board of Trustees elected Brown its first female member. She served in that capacity until her death in 1948.[85]

Perhaps the most influential woman in African American higher education during the first half of the twentieth century, however, was Lucy Diggs Slowe.[86] A Howard University graduate who returned to her alma mater to become the first dean of women, Slowe's work brought into sharp relief the ways that an ethos of commercialism infused American higher education in the decades prior to the Second World War, even while civic-mindedness and practicality continued to assert an influence on college and university campuses.[87]

Born in Virginia on the Fourth of July, 1885, and orphaned at the age of six, Slowe was taken in by her aunt, Martha Price, who moved her family from Virginia to Baltimore so that Slowe could attend that city's "colored" high school. Graduating at the top of her class, Slowe won a scholarship to Howard. Aware that limited financial resources would hamper her effort to acquire a higher education, Slowe decided to work her way through school, taking clerical jobs during the academic year, soloing in local church choirs, and eventually becoming employed as a student assistant to English professor

George William Cook. In addition to correcting student essays for Cook, the Howard administration assigned her the task of chaperoning female students during off-campus excursions, giving Slowe her first experience supervising undergraduate women.[88]

By the time Slowe attended Howard, the university had become the largest HBCU in the nation, enrolling over twelve hundred, including students from Puerto Rico, the British West Indies, Africa, India, and Latin America.[89] As Howard's newly inaugurated president, John Gordon, declared in 1904, the university was becoming a school for the "colored races of all continents."[90] By all accounts, Slowe took full advantage of what Howard University had to offer in the first decade of the twentieth century. Unlike many young women who enrolled in what had become the University's Teachers College, Slowe pursued a bachelor's degree in English in the College of Arts and Sciences and engaged in the full range of extracurricular activities that were becoming popular on campuses across the United States. Having participated in high-school athletics, she joined and was elected president of the Howard Women's Tennis Club, served as president of the faith-based service group the Young People's Society of Christian Endeavor, was vice president and secretary of the Alpha Phi Literary Society, and was an active member of the Culture Club—a student group that hosted and participated in discussions with prominent political, economic, and social leaders.[91]

Slowe also happened to be attending Howard during two events that undoubtedly gave members of the Culture Club much to discuss. The first was the university's fortieth anniversary celebration, which coincided with the inauguration of a new president, the Reverend Wilbur Patterson Thirkiel. Festivities included speeches by US President Theodore Roosevelt and industrialist Andrew Carnegie, with the university simultaneously marking the occasion by observing its first Founders Day.[92] The second event, which occurred off of Howard's campus but surely influenced members of the university community, was the founding of the Niagara Movement. Launched in 1905 by African American leaders, including W.E.B. DuBois and William Monroe Trotter, the Niagara Movement established a national strategy board for the purpose of opposing the conciliatory racial policies of Booker T. Washington and others. Although the initial organization was short-lived, it served as a precursor to the 1909 establishment of the National Association for the Advancement of Colored People.[93]

With progressive social movements such as African American civil rights and woman suffrage shaping her development, Slowe joined with Ethel Hedgeman and seven other Howard students in 1908 to establish the first Greek-letter sorority for African American college women in America.[94] Formed just two years after Cornell University students founded the nation's first black fraternity, Alpha Kappa Alpha shared its male predecessor's goals of racial solidarity and service to the black community.[95] And yet, as Michael H. Washington and Cheryl L. Nuñez describe, Alpha Kappa Alpha's founders, in contrast with previous black college graduates, placed "a greater emphasis" on community service "as preparation for their lives as professional women."[96] As with students on the campuses of predominantly white universities, commercialism, with its accompanying emphasis on professional status and personal success, influenced the post-graduation plans of many African American students, including sorority members such as Lucy Diggs Slowe. Unlike most of her classmates, however, Slowe would eventually become responsible for not only her own career but, in her capacity as Howard University Dean of Women, for advising female undergraduates on which academic programs to undertake and what personal and professional goals to pursue.

Following her graduation as class valedictorian in 1908, Slowe sought employment to support herself, becoming a teacher at her former Baltimore high school before serving as founding principal of the first African American junior high school in Washington, DC. During this time Slowe also obtained a master's degree in English from Columbia University and, having developed a passion for tennis, became the nation's first African American women's national tennis champion when she won the singles title at the inaugural American Tennis Association national tournament in 1917.[97] Five years later, James Stanley Durkee, who had been appointed to Howard's presidency in 1919, recruited Slowe to the post of Dean of Women. Howard University had never had such a position, however, and Durkee expected Slowe to assume the role as well as undertake the task of defining exactly what it entailed.

University of Chicago President William Rainey Harper created the first dean of women position in 1892 when he recruited Alice Freeman Palmer to the newly established institution in an effort to make the campus—located in a city better known for stockyards than universities—seem a more acceptable place for young women to live. Palmer, who by the time of her appointment was nationally renowned as having been the first female college president in the nation (at Wellesley), accepted the position. She commuted from Cambridge, Massachusetts (where her husband, George Palmer, taught at Harvard) to Chicago for the next three years. From that point forward, coeducational colleges and universities slowly began adopting the position of dean of women on their campuses.[98]

The dean of women's position eventually became one manifestation of a larger "personnel perspective" that colleges and universities adopted following the First World War.[99] Higher-education enrollments rose by 84 percent during the 1920s, reaching one million students for the first time in history.[100] Simultaneously, college and university administrators became increasingly concerned about the number of students who dropped out (approximately 35 percent in their first year) as well as students' emotional health and well-being. To address these problems, according to historian Christopher Loss, higher-education officials "turned to the new psychological sciences for solutions."[101] Accordingly, the field of student personnel work developed in order to train specialists for employment on college and university campuses. Slowe both participated in and became a leader in this field, eventually enrolling in a student personnel PhD program at Columbia University's Teachers College.[102]

The Howard University to which Slowe returned as an employee in 1922 reflected developments in American higher education more broadly. Undergoing its own period of expansion (partly due to increased federal appropriations beginning in 1920), Howard enrolled approximately two thousand students by 1925, almost one-sixth of the nation's college and university black student population.[103] The institution employed over 150 faculty members and, in addition to undergraduate programs in arts and sciences, engineering, architecture, education, home economics, and commerce, was home to graduate schools of theology, law, medicine, dentistry, and pharmacy.[104]

With only 170 of the University's 452 female undergraduates living on campus at the time she was hired, Slowe used her new position to immediately advocate for the development of a women's campus and recreational center located near but "separated from the physical center of all other phases of university life."[105] Informing Durkee of the need for more women's dormitories, she urgently lobbied for their construction.[106] In December 1931, her efforts were rewarded when the Howard University student newspaper reported the completion of three new "stately architectural creations" to house female students. The buildings' opening ceremonies, *The Hilltop* noted, "marked the realization of a long planned dream of Dean Slowe."[107] Yet the new construction, according to Slowe, did more than simply improve housing conditions. The buildings provided, she claimed, cultural and educational spaces that afforded young women opportunities to develop leadership skills through the formation of, for instance, a Students' House Government Association.[108]

Historian Linda Perkins has described Lucy Slowe as a "champion of the self-determination of African American women in higher education." Indeed, much of Slowe's work sought to foster leadership and a sense of agency among young black women.[109] In an essay published in *The Journal of Negro Education* and titled "Higher Education of Negro Women," the dean argued that "developing initiative" among young African American women was especially difficult because of the religious-oriented, patriarchal culture in which most were raised.[110] Consequently, Slowe established a Women's Student League at Howard "to increase fellowship and intelligent leadership on the campus and in the community" and organized an annual conference at the university "to further the training of student leaders on campus."[111] In addition, and given her commitment to fostering a sense of independence among young Howard women, Slowe dedicated much of her energy to providing students with career and vocational guidance. Acutely aware of the double challenge that race and gender posed to university-educated African American women who sought meaningful careers, Slowe observed in 1937 that HBCUs such as Howard had been extremely slow to provide young women with guidance in choosing a career. "Here and there," she claimed, "Negro colleges are offering their students expert advice in the field of vocational guidance, but it is the exception rather than the rule. This guidance is even more important for Negro women than it is for white women because the former have to be guided not only with reference to their aptitude, but because of racial identity, also, with reference to possible opportunities for work. Negro women cannot assume that because they are prepared efficiently as individuals they will receive the same consideration as others when they apply for work."[112]

Slowe was not satisfied with black female college graduates simply entering traditionally feminized lines of work such as teaching. Instead, she sought for them to engage in what she called the "modern" world. Arguing that commercialism had forever altered "the routine of life" that existed prior to the Civil War, she asserted that women had been propelled out of "home occupations" and into "industrial and commercial pursuits." Any "discussion of the education of women," she concluded, "must take into consideration the present status of women, their opportunities and their chances for achievement in the new order."[113] Yet when Slowe administered a National Association of College Women survey of forty-four higher-education institutions enrolling African American women, she found that only 7 percent of those students studied sociology, 4 percent political science, and 4 percent economics—all subjects that were, she claimed, "basic to understanding modern life."[114] At Howard, she identified the same trend. Most black college and university women, she confirmed, continued to prepare themselves for a teaching career.[115]

Accordingly, and in keeping with a dominant ethos of commercialism, Slowe counseled students to pursue studies that would prepare them for careers leading to professional advancement and personal success. "Women are making successes in the both the business and professional worlds," Slowe pronounced in the first address ever delivered by an African American women to the National Association of Deans of Women, "but not enough of them are going into these vocations. My feeling is that our women have a great contribution to make in fields of science, business, and politics."[116] Simultaneously, Slowe urged students to prioritize their role as leaders of society engaged in promoting the common good through race uplift. As she declared in a 1934 speech to the National Association of College Women, "It seems to me that the first duty of college women is to inform themselves thoroughly on economic and political problems confronting our citizens and to furnish the masses of our people with guidance in a democratic state."[117] Again, rather than encouraging students to embrace teaching—the traditional method through which African American women engaged in race uplift—Slowe took it upon herself to widen their occupational horizons. "College women need guidance in their choice of vocations in the light of the realities which they will face after they leave college," Slowe claimed, "and it is the business of the Dean of Women to see that such guidance is furnished."[118]

Slowe's untimely death at the age of fifty-two brought an abrupt end to her ascending career and growing national reputation. As a founding member of the National Association of Deans of Women and Advisors to Girls in Negro Schools, the first executive secretary of the National Council of Negro Women, and a charter member of the Washington, DC College Alumnae Club (a forerunner of the National Association of University Women, of which she served as president from 1924–1929), Slowe contributed to establishing organizations that supported African American college graduates in their efforts to advance both personally and professionally. An inspiring speaker, she was invited to address both HBCUs and predominantly white colleges and universities. Shortly before her passing, she became a more outspoken critic of racism in America, delivering a radio address in which she forcefully criticized the nation's capital for continuing to enforce "jim-crowism."[119]

Slowe's experiences at Howard University reflected many of the changes that occurred in black higher education following the turn of the twentieth century. As a young woman, she sought to better herself and her race by acquiring a university education and becoming a teacher. She also valued the status that accompanied professionalism and spent her entire career at Howard demanding that the dean of women be treated as a professional equal to the dean of men rather than a glorified matron (dormitory supervisor). Writing of "The Business of Being a Dean of Women," she asserted, "Being a Dean of Women . . . has passed from its early state of vagueness as to purpose and function to a business or as we Deans of Women like to think, to a profession."[120] By the late 1920s, although Slowe continued to support the notion of college-educated women contributing to race uplift, she argued that black colleges and universities were obligated to provide female undergraduates with the training and opportunities necessary to break out of the traditional means of service through teaching.

Unlike W.E.B. DuBois, who harshly criticized Howard students in 1930 for their frivolity, Slowe argued that there were generally two types of students who sought a higher education: "Namely, those who come for what they call 'college life,' and those who still come for a very serious intellectual experience." If colleges and universities such as Howard were "properly organized," she claimed, all students would, regardless of their initial reasons for enrolling, receive "some benefit—social and intellectual—from their stay."[121] Slowe's optimism undoubtedly resulted from her own higher-education experiences during the early part of the twentieth century. She began as a Howard student who played a central role in founding one of the Greek-letter societies that DuBois eventually railed against and concluded her career as a dean of women who encouraged young women to pursue professional status and success while also serving their communities. The timing of her passing in 1937 meant that Slowe did not live to see the even greater transformation that American higher education was about to undergo, as economic depression gave way to war and an ethos of commercialism gave way to the birth of an affluent America.

Conclusion to Part III

Whether through Leland and Jane Stanford's hope to promote the public welfare, Sophia Smith's intention to redress the wrongs women had suffered, or Oliver Otis Howard's desire to serve newly emancipated people, Stanford University, Smith College, and Howard University all took advancing the common good as a central concern, collectively increasing access to higher education for African Americans, women, and students from lower socioeconomic backgrounds. By the end of the First World War, however, a social ethos of commercialism, with its accompanying emphasis on occupational success and individual gain, came to predominate on these campuses, guiding the institutions in their development and influencing students' educational decisions.

The financial constraints imposed by the Great Depression during the 1930s posed significant challenges to all three institutions. Yet, unlike many other colleges and universities, Stanford, Smith, and Howard survived the crisis and were poised to resume their progress when the exigencies of World War II brought their advancement to a halt. As the armed forces depleted male higher-education enrollments following the lowering of the draft age from twenty-one to eighteen in 1942, work in defense industries as well as service branches such as the Women's Army Corps (WAC) and Women Accepted for Volunteer Emergency Service (WAVES) drew women away from campus. Consequently, higher-education institutions across the United States suffered the loss of students and their tuition dollars for the second time in just over a decade.[122]

Many colleges and universities responded to wartime challenges by negotiating contracts with federal agencies to take advantage of their suddenly underutilized facilities and personnel. Stanford and Howard hosted Army Specialized Training programs to train military recruits, while Smith was home to the first WAVES Officers Training Unit. Emerging research universities also negotiated agreements with the federal government and defense industries to conduct war-related research. These institutions increasingly aligned their educational missions with national defense priorities and emphasized technical training and applied research. Competition for lucrative federal contracts became a mainstay of the Cold War university.[123] By 1960, 39 percent of Stanford University's operating budget came from the federal government, with 80 percent of that amount going directly to research in engineering and physics.[124]

In the decades immediately following World War II, however, American higher education experienced two major developments that led many to portray the postwar period as a "golden era" for colleges and universities.[125] First, enrollments skyrocketed 227 percent between 1950 and 1970; by 1970 over one-third of Americans between the ages of 18 and 24 were enrolled in a college or university. Second, public institutions met much of this demand. In 1970, three-quarters of America's higher-education student population attended public colleges and universities, with about one-fourth of the total number enrolling in two-year colleges.[126] And although veterans' benefits such as the GI Bill led to a significant increase in male enrollments immediately following the war (and, consequently, a decline in women's proportional representation), in absolute numbers women's participation in higher education during the early 1950s surpassed their prewar enrollment peak by more than fifty thousand students. Indeed, more women are estimated to have received bachelor's degrees in 1952 than at any prior time in US history. The same held true for master's degrees: colleges and universities conferred almost twice as many of these on women in 1952 than in 1940, this during a period when many institutions limited the number of women they admitted in an effort to make room for returning veterans.[127]

With World War II boomtowns accelerating the process of urbanization during the 1940s, much of the nation's demographic growth occurred in and around cities. Consequently, many states constructed entirely new colleges and universities in major metropolitan areas to serve hundreds of thousands of students who previously had little or no access to higher education. Urban public universities, such as the University of South Florida, and two-year community colleges, such as the ones in Rhode Island and New Mexico to be profiled in later chapters, catered to "nontraditional" students, especially racial and ethnic minorities, immigrants, and working class youth and adults.

Portrayals of the postwar period as higher education's golden era belie the many challenges that institutions confronted during this period. Ultimately, however, it was the rise of an affluent society, beginning in the 1920s and catalyzed by robust post–World War II economic expansion, that transformed American higher education once more. In an age of commercialism, acquiring a college or university degree became essential to achieving personal status and professional success in one's chosen occupation. A social ethos of affluence amplified this new reality, shifting higher education's central purpose toward providing a credential that helped men and women procure the wealth necessary to fully partake in the nation's consumer culture.

THE COLD WAR THROUGH THE TWENTY-FIRST CENTURY

9

"A WEDDING CEREMONY BETWEEN INDUSTRY AND THE UNIVERSITY"

The Urban University in the Southeast

Just months before the newly established University of South Florida (USF) opened in Tampa in May 1960, the university's director of institutional research, Lewis B. Mayhew, released results of a survey his office had conducted of high-school seniors in the surrounding region. A public four-year institution founded with the aim of serving a "nontraditional" urban student population, USF expected to draw most of its initial enrollment from within a forty-five-mile radius, where almost 25 percent of Florida's population resided.[1] The survey results confirmed much of what USF's first president, John S. Allen, had anticipated. Of the 607 prospective applicants, most had parents who had not attended college, while the parents of a substantial minority (235) had not graduated from high school. A majority of the students planned on living at home and commuting to the university—in large part to save on the cost of housing—while many intended to enroll part-time and work part-time to finance their studies.[2]

The survey also revealed a central challenge to Allen's plans. Publicly celebrating USF as "a completely new and separate institution, rather than a branch of one of the existing state universities," he characterized it as "the first modern state university conceived, planned, and built in the United States in the 20th century."[3] Yet in guiding the development of this "modern" university's curriculum, Allen looked not to the nation's flourishing research universities but to the traditional liberal-arts college as a model for an urban institution that would foster civic-mindedness among students. Consequently, Mayhew noted the potential conflict that prospective USF students' educational objectives posed to Allen's intended mission. Of the reasons students gave for wanting to attend college, the greatest number (228 males and 146 females) indicated "prepare for work," while far fewer (seventy-one males and fifty-six females) specified "become generally educated." Of the specific occupations in which young men expressed an interest, well-paying fields such as business, engineering, and "pre-professional" were the leading choices, whereas young women ranked education (schoolteaching) and pre-professional as their preferences.[4] This data, Mayhew advised Allen, "presents evidence which is of considerable significance to the faculty of the University of South Florida." He continued, "The institution has been organized to give major emphasis to the Liberal Arts and Sciences. This institutional orientation needs to be reconciled with the overwhelming vocational concern of the first freshman class. This is not to say that these two are irreconcilable or antithetical. It does place the burden of motivation on the faculty. Students will need to be shown the explicit relevance of courses in the Liberal Arts for their personal aspirations."[5]

The tension that Mayhew identified between Allen's civic-minded goals and students' "overwhelming vocational concern" was hardly unique to USF. Rather, it was one that many higher-education institutions confronted in the decades following World War II. Harvard University responded to this tension as early as 1945 in a report entitled *General Education in a Free Society*. Popularly known as the *Harvard Red Book* because of its crimson cover, the report highlighted a distinction between "general" education, which it described as being that part of a student's education "which looks first of all to his life as a responsible human being and citizen," and "special" education, which it claimed "looks to the student's competence in some occupation." The authors concluded that, although all students should receive both forms of education, general education was crucial to the growth of democracy, should emphasize the humanities as the basis of the liberal arts, and would consist of courses taken by all of the university's undergraduate students.[6] Just two years later, *Higher Education for American Democracy*, the national report issued by US President Harry S. Truman's Commission on Higher Education, similarly grappled with the tension between general and vocational education.[7] Differing slightly from the Harvard committee in their response, Truman Commission members proposed a program of general education designed to "inculcate in students the qualities necessary for citizens in a democracy, including knowledge of international affairs and domestic politics, the capacity for social analysis, self-understanding, and self-expression, and the exploration of vocation and other adult responsibilities."[8]

John Allen similarly claimed that USF should maintain as its primary concern the education of competent citizens, while also providing students with opportunities to prepare for future vocations. In an address to the university's first faculty, he observed, "We believe that education for a person's civic responsibilities, education for personal responsibilities and education for family responsibilities, i.e., education for citizenship—if you will give a very broad definition to the term 'citizenship'—is too important to leave to chance. We are all citizens, members of families, and members of community groups. We must *all* understand human behavior, government, international relations, science, mathematics, philosophy, literature and fine arts."[9]

Weeks later, Florida governor LeRoy Collins delivered a convocation address to USF's charter class in which he affirmed Allen's characterization of the university's mission. Having remarked two years earlier at the groundbreaking ceremony that "no task" was "more commanding upon our civic consciences or more satisfying to our desire to contribute to the public good" than establishing the university, Collins returned to that theme. Criticizing the "egoism and self-centeredness" that some Americans demonstrated by being concerned only with financial success (a group he described as "living in ranch-style houses and driving expensive cars"), Collins observed, "The extreme of these citizens say unto themselves: Nothing in this world is really worthy of me. Some of the less extreme will say that nothing is worthy of me but my family, or my business, or my profession. But basically, they absolve themselves of responsibility of their local communities, their state, their nation and the world by telling themselves that there is nothing outside their own little spheres that deserve their allegiance in a struggle against wrong and injustice." Then, echoing the inaugural address Joseph McKeen had delivered at Bowdoin College more than 150 years earlier, Collins urged the assembled students not to use their higher educations for private advantage but, rather, to contribute to the common good: "Seek out the opportunities for leadership through which you may repay society and enrich the democratic process which has made it all possible. This, students, will be Florida's claim upon you."[10]

Allen's and Collins's comments were not simply rhetorical. One of USF's early marketing brochures, entitled *The University of South Florida: An Invitation to Learn*, urged students *not* to attend the university if what they wanted was simply to "prepare for a job." If this was the case, it advised, "Consider a technical or trade school."[11] Similarly, the university's first catalogue urged students to "think twice" about enrolling if their primary objective was to achieve social status through a university degree: "While a college experience may be important to some persons for its supposed values of social prestige, this should not be the determining factor in deciding to go to college. There are many other ways to achieve such values and college is not designed as a place to spend four pleasant socializing years—and a good bit of Dad's bank account—waiting to grow up."[12]

Many students, however, had other ideas.

In 1958—two years after USF's establishment and two years before it opened to students—economist John Kenneth Galbraith published *The Affluent Society*, in which he observed that changes to the nation's political economy resulting from World War II had generated unprecedented affluence in the United States.[13] Galbraith argued, however, that America's newly affluent society violated the "conventional wisdom" by which free-market economies operated because it had become one in which producers, rather than merely satisfying consumer wants, created them through means such as advertising and salesmanship. Consequently, consumer wants became insatiable, while social status became tied firmly to material acquisition. "As a society becomes increasingly affluent," Galbraith explained, "wants are increasingly created by the process by which they are satisfied. . . . Expectation rises with attainment."[14] The problem with postwar material abundance, he concluded, was that "The more wants that are satisfied, the more new ones are born."[15]

The rising ethos of affluence that Galbraith identified had profound implications for colleges and universities. Whereas earlier in the century commercialism had led a growing but still relatively small number of Americans to value higher education as a means by which to achieve professional success in an increasingly competitive job market, many people now concluded that a university degree was a ticket to the good life—a passport to the American Dream—practically guaranteeing the wealth necessary to fully participate in the nation's expanding consumer culture and achieve elevated social status.[16] As W. Norton Grubb and Marvin Lazerson have written of higher education during this period, many students enrolled in colleges and universities not to acquire "useful knowledge" or even practical skills, but solely because of "the possibilities for individual gain."[17]

In addition to demonstrating the effects of a social ethos of affluence on students' approaches to higher education, the history of the University of South Florida illustrates how colleges and universities similarly prioritized acquiring wealth during the second half of the twentieth century. Although established as a low-cost institution dedicated to undergraduate instruction, USF eventually sought to become an affluent "multiversity" by pursuing lucrative research contracts, establishing technology transfer and patent and licensing offices, and raising revenue by increasing the cost of undergraduate education, all in an effort to generate financial resources and elevate institutional prestige.[18]

Moreover, USF's location in a growing Southern metropolitan area—part of the nation's expanding Sunbelt—reflected many of the social, political, and economic changes that took place in the United States in the decades following the Second World War.[19]

In 1954, state legislators representing Florida's Hillsborough County, which included the Tampa metropolitan area, sought to capitalize on a recently released report encouraging the expansion of higher-education opportunities throughout the state.[20] As with the Truman Commission's *Higher Education for American Democracy, Higher Education and Florida's Future* urged dramatically increased access to colleges and universities for the state's residents. Predicting that Florida's rapidly rising population would lead enrollments to skyrocket from 36,000 to over 132,000 students by 1970 (a number the report significantly underestimated), it called on the legislature to establish at least one public degree-granting institution and eighteen new community colleges throughout the state.[21] Yet it was economic concerns that primarily drove the proposed expansion. Describing Florida as one of the fastest-growing states in the nation, a promotional bulletin that higher-education boosters provided to state legislators noted that limited access to higher-education institutions led to Florida's being ranked thirty-sixth in the nation in the number of students enrolled in a college or university. "Florida cannot expect to continue its remarkable rate of economic growth," the bulletin read, "unless it provides higher education facilities comparable to its neighboring states [with] which it competes for population, industry and investment capital."[22]

Growth in and around the Tampa Bay area was indeed extraordinary, with the metropolitan region's population increasing from approximately 209,000 residents to more than a million and a half between 1940 and 1980.[23] By 1970, the Tampa Bay region was the third-largest metropolitan area in the South.[24] This transformation resulted from a confluence of factors.[25] First, the area had multiple population centers. Tampa's "Latin" quarter, for instance, known as Ybor City, comprised thriving Cuban, Italian, and Spanish communities. Economically, the area was a major center of US cigar production.[26] The region also had vibrant African American and Bahamian communities and was home to a variety of black social and political organizations, including the Knights of Pythias, the Prince Hall Masons, and the City Federation of Colored Women's Clubs.[27] Second, as part of mobilizing for national defense in the years leading up to World War II, the federal government converted Drew Field Municipal Airport to military use, established the two-thousand-acre Hillsborough Army Air Field in northeast Tampa as a training base, and constructed MacDill Air Field at the lower end of the Interbay Peninsula. At the height of the war, the Army Air Corps stationed more than forty thousand soldiers at the three installations; many veterans would later return to the area and make it their home.[28] Third, defense industries sprang up throughout the region, luring thousands of Americans still reeling from effects of the Great Depression to relatively well-paying jobs. The Tampa shipyards, for instance, constructed by industrialist Matthew McCloskey in 1942 to equip the US Maritime Commission, employed sixteen thousand civilians and maintained a payroll of three quarters of a million dollars a week.[29] The city of St. Petersburg, located directly across the bay, amplified these developments, growing even faster in population than Tampa proper throughout the 1940s.[30]

The Tampa Bay region's growth was not unusual, however. Part of the nation's emerging Sunbelt, which stretched from coast to coast along the southern part of the United States, Tampa's experience was shared by metropolitan areas such as Los Angeles, Phoenix, Dallas, and Charlotte. Historians have published dozens of studies examining the Sunbelt and its origins, its significance, and, perhaps most importantly, whether the term describes an identifiable region with a shared political, economic, and social culture or, instead, a "state of mind" characterized by "an evolving brand of modern conservatism."[31] Amidst scholarly disagreement, most historians nevertheless contend that economic development stimulated by federal subsidies and tied to industrial growth in the areas of national security, defense contracts, military expansion, and technology catalyzed the Sunbelt's rise. This growth, according to Sean Cunningham, was "concurrently fueled by and cyclically reflected in" the expansion of postindustrial sectors of the economy, such as real estate, finance, tourism, retail, and especially higher education.[32]

Although Florida's population had been on the rise for decades, the state experienced what historian Gary Mormino has described as the "Big Bang" following World War II.[33] In 1950, approximately 2.7 million people called the state home. Twenty years later, that number had reached over 6.7 million. "No other state matched Florida's velocity," Mormino writes, "and only California attracted more new residents during the 1950s." (Florida would continue its remarkable growth, with a sixfold population increase between 1950 and 2000, a rate two times that of California.)[34] As members of the state's Council for the Study of Higher Education observed, however, educational provision failed to keep up with the expansion. In 1954, nine accredited private colleges and universities, three state universities, and five two-year junior or community colleges enrolled a total of only thirty-six thousand students across Florida.[35] Moreover, these institutions were segregated, severely limiting educational opportunities for racial and ethnic minorities, particularly African Americans.

The council acknowledged that Florida's greatest areas of population growth were remote from the established public universities: the University of Florida in

Gainesville and two Tallahassee institutions, Florida State University and the historically black Florida Agricultural and Mechanical University. To compensate, they proposed building commuter institutions in high-growth regions, which would permit the state to save on the cost of dormitory construction, while students (whom they expected would live at home while enrolled) would save on the cost of room and board. Accordingly, Florida's Board of Control, the body that held authority over the state's public higher-education institutions, took initial steps to establish a new university in the Tampa Bay area. After much wrangling over whether to build in the city of Tampa or St. Petersburg, the board chose a 1,694-acre tract near the northeast edge of Tampa.[36]

The board's plan for the university thoroughly reflected the characteristics of a rising Sunbelt metropolis. Rather than building the institution in the city center, they located it in an area of anticipated growth about nine miles from Tampa's central business district, on a barren site near the former Hillsborough Army Air Field (which the federal government had turned over to Hillsborough County following the end of World War II; figure 9).

FIGURE 9.   Billboard advertising the opening of the University of South Florida, c.1958. Courtesy of the Special & Digital Collections, Tampa Library, University of South Florida.

Developers constructed an industrial park nearby that, when combined with the new university, was expected to promote regional commercial and residential development as well as tourism. (August Busch Jr., would open his brewery and beer garden in the vicinity just three years later.[37]) Funds from the 1956 Federal Highway Act supported building roads and highways that dramatically increased access to the unincorporated area, while the conversion of Drew Field (also decommissioned following the war) into an international airport further improved access into and out of the region.[38]

It was in that expanding metropolitan locale that John S. Allen began the process of building a new four-year state university from "the ground up," as he liked to claim.[39] With the legislature appropriating eight and a half million dollars for construction and equipment and $140,000 for salaries and planning, Allen began working with architects and hiring faculty and staff.[40]

Allen had a distinguished career prior to arriving at USF. Having served as a faculty member at the University of Minnesota and Colgate University, directed the New York State Board of Regents Division of Higher Education, and held the positions of vice president and acting president of the University of Florida, he had significant experience managing both personnel and facilities. Perhaps his greatest influence on USF, however, was his commitment to general studies rooted in the liberal arts for the express purpose of educating citizens. Just days following the launch of the first Soviet Sputnik satellite in 1957, local reporters pressed Allen to explain why American higher education had failed to maintain US technological superiority. "It is clear we need more scientists and engineers," he responded, "but we do not need scientists and engineers who are politically naïve or economically illiterate." Allen later acknowledged that it was a "matter of national concern" that in the same year the US graduated twenty-two thousand students with bachelor of science degrees, the Soviet Union graduated sixty thousand with master's degrees in scientific fields. However, he observed, there was "one principal difference" between US and Soviet scientists. Theirs were "selected for training on the basis of political reliability, while ours are free to think for themselves and serve humanity in many ways. In this connection, let us remember that atomic power cannot teach a Sunday school class, write a poem or compose a song. Scientists must be citizens in the fullest sense if their country is to perform its responsibilities to the world at large."[41]

To provide the liberal education necessary to educate citizens, Allen led the development of an academic program that began with coursework taken primarily in a College of Basic Studies.[42] This offered seven full-year courses in the following areas: Functional English (writing, reading, speaking, listening); Functional Foreign Language (French, German, Russian, or Spanish); Human

Behavior—Effective Living and Thinking (psychology, anthropology, sociology, logic); The American Idea—America and the World (history, government, geography, economics, sociology, and anthropology); Natural Science (a choice of biological science—botany, physiology, zoology—or physical science—astronomy, chemistry, geology, physics); Mathematics (algebra, geometry, trigonometry, calculus, statistics); and the Humanities (philosophy, literature, religion, intellectual history, drama, painting, sculpture, music).[43] During their first two years, all undergraduates took Functional English and five out of the six remaining courses. Faculty offered honors sections of each course to students with more rigorous academic preparation.[44]

During the junior and senior years, students pursued a major in one of the university's three additional colleges: Liberal Arts, Business Administration, and Education. Although many students, especially those intending to pursue graduate and professional study in law, medicine, or engineering, enrolled in the College of the Liberal Arts, the colleges of Business Administration and Education offered professionally oriented coursework. Even in these colleges, however, the curriculum tended toward liberal studies. USF's first catalogue described the College of Business Administration as serving a "specialized function" in preparing students for "responsible positions in business and industry," while also characterizing the program as "broadly conceived to provide a sound, fundamental education in the field rather than to train narrowly for specific jobs." It continued, "These broad foundations serve as well for the longer future when new responsibilities come to those who are prepared to receive them in a day when change is the rule we must live by."[45] Course offerings ranged from labor economics, international commercial policies, and principles of investment to accounting, marketing, secretarial studies (typing and shorthand), and business machines.[46]

The College of Education served a similarly specialized role, training students for employment in schools and classrooms rather than the front office. Describing teacher preparation as an "all-university function," the catalogue echoed the Wisconsin Idea when it described the education of effective teachers as a civic obligation that public institutions of higher education undertook to serve the common good.[47] One USF administrator recalled that the decision to establish a College of Education resulted from a combination of the institution's awareness of "pressing community needs" for well-trained teachers and an acceptance of public universities' responsibility to meet those needs.[48]

Meeting "pressing community needs" was a priority many universities located in urban areas adopted during the second half of the twentieth century. America's "urban crisis," which began in the 1950s and continued for almost four decades, consisted of the economic decline of major US cities as well as the descent of extremely poor city neighborhoods into severe social distress. The product of racial and class segregation, federally subsidized suburbanization, job discrimination, urban redevelopment projects that frequently displaced the poor, and the flight of capital from cities to the suburbs, inner-city "ghettos" were marked by high unemployment, rising crime rates, civil unrest, and poverty.[49] Urban universities often responded to these conditions by seeking to ameliorate them in areas surrounding their campuses.[50] Undoubtedly motivated by institutional self-interest—and sometimes doing more harm than good—many such institutions claimed that their service efforts were linked to higher education's civic obligations.[51]

In 1964, President Lyndon Johnson offered a specific example of this commitment by drawing a direct comparison between the service that institutions such as the Michigan Agricultural College had performed through the Morrill Act and the role that higher education might play in confronting the nation's urban crisis. "A century ago we were a nation of farms and farmers," Johnson observed. "Congress passed legislation to apply the science of our learning to the secrets of our agriculture—and our colleges and universities set out to change our farms. I expect higher education in America to cross many new frontiers and one of the most critical is the frontier of city life."[52] The following year, he signed the Higher Education Act into law. With the legislation providing financial support, colleges and universities such as USF established extension services in urban areas that emulated agricultural extension programs founded in the nineteenth and early twentieth centuries.

Unlike institutions such as Columbia University and the University of Chicago, which were located in or close to their respective city centers, USF was located on Tampa's outskirts.[53] In its early years, then, the university had the luxury of selecting which urban problems it wished to address. The College of Education, for example, designed its program around improving urban schools in the Tampa metropolitan area, with faculty assisting teachers in developing curriculum and the college opening to pupils at local schools on Saturdays for academic enrichment programs.[54] Yet the greatest service that USF administrators claimed to perform during this period was providing an accessible, affordable, teaching-oriented four-year undergraduate education to nontraditional students. As College of Liberal Arts dean Russell M. Cooper later recalled, the university's faculty were selected based primarily on "evidence of active, provocative engagement with students in the process of learning" and the "most important criterion for advancement in faculty rank and salary was effective teaching."[55] Lewis B. Mayhew, in his capacity as chairman of the institution's "Role and Scope Committee," affirmed the university's emphasis on teaching when he drafted its mission statement, writing, "Since the University is to be essentially an undergraduate institution and since undergraduate students pose particular instructional problems, the importance of teaching and learning will be stressed. During its formative years graduate research will not be central but teaching will be all-important."[56]

With USF's institutional priorities established, academic program in place, and opening scheduled for September 26, 1960, the registrar's office began processing applications from a range of students, male and female, young and old. The first student to enroll reflected the student demographic the institution anticipated serving. Barbara Campbell had graduated from a local high school, married, and had three young children. At her mother's and husband's urging, she decided to apply to USF to study elementary education. Upon Campbell's admission to the university, the Campus Edition of the *Tampa Daily Times* (which served as the campus newspaper until students established their own in 1966) illustrated the community's awareness of the nontraditional students USF intended to enroll, noting, "Had it been planned, there could not possibly be a better, more suited person to be the number one student at USF than Barbara Campbell."[57] Altogether, that year the university admitted 1,996 students between the ages of sixteen and sixty-eight who paid a modest $180 per year in tuition.[58]

Within a year, USF enrollments surged to 2,698 (1,590 men and 1,108 women).[59] Almost all commuters, they nevertheless began establishing a student culture on the campus, which, despite landscapers' efforts in planting five hundred trees, experienced frequent sandstorms.[60] In an effort to maintain what he called an "accent on learning," Allen insisted that USF neither participate in intercollegiate athletic competitions nor form a football team. Students responded by establishing intramural sports clubs as well as a host of other extracurricular activities.[61]

During the university's first decade, Allen experienced a series of unanticipated challenges to his leadership. Just months after the university opened to students, the McCarthyist-influenced Florida Legislative Investigating Committee—more popularly known as the Johns Committee—conducted what amounted to a communist witch-hunt on campus. Soon after, the American Association of University Professors censured USF for violating academic freedom when Allen revoked the appointment of a controversial scholar to a one-year, halftime position. In the years that followed, student activists held a series of demonstrations in opposition to the Vietnam War (although USF experienced relative calm in contrast to the level of disruption that took place on many other campuses).[62] And as the civil rights movement gained momentum in the United States, conservative critics lambasted USF's policy of racial and ethnic integration, while African American students, in particular, accused it of doing little to remedy racial and ethnic discrimination.[63]

Given its commitment to increasing access to higher education for nontra-ditional urban students, this last issue was particularly salient for the university. Prior to USF's establishment, Florida's public higher-education institutions were unequivocally segregated, with black students attending the state's Agricultural and Mechanical University. As Larry Johnson, Deirdre Cobb-Roberts, and Bar-bara Shircliffe have demonstrated, Florida state officials, and especially the Board of Control, provided "enlarged, but still not equal" higher-education opportuni-ties to African Americans and other minorities in the wake of the 1954 *Brown v. Board of Education* decision.[64] Board of Control members, for instance, supported by Florida State Supreme Court rulings, attempted to prohibit Virgil D. Hawkins, a black man, from enrolling in the University of Florida Law School even after the US Supreme Court ruled in Hawkins's favor in 1956.[65] It took another two years before the first African American gained access to the University of Florida Law School.[66]

USF, however, was a relative exception to the state's extreme practices of racial exclusion. When established, the university was open to women and men, whites as well as racial and ethnic minorities. Although the institution did not at first actively recruit students of color, it admitted Ernest Boger, USF's first African American student, just one year after opening. Boger later recalled that he "par-ticipated fully in all the college activities," served as a student assistant in the psy-chology and music departments, and lived on campus during his junior year. He remembered experiencing relatively few instances of "ugliness" as a consequence of his race. "We did have a different, progressive environment here at South Flor-ida," Boger observed, "and I've always been very proud of that."[67] Indeed, before construction began on USF's first building, state officials considered convert-ing a private but foundering institution, the University of Tampa (UT), into the new state university. Following the *Brown* decision in 1954, however, UT trustees rejected state overtures because they believed that white students would "flock" to their private, segregated institution rather than attend the public, integrated University of South Florida.[68]

Even so, African Americans comprised only 2 percent of USF's 12,500 stu-dents by 1968.[69] As at colleges and universities across the nation, black student activists responded to the status quo by agitating for change. Forming One-to-One, an organization that sought to educate whites "about the nature of the black struggle in America," members of the group rallied for increased access to higher education for students of color while seeking to engage the university commu-nity in "working more closely with residents of the inner-city for the betterment of the total society." Consequently, members claimed that One-to-One had "the implied, yet imperative objective of mounting a massive, concerted, and calcu-lated war on poverty, ignorance, discrimination, racism, bigotry, and oppression,

since they are all interrelated and involved in the dynamics of the current crisis."[70] Over the next several years, One-to-One members participated in Get Out
the Vote campaigns sponsored by the National Association for the Advancement
of Colored People (NAACP) and the Southern Christian Leadership Conference (SCLC), volunteered with a variety of Tampa social-service organizations,
hosted panels on racial oppression in American society, and published a newsletter promoting Black Power. "The Civil Rights Movement is dead," declared one
such issue, "destroyed by the position of its own short-sightedness, naivete, and
miscomprehension. Now is the age of the human rights and Black power, distinguished by its unmistakable turnabout in mood, direction, and leadership—
Black Leadership."[71]

USF officials responded to student activism, as well as pressure resulting
from federal legislation such as the 1964 Civil Rights Act, by developing an
affirmative-action program to recruit and support "disadvantaged" students—
a euphemism for students of color, particularly African Americans. In their
program proposal to the faculty, Dean of Women Margaret E. Fisher and College of Basic Studies Dean Edwin P. Martin claimed, "The history of the Negro
student population, has been discouraging to those of us who feel strongly
that education is the Negro's major access to eventual full membership in society. . . . Clearly, the absence of discrimination, although necessary, is sufficient
neither to attract potential Negro graduates nor to promote their success on
the campus." The program, which the USF Faculty Senate approved after only
a fifty-five-minute debate, included faculty members visiting regional high
schools to recruit and interview African American candidates; admitting applicants regardless of their test scores and high-school records; allowing recruited
students to remain at USF for two years despite poor academic performance;
providing housing, financial assistance, remedial counseling and other support services; and developing a targeted advising program that paired students
with faculty members who served as "sponsors" throughout the entire time
the students remained undergraduates.[72] "Let me emphasize that you alone
are the judge of whether these students will be admitted and continued in the
university," Martin wrote to participating faculty after USF officially launched
the program. "None of them is admissible according to routine procedure, but
we are, in effect, betting that some of them can become successful students
because of the help you will give them during a transition period between high
school and college."[73]

Beginning with twenty students, the university's program for disadvantaged
students quickly expanded, partly because it benefited from Upward Bound, a
federally subsidized program established on the USF campus in 1965. Upward
Bound supported talented low-income students, mostly racial and ethnic

minorities, in succeeding in high school and preparing for college. Of the ninety students who completed USF's Upward Bound program as high-school seniors in 1968, the university admitted eighty.[74] Consequently, John Allen felt confident enough in USF's efforts to recruit and support students of color to include a section in his 1969 State of the University address to faculty and staff on the institution's commitment to diversity. He reported, "For the past several months, we have had a group of black students acting as advisors to our Director of Admissions. Their particular duty has been to seek out additional black students who have the potential to succeed at the University of South Florida, but who may or may not yet have shown or developed their full potential." Allen then announced progress in USF's efforts to establish an Afro-American Studies program. "We have been fortunate," he reported, "in securing three highly qualified black professors to teach courses in our Afro-American studies program which begins this Fall. Using core courses in Afro-American studies, on the same basis as our baccalaureate programs in Latin American and American Studies, we have proposed to the Board of Regents that we be allowed to offer a bachelor's degree in Afro-American Studies."[75] Finally, he reminded his audience that the university had adopted an affirmative-action plan "to insure equal opportunity for all persons, regardless of race, religion, sex, or national origin," emphasizing that it "applies to students, faculty, administration and staff alike."[76]

Although Allen undoubtedly portrayed USF efforts on behalf of racial and ethnic minorities in the most positive light possible, evidence suggests that the university was indeed ahead of Florida's other public higher-education institutions on issues of civil rights and affirmative action. For instance, when US Office for Civil Rights Regional Director Paul M. Rilling wrote to Florida Board of Regents Chancellor Robert B. Mautz in February 1970 to report on college and university compliance reviews recently conducted throughout the state, he asserted that "nearly all of the institutions reviewed" had failed to discharge their "affirmative duty to adopt measures necessary to overcome the effects of past segregation." USF, however, provided an exception. Rilling observed, "The University of South Florida has established an affirmative-action program which indicates that it has set goals and is making progress toward these goals in adding minority faculty members and students. Such actions on the part of other universities would suggest that they would be moving in a desirable direction toward providing equal educational opportunities for all students in the State of Florida."[77]

In an effort to further increase enrollment of students of color, Allen hired former Harlem Globetrotter Troy Collier to serve as assistant to the vice president for student affairs. Tasked with reaching out to minority communities and encouraging students of color to apply to the university, Collier explained the disproportionately low enrollment of African American students as partly a result of mistrust between members of the black community and the predominantly white university. "Our main problem," he claimed, "is to get everyone informed with the real facts—and to get those facts believed. Minority group people need to have confidence that we are doing everything we can to help and that they are really wanted and have at least a few friends."[78] Over the next three years, Collier led an aggressive recruiting program that expanded the number of African American students on campus from approximately two hundred to more than a thousand, with total minority enrollment rising to just over 1,700. The growth, Collier noted, placed USF within its 1974–1975 equal opportunity goals. However, a decade's worth of increases had led USF's total enrollment to climb to twenty-one thousand. Consequently, minority enrollment rose to a mere 8 percent of the student body. "We are about 50 per cent of where we should be," Collier concluded. "We need large increases."[79]

Combined with the Higher Education Act, which established the first major federal student financial aid program, affirmative-action efforts such as USF's increased access to higher education for minority youths, many of whom came from disadvantaged backgrounds. Nevertheless, the large majority of students at USF between 1960 and 1980—as well as those at most large urban public institutions nationally—were nontraditional mostly to the extent that they lived at home and commuted to campus. As Dongbin Kim and John L. Rury have demonstrated, although students aged nineteen and twenty residing with parents and commuting became the largest category of beginning college and university students during this period, these young men and women were primarily white and from solidly middle- and upper-class backgrounds.[80] Another decade would pass before urban public universities, including USF, began enrolling a significant proportion of low-income students and students of color.

In 1970, John Allen announced his retirement at the age of sixty-three. Reflecting the so-called "golden age" in higher education, the years of his tenure witnessed dramatic growth at the University of South Florida. When the university first opened, it had a budget of $2.4 million, ten buildings, 341 employees (including 109 full-time faculty), and fewer than two thousand students. By the time he retired, the budget was $38.4 million and the institution comprised seventy-three buildings, over 1,700 employees (834 full-time faculty), almost eighteen thousand students, and both the main campus and a branch in St. Petersburg.[81] Throughout this period, Allen maintained the institution's focus primarily on teaching and educating for citizenship. Yet, USF was not insulated from the rapidly expanding influence of a social ethos of affluence in America.

When the Florida Board of Regents appointed M. Cecil Mackey as USF's second president in February 1971, it hired an administrator who, as Florida State University executive vice president, had already worked to elevate the wealth and status of a public university.

Mackey later recalled that his first impressions of USF included "that a lot of people believed in the institution." He remembered, "They were glad to be here, they thought there were important things to do for the community, and they were committed to doing the best they could for USF as they perceived it." However, he also believed that the university lacked a "cohesive vision," a "decision about where it should be going, what the future was to be in terms of the quality, the breadth, the scope of the institution."[82] Mackey concluded that the university's emphasis on teaching was too narrow a priority and that USF could better serve the Tampa metropolitan area, the State of Florida, and the nation by becoming a research university. He later recalled,

> I looked on one of my first and highest priority assignments to be to try to figure out what the university was capable of, what its true role and mission should be for the long haul, and then assess the quality of what we had, and see how that related to where we might want to go. . . . The scope that it had so far at that point had been much more limited to teaching with relatively little emphasis on research. . . . I thought that was much too limiting for what the university was capable of being.[83]

Mackey accurately assessed USF as an institution that prioritized undergraduate teaching. Yet graduate study, as well as scholarly and applied research, had slowly begun expanding as early as its first decade. The Florida Board of Control authorized the university to confer its first graduate degree (in Education) in 1964. By 1971, USF offered doctoral degrees in three disciplines and master's degrees in forty. Moreover, as early as 1962, John Allen publicly acknowledged faculty for successfully acquiring research grants from external agencies such as the National Science Foundation, the Atomic Energy Commission, and the National Institutes of Health.[84] Just two years later, following the establishment of an Office of Sponsored Research to assist faculty in acquiring external support, Allen noted in his annual report that faculty had received forty-four sponsored research grants totaling approximately $750,000.[85] By 1970, the university's research funding grants totaled more than five million dollars.[86] Nevertheless, compared to other institutions of its size, USF trailed significantly in obtaining sponsored research.

Prior to World War II, very few higher-education institutions received significant federal research support. In 1940, private industry accounted for almost 70 percent of total expenditures for research and development (R&D), with the federal government accounting for only 20 percent.[87] However, wartime technological advances resulting from university-based research, such as the atom bomb, led policymakers to urge dramatically increased financial investments in basic research, especially in mathematics and the sciences.[88] In addition, the rise of the Cold War and the launch of the Soviet Sputnik satellites catalyzed federal spending.[89] Within two decades of the end of World War II, federal investments in university research had risen almost 900 percent.[90] Consequently, many university faculty turned their attention away from local or regional concerns in order to "follow the money," as historian Margaret P. O'Mara writes, and pursue federal research grants for programs "of national significance and scope."[91]

To tap into federal largesse and make USF into a "first-class research oriented university," Cecil Mackey hired University of Oklahoma Vice President for Research and Graduate Studies Carl Riggs to serve as the institution's vice president for academic affairs.[92] Riggs later recalled that when he arrived at USF in August of 1971, "much of the University still believed it would continue to be a relatively small, essentially liberal arts institution." He continued, "During my recruiting visits to the campus, President Mackey and I had an easily made agreement that the University had to be gently moved toward the large, complex, multi-campus institution that it was destined to be, and that the change had to include much more emphasis on research."[93]

Mackey and Riggs led USF's transformation into what University of California president Clark Kerr had characterized several years earlier as a "multiversity": an institution committed to many purposes, especially scholarly and applied research.[94] Pursuing the status that accompanied becoming a Research 1 (R1) University, USF recruited recognized scholars as well as newly minted PhDs with established interests in research and publication, while elevating publication requirements for promotion and tenure.[95] Consequently, the university's founding commitment to undergraduate instruction began to dissolve. "If you name off the ten best universities in the US," USF Vice Provost for Research and Graduate Studies George R. Newkome later claimed, "they are known for their research aspects, not for their undergraduate pedagogical studies. The only way we're going to become known is to establish a very strong, dynamic research–graduate studies base."[96]

The Carnegie Foundation for the Advancement of Teaching established the R1 category in 1970 using two criteria: annual total federal research support and annual number of doctoral degrees awarded.[97] When the foundation first published its "Classification of Institutions of Higher Education" three years later, institutional status almost immediately became attached to a college or university's place in the rankings. The *Chronicle of Higher Education*, which began publication a few years earlier, made these rankings (along with a similar set of standings issued by the National Science Foundation) an annual feature story.[98] In turn, many higher-education institutions reoriented their priorities toward moving up in the rankings, with universities such as USF establishing research institutes as well as colleges of engineering, medicine, and nursing with substantial research components in an effort to elevate institutional prestige.[99] As College of Liberal Arts dean Russell M. Cooper would later write of this transformation, "Financed primarily by external subventions, professors in research institutes tended to become more and more detached from the general life and work of a university as well as from its general administration and budget, less and less involved in teaching and mutual concerns of faculty and student colleagues.... After 1971, the University's emphasis upon integrated general, liberal, and professional education dissipated."[100]

In addition to pursuing prestige, higher-education institutions such as USF sought to expand contracted research programs because they offered alternative sources of revenue. Nationally, public universities' share of state appropriations decreased from 54 to 46 percent between 1968 and 1977, triggering frequent funding crises on campuses throughout the country.[101] At USF, a proposed 20 percent cut to the university budget in 1975 led to slashing everything from travel and library hours of operation and book orders to faculty and staff positions. One year later, Mackey resigned the presidency, in part because of the state's failure to adequately finance the institution. By 1980, the financial situation at USF had grown so dire that the university could not pay its annual utility bill; administrators began to consider implementing a four-day workweek.[102] Consequently, higher-education institutions in Florida and elsewhere increasingly relied on federal and state research grants and private sources of financial support, such as endowment earnings, gifts, and especially tuition, to support their annual operations.[103] Yet popular backlashes against soaring tuition bills, especially at public colleges and universities that continued to declare a commitment to access and affordability, eventually limited the size of the increases they could implement.[104]

A persistent decline in state appropriations, restrictions on tuition increases, and the lucrative provisions and elevated institutional status accompanying sponsored research awards eventually gave birth to what has been called the "entrepreneurial university."[105] Although Stanford University (and its role in the growth of Silicon Valley) is often cited as the preeminent model of academic entrepreneurship, universities across the nation adopted entrepreneurial practices during the latter part of the twentieth century in an effort to generate wealth.[106] The establishment of research parks, technology transfer, and patents and licensing offices, for instance, provided the partnerships, capacity, and expertise necessary for universities to commercialize intellectual property. Moreover, the Bayh-Dole Act of 1980 provided the legal foundation for higher-education institutions to profit significantly from their research programs.

Prior to 1980, the federal government retained the rights to results generated by federally sponsored research at colleges and universities. Yet the government rarely licensed or capitalized on those results. Congressional approval of the Bayh-Dole Act dramatically altered those conditions, legislating that the organizations and institutions conducting the research retained the rights to those results. Accordingly, many universities were positioned to generate tremendous wealth from grant-funded research and corporate partnerships.[107] As Roger Geiger's observations on higher education during the 1980s suggest, the Bayh-Dole Act permitted an ethos of affluence to fully infuse these institutions, transforming their priorities and practices. "The university's embrace of commercial endeavors typified a mode of behavior evident in many realms during that decade," he writes. "The spirit of excess that characterized financial markets and personal consumption seemed to have an analog among research universities as well, which paid little heed to reservations that might formerly have restrained them. Broadened involvement with donors, industry, and commercial markets provided examples of consequential and most likely irreversible change."[108]

USF fully embraced the model of the entrepreneurial university by engaging in a wide range of wealth and status-generating projects and programs. In 1982, it established the Center for Electronic Development and Research (CEDAR) in collaboration with the Honeywell Corporation to more closely align engineering research with corporate needs.[109] As Congressman Sam Gibbons proclaimed at the center's ribbon-cutting, "What we are witnessing today is a wedding ceremony between industry and the University."[110] Reflecting the close partnership that USF and Honeywell developed, the center was initially located in a ten-thousand-square-foot space at the company's north Tampa plant. (It would later move into the university's new $10 million College of Engineering building.) Upon its opening, USF Electrical Engineering Department chair and CEDAR Executive Director Michael Kovac explained that the center would engage primarily in applied engineering research: "It signals the beginning of much closer cooperation between academia and industry—for their mutual benefit."[111] Honeywell executive Richard Mayer concurred: "Honeywell feels there must be a strong alliance between universities and industry."[112]

USF administrators anticipated that the research conducted at the growing number of university centers and institutes across campus—not only CEDAR, but the Center for Microelectronics Design and Test (established 1985), the Moffitt Cancer Center (1986), the Center for Urban Transportation Research (1988), the Institute for Biomolecular Science (1988), and the USF Eye Institute (1989)—would result in a rise of patentable discoveries.[113] Consequently, the university followed a growing trend in higher education toward assuming institutional responsibility for facilitating the commercialization of research results by establishing a technology transfer office (TTO).[114] Although TTOs vary in size and responsibilities, they commonly perform four tasks: receiving disclosures from faculty, staff, and students regarding potential inventions; assessing these disclosures for potential commercialization; conducting the patenting process; and managing the licensing process (identifying licensees, negotiating agreements, and overseeing enforcement).[115] By the close of the twentieth century, research-university faculty nationwide earned more than $1 billion per year in royalties and fees, in part through the resources and support provided by TTOs.[116]

USF similarly assumed an active role in regional business development by establishing a service called USF Connect, through which it provided small business professionals and entrepreneurs access to a wide range of university resources, including technology, marketing, financing, management, and legal advice.[117] Associate Vice President for Economic Development Rod Casto said of the service, "Whether it's taking a new product to the marketplace, developing a solid business plan, securing financing, creating partnerships or simply exploring opportunities for the next stage of business development, we know what it takes."[118] Intended especially to serve science faculty seeking to capitalize on their discoveries, USF Connect adopted the slogan "The Business of Science" and incorporated a technology incubator and research grants program into its operations.[119] The university simultaneously began constructing a new 230,000-square-foot research park.

University-based research parks have traditionally operated under the principle that the spatial proximity of university and industry will promote profitable collaboration.[120] Accordingly, universities have sold or leased land or buildings to businesses with the intent of partnering in developing new products or processes.[121] The rise of technology transfer during the 1980s catalyzed the establishment of these parks on campuses throughout the United States. Although twenty-four had been created by 1979, almost twice that number opened between 1980 and 1984, a rate that continued throughout the decade. In 1990, almost 80 percent of university-related research parks were less than ten years old.[122]

USF was comparatively slow in establishing its park. A Florida state commission approved its creation as early as 1979, and a number of real-estate developers partnered with the university in planning off-campus research facilities. Debate over where to build on campus, however, as well as how the park would fit into the university's organizational scheme, consistently delayed its development.[123] Nevertheless, after becoming president in 1988, Francis T. Borkowski spearheaded an effort to establish a "University Technology Center" at USF as an anchor for a Research and Development Park. "Only by pooling resources into strong, powerful consortia," Borkowski was quoted in the Center's promotional materials, "by working closely with higher-educational institutions—staying close to research—will industries be able to compete."[124] Given that sponsored research at USF had increased 250 percent during the previous five years, particularly in biomedical technology, natural sciences, and engineering, Borkowski committed the institution's mission, resources, and faculty "to economic growth through the transfer to industry of newly developed technology."[125]

Although USF did construct its Technology Center, it was not until the year 2000, when Judy Genshaft assumed the presidency, that the institution launched the development of a major on-campus biotechnology and life-sciences research park. As provost of the University at Albany (State University of New York), Genshaft had participated in establishing an interdisciplinary research center and business incubator at a public, metropolitan university. She later recalled that during her interview with the presidential search committee she expressed her interest in constructing a similar park at USF. In explaining her support for the project, Genshaft observed, "I think that the twenty-first century... is looking to... research universities to present the start-up of economic development: companies." She then described the financial benefit she anticipated USF faculty and students gaining from the park: "We have some USF researchers who have already started a company, and their company has grown to the point that they were looking to move it to Virginia, but now that we have a research park they're staying here. That's exactly what we want. We want our students and our faculty to develop spin-off companies that can go right into the park."[126]

Plans for the new venture were extensive. In 2004, USF Chief Financial Officer Carl Carlucci explained that it would include two state-of-the-art buildings, with the $40 million construction cost shared among the Hillsborough County Commission, the city of Tampa, private investors, and the university.[127] When the park opened a year and a half later, it indeed reflected the priorities of an entrepreneurial university. In addition to providing space for sponsored research, the Interdisciplinary Research Building housed the Center for Biological Defense, a US Department of Defense–funded center for applied biodefense and emerging infectious disease research. The Business Partnership Building opened with twenty businesses leasing space, eight of which were faculty startups.[128] In addition, the building served as home to the USF Center for Entrepreneurship. Designed to provide entrepreneurial education and training and research in the fields of business, engineering, and health sciences, the Center claimed to foster "the critical skills necessary to identify new business opportunities, accelerate the commercialization of new technologies, and create and grow successful new business ventures through entrepreneurship."[129]

Yet throughout this period, while USF actively pursued an R1 designation by investing heavily in research and promoting the commercialization of intellectual property, many undergraduate students—both at USF and on campuses throughout the nation—enrolled for reasons that had relatively little to do with contracted research and technology transfer. In 1974, *The Chronicle of Higher Education* reported on a "new vocationalism" in higher education, which it identified as the "most notable trend" among currently enrolled college and university students.[130] Although many undergraduates had previously pursued higher education as a means of professional preparation, the paper reported, students were now "very, very worried" about being gainfully employed immediately following graduation. Consequently, they were "abandoning theoretical, abstract, and purely academic fields" for those that led directly to lucrative jobs. One survey the article cited revealed that the number of students who planned to "start making it" upon graduating had increased by over 10 percent in just one year. In contrast, the percentage of students surveyed who indicated that they planned to "work for political or social change" dropped to less than 1 percent.[131] Similarly, a Carnegie Foundation report indicated that the number of undergraduates majoring in the "professions," including vocational and occupational programs, increased from 38 to 58 percent between 1969 and 1976.[132]

One explanation for the rise of the new vocationalism among students nationally was the enrollment growth at public urban universities such as USF. As J. Martin Klotsche, chancellor of the University of Wisconsin, Milwaukee, observed in 1966, "The fact that large numbers of urban students work while attending the university causes them to be job-oriented to their course of study."[133] Klotsche had direct experience with students' occupational orientation. His branch campus was established in 1956—the same year as USF—and, like USF, served a nontraditional, urban student population. Within a decade of the Milwaukee campus's opening, the institution began responding to students' anxieties over future careers by offering an educational program that, according to Klotsche, "overstressed" vocational or professional concerns, resulting in a disproportionate enrollment in programs such as engineering, commerce, and pharmacy.[134]

As both Klotsche and the prospective USF student survey that Lewis Mayhew conducted in early 1960 suggested, the new vocationalism had been years in the making, with higher-education institutions responding to it for almost as long. During the 1960s, for example, USF had met increasing demands for occupational training by implementing a Cooperative Education Program to provide students with work experience. "Students today are frequently heard to demand that their education be made more 'relevant,'" John Allen announced by way of describing the program. "I believe that the Cooperative Education Program is one of the most effective answers we have developed to this demand for relevance. A Co-op student alternates a term in college with a term on a job in business, industry, science or government where he learns to apply his knowledge and theories to practical matters."[135]

By placing students with national agencies such as the US Food and Drug Administration, US Weather Bureau, and Smithsonian Institution, as well as with regional offices and corporations such as the Florida Power Corporation, the General Telephone Co., and Pratt & Whitney, cooperative education allowed Allen to maintain the integrity of the university's liberal arts–oriented academic program while responding to student demands for relevance.[136] Given how many USF students sought well-paying jobs, however, cooperative education served relatively few. Consequently, as at the University of Wisconsin–Milwaukee, student concerns led USF to transform its curriculum during Cecil Mackey's tenure. Mackey eliminated the College of Basic Studies and developed an academic program that increasingly stressed vocational and professional interests, including (again, as at Milwaukee) engineering and nursing as well as mass communication, finance, marketing, and international business. USF also continued to establish branch campuses that offered a greater variety of pre-professional, technical, and occupational coursework.[137]

Students' growing concern with lucrative employment and material success reflected a rising ethos of affluence in America, one that had important ramifications for higher education. Jack E. Fernandez, whose career began in 1960 as a USF assistant professor of chemistry and physical science and continued through the beginning of the twenty-first century, was well positioned to observe the influence of this ethos over time. In 2003, the Florida Studies Center interviewed Fernandez about the changes he had observed on campus over the course of his career. When asked specifically about students' reasons for enrolling, he claimed that students in the 1960s were, for the most part, vocationally oriented. "These kids wanted to get their degree and do their profession, whatever that was," he recalled. When then asked to compare those students to the ones with which he more recently worked, he said, "The impression I have is that students now are more preoccupied, not with fulfilling a dream or some kind of work they want, as they are with making money."[138]

In 2000, the Carnegie Foundation began the process of revising its higher-education classification scheme, eliminating the R1 category and replacing it with "Doctoral Research Universities—Extensive." For the first time, Carnegie included USF among its top-tier research universities.[139] Four years later, President Genshaft announced a "Top 50 in Five Years" initiative to further increase research expenditures and elevate endowment income and annual giving, with the objective of becoming one of the top fifty research universities in the United States. The following year, she launched "USF: Unstoppable," a major gifts campaign with a $1 billion goal. She also announced the university's intention to join the Big East Athletic Conference.[140] Having broken with John Allen's prohibition of football in order to maintain an "accent on learning," USF fielded its first intercollegiate football team in 1997. Only three years later, the university entered NCAA Division I-A athletics and, in 2005, joined the Big East. Genshaft called this move "a great opportunity to be affiliated with great institutions that see USF the way I see USF. These are universities that will be solid university partners over the next decade, and I believe our affiliation with them will advance our brand as a national research university."[141]

Many of USF's research programs, especially in the health sciences, resulted in discoveries that significantly benefited the common good. Yet as an ethos of affluence became a driving force at the university, John Allen's early emphasis on educating for citizenship by prioritizing teaching gave way to the entrepreneurial priorities of generating wealth and increasing institutional prestige. Accordingly, by the turn of the twenty-first century, USF began abandoning its commitment to nontraditional commuter students. Genshaft, for instance, sought to elevate admissions standards to attract better academically prepared students, including raising minimum SAT scores and admitting more National Merit Scholars, while simultaneously transforming the university into a residential institution. She explained, "I want the University of South Florida to be among the top twenty-five American universities. In order to do that... there is a quality of student that you need to have on the campus that is committed to full-time study so that you have that intellectual dialogue. . . . You don't get that if you're just driving on, taking a class, and leaving."[142]

When the Florida Council for the Study of Higher Education recommended establishing USF in 1956, it did so with the intent of meeting the needs of students in the Tampa metropolitan area who, because of lack of opportunity, would not have previously pursued higher learning. Over time, however, as USF increasingly sought wealth and status, it distanced itself from its original student demographic. Yet council members, in an effort to provide publicly supported higher education to all Florida residents, had also recommended establishing eighteen two-year community colleges that, when combined with the existing five, would place over 99 percent of the state's population within commuting distance.[143] That recommendation repeated a 1947 Truman Commission on Higher Education proposal calling for the dramatic expansion of public community colleges across the nation. Many states in addition to Florida—Rhode Island and New Mexico among them—implemented the proposal. It is with those states' efforts to provide low-cost two-year postsecondary education that this book concludes.

10

"TO MEET THE TRAINING AND RETRAINING NEEDS OF ESTABLISHED BUSINESS"

Community Colleges in the Northeast and Southwest

The community college is the workhorse of American higher education—and it has never been more popular. In 2013, approximately 46 percent of the US undergraduate population enrolled in community colleges. In comparison to higher-education enrollments nationally, these students were disproportionately of color: approximately 57 percent of the total were Hispanics, 52 percent African Americans, and 43 percent Asian-Pacific Islanders.[1] In addition, almost 61 percent of Native American undergraduates were enrolled in community colleges, many at one of twenty-five two-year tribal colleges spread throughout the Midwest, Southwest, and Western United States and Alaska.[2] Community colleges also serve a significant proportion of disadvantaged and first-generation college students. Of undergraduates from families with incomes of less than $25,000 a year, 44 percent attend community college, as do 38 percent of those whose parents did not graduate from a college or university.[3]

Yet community colleges have received relatively little attention from historians, an unfortunate shortcoming both because the community college is the single form of higher education that Americans can lay legitimate claim to having "invented" and because the institution has undergone a remarkable historical transformation.[4] Beginning in the early twentieth century as "junior colleges," community colleges were designed to provide the first two years of undergraduate study leading to the bachelor's degree. Over time, however, many became training grounds for individuals seeking occupational certification while also serving as resources for small-business development and agents of small-scale technology transfer.[5]

Scholars have provided a wide range of explanations for the junior college's transformation. As Kevin Dougherty describes in *The Contradictory College*, one interpretation contends that junior-college occupational training arose "out of the demand of students for remunerative work and of society for a trained labor force," while another claims that "occupational education stemmed from the demands of the capitalist class for publicly subsidized employee training and a means to maintain the educational gap between the social classes." Still another analysis asserts that junior colleges "vocationalized themselves" with the intention of "carving out a secure, if subordinate, training market," while Dougherty concludes that "self-interested, relatively autonomous government officials" were largely responsible for the junior college's shift to vocational education.[6]

To be sure, all of these interpretations offer some insight into the institution's conversion from a pre-baccalaureate, academically oriented college to a site of occupational training. Yet, all also tend to treat the changes that occurred among junior colleges as distinct from those that characterized American higher education more generally. When viewed in this broader context, the rise of an ethos of commercialism during the first half of the twentieth century can be seen influencing junior colleges in a fashion similar to that of four-year colleges and universities. Whereas four-year institutions such as Stanford University introduced applied courses of study and established professional schools, junior colleges maintained academic programs of collegiate grade while expanding vocational education opportunities. Indeed, what historian Roger Geiger writes of the research university between 1900 and 1940 may be applied in only slightly modified form to the junior college during this same period. These two-year institutions met the needs of a particular demographic group in American society by offering "the possibility of proximate social mobility: students could now forgo the arcane rites of the ancient languages, study practical subjects, and prepare for definite careers."[7] In the decades following World War II, this institutional transformation only accelerated, as an ethos of affluence catalyzed the dramatic nationwide expansion of higher-education institutions dedicated to occupational training.

Some historians have undoubtedly shunned the community college as a subject because of its low status in the higher-education hierarchy. Even those who have sought to investigate it, however, have been challenged by a lack of historical archives. Community colleges' limited financial resources have typically prevented their cataloging and preserving institutional documents, making researching and writing a comprehensive history of the American community college especially difficult. Given the significant number of community colleges established during the 1960s, however, many have recently begun to uncover their histories in anticipation of founding anniversaries, especially fifty-year celebrations. Accordingly, some colleges have begun gathering historical data, conducting oral histories, assembling archives, and producing documentary films.

This chapter takes advantage of just this development at the Community College of Rhode Island (which celebrated its golden anniversary in 2014) and Santa Fe Community College (which marked a thirtieth anniversary in 2013). Beginning by examining the history of the junior college through World War II, it investigates conflicts over the institution's primary educational purpose before briefly tracing postwar changes, including the dramatic growth in the number of junior colleges nationally and their eventual conversion to community colleges. Finally, it uses the cases of Rhode Island and Santa Fe to illustrate how a rising ethos of affluence guided the transformation of community colleges in ways that paralleled (while not replicating) changes at four-year institutions in the decades leading to the twenty-first century.

The primary motivating force behind establishing junior colleges in the United States arose from the expansion of mass public secondary schooling. Between 1890 and 1940, US public high-school enrollments almost doubled every ten years, from 203,000 to 4,399,000 students.[8] In just the decade following World War I, the proportion of American children of high-school age in school increased from 20 to 50 percent.[9] In addition to rapidly rising attendance, the period witnessed steadily increasing high-school graduation rates. In 1900, approximately six high-school students graduated for every one hundred seventeen-year-olds in the United States. By 1920, that number had almost tripled, to seventeen; then it continued its ascent to twenty-nine in 1930, fifty-one in 1940, and fifty-nine in 1950.[10] Many of these graduates pursued some form of postsecondary learning, leading higher-education enrollments to rise from over 237,000 students in 1900 to almost 2.5 million by 1950.[11] Such an increase put pressure on colleges and universities across the nation to enlarge the size of their student bodies. Simultaneously, the emergence of the research university, with its commitment to scholarship and graduate education, led some university administrators to seek to move the first two years of undergraduate education down to the high schools.[12] Reformers consequently designed junior colleges to both expand access to higher learning and free universities of the responsibility of educating "lower division" freshmen and sophomores. This resulted in a uniquely American type of higher-education institution devised to serve students who, rather than graduating upon completing their coursework, would transfer to a four-year college or university.[13]

Beginning in 1901 with Illinois's founding of Joliet Junior College (the result of a collaboration between University of Chicago president William Rainey Harper and Joliet High School principal J. Stanley Brown), public junior colleges expanded rapidly.[14] Typically housed in existing secondary-school buildings, 85 junior colleges nationwide served approximately 4,500 students in 1918, or almost 2 percent of US undergraduates. During the interwar years, the pace of expansion accelerated swiftly—so much so that no segment of higher education grew more rapidly than the junior college. Throughout the 1920s, as the total number of higher-education institutions in the United States rose from 670 to 1,076, junior colleges accounted for almost half the increase, with the greatest growth occurring in California.[15] By the late 1920s, this single state enrolled nearly fourteen thousand junior-college students. Although some of these colleges were private, a large majority were publicly established and locally funded, typically as part of public school districts.[16]

Concurrently, many normal schools and agricultural colleges began developing into state colleges, providing preparation for occupations such as teaching, journalism, social work, agricultural science, and midlevel government service.[17] With elevated standards of admission and rising tuition costs accompanying this transformation, institutions that had previously been both accessible and affordable to students from low socioeconomic backgrounds became increasingly restrictive. The junior college thereby assumed responsibility for providing access to higher learning for these students, leading it to become known popularly as the "people's college."[18]

Although businesses and chambers of commerce frequently supported junior colleges for the economic benefits they brought to local communities, employment training initially made up only a very small part of the curricular offerings. Even in states such as California, where junior-college advocates typically favored occupational coursework, a two-year collegiate curriculum prevailed, with a large majority of students expressing an intention to transfer to four-year institutions.[19] Over time, however, although many students continued to enroll with the aim of completing a bachelor's degree, a slowly increasing number registered for vocational training programs.[20]

Junior colleges offered vocational curricula prior to World War I, but it was not until the 1920s that a broader educational shift toward vocational education in the United States led these courses of study to expand. In 1917, Congress passed the Smith-Hughes Act, directing federal funds to the development of secondary-school vocational programs. One year later, the National Education Association's Commission on the Reorganization of Secondary Education identified vocational education as one of secondary schools' seven "cardinal principles."[21]

Occupational education's proponents claimed that what they characterized as two-year "terminal" programs met the needs of students who, either because they were unable or uninterested, did not pursue bachelor's degrees. The American Association of Junior Colleges (AAJC) signaled the growing strength of this stance in its rapidly changing definition of junior colleges. Established in 1920, the AAJC sought to develop a junior-college identity along with a corresponding set of institutional objectives. Shortly after its founding, the organization defined the junior college as "an institution offering two years of instruction of strictly collegiate grade." In 1925, however, as vocational curricula continued to spread, it revised its definition to include "the larger and ever-changing civic, social, religious, and vocational needs of the entire community."[22]

Yet public high schools already offered basic forms of vocational education (in carpentry and metal work, for instance), posing a problem for junior-college advocates who sought higher institutional status than that held by secondary schools (even if most junior colleges continued to be housed in high-school buildings). Proponents of occupational training therefore identified particular kinds of vocations for which junior colleges would prepare students, labeling them "semiprofessional." As one speaker at the 1928 AAJC annual conference described, junior-college occupational courses would be "above the level of routine and handicraft vocational courses that are given in high school. . . . Junior engineers in architects' and engineers' offices will be examples. The nursing profession is another. People who enter these vocational fields will be the masters of certain definite bodies of technique and will be expected to use intelligence of a rather high order in their work." Further distinguishing between the junior college and four-year institutions, the speaker added that such courses were "definitely below the highly professional specialization that takes place on the university level."[23]

Although the push to provide semiprofessional training in fields that did not require additional higher learning grew throughout the 1920s, that push became a shove when the Carnegie Foundation for the Advancement of Teaching's Commission of Seven endorsed the move toward occupational education in a report on California's junior colleges in 1932. Following higher education's explosive growth throughout the state in the 1920s, and the onset of the Great Depression at the end of the decade, California legislators commissioned the Carnegie Foundation to study the state's burgeoning but haphazard collection of public colleges and universities. The resulting report, authored by preeminent educators from across the nation (who were undoubtedly influenced by the nation's financial crisis) urged efficiency and coordination while providing a rough blueprint for what California would eventually adopt in 1960 as its higher-education "master plan."[24]

The foundation provided substantial support for occupational training proponents by encouraging the state to systematize its higher-education sector through institutional differentiation. The flagship university—the University of California, Berkeley—would be the only institution approved to grant both doctoral and professional degrees, while the rest of the University of California branch campuses would award bachelor's and master's degrees. Accordingly, the teachers colleges (most of which began as normal schools) would grant bachelor's degrees and a single master's degree (in Education). Importantly for the junior colleges, rather than affirming their role in providing the first two years of undergraduate coursework, the report assigned them the task of offering semi-professional programming that would, in the words of University of California President Robert G. Sproul, "suitably train those students and get them in their lifework sooner."[25] As historian David Levine writes, the public junior college became "a terminal institution where most young people of limited means and allegedly limited abilities and aspirations concluded their education by preparing for a semi-professional occupation."[26]

Despite the Carnegie Foundation's recommendations and the expansion of occupational offerings in junior colleges across the United States, two-year terminal degrees remained relatively unpopular with students throughout the beginning of the World War II era.[27] With junior-college enrollments surging during the 1930s (partly because attending provided a low-cost alternative to entering a dramatically shrinking job market), many students continued to declare that their primary interest was obtaining a bachelor's degree.[28] Nevertheless, in the years following the Second World War, the Truman Commission on Higher Education advocated expanding the number of junior colleges in the United States while echoing the Carnegie Commission's recommendation that they emphasize terminal programs.[29] The Truman Commission further borrowed from the Carnegie report when it urged a change in the descriptor "junior college" to "community college," tying its justification directly to the push toward vocational training. Commission members deemed the former too closely linked to the institution's college-preparatory role, while the latter better characterized an institution tied to a community's economic and social needs.[30]

It was also during the postwar era that junior colleges increasingly became targets of criticism. Legislators nationwide showed the same support during the 1950s that Florida's did in establishing both public junior colleges and commuter institutions such as the University of South Florida. They extolled junior colleges for contributing to the common good by providing an accessible and affordable form of higher education. However, as the number of students who used two-year institutions as stepping-stones to bachelor's degrees decreased over time, a

growing number of critics accused junior colleges of limiting, rather than fulfilling, student aspirations. As early as 1960, sociologist Burton Clark made this
claim forcefully when he coined the phrase "cooling out" to describe how community colleges, instead of encouraging students to complete two years of study
before transferring to a four-year institution, actually discouraged them from
doing so.[31]

Clark's study was part of a wider examination of educational institutions
in the United States conducted by scholars who concluded that public schools
and community colleges often failed to provide students, especially "nontraditional" students, with pathways of opportunity for social mobility. Instead, they
claimed, these institutions reproduced social and economic class relations in
America.[32] According to Clark, they used vocational aptitude testing, guidance,
and career counseling to dissuade students from pursuing four-year bachelor's degrees. A series of studies followed Clark's, including K. Patricia Cross's
Beyond the Open Door, L. Steven Zwerling's *Second Best*, and David Nasaw's
Schooled to Order, all of which argued that, rather than supporting aspiring
students' educational goals, community colleges (as well as public education
more broadly) redirected them toward the "lower ranks of the industrial and
commercial hierarchy."[33]

In 1989, Steven Brint and Jerome Karabel published what one scholar has
described as the "most acclaimed and sophisticated work" on the controversy
over the community colleges' educational role. Although the authors credited
community colleges with providing nontraditional students access to higher
education, the title of their work, *The Diverted Dream*, reflected their claim that
these institutions sidetracked students who might otherwise have completed
four-year degrees.[34] "The very real contribution that the community college has
made to the expansion of opportunities for some individuals," they concluded,
"does not . . . mean that its *aggregate* effect has been a democratizing one. On the
contrary, the two-year institution has accentuated rather than reduced existing
patterns of social inequality. Indeed, in both the social origins and the occupational destinations of its students, the community college clearly constitutes the
bottom tier of a class-linked tracking system in higher education" [emphasis in
the original].[35]

In their study, Brint and Karabel described the years between 1970 and 1985
as a time of "great transformation" for community colleges because of the ways
in which most institutions substantially reoriented course offerings around
vocational education. In retrospect, it comes as little surprise that the transformation occurred when it did. Until that period, the collegiate curriculum
remained fundamental at most two-year institutions, although it often existed
in tension with a growing vocational emphasis. Beginning in 1970, however,

the nation's retrenchment led colleges and universities across the nation, especially public institutions, scrambling for financial resources. With government-funded employee-training programs providing alternate sources of revenue and students aggressively seeking job security following the onset of the recession in 1973, most community colleges eagerly adopted occupational training as a core institutional function. As John Grede, former Chicago City Colleges vice chancellor for occupational education, observed regarding the decade from 1970 to 1980, "The occupational people have always been criticized by the old-line liberal-arts transfer element for always responding to money, and I think it was true. The advent of getting some additional funding from the outside, both federal and state, was quite attractive."[36] Indeed, as government increased support for employee training and investments in what became known as "career education," businesses began investing in community colleges because they reaped benefits from the institutions' publicly subsidized, low-cost job-training programs. Students responded by enrolling in programs they believed would provide a secure route to well-paying employment in fields such as accounting, hotel management, medical technology, secretarial work, and computer programming.[37] As a result, students at community colleges "cooled out" in ever-greater numbers throughout the remainder of the twentieth century.

As with most public higher-education institutions in the final decades of the twentieth century, declining state appropriations drove community colleges to become increasingly entrepreneurial. In the 1980s, as US deindustrialization compelled states to adopt new economic policies emphasizing investments in human capital and high-tech business development, many community colleges seized the opportunity to adapt their institutional missions to become economic-development partners.[38] As described by John G. Melville, senior policy analyst at SRI's Center for Economic Competitiveness, and Thomas J. Chmura, deputy director of the Greater Baltimore Committee (a business development and advocacy organization), community colleges during the 1980s "turned out to be excellent sources of management and technical assistance for new small businesses. Also, they were well positioned to provide basic technology transfer services to existing businesses. And, they could provide information and insights useful in the development of business attraction strategies."[39] In Oregon, for instance, state and federal funding permitted the expansion of a successful pilot project at Lane Community College in Eugene that resulted in two-year colleges serving as small-business development centers. The colleges created programs to support "clients" in developing marketing plans and advertising strategies, while also organizing conferences on topics such as how to successfully compete for federal and state business development grants.[40]

Alternatively, Illinois state officials established the Illinois Economic Development Grant Program to provide both incentives and rewards for community-college entrepreneurialism. To qualify for grants ranging from less than $50,000 to over $350,000, community colleges established offices of economic development, which provided customized employment training for businesses, assistance in developing industrial recruitment strategies, and an array of other services.[41]

Many community colleges during this period also capitalized on state incentives to become technology-transfer agents. In contrast with research universities' previous adoption of technology transfer, in which the institution supported both the research and the commercialization of research results, the community college—as an agent—assisted in introducing technology to the marketplace.[42] In Ohio, for example, the state-level Technology Transfer Organization provided the financial resources necessary for community colleges in Lorain and Cuyahoga Counties to assist local manufacturers in becoming familiar with new technologies in robotics, microelectronics, and computer-aided design.[43] At breakfast meetings, luncheons, and seminars, college instructors educated potential customers about new processes and products before demonstrating new equipment and software. In return, the colleges received state economic development aid as well as the fringe benefit of equipment donations for its "indirect marketing" of the technologies to local businesses.[44]

Throughout the final decades of the twentieth century, community colleges also became a primary source of contracted employment training for major industries, local businesses, and state agencies. During the 1970s and '80s, state governments adopted subsidized job-training programs as a strategy for both reducing unemployment and inducing corporations to relocate to their states. Florida's Sunshine State Skills Corporation, Iowa's Industrial New Jobs Training Program, Maryland's Partnership Through Workforce Quality, and Massachusetts's Bay State Skills Corporation all facilitated industries' contracting of community colleges to provide employment training.[45] By 1990, these programs had become so popular that almost every US state operated one.[46] Frequently, however, the job-training contracts into which community colleges entered did not provide courses for regularly enrolled students. Rather, the colleges contracted with specific corporations and businesses, many of them high-tech industries, to provide specialized training programs "custom tailored to meet the needs of specific firms" and thus distinct from the courses available to tuition-paying students.[47] Characterized as "public-private partnerships," contracted employment-training programs provided such a significant source of revenue for community colleges that more than three-quarters of the nation's two-year colleges reported offering such training by 1990.[48]

The transformation of many community colleges into engines of local economic development exemplified these entrepreneurial activities. In the process, the institutions received significant state, federal, and corporate funding, permitting them to expand programming, facilities, and staff. Nevertheless, their pursuit of wealth has come at a cost. As John S. Levin, director and principal investigator of the California Community College Collaborative, describes, "In the decade of the 1990s, community colleges became more overtly connected to the marketplace and to the ideologies of the neo-liberal state. That is, community-college behaviors resembled those of private business and industry, pursuing competitive grants, relying more and more on the private sector for its revenues, privatizing services and education, securing contracts with both the private and public sectors, and simply 'economizing': letting financial rationales take precedence over others."[49]

Decades earlier, however, as junior colleges underwent the "great transformation" that Brint and Karabel described, the term "community college" had just begun to enter popular use, a majority of students had for the first time enrolled in vocational programs, and the institution had, along with the rest of American higher education, experienced a "golden age."[50] Indeed, the period between the end of World War II and the early 1970s might be more accurately characterized as a "platinum era" for community colleges, as enrollments soared from approximately 156,000 students to over 2.3 million.[51] In some states, including California, the expansion of an already-vibrant community-college system characterized this growth. In others, such as Rhode Island, the period witnessed the creation of entire community-college systems where none had previously existed.[52]

Members of the Rhode Island General Assembly legislated the founding of a statewide system of community colleges in 1960.[53] Four years later, the Board of Trustees of State Colleges appointed William F. Flanagan president of Rhode Island Junior College (RIJC).[54] Flanagan, who had served as director of graduate studies at Rhode Island College, began to plan for the institution's opening just six months later in the former Brown and Sharpe factory building on Promenade Street in the state capital of Providence. Having received funding to enroll two hundred students, Flanagan requested a special appropriation from Governor John Chafee to increase the number to 325 after the college received more than eight hundred applications. Although Chafee, a strong supporter of the college, granted the additional funds, RIJC still turned away hundreds of students due to a lack of capacity.[55]

In his first presidential report, Flanagan described the multiple objectives he believed the new college should seek to accomplish. "In no sense of the word do we wish to become merely the first two years of a state institution of higher learning comparable to the first two years at our sister institutions," he wrote. "We do not wish to become a vocational institution isolated from the broad academic disciplines that are now almost a requisite for an educated citizenry in the American society of the late twentieth century."[56] Instead, he claimed, the college would provide a collegiate-level transfer program as well as terminal programs including "both the cultural and vocational aspects of collegiate life." Through the vocational programs, specifically, Flanagan hoped, "to have an opportunity for training in those technical disciplines that will provide our students with a saleable skill which may in turn be transferred by them into instruments of their own economic self-sufficiency as well as contribute to the economy of our state."[57]

Throughout his tenure, Flanagan consistently emphasized the important role he believed RIJC played in providing the career training necessary for students to achieve economically prosperous futures. "The transition from secondary school to college is fraught with new freedoms and new responsibilities," he advised students. "Here is the golden door to a number of career choices that can affect your whole life."[58] Yet Flanagan also reflected a civic-minded ethos when he characterized the "broad academic disciplines" that made up the liberal arts as "almost a requisite for an educated citizenry" and claimed that the college should not favor a strictly vocational program of study. Similarly, while urging students to make wise career choices, Flanagan enjoined them to contribute to the public good: "Use your time well. Seek counsel before you act. Work before you seek pleasure. Study before you play. But do not hesitate to give of yourself and sacrifice some of your self interests for the common good of your school and the greater community of which we are all members."[59]

RIJC's course of study reflected the multiple objectives Flanagan held for the institution. It began with an associate in arts (AA) degree based primarily in a liberal arts curriculum, including courses in English, mathematics, the sciences, foreign language, fine arts, and social studies. After successfully completing AA degree requirements, students could conclude their college careers or apply for transfer to a four-year institution. The college also offered an associate in science (AS) degree that, unlike the single curriculum comprising the AA, provided students with a range of options. They could obtain a general AS degree by fulfilling requirements in English, biology, chemistry, physics, mathematics, and foreign language (and then, as with AA recipients, conclude their college careers or apply for transfer). Alternatively, students pursuing an AS could meet the requirements of the "engineering transfer curriculum" with the intent of transferring to a four-year university engineering program. They could also concentrate in one of a number of career-related studies to prepare for semiprofessional work in the fields of business administration (including accounting and management), chemical technology, electronic technology, mechanical technology, or nursing.[60] Advertising these offerings, the college informed students interested in chemical technology, "Chemical laboratory assistants are always in demand. Industries depend upon their own or upon consulting laboratories for information about raw materials, tests on new materials and the maintenance of quality. Almost two-thirds of this testing can be done by men and women with the kind of training offered in the two-year terminal program in Chemical Technology at Rhode Island Junior College."[61]

Of all these options, the liberal-arts curriculum initially enrolled the greatest number of students (approximately 60 percent) and business administration the second largest (almost 25 percent).[62] Over the next few years, however, as the college established a vocational-technical program in response to federal- and state-level calls for increased employee training, the proportion of students enrolling in both liberal arts and business declined while "vo-tech" enrollments increased. Beginning with 105 students, RIJC's vocational-technical program included courses in data processing, industrial chemistry, machine processes, mechanical design, industrial electronics, and instrumentation. The college developed its program in consultation with an advisory committee comprising members of local businesses and industry so that course curricula would, according to Flanagan, "prepare students to qualify for positions in a cluster of present and reasonable predictable future employment opportunities."[63] By 1970, almost six hundred students were enrolled in what had become an expanded Vocational-Technical Division.[64] Incorporating a cooperative work experience program, the division also provided students with short-term job placements in companies ranging from General Electric to Sears, Roebuck, Stop & Shop to Citizens Savings Bank.[65]

Although administrators did not record students' racial and ethnic composition during the college's early years, yearbook pictures of the first graduating class in 1966 suggest that a large majority of the students were white, with men outnumbering women two to one.[66] These students, who were nontraditional in that they mostly likely would not have pursued higher education had RIJC not provided a local, accessible, and affordable option, came to college primarily from the surrounding region. All commuters, they nevertheless created a vibrant student life on campus, establishing a variety of clubs and activities, including a band, glee club, and international relations club as well as a student government, junior chamber of commerce, and dramatic group called the Gamma Tau Players. Students also published a newspaper and literary magazine, while the college fielded basketball, baseball, golf, and outdoor track teams and a cheering squad, and hosted a ROTC program.[67]

Just one year following RIJC's first commencement, and in desperate need of space to meet the demands of increasing enrollments, state and college officials

broke ground for a permanent facility. Having received an eighty-acre donation from Royal Webster Knight (a descendant of a prominent Rhode Island
family), they built the campus in the city of Warwick, twelve miles south of
downtown Providence. Controversy erupted over the master site plan, however. Some people urged construction of a traditional New England–style
campus with ivy-covered brick buildings. Others wanted to accommodate
all of the college's programs, classrooms, laboratories, and offices in a single
380,000-square-foot "megastructure" designed in the brutalist architectural
style and made entirely of poured concrete.[68] Although proponents of the latter won out—the choice remained controversial decades later—RIJC became
the fastest-growing college in the state even prior to the building's completion
in September 1972. With enrollments increasing more than tenfold and the
number of full- and part-time faculty paralleling the rise, state and college
officials began planning a second RIJC campus in the city of Lincoln, seventeen
miles north of Warwick.[69]

When William Flanagan retired two years after the Lincoln campus's opening in 1976, the trustees hired an administrator who had substantial previous
experience leading two-year institutions. Edward J. Liston had been the founding president of Connecticut's Housatonic Community College and also led
Pierce College, a two-year institution in Woodland Hills, California. Liston later
acknowledged the influence that working in a California community college
had on his leadership of RIJC. Describing the junior college throughout history as "primarily a liberal arts college, designed for the transfer to four-year
colleges," Liston observed that California had led the nation in establishing
community colleges with a "three-fold mission," including providing prebac-
calaureate education for students seeking to transfer, "professional and technical
education" for those seeking to enter the workforce, and community services in
the form of noncredit courses and "the sponsorship of forums and other community events."[70]

Upon assuming the presidency, Liston decided that RIJC needed to take "a
great leap forward" in developing the latter two parts of the community-college
mission. He extended the college's presence throughout the state by establishing
satellite centers and instituting televised courses through the public broadcasting
system.[71] He was reportedly also concerned about the college's reputation among
state residents. Learning that some people had taken to calling it "REJECT" after
its abbreviation "RIJC," Liston proposed renaming the institution the Community College of Rhode Island (CCRI), a change the state's General Assembly enacted in 1980.[72] Moreover, in a combined effort to increase the college's
institutional status as well as raise revenue, Liston directed his attention toward
developing ties to business and industry.

With the US economy in recession and inflation on the rise, public funding for higher education in Rhode Island had been declining for several years. Consequently, just months following Liston's inauguration, faculty struck over a salary dispute.[73] Lasting only nine days, the strike nevertheless highlighted the increasing fiscal challenges confronting the institution. A year later, Liston announced that he would request a $360,000 supplemental appropriation from the state legislature just to cover the college's energy and telephone bills.[74] Seeking to remedy the damage caused by rising deficits and hoping to elevate CCRI's reputation, Liston increasingly promoted its capacity to meet the needs of business and industry through lucrative training contracts.

In June 1982, the college announced a partnership with the local chapter of the National Tooling and Machine Association to provide classroom instruction necessary for apprentices to earn a journeyman's certificate through which students could simultaneously earn CCRI credit.[75] "We are quite excited about this new relationship with industry," Liston announced regarding the program, "a partnership that benefits both the college and the machine tool industry."[76] Later that December, he formed a Business and Industry Advisory Council made up of representatives of Rhode Island companies and CCRI faculty and administrators. Among other tasks, Liston requested that council members "identify areas of mutual interest between the college and the community; determine educational needs of Rhode Island industry and make college services better known to industry . . . develop employment and advisory support from business; and strengthen the link between the classroom and the 'world of work.'"[77]

Simultaneously, CCRI established an Office of Off-Campus Courses for Business and Industry to better advertise its customized employee training programs.[78] Later renamed the Center for Business and Industrial Training, the office became central to the college's decades-long efforts to obtain private contracts.[79] In 1983, for instance, CCRI contracted with General Dynamics Electric Boat (the company's submarine-building division) to provide training to apprentice production welders, shipfitters, pipefitters, marine-assembly machinists, and sheet-metal mechanics. As with the college's partnership with the National Tooling and Machine Association, apprentices received college credit for classroom instruction, which occurred at the company's facilities in Quonset Point.[80] Similarly, CCRI partnered with the University of Rhode Island (URI) to provide a customized engineering development program for the Raytheon Corporation's Submarine Signal Division in Portsmouth. Under this contract, CCRI faculty taught the courses comprising the first two years of a bachelor of science degree in engineering to qualifying employees at the Raytheon plant (with URI instructors teaching the second two).[81]

By the end of the 1980s, the Center for Business and Industrial Training provided programming for almost twenty companies and organizations annually, involving over 1,300 employees. These contracts provided a crucial revenue stream for the college that was relatively unaffected by the erosion of state appropriations.[82] Yet this growth represented only the beginning of CCRI's involvement with private enterprise, which it actively expanded throughout the 1990s. "Because of the changing nature of work," Liston later recalled of the expansion, "the task of educating and re-educating the workforce is now recognized as a never-ending one. Much of this is caused by the rapid developments in the use of new technology as well as the general explosion of knowledge made possible by technology that continually changes the way work is being done." He further explained, "Recognizing this, CCRI in 1996 began to focus on workforce development as a vital, integral factor in the future planning of the college. . . . The goal was to position the college to be the premier deliverer of workforce training in the state" (figure 10).[83]

Liston observed that federal and state grants provided an important source of funding for the college throughout the 1980s, allowing it to "significantly expand" programs and services.[84] In 1982, he announced the receipt of a three-year, $600,000 federal grant to develop a computer literacy program designed to offer "'state of the art' technical education in order to provide students with the skills they will need in today's increasingly technological society."[85] A year later, CCRI received another high-tech grant, this one from the state: $480,000 to increase student access to computers and computer training. Liston announced, "Governor [J. Joseph] Garrahy has given the college an opportunity to better serve the needs of our students and the state of Rhode Island through the high tech initiative. As businesses and industries embrace high technology, there will be a need for persons who design, operate and repair sophisticated equipment. CCRI can assist in securing a brighter economic future for the state by providing students with the skills needed to move Rhode Island industry into the future."[86]

While administrators prioritized obtaining private contracts and government grants to finance the college's work, they simultaneously and increasingly expressed a commitment to expanding higher-education access to low-income and first-generation students of color. In March 1980, Liston hired John White, a former minority affairs assistant in the US Navy and employee of the Rhode Island Office of Equal Opportunity, to enhance the college's affirmative-action policies and recruit an increasing number of minority faculty, staff, and students.[87] CCRI also established the Minority Mentor Program within its Office of Affirmative Action and Minority Student Affairs to provide students with mentors to assist them in completing such unfamiliar tasks as submitting financial-aid forms and selecting courses.[88] As a result of these recruitment, support, and retention efforts, minority student enrollment slowly increased over time.[89]

CCRI
Serving
the
Rhode
Island
business
community

Customized training programs
Business/industry partnerships
Workforce development initiatives
Cooperative education opportunities
Entrepreneurial skills training

Community College of Rhode Island

FIGURE 10. Community College of Rhode Island promotional literature, 1996. In the author's collection.

Yet the college's most tangible expression of its commitment to the state's low-income and minority residents arguably occurred in 1990, when CCRI opened a campus in downtown Providence.

Although founded in the state's capital city, CCRI nevertheless lost much of its connection to Providence after it moved south to Warwick. Rhode Island College, however, a public four-year institution located in the city's Mount Pleasant section, had established a downtown Urban Education Center in 1968 to serve the needs of low-income and unemployed residents caught in the wake of the nation's spiraling urban crisis. Offering high-school equivalency preparation and testing, educational and employment guidance and counseling, and college-level courses, the center served a significant number of adult students of color.[90] Beginning in the early 1980s, a state-mandated reorganization of public higher-education institutions led to CCRI's joining Rhode Island College in administering the center. Several years later, CCRI assumed full responsibility.[91] When, in 1989, state officials granted CCRI approval to acquire a facility in South Providence that could meet the needs of a new campus, the college seized the opportunity.[92] Housing the Urban Education Center as well as the Rhode Island Educational Opportunity Center (a federally funded program designed to recruit and assist "low-income and minority persons to enter postsecondary education relevant to their career goals"), the Providence campus also offered a full range of two-year courses of study.[93] "Most community colleges are located in urban areas because they can offer educational opportunities for individuals who have neither the time nor the money to travel any distance to classes," Liston explained at a news conference at which he announced the campus' founding. "Our presence in Providence is essential if we are to fulfill our mission of offering access to all Rhode Island residents."[94]

One year following the Providence campus's opening, CCRI's enrollment exceeded sixteen thousand for the first time. The student body comprised 63 percent women and 12 percent students self-reported as members of ethnic minority groups. Almost twice as many enrolled in courses of study labeled "business and commerce technologies" as they did liberal-arts programs.[95] In the same year, the college received nearly $3 million in grants—a record high.[96] But even with the financial benefits that grants and private contracts generated, CCRI continued to suffer from declining state appropriations. As a percentage of total revenue, the college's state contribution decreased from 81 percent in 1976 to 65 percent in 1990.[97] In response, CCRI began raising the cost of tuition, a move that secured some degree of financial stability but one that also ultimately made the college less affordable to the very students it sought to serve.[98]

While Liston grappled with the challenge of expanding higher-education access in Rhode Island during an era of retrenchment, educators and local

officials more than two thousand miles away, in Santa Fe, New Mexico, were similarly seeking to expand higher-education opportunities in their city. Although
the New Mexico Legislature had passed a Junior College Act almost twenty years
earlier (just months prior to CCRI enrolling its first students), the state capital
had yet to establish a two-year college.[99] Santa Fe was New Mexico's second-
largest city after Albuquerque, however, and the 1980 census indicated it was
growing, with the city's population increasing almost 20 percent between 1970
and 1980 and the number of Santa Fe County residents by twice that much.[100]
Consequently, in 1982 the Santa Fe School Board conducted a needs assessment,
which revealed that relatively few regional postsecondary educational opportunities existed for low-income residents, most of whom worked during the day
to support themselves and, often, their families. Given the limited educational
opportunities at working students' disposal, the board concluded, "It would be
difficult, if not impossible," for them "to pursue a substantial training program in
the evening."[101] Identifying an especially urgent need for low-cost occupational
training, the board, with State Board of Educational Finance approval, proposed
establishing a new public community college.[102]

By the time Santa Fe founded its community college, many two-year institutions elsewhere, including CCRI, had already adopted occupational training as
central to their work. Santa Fe Community College (SFCC) supporters publicized
the benefits businesses would reap from having the institution located in their city.
The city school board reported, "Businesses are not satisfied with vocational and
technical training in Santa Fe. In their view, adequate courses are not available and
there is concern for the quality of existing programs."[103] School Superintendent
James P. Miller lobbied residents to approve a tax in support of the institution
by claiming the college would provide prospective students with "the training
they need for jobs, for promotions, for new careers." He continued, "Business and
industry which might be interested in Santa Fe always ask 'can we get trained people?.' A community college is itself a clean, smokeless, high-level 'industry' which
will employ many people in Santa Fe. The local required tax support for a community college is an investment in the prosperity of our community."[104]

Arguments such as Miller's convinced Santa Fe residents to vote overwhelmingly in support of establishing the college, and on March 17, 1983, Governor
Toney Anaya appropriated $400,000 in startup funds.[105] The following month,
the state legislature approved a bill establishing the Santa Fe Junior College District, appropriating $1.1 million in projected first-year operating costs.[106] On
September 12, 1983, SFCC opened to students in leased facilities across the city,
including a local industrial park (figure 11).

At the time New Mexico established SFCC, Hispanic residents were just under
two-thirds of Santa Fe's population, while one-third was white (non-Hispanic).

The remaining residents were Native American, African American, and Asian American.[107] Many of the city's residents were low-income and had either not graduated from high school or not pursued postsecondary education.[108] Based on these demographic factors, as well as the experiences of other community colleges in the state, SFCC officials correctly anticipated that residents would take advantage of the educational opportunities the college offered provided that admissions standards were low and tuition affordable. They also predicted that inexpensive two-year postsecondary education would attract a minority of middle-class students who would take advantage of SFCC's low cost and begin their studies there before transferring to one of the state's universities.[109] Acting on these projections, SFCC declared itself an "open enrollment, local District, locally controlled community college which will admit students who demonstrate a desire to learn, have an ability to profit from its educational programs, and who exhibit appropriate standards of conduct."

Accordingly, the college described its extremely flexible admissions criteria as "high school diploma or General Education Development (GED) Certificate; college transfer; provisional enrollment for adult students who are non–high school graduates or non-GED holders; concurrent enrollment for qualified high school second semester juniors and seniors; and early enrollment for outstanding high school seniors."[110] That is to say, almost any resident, including students currently enrolled in high school, could attend SFCC. The college then set its costs for tuition and fees comparatively low: $13 per credit hour to a maximum of $156 per semester.[111] Tuition for out-of-district residents was set at $16 per credit hour to a maximum of $192 per semester, while out-of-state residents paid $40 per credit hour to a maximum of $480 per semester.[112] Finally, SFCC issued an equal educational opportunity policy stating that the institution was committed to providing higher learning to students regardless of their sex, marital status, color, race, religion, age, national origin, or physical handicap in all areas of college life, including "admission, recruitment, extracurricular programs and activities, access to course offerings, counseling and testing, and financial assistance."[113]

SFCC pronounced in its first catalogue that its "guiding principle" was to remove for students "the geographic, economic, and cultural barriers" to participating in educational programs. Here, it emphasized, "All citizens shall be encouraged to continue their education."[114] Accordingly, the college scheduled many course offerings for the convenience of working adults, granting access to students who were historically labeled "nontraditional" but who, by the time of SFCC's establishment, had become a major segment of America's higher-education student population. Doing so attracted over 7,800 students to the institution in its first year (1,054 of them to credit-bearing courses).[115] Women who had begun but never completed a higher education constituted a large majority of the

FIGURE 11. Santa Fe Community College promotional poster, c. 1983. In the author's collection.

enrollees; many other students, both men and women, had never been to college. Most students were Hispanic. Their average age was twenty-nine, and almost all registered part-time, taking afternoon and evening courses that permitted them to work (often full-time) while remaining enrolled.[116]

Seeking to provide "occupational education and training at a semi-professional level" leading to "employment in business, industry, and government," the college unabashedly advertised the private advantage it claimed students would reap from enrolling.[117] Rather than emphasizing a two-year collegiate course of study with the aim of student transfer to a four-year institution, SFCC affirmed many students' occupational interests and desire to obtain jobs in relatively well-paying fields of employment. This personal-advancement-through-occupational-success mission imbued the college, from the slogan on its first advertising poster—"Where Success Begins"—to the library's prioritizing the acquisition of an "occupational collection," to the first section of the student handbook, which encouraged students to visit the college's Career Development Center so as to assess their "interests, skills and abilities in order to set appropriate career goals."[118]

The college's first president, William C. Witter, organized SFCC into five divisions. "Administrative" held responsibility for the college's management and governance. "Community Relations" handled marketing and advertising, oversaw college publications, and served as liaison to local and state governments. "Student Services" directed admissions, registration, and financial aid; provided guidance, counseling, and career advice; and administered special services for disabled students. "Instruction" offered the courses for associate's degrees and occupational training. "Community Services" provided students with non-credit-bearing courses, workshops, and other activities that were designed, according to college officials, "to help participants become more proficient in their chosen occupations and professions" and "enrich their personal and family lives, enjoy their leisure time and gain a deeper appreciation of their culture and environment."[119] College officials further subdivided the Instruction division (which they anticipated would fulfill the institution's primary educational aims) into Business and Occupations, Arts and Sciences, and Developmental Studies. Of the three, Business and Occupations employed the largest number of faculty and staff, offered the greatest number of courses per year, and enrolled the highest number of students.[120]

Within two years of opening, SFCC had developed a substantial list of approved degrees and certificates. The associate in arts degrees in business, liberal arts, and Southwest studies, as well as associate in science degrees in computer science and pre-engineering, enrolled students who intended to transfer to four-year institutions. By contrast, the associate in applied science degree in occupational and/or technical education prepared students "to enter a career upon completing the degree with no further study required."[121] Many of the fields in which students pursued an applied science degree reflected the program's semi-professional orientation, including criminal justice, drafting technology, hotel/motel restaurant management, paralegal studies, and real estate. The college also offered non-credit-bearing certificates in many of these fields for students who did not complete the entire course of study.[122]

As at the Community College of Rhode Island, SFCC student enrollments began to exceed projections soon after the college's establishment, leading administrators to announce a fundraising effort to construct permanent facilities. Local developers responded by offering 166 acres of land on which to build a campus, eight miles south of downtown Santa Fe. The location was not ideal. Without public transportation to the site, college officials anticipated some students confronting logistical challenges in attending class. Still, SFCC accepted the million-dollar donation and voters approved a $5 million dollar bond issue to finance construction.[123] A special session of the state legislature consequently approved an additional $5 million capital outlay request which, when combined with the voter-approved bond, gave college officials $10 million for the construction of a campus.[124]

Even prior to securing property and funding for a permanent facility, William Witter turned his attention toward generating increased revenue for the college, announcing that "economic trends" and "industry and community needs" would be central to institutional planning and program development. Again as at CCRI, college officials responded to the growing use of microcomputers during the 1980s by creating courses in computer science, computer and communications technology, "computers in small businesses," and computer repair and maintenance. In later years, SFCC expanded its offerings to include technologies such as solar photovoltaics and fiber optics. Moreover, as early as his first annual report, Witter described the college as "actively working to identify and develop programs to meet the training and retraining needs of established business, industry and government agencies as well as those which may choose to relocate or expand in the area."[125] For instance, SFCC contracted with the New Mexico Department of Corrections, which had initiated a prisoner rehabilitation program to provide instruction to inmates at prisons in Santa Fe, Los Lunas, Grants, and Las Cruces. By 1988, the Corrections Education Program employed a director and fifteen instructors and enrolled almost two thousand inmates. Students could choose from thirteen instructional programs (most modeled on courses the college offered through its Division of Business and Occupations) and had the opportunity to acquire an occupational training certificate or associate's degree.[126]

SFCC also undertook the development of a federally funded initiative to serve disabled residents. The Handicapped Outreach and Support program provided "appropriately modified specialized vocational technical programs to handi-capped adults with full access to all support services of SFCC in coordination with agencies and organizations serving handicapped individuals."[127] As imple-mented, the program offered participants occupational instruction as well as career guidance and support services so that they might become more indepen-dent and self-supporting. Four hundred and twenty-six students participated in the program in its first year, including seventeen the college labeled as mentally retarded, nineteen hard of hearing, six deaf, three speech-impaired, nine visually handicapped, 237 seriously emotionally disturbed, nineteen crippled (orthope-dically impaired), sixty-four other health impaired, four multihandicapped, and forty-eight with specific learning disabilities.[128]

The Handicapped Outreach and Support and Corrections Education pro-grams were significant both because they served student populations frequently marginalized in US higher education and because they supplemented declining state appropriations. When New Mexico first established SFCC, the state provided a million-dollar appropriation to the college and local government an additional half-million dollars; tuition and fees amounted to just over $175,000.[129] By the turn of the twenty-first century, SFCC's annual state appropriation, although increased to over $7 million to sustain the college's consistently expanding enrollments, facilities, and programs, decreased from 60 percent of the institu-tion's total revenue to just over 25 percent. Local support also declined, although less dramatically, from 30 to 22 percent.[130]

By the beginning of the twenty-first century, contracts and grants provided a full quarter of SFCC's operating budget.[131] To capitalize on this growth, in 2005 the college established the Training Center Corporation, an organization that undertakes many of the functions of a major university research park, albeit on a smaller scale. This permits the college to "form partnerships with businesses and create cooperative technological ventures to foster local economic development and jobs," to "acquire, hold and dispose of intellectual property and technologi-cal innovations," and to "cooperatively market educational programs with busi-nesses and other organizations."[132] In these ways, the center generates revenue by serving as a technology-transfer agent, a marketing firm, and a small-business development office, particularly through the center's Entrepreneurship Training Program.

Engaging in a wide range of revenue-generating projects and programs, com-munity colleges have most recently sought to increase status by either closely affiliating with four-year institutions or obtaining the authority to confer four-year degrees. When SFCC was established, no public four-year postsecondary institution existed in Santa Fe to which students could transfer, requiring those who wanted to continue their educations to relocate to Albuquerque, Las Cruces, or Las Vegas (New Mexico). In 2009, however, SFCC collaborated with the Institute of American Indian Arts, New Mexico Highlands University, and the University of New Mexico—all four-year degree-granting institutions—to receive state approval to establish a Higher Education Center (HEC). The HEC provides students the opportunity to complete their first two years of undergraduate study on the SFCC campus and begin their third year of coursework without having to relocate. Students whose applications are accepted enroll in one of the consortium's member institutions. They then attend classes at SFCC and/or take classes online. Since the HEC opened in 2011, New Mexico State University has joined the consortium and Santa Fe residents have approved a multimillion-dollar bond measure to construct a new HEC facility closer to downtown.[133]

In announcing the center's establishment, SFCC emphasized the convenience it afforded students who planned on obtaining bachelor's degrees. "Your path to a better future just got EASIER!" declared one advertisement.[134] Indeed, one of the center's primary goals is to permit students to "seamlessly" transfer SFCC credits to their new institution, reducing the possibility of wasting time, energy, and financial resources by taking courses that will not count toward a four-year degree.[135] SFCC's consortium-oriented strategy for increasing access to four-year degree opportunities is relatively uncommon. Instead, many community colleges throughout the United States have begun to seek, and some have been granted, institutional authority to award four-year diplomas.

In 2015, community colleges in twenty-two states awarded bachelor's degrees, and the State of California launched a pilot program permitting fifteen community colleges to offer the degree in such applied fields as biomanufacturing, respiratory care, industrial automation, and mortuary science.[136] These approvals have been extremely controversial because they undermine long-held assumptions regarding community colleges' educational role in American society as well as challenge the existing institutional status hierarchy in higher education.[137] Going forward, however, the number of traditional two-year institutions conferring the bachelor's degree will likely grow, if for no other reason than to meet consumer demand by providing occupationally oriented four-year degree programs at a lower cost than many public, four-year colleges and universities.[138]

Conclusion to Part IV

As in the past, large majorities of community-college students continue to identify their primary educational objective as obtaining four-year diplomas. Yet, even with an increasing number of community colleges awarding bachelor's degrees, few students actually achieve this goal. A US Department of Education survey conducted in 2009 reported that over 80 percent of all first-time community-college students expressed an interest in pursuing a bachelor's degree. This desire, according to Stephen J. Handle, former executive director of the College Board's National Office of Community College Initiatives, was especially strong among Latinos (85 percent), African Americans (83 percent), and students in the lowest income quartile (84 percent).[139] According to a 2012 study, however, only 15 percent of students who started at two-year institutions in 2006 completed a degree at a four-year college or university within six years.[140] Although a range of factors, especially increasing tuition costs, have contributed to this outcome, such a gross disparity between the number of community-college students who declared their intentions to complete bachelor's degrees and those who followed through suggests that the phenomenon Burton Clark termed "cooling out" continues to divert students from fulfilling their aspirations.

Federal officials, including President Barack Obama, have recently expressed increased support for two-year colleges, given the role these institutions play in contributing to the nation's economic prosperity. Announcing a proposal that would pay community-college tuition for millions of qualifying students, Obama declared in January 2015, "It's something that we can accomplish, and it's something that will train our work force so that we can compete with anybody in the world."[141] The president's concern for community colleges is certainly well placed. While the nation's top twenty-five universities and top twenty-five liberal arts colleges receive frequent attention from the media and government officials, these institutions collectively educate fewer than 350,000 students each year. By contrast, over twelve million students were enrolled in community colleges in 2015.[142]

Obama's proposal would most certainly enable a greater number of community-college students to complete two-year collegiate programs, permitting them to transfer to four-year institutions. Nevertheless, his administration's emphasis on occupational training at the community-college level parallels a decades-long expansion of occupational offerings at four-year institutions, such as the University of South Florida. Just as USF's early survey of prospective students revealed that most intended to pursue higher education in order to "prepare for work," many Community College of Rhode Island and Santa Fe Community College students have also sought pre-employment training. Accordingly, just as USF prepared graduates for jobs in accounting, banking, merchandising, and other professional fields that emphasized financial reward and status, CCRI and SFCC offered training for semiprofessional careers in criminal justice, real estate, and medical technology. In many cases, these students enrolled in colleges and universities precisely because of the lucrative benefits they believed higher education furnished. It comes as little surprise, then, that the Higher Education Research Institute's American Freshman Survey, which has tracked student attitudes toward postsecondary education for almost fifty years, reports that the percentage of students who claim that becoming "very well off financially" is an "essential or very important" reason for enrolling in college or university has doubled since 1967—to 85 percent.[143]

In recent decades, the pursuit of wealth and status has characterized students and institutions alike. Public colleges and universities, which have grappled with the challenges of declining state appropriations since the 1970s, have increasingly sought private contracts and government grants. Research universities have pursued the financial advantages and elevated institutional status that accompanies sponsored research awards, while community colleges have looked to private enterprise and federal and state agencies to provide the funding necessary to expand operations and rise in higher education's institutional hierarchy. The shift toward more entrepreneurial institutions has also been a response to pressures to limit tuition increases so as to not exclude the students that many of these institutions were established to serve. It is just these issues, however, including access, affordability, and "mission creep," that have become central factors in the so-called crisis that many believe higher education in the United States currently confronts.

Epilogue

By the beginning of the twenty-first century, a social ethos of affluence dominated American higher education—a transformation that has hardly gone unnoticed. In *Higher Education and the American Dream,* historian Marvin Lazerson observes that colleges and universities have been wildly successful in assuming responsibility for preparing skilled labor, providing expert knowledge, and conducting scientific research—success that has "brought with it millions and millions of dollars from public and private sources." As with John Kenneth Galbraith's examination of *The Affluent Society,* however, Lazerson concludes that for higher-education institutions, "expectation" has risen "with attainment." He writes, "Higher education's success in attracting money stimulates the desire for even more money. The search for gold has become an ever-present phenomenon."[1] In a comparable vein, Lazerson and W. Norton Grubb note how recent proposals to enroll all high-school graduates in some form of postsecondary education—from low-cost, two-year community colleges to elite four-year institutions—is almost solely predicated upon higher education's claim to promote private gain: "The rhetoric of college for all advocates college education not as a way of developing moral leadership for religious and secular society, as in the eighteenth and nineteenth centuries, but as a way to increase individual status and income."[2] Similarly, after spending a year studying undergraduates at Northern Arizona University, anthropologist Cathy Small concluded that twenty-first-century students enroll in higher education primarily for the purpose of obtaining lucrative employment and acquiring wealth. "College," she determined, "is all about positioning yourself for a good job and an affluent future."[3]

Most recently, the already-aggressive pursuit of wealth by both educational institutions and their students has intensified through what many observers have labeled the corporatization of higher education. Titles of current books reflect this trend, including Jennifer Washburn's *University, Inc.*, Eric Gould's *The University in a Corporate Culture*, Derek Bok's *Universities in the Marketplace*, and James E. Côté and Anton L. Allahar's *Lowering Higher Education: The Rise of Corporate Universities and the Fall of Liberal Education.*[4] Few of these works conclude that colleges and universities benefit in any meaningful way from adopting corporate practices. In fact, many attribute the current "crisis" in higher learning to these, including soaring tuition costs, limited student learning, the decline of the humanities, increasing class stratification, and the "unmaking of the public university."[5] Of course, corporate values have been influencing higher education for well over a hundred years. Thorstein Veblen's *The Higher Learning in America* provides just one instance of the concern Americans expressed at the beginning of the twentieth century over commercialism's influence on higher education. In recent decades, however, the change has been of a much greater magnitude in both style and substance, as affluence-oriented colleges and universities have shifted from being *influenced* by commercial values to *becoming* corporate entities, with some higher-education institutions being established as for-profit corporations.

In 2003, just two US colleges charged more than $40,000 a year for tuition, fees, room, and board. Six years later, over two hundred did.[6] The beginning of the Great Recession in 2008 catalyzed this spike in cost, driving down endowments and accelerating already-declining state support for higher education. One important ramification is that tuition at four-year public institutions, nationally, has come to provide a greater source of revenue than state appropriations. Yet as Nicolaus Mills observes, it is not simply the nation's economic climate that now dictates what colleges and universities charge. It is the adoption of a corporate model that has already proven remarkably expensive to operate and extremely difficult to reform because of its overwhelming preoccupation with status, as the experience of Virginia's Sweet Briar College indicates.[7]

Founded in 1901 as a women's liberal arts college, Sweet Briar survived the maelstrom of the twentieth century, including two world wars and an economic calamity, only to announce in 2015 that it was closing. Although the particular challenges confronting rural women's colleges undoubtedly played a role in the institution's financial decline, the combination of a corporate model of operation and the effects of the recession led to college officials' announcing that the institution would end operations following the close of the academic year.[8] "There are some liberal arts colleges—places such as Williams, Amherst, Bowdoin, and Middlebury Colleges—that have prestige to attract students and the financial means to promote both constant campus activities and plenty of opportunities for urban experiences," reported Scott Jaschik for *Inside Higher Ed*. "But," he quoted Sweet Briar president James F. Jones as saying, "it is increasingly difficult for other colleges to compete."[9] Legal action combined with strong alumnae support ultimately saved Sweet Briar. Yet, Moody's Investor Service has estimated that the number of four-year public and private higher-education institutions that will go out of business over the next few years could triple, from five to fifteen annually.[10]

In 1983, *US News and World Report* published its first "Best Colleges" guide. The magazine's approach to rating higher-education institutions was hardly new. As discussed in chapter 9, the Carnegie Foundation for the Advancement of Teaching had been ranking institutions based on federal research support and annual number of doctoral degrees awarded for over a decade. By the end of the century, however, the *US News* rankings provided not just research universities but all higher-education institutions with a "bottom line" against which to judge their "productivity" vis-à-vis "the competition." In turn, colleges and universities reoriented their institutional priorities toward rising in the rankings. In an effort to increase "selectivity," for instance, many began recruiting an increasing number of applicants, all the while knowing they had not proportionally increased the number of spots available to those students. Average SAT score is also a ratings criterion, and so institutions began shifting financial-aid resources from need-based to merit-based in an effort to appeal to high scorers. Given that SAT scores correlate with family income, one harmful result has been that a greater number of students who do not need aid receive it, leaving less available to those who do.

Strenuous efforts to attract ever-more academically able students, particularly those whose families could afford to pay "full freight" (the total cost of tuition, fees, room, and board without the support of financial aid), coincided with colleges' and universities' growing treatment of students as customers who could be lured away by the competition. As James Engell and Anthony Dangerfield write in their work *Saving Higher Education in the Age of Money*, "It has become common practice in the last decade to declare that students paying tuition are consumers or customers, not students. The common denominator of these phenomena is an overwhelming concern, even an obsession, with money."[11] One consequence of the "student as consumer" approach to higher education, according to William Deresiewicz, is that higher-education institutions have begun to "pander" to undergraduates rather than challenge them. "You can fairly smell it on the campuses," Deresiewicz writes in his provocative style, "where the students are so unmistakably in charge."[12] After describing grade inflation as attributable to students feeling "that they're paying for A's," Deresiewicz observes, "The customer-service mentality is also responsible for the profusion of swanky new dorms, gyms, and student centers—a building boom that . . . was financed by a mountain of debt, and that has been a major factor in tuition growth. Colleges now sell themselves to kids in terms of what they can give them, not what they plan to expect of them."[13] In their theory of "academic capitalism," however, Sheila Slaughter and Gary Rhoades claim that higher education has already moved beyond simply "thinking of the student as consumer" to "the institution as marketer." The scholars note, "When students choose colleges, institutions advertise education as a service and a life style." Once students enroll, "their status shifts from consumers to captive markets, and colleges and universities offer them goods bearing the institutions' trademarked symbols, images, and names at university profit centers such as unions and malls."[14]

Yet to remain competitive, higher-education institutions seek to cut costs as well as increase revenues. Given that personnel expenses are frequently the greatest drain on college and university financial resources, that is precisely the area that administrators have targeted. As Frank Donoghue has demonstrated in *The Last Professors: The Corporate University and the Fate of the Humanities*, adjunct instructors, who are frequently part-time employees, compensated per course taught, and rarely receive benefits, now make up an astonishing 65 percent of college and university instructors, with the remaining 35 comprising tenured and tenure-track professors.[15] Perhaps more disturbingly, this situation is at its worst at community colleges where, nationally, 80 percent of instructors are not on the tenure track. As Donoghue notes, there are community colleges in the United States in which the entire faculty may consist of adjuncts paid by the course. "There seems no doubt . . . ," he concludes, "that the trend toward increased use of adjunct teachers will continue. It is . . . the cheapest way to run a university. The heavy use of adjunct labor accords with the bedrock corporate values of efficiency and accountability that are now embraced by growing numbers of university administrators."[16]

Of course, the most conspicuous illustration of higher education's corporatization is found in the for-profit sector, with one example having an antecedent in what historian John Thelin describes as a "distinctly American contribution" to higher learning: the diploma mill.[17] Established primarily as profit-making enterprises (like paper- or sawmills), diploma mills have existed in the United

States since at least the early nineteenth century, taking the form of unaccredited higher-education institutions that award illegitimate degrees for a fee. Today, these enterprises hawk their degrees online, offering unsuspecting consumers the opportunity to acquire a bachelor's or master's degree within four to six weeks based on previous work experience.[18]

Much more widespread, however, is the growth of degree-granting, for-profit colleges and universities that function as chain stores and provide a significant portion of their educational services online.[19] Enrollment in so-called for-profit colleges has skyrocketed over the past two decades. In the year 2000, approximately 450,000 students enrolled in for-profit institutions—less than 3 percent of total higher-education enrollment in the United States. By 2015, that figure had increased to 2.4 million, or approximately 10 percent of the total. And the number continues to rise. Between 2007 and 2010, one in every three new college students enrolled in a for-profit institution.[20] These colleges and universities are owned by vast for-profit private enterprises, such as the Apollo Group's University of Phoenix and the Graham Holdings Company's Kaplan University.[21] Most of these companies advertise heavily and charge substantial tuition. In 2012–2013, the average for-profit college undergraduate paid $15,172 per year in tuition in contrast to $8,655 at four-year public universities and $3,131 at community colleges. Moreover, although for-profit colleges are private businesses, most of their revenues come from tax dollars in the form of federal student aid. Public funds have provided 86 percent of these revenues in recent years, amounting to $32 billion annually. Accordingly, students who enroll in for-profit colleges assume a greater debt burden than their peers at public and private nonprofit colleges and universities. (For 2008 bachelor degree recipients, the figures were $32,700, $22,400, and $17,700, respectively.) As a result, for-profit borrowers also have the highest default rate of the three groups, accounting for almost half of all student loan defaults each year.[22]

There is no evidence that these institutions have a greater success rate in assisting students achieve their educational and career goals than do public and private nonprofit colleges and universities. On the contrary, recent studies suggest that for-profit college students experience higher unemployment rates than their peers at other kinds of institutions and, when they are employed, receive lower wages.[23] As a result, the future of for-profit colleges and universities is unclear.[24] In 2014, Corinthian Colleges, which operated the widely advertised Heald, Everest, and WyoTech campuses and at its peak enrolled seventy-two thousand students, effectively went out of business. Experiencing severe financial difficulties and under federal investigation for allegedly falsifying job placement rates, the enterprise negotiated an agreement with the US Department of Education to sell eighty-five of its campuses and liquidate the remaining twelve.[25] Two years later, ITT Technical Institutes, which in 2010 had received over $1 billion in federal financial aid and GI Bill benefits, similarly shut its doors, leaving thirty-five thousand students stranded.[26] Investigated by the US Attorney's Office in 2004 for fraud relating to student recruitment, dropout rates, grade inflation, and falsified job placement and salary reports, ITT survived in part because the 2008 financial crisis triggered a sudden increase in enrollments by people who had lost their jobs and hoped to acquire marketable skills. Over time, however, as former students and watchdog groups increasingly filed complaints against the company, the US Department of Education began monitoring ITT's finances. In September 2016, government officials announced that they were banning the company from enrolling new students receiving federal financial aid. Just one month later, ITT Services closed.[27]

Given the experiences of Corinthian Colleges and ITT Services, it would be reasonable to assume that for-profit postsecondary institutions are on the decline. However, as Paul Fain and Doug Lederman explain in their study of profit-driven higher education, descriptively entitled "Boom, Regulate, Cleanse, Repeat," it is more likely that for-profit enterprises will continue to expand over the long term even while they experience recurring short term cycles of growth and retrenchment.[28]

For-profit colleges reflect the apotheosis of affluence in higher learning. Treating educational provision as an extractive rather than additive enterprise, these corporations seek to accumulate wealth by transferring billions of public dollars to private shareholders, an approach that has failed to guarantee either student success or corporate profitability. Fortunately, most higher-education institutions have resisted this extreme form of corporatization. While an ethos of affluence has undoubtedly shaped contemporary higher education, most colleges and universities continue to be guided by the tension between this and civic-mindedness, practicality, and commercialism. For some critics, this tension results in inefficient institutions with conflicting purposes that are desperately in need of disruption.[29] Yet US colleges and universities have become the envy of the world, at least in part because they sustain multiple purposes, not the least of which is serving the common good. Rather than a problem in need of a solution, this characteristic may very well be American higher education's greatest strength.

This is not to say that higher education's commitment to the common good has remained immutable. History is the study of change over time and few central social institutions better lend themselves to that study than colleges and universities. Especially in form but also in function, higher education in the United

States has undergone dramatic transformation over the past two hundred years. During the early nineteenth century, institutions such as South Carolina College sought to inculcate civic virtue in students largely by maintaining a regimented residential system designed to severely regulate their behavior. (Evidence for both the centrality and severity of this regimentation is found in the extent to which students frequently chafed at and occasionally revolted against it.) In notable contrast, commuter institutions established following World War II, such as the University of South Florida, expected to have little influence over students outside of the classroom. As USF director of institutional research Lewis B. Mayhew observed in 1960, the importance of the faculty's role was "heightened" at USF because most students intended to live at home and commute to school. "In such a University," he claimed, "many of the values which could be inculcated in students through residence in college must be gained through the classroom or not at all."[30]

Indeed, the most pertinent example of the sweeping changes that occurred in American higher education over the course of the nation's history is evident in the wide range of institutional types that developed. Many of these varieties eventually merged with or grew into comprehensive institutions that shared similar characteristics, leaving most Americans unaware of the ways in which these schools, colleges, and universities represented distinctive, sometimes radical breaks with tradition during the eras in which they were founded.

The residential colleges that make up England's Oxford and Cambridge Universities served as models for many American colleges during the early national period. And although regional distinctions took on greater importance at colleges such as Bowdoin, South Carolina, and Georgetown in the years leading up to the Civil War, these institutions frequently shared educational goals, pedagogical methods, and curricula. During the antebellum era, however, Americans began to question the efficacy of a higher education predicated primarily on the mental discipline associated with memorizing and reciting the classics, which led to the establishment of new kinds of institutions. Borrowing again from European models but modifying them for an American context, agricultural and technical colleges such as the Agricultural College of the State of Michigan and teacher-training institutions such as the California State Normal School provided students with a very different kind of higher learning, much of it specialized and practice-based.

Political, economic, and social upheaval accompanying the Civil War led Americans to once again form new kinds of higher-education institutions that they believed would better meet the needs of a reconstructed nation. Howard University and Smith College provided educational opportunities for men and women previously marginalized, if not expressly excluded, from other colleges and universities. Similarly, the emergence of universities such as Stanford, intended to both prepare students for personal success in their chosen careers and engage scholars in research and publication, resulted in part from changes to the nation's political economy. Following two world wars and the Great Depression, Americans further reconceived of higher education, with urban commuter universities such as the University of South Florida and two-year institutions such as Rhode Island Junior College and Santa Fe Community College responding to postwar economic imperatives and an increasingly diverse student population.

During each of these periods, changes to the nation's prevailing social ethos led Americans to establish new kinds of higher-education institutions that reflected the priorities of their day; to paraphrase educational reformer Abraham Flexner, higher-education institutions have been expressions of their age. As each ethos gained predominance at different moments in the nation's history, it reshaped the terms of institutional debates and propelled changes in higher education more broadly, playing an especially influential role in colleges' and universities' commitment to the common good.

From a twenty-first-century vantage point, it is relatively simple to appreciate the early national period as an era when colleges and universities earnestly claimed to advance the public good. During this period, an ethos of civic-mindedness led higher-education institutions to ascribe "peculiar obligations" to graduates to use higher learning to benefit public rather than private interests. Over time, however, practicality, followed by commercialism and finally affluence, increasingly prioritized individual advancement and private gain over the public welfare. While colleges and universities in the United States today continue to publicize their contributions to the public good, they fervidly prioritize the acquisition of wealth—both their own institutional gains and graduates' future earnings.

Nevertheless, American higher education remained committed to the common good over time even as social, political, and economic forces pushed it in an opposing direction. Although civic-mindedness predominated at colleges and universities during the early national period, relatively few students ever gained admission to these institutions. Over the course of the next century and a half, higher education consistently expanded access to include poor and working-class students, women, and racial and ethnic minorities, making possible the "democratized" higher education that characterizes the modern day. In addition to becoming more inclusive, colleges and universities contributed to meeting societal needs. In 1916, when Stanford University President Ray Lyman Wilbur pronounced that "knowledge—education" was necessary for Americans to work together "for common ends and for the common good," he reaffirmed a role for American higher education that prioritized service to society.[31] Under Wilbur's leadership, Stanford faculty and students actively sought to resolve what seemed intractable problems in a nation experiencing rapid industrialization, corporate greed, unprecedented immigration, political corruption, labor unrest, and dramatically expanding income inequality. Wilbur elaborated on proclamations issued by many college and university administrators during the era, including University of Wisconsin President Charles Van Hise, who gave meaning to the "Wisconsin Idea" when he pronounced that the "beneficent influence of the university" should reach "every family in the state." One hundred and ten years later, in 2015, when Governor Scott Walker of Wisconsin proposed replacing the "Wisconsin Idea" with the far narrower objective of meeting "the state's workforce needs," popular backlash led him to quickly abandon the idea.[32]

The rejection of Walker's proposal offers just one of many examples of Americans' continued faith in higher education's capacity to contribute to the common good. In 2013, when an Arizona community college enrolling over forty thousand students moved to tighten its admission standards in the face of community opposition, its regional accreditor, the Higher Learning Commission of the North Central Association of Colleges and Schools, penalized it for demonstrating "a lack of understanding of its role in serving the public good in its community."[33] More recently, a national dialogue has arisen challenging the ways in which current four-year college and university admissions processes favor affluent families by rewarding the kinds of experiences the wealthy can provide their children, including well-resourced public schools offering a range of Advanced Placement courses, summer enrichment programs, and the time necessary for community service, unpaid internships, and volunteering abroad.[34] This dialogue took on greater urgency when Harvard University researchers surveyed ten thousand middle- and high-school students about what was most important to them: high individual achievement, happiness (feeling good most of the time), or caring for others.[35] Surprised to find that only 22 percent of the students reported caring for others, and knowing that higher-education admissions criteria influence millions of students' behavior, they released a report urging college and university admissions offices to prioritize ethical engagement, "especially concern for others and the common good," as well as intellectual engagement."[36] Dozens of higher-education administrators across the institutional spectrum, from small liberal-arts colleges to major research universities, quickly endorsed the report, reaffirming higher education's acceptance of a responsibility for fostering the common good in American society.

Of course, it is unlikely that any one report will overcome the powerful hold that an ethos of affluence currently has on either higher education or

American society. Indeed, with critics blaming colleges and universities for not providing the critical thinking, problem solving, and communication skills necessary for graduates to succeed as "aspiring adults"—and state and federal lawmakers demanding that these same institutions limit costs while increasingly holding them accountable for learning outcomes—colleges and universities in the twenty-first century are against the ropes. Still, history has shown higher education to be remarkably resilient. Even now, a dedication to the public good animates many college and university communities while motivating students, faculty, and administrators to fulfill the promise that the Reverend Joseph McKeen articulated in his Bowdoin College inaugural address over two centuries ago, that "literary institutions are founded and endowed for the common good, and not for the private advantage of those who resort to them for education."[37] As long as they hold true to this ideal, colleges and universities will produce more than just knowledge that contributes to the next great technological innovation or a workforce that successfully competes in a global economy. They will foster the civic capability and commitment to the public good necessary for American democracy not to simply survive but to flourish for decades to come.

Notes

PROLOGUE

1. Richard Arum and Josipa Roksa, *Academically Adrift: Limited Learning on College Campuses* (Chicago: University of Chicago Press, 2010); *Aspiring Adults Adrift: Tentative Transitions of College Graduates* (Chicago: University of Chicago Press, 2014).

2. Kevin Carey, *The End of College: Creating the Future of Learning and the University of Everywhere* (New York: Riverhead Books, 2015).

3. "Bill to Establish a College at Columbia," November 23, 1801, Journals of the House of Representatives, Archives of the Historical Commission of South Carolina. Reproduced in Edgar W. Knight, ed. *A Documentary History of Education in the South before 1860*, vol. 3 of 5 (Chapel Hill: University of North Carolina Press, 1952), 44–46.

4. "The Inaugural Address, Delivered in Brunswick, September 2, 1802, by the Rev. Joseph McKeen, A.M. & A.S.S.," Box 1, Folder "Presidential Inauguration 1802," Catalogue 1.2.1, Department of Special Collections, Bowdoin College Archives.

5. "Proposals for Establishing an Academy at George-town, Patowmack-River, Maryland," Box 19, Folder 6, Georgetown College Varia (1791–1844) [56 Z1–5], Archives, Maryland Province, Society of Jesus, Special Collections Research Center, Georgetown University Library, Washington, DC.

6. See, for instance, Robert Church, "Conversation: Renegotiating the Historical Narrative: The Case of American Higher Education," *History of Education Quarterly* 44, no. 4 (2004): 585–89.

7. Regarding the notion of a "social ethos," I borrow from political scientist and philosopher Joshua Cohen, who writes that a social ethos is composed of "socially widespread preferences and attitudes about the kinds of rewards it is acceptable to insist on, and associated with those preferences and attitudes, a sense about the ways of life that are attractive, exciting, good, worthy of pursuit." Joshua Cohen, "Taking People as They Are?," *Philosophy and Public Affairs* 30, no. 4 (2002): 365.

8. See, for instance, Robert E. Shalhope, "Republicanism and Early American Historiography," *The William and Mary Quarterly* 39, no. 2 (1982): 334–56.

9. Gordon S. Wood, *The Creation of the American Republic, 1776–1787* (Chapel Hill: University of North Carolina Press, 1969), 53–65.

10. Barry Alan Shain, *The Myth of American Individualism: The Protestant Origins of American Political Thought* (Princeton: Princeton University Press, 1994), 3, 47.

11. Kevin Carey, "Meet the Man Who Wrote the Greatest Book about American Higher Ed," *The Chronicle of Higher Education*, October 29, 2015.

12. Laurence R. Veysey, *The Emergence of the American University* (Chicago: University of Chicago Press, 1965).

13. Julie A. Reuben, "Writing When Everything Has Been Said: The History of American Higher Education following Laurence Veysey's Classic," *History of Education Quarterly* 45, no. 3 (2005): 413.

14. Julie A. Reuben, *The Making of the Modern University: Intellectual Transformation and the Marginalization of Morality* (Chicago: University of Chicago Press, 1996), 12.

15. See, for instance, Helen Lefkowitz Horowitz, "In the Wake of Laurence Veysey: Re-Examining the Liberal Arts College," *History of Education Quarterly* 45, no. 3 (2005):

420–26; Hugh Hawkins, "The Making of the Liberal Arts College Identity," *Daedalus* 128, no. 1 (1999): 1–25; W. Bruce Leslie, *Gentlemen and Scholars: College and Community in the "Age of the University," 1865–1917* (University Park: Pennsylvania State University Press, 1992); James Axtell, "The Death of the Liberal Arts College," *History of Education Quarterly* 11, no. 4 (1971): 339–52.

16. Thomas D. Snyder, ed. *120 Years of American Education: A Statistical Portrait* (Washington, DC: US Department of Education National Center for Education Statistics, 1993): Table 24, 77.

17. Steven Brint and Jerome Karabel, *The Diverted Dream: Community Colleges and the Promise of Educational Opportunity in America, 1900–1985* (New York: Oxford University Press, 1989): 83–84, 101.

18. Veysey, *Emergence*, 338.

19. Henry M. Levin, "Educating for a Commonwealth," *Educational Researcher* 30, no. 6 (2001): 30.

20. Ibid.

21. Jack C. Lane, "Yale Report of 1828 and Liberal Education: A Neorepublican Manifesto," *History of Education Quarterly* 27, no. 3 (1987): 329–30.

22. Alan Trachtenberg, *The Incorporation of America: Culture and Society in the Gilded Age* (New York: Hill and Wang, 1982), 5.

23. *Stanford University: The Founding Grant with Amendments, Legislation and Court Decrees*, (Stanford, CA: Stanford University Press, 1971), 1.

24. John Kenneth Galbraith, "The Affluent Society," in *John Kenneth Galbraith: The Affluent Society and Other Writings, 1952–1967*, ed. James K. Galbraith (New York: Library of America, 2010), 472.

25. See, for instance, Arthur M. Cohen, *The Shaping of American Higher Education: Emergence and Growth of the Contemporary System* (San Francisco: Jossey-Bass, 1998), 175; Marvin Lazerson, "The Disappointments of Success: Higher Education after World War II," *Annals of the American Academy of Political and Social Science* 559 (1998): 68.

26. Russell M. Cooper and Margaret B. Fisher, *The Vision of a Contemporary University: A Case Study of Expansion and Development in American Higher Education, 1950–1975* (Tampa: University of South Florida Press, 1982), 69; Mark I. Greenberg, Andrew T. Huse, and Marilyn Keltz Stephens, *University of South Florida: The First Fifty Years, 1956–2006* (Tampa: University of South Florida, 2006), 79.

27. Frederick Rudolph, *The American College and University: A History* (New York: Knopf, 1962), 356.

1. "LITERARY INSTITUTIONS ARE FOUNDED AND ENDOWED FOR THE COMMON GOOD"

1. On the history of Bowdoin College, see Nehemiah Cleaveland, *History of Bowdoin College* (Boston: J. R. Osgood & Co., 1882); Louis C. Hatch, *The History of Bowdoin College* (Portland, ME: Loring, Short & Harmon, 1927); William B. Whiteside, *The Will to Learn: Education and Community at Bowdoin College* (Brunswick: Bowdoin College, 1970); Ernst Christian Helmreich, *Religion at Bowdoin College: A History* (Brunswick: Bowdoin College, 1982).

2. Charles C. Calhoun, *A Small College in Maine: Two Hundred Years of Bowdoin* (Brunswick: Bowdoin College, 1993), 5.

3. David B. Potts, "American Colleges in the Nineteenth Century: From Localism to Denominationalism," *History of Education Quarterly* 11, no. 4 (1971): 363–80.

4. Ibid., 368–69; Calhoun, *A Small College in Maine*, 3–6.

5. Hatch, *The History of Bowdoin College*, 16.

6. "The Inaugural Address, Delivered in Brunswick, September 2, 1802, by the Rev. Joseph McKeen, A.M. & A.S.S.," box 1, folder "Presidential Inauguration 1802," Catalogue 1.2.1, Department of Special Collections, Bowdoin College Archives.

7. Ibid.

8. On the liberal professions for which New England colleges educated students, see Jurgen Herbst, "The Yale Report of 1828," *International Journal of the Classical Tradition* 11, no. 2 (2004): 227; David F. Allmendinger, *Paupers and Scholars: The Transformation of Student Life in Nineteenth-Century New England* (New York: St. Martin's Press, 1975), 18.

9. "The Inaugural Address."

10. William G. Bowen, Martin A. Kurzweil, and Eugene M. Tobin, *Equity and Excellence in American Higher Education* (Charlottesville: University of Virginia Press, 2005), 19.

11. Julie Reuben, "Patriotic Purposes: Public Schools and the Education of Citizens," in *The Public Schools*, ed. Susan Fuhrman and Marvin Lazerson (Oxford, UK: Oxford University Press, 2005), 2; and Carl F. Kaestle, *Pillars of the Republic: Common Schools and American Society, 1780–1860* (New York: Hill and Wang, 1983), especially chapters 1 and 5.

12. Quoted in John R. Thelin, *A History of American Higher Education* (Baltimore: Johns Hopkins University Press, 2004), 26.

13. Herbst, "The Yale Report," 222.

14. Frederick Rudolph, *The American College and University: A History* (New York: Knopf, 1962), 58–59.

15. Jesse Appleton, *The Works of Rev. Jesse Appleton, D.D., Late President of Bowdoin College: Embracing His Course of Theological Lectures, His Academic Addresses, and a Selection from His Sermons*, vol. 2 of 2 (Andover: Gould and Newman, 1836), 289.

16. *General Catalogue of Bowdoin College and the Medical School of Maine, 1794–1894* (Brunswick: Bowdoin College, 1894), xxxii.

17. Ibid.

18. Ibid., lxiv–lxvii.

19. Kenneth Nivison, "'But a Step from College to the Judicial Bench': College and Curriculum in New England's 'Age of Improvement'," *History of Education Quarterly* 50, no. 4 (2010): 460–87.

20. Caroline Winterer, *The Culture of Classicism: Ancient Greece and Rome in American Intellectual Life* (Baltimore: Johns Hopkins University Press, 2002), 29.

21. Quoted in Christopher J. Lucas, *American Higher Education: A History*, 2nd ed. (New York: Palgrave Macmillan, 2006), 133.

22. Ibid., 135–37.

23. Hatch, *The History of Bowdoin College*, 28–29.

24. Margaret Sumner, *Collegiate Republic: Cultivating an Ideal Society in Early America* (Charlottesville: University of Virginia Press, 2014), 56–57.

25. Calhoun, *A Small College in Maine*, 101–5.

26. *General Catalogue, 1794–1894*, lxviii.

27. Cyrus Hamlin, *My Life and Times* (Boston: Congregational Sunday School and Publishing Society, 1893), 92.

28. Quoted in Appleton, *The Works of Rev. Jesse Appleton*, 2.

29. Thelin, *A History of American Higher Education*, 65.

30. Hamlin, *My Life and Times*, 103–4.

31. Calhoun, *A Small College in Maine*, 131.

32. Wilmot Brookings Mitchell, *A Remarkable Bowdoin Decade: 1820–1830: A Paper Read at the Town and College Club in Brunswick, Maine, December 1, 1950* (Brunswick: Bowdoin College, 1952).

33. Quoted in *General Catalogue, 1794–1894*, xxxv–xxxvi.

34. Ibid., lxviii.

35. Joseph F. Kett, *The Pursuit of Knowledge under Difficulties: From Self-Improvement to Adult Education in America, 1750–1990* (Stanford, CA: Stanford University Press, 1994), 14–15.

36. Quoted in Hatch, *The History of Bowdoin College*, 304.

37. Ibid., 305–6.

38. Ibid., 306.

39. Ibid., 309.

40. Hamlin, *My Life and Times*, 121.

41. Hatch, *The History of Bowdoin College*, 310.

42. Nehemiah Cleaveland, *An Address, Delivered at Bowdoin College, before the Peucinian Society, at Their Annual Meeting, September 3, 1821* (Brunswick: Joseph Griffin, 1821), 16.

43. Ibid., 30.

44. Robert Page, *Sketch of the Class Which Graduated at Bowdoin College in 1810* (Concord, NH: McFarland & Jenks, 1852).

45. *General Catalogue, 1794–1894*, 28.

46. Mitchell, "A Remarkable Bowdoin Decade," 6–7.

47. Allmendinger, *Paupers and Scholars*; Hatch, *The History of Bowdoin College*, 225–29.

48. In 1829, for instance, twenty-eight students, or one-quarter of Bowdoin's student body, relied on more than one of these forms of financial support. Allmendinger, *Paupers and Scholars*, 12.

49. Alpheus S. Packard, "Characteristics of a Good District School: An Address Delivered before the Teachers' Association of Bowdoin College." (Brunswick: Press of J. Griffin, 1838), 33–34.

50. Allmendinger, *Paupers and Scholars*, 86.

51. Diary entry entitled "Thoughts on My Birthday" by George F. Talbot, January 16, 1836, Catalogue 1.3.3, Volume 22, Jan. 24, 1835–Feb. 11, 1836, Department of Special Collections, Bowdoin College Archives.

52. Diary entry by George F. Talbot, November 27, 1836, Catalogue 1.3.3, Volume 23, Feb. 12, 1836 – Feb. 14, 1837.

53. *General Catalogue of Bowdoin College and the Medical School of Maine: A Biographical Record of Alumni and Officers, 1794–1950*, Sesquicentennial Edition (Brunswick: President and Trustees of Bowdoin College, 1950).

54. Diary entry by John Marsh Mitchell, September 28, 1839, Catalogue 1.1.3, Volume 49, Sept. 28, 1839 – Feb. 12, 1842, Department of Special Collections, Bowdoin College Archives.

55. *General Catalogue, 1794–1950*.

2. "THE GOOD ORDER AND THE HARMONY OF THE WHOLE COMMUNITY"

1. Daniel Walker Hollis, *University of South Carolina*, vol. 1 of 2 (Columbia: University of South Carolina Press, 1951), 3–21.

2. Walter B. Edgar, *South Carolina: A History* (Columbia: University of South Carolina Press, 1998), 297.

3. "Bill to Establish a College at Columbia," November 23, 1801, Journals of the House of Representatives, Archives of the Historical Commission of South Carolina. Reproduced in Edgar W. Knight, ed. *A Documentary History of Education in the South before 1860*, vol. 3 of 5 (Chapel Hill: University of North Carolina Press, 1952), 44–46.

4. Maximilian LaBorde, *The History of the South Carolina College* (Charleston: Walker, Evans & Cogswell Printers, 1874), 11.

5. Quoted in LaBorde, *The History of the South Carolina College*, 8.

6. For an analysis of sectionalism in South Carolina, see Edgar, *South Carolina*, especially chapter 12.

7. Quoted in LaBorde, *The History of the South Carolina College*, 9.

8. Quoted in Hollis, *University of South Carolina*, 17.

9. Edwin L. Green, *A History of the University of South Carolina* (Columbia: The State Company, 1916), 14.

10. Hollis, *University of South Carolina*, 23.

11. Green, *A History of the University of South Carolina*, 12.

12. Ibid., 17.

13. George Paul Schmidt, *The Old Time College President* (New York: Columbia University Press, 1930), 146–47.

14. Ibid., 69–70.

15. Jurgen Herbst, *From Crisis to Crisis: American College Government, 1636–1819* (Cambridge, MA: Harvard University Press, 1982), 210.

16. Hollis, *University of South Carolina*, 3.

17. Knight, *A Documentary History*, 80–81.

18. Chalmers G. Davidson, *The Last Foray: The South Carolina Planters of 1860* (Columbia: University of South Carolina Press, 1971), 18–53. Also see Jon L. Wakelyn, "Antebellum College Life and the Relations between Fathers and Sons," in *The Web of Southern Social Relations: Women, Family, & Education*, ed. Walter J. Fraser, R. Frank Saunders, and Jon L. Wakelyn (Athens: University of Georgia Press, 1985), 111.

19. See, for instance, Lorri Glover, "An Education in Southern Masculinity: The Ball Family of South Carolina in the New Republic," *The Journal of Southern History* 69, no. 1 (2003): 39–70.

20. Drew Gilpin Faust, *James Henry Hammond and the Old South: A Design for Mastery* (Baton Rouge: Louisiana State University Press, 1982), 13.

21. *By-Laws of the South Carolina College, December 1807* (Columbia, SC: A. S. Johnston, 1808).

22. See Glover, "An Education in Southern Masculinity"; Wakelyn, "Antebellum College Life and the Relations between Fathers and Sons"; and Steven M. Stowe, *Intimacy and Power in the Old South: Ritual in the Lives of the Planters* (Baltimore: Johns Hopkins University Press, 1987); among others.

23. Bertram Wyatt-Brown, *Southern Honor: Ethics and Behavior in the Old South* (New York: Oxford University Press, 1982), 154.

24. Religious commitments and/or commercial apprenticeships frequently dictated the terms of adolescent socialization in the North, whereas during the early nineteenth century access to evangelical zeal and commercial enterprise was more restricted in the South. Wyatt-Brown, *Southern Honor*, 164.

25. Ibid., 164–66.

26. For a complete list of the laws in 1807, see Knight, *A Documentary History*, 102–3.

27. *By-Laws of the South Carolina College*, 12.

28. John A. Reesman, "A School for Honor: South Carolina College and the Guard House Riot of 1856," *The South Carolina Historical Magazine* 84, no. 4 (1983): 205.

29. Ibid., 208.

30. Richard J. Calhoun, ed. *Witness to Sorrow: The Antebellum Autobiography of William J. Grayson* (Columbia: University of South Carolina Press, 1990), 80.

31. Hollis, *University of South Carolina*, 54.

32. Quoted in Glover, "An Education in Southern Masculinity," 45.

33. Letter from Jonathan Maxcy to the board recommending the expulsion of "John Gaillard, of the Junior Class," November 26, 1813, Jonathan Maxcy Papers, South Caroliniana Library, University of South Carolina.

34. LaBorde, *The History of the South Carolina College*, 63.

35. Knight, *A Documentary History of Education in the South before 1860*, 85.

36. Ibid., 95.

37. LaBorde, *The History of the South Carolina College*, 66–69; Hollis, *University of South Carolina*, 62–63.

38. *By-Laws of the South Carolina College*, 25.

39. Letter from William C. Preston to the trustees of the South Carolina College, May 6, 1846, South Caroliniana Library, University of South Carolina.

40. Reesman, "A School for Honor," 205.

41. Louis P. Towles, "A Matter of Honor at South Carolina College, 1822," *The South Carolina Historical Magazine* 94, no. 1 (1993): 6–18.

42. Robert F. Pace and Christopher A. Bjornsen, "Adolescent Honor and College Student Behavior in the Old South," *Southern Cultures* 6 (2000): 10.

43. Ibid., 12.

44. Knight, *A Documentary History of Education in the South before 1860*, 103.

45. *By-Laws of the South Carolina College*, 26.

46. *By-Laws of the South Carolina College*, 24.

47. Edgar, *South Carolina*, 306.

48. Stowe, *Intimacy and Power in the Old South*, 5.

49. Edgar, *South Carolina*, 306.

50. Hollis, *University of South Carolina*, 138–39.

51. Eric H. Walther, *The Fire-Eaters* (Baton Rouge: Louisiana State University Press, 1992), 176–77.

52. Ibid., 173–74.

53. Letter from William C. Preston to General Thompson, February 12, 1857, William Campbell Preston (1794–1860) Papers, South Caroliniana Library, University of South Carolina.

54. LaBorde, *The History of the South Carolina College*, 19.

55. Patrick Scott, "From Rhetoric to English: Nineteenth Century English Teaching at South Carolina College," *The South Carolina Historical Magazine* 85, no. 3 (1984): 233–43.

56. *By-Laws of the South Carolina College*, 28–29.

57. Colin Bennett, "Compacts and Compromises: Thomas S. Twiss and West Point Influence in the Antebellum South Carolina College," *The South Carolina Historical Magazine* 109, no. 1 (2008): 7–37.

58. Report by Thomas Twiss to President Barnwell, November 23, 1836, Thomas S. Twiss Papers, South Caroliniana Library, University of South Carolina.

59. For a detailed analysis of these characteristics of the curriculum, see Michael Sugrue, "'We Desired Our Future Rulers to Be Educated Men': South Carolina College, the Defense of Slavery, and the Development of Secessionist Politics," in *The American College in the Nineteenth Century*, ed. Roger Geiger (Nashville: Vanderbilt University Press, 2000), 91–114.

60. See H. M. Ellis, "Thomas Cooper: A Survey of His Life," *South Atlantic Quarterly* 19, no. 1 (1920): 24–42; Dumas Malone, *The Public Life of Thomas Cooper, 1787–1839* (New Haven: Yale University Press, 1926); Stephen L. Newman, "Thomas Cooper, 1759–1839: The Political Odyssey of a Bourgeois Ideologue," *Southern Studies* 24, no. 3 (1985): 295–305; Daniel Kilbride, "Slavery and Utilitarianism: Thomas Cooper and the Mind of the Old South," *The Journal of Southern History* 59, no. 3 (1993): 479–86.

61. Ellis, "Thomas Cooper," 24–35.

62. While President of South Carolina College, Cooper would seek redress. See Thomas Cooper, "Letters of Dr. Thomas Cooper," *American Historical Review* 6, no. 4 (1901): 725–36.

63. Hollis, *University of South Carolina*, 74–76.

64. Ibid., 104.

65. Thomas Cooper, *Lecture on the Elements of Political Economy* (Columbia, SC: McMorris & Wilson, 1829); Thomas Cooper, *A Manual of Political Economy* (Washington, DC: Duff Green, 1834).

66. Cooper, *Lecture on the Elements of Political Economy*, 62–63.

67. Thomas Cooper, *A Tract on the Proposed Alteration in the Tariff* (New York: Clayton and Van Norden, 1824).

68. Quoted in Edgar, *South Carolina*, 331.

69. Herman Belz, ed. *The Webster-Hayne Debate on the Nature of the Union* (Indianapolis: Liberty Fund, Inc., 2000), 24.

70. Notebook with lecture notes & "Questions & Answers Adapted to Four Lectures Delivered by Professor R. Henry on the Constitution of the United States," John Creighton McMaster Papers, South Caroliniana Library, University of South Carolina.

71. Moral Philosophy notes on Paley (Book III, Part 2, Chapter 3, p. 150), Robert Henry Papers, South Caroliniana Library, University of South Carolina.

72. Green, *A History of the University of South Carolina*, 264–65.

73. Euphradian Society Constitution, Clariosophic Literary Society Records, South Caroliniana Library, University of South Carolina.

74. Glover, "An Education in Southern Masculinity," 55.

75. Richard Croom Beatty, ed. *Journal of a Southern Student, 1846–1848* (Nashville: Vanderbilt University Press, 1944), 34.

76. "Debate Topics," Clariosophic Literary Society Records and Euphradian Society Records, South Caroliniana Library, University of South Carolina.

77. Walter Brian Cisco, *States Rights Gist: A South Carolina General of the Civil War* (Shippensburg, PA: White Maine Publishing Co., 1991).

78. Journal entry entitled "For the Telegraph" by James Ward Hopkins, signed "A Junior of 1851," March 1851, Journal, 1848–1867, James Ward Hopkins, South Caroliniana Library, University of South Carolina.

79. Michael David Cohen, *Reconstructing the Campus: Higher Education and the American Civil War* (Charlottesville: University of Virginia Press, 2012), 44–46.

3. "TO PROMOTE MORE EFFECTUALLY THE GRAND INTERESTS OF SOCIETY"

1. For an early history of Georgetown University, see John Gilmary Shea, *Memorial of the First Centenary of Georgetown College, D.C., Comprising a History of Georgetown University* (Washington, DC: Pub. for the College by P. F. Collier, 1891).

2. For one interpretation of why college officials did not seek a state charter from Maryland upon the institution's establishment, see Jurgen Herbst, *From Crisis to Crisis: American College Government, 1636–1819* (Cambridge, MA: Harvard University Press, 1982), 201–2.

3. "An Act Concerning the College of Georgetown, in the District of Columbia," box 19, folder 6, Georgetown College Varia (1791–1844) [56 Z1–5], Archives, Maryland Province, Society of Jesus, Special Collections Research Center, Georgetown University Library, Washington, DC; James Stanislaus Easby-Smith, *Georgetown University in the District of Columbia, 1789–1907*, vol. 1 of 2 (New York: Lewis Publishing Company, 1907), 49–50.

4. Robert Emmett Curran, *The Bicentennial History of Georgetown University: From Academy to University, 1798–1889*, vol. 1 of 2 (Washington, DC: Georgetown University Press, 1993), 76–77.

5. "Proposals for Establishing an Academy at George-Town, Patowmack-River, Maryland," box 19, folder 6, Georgetown College Varia (1791–1844) [56 Z1–5], Archives,

Maryland Province, Society of Jesus, Special Collections Research Center, Georgetown University Library, Washington, DC.

6. "College Prospectus—1798," box 19, folder 4, Georgetown College Varia (1787–1922) [56 P1-R6], Archives, Maryland Province, Society of Jesus, Special Collections Research Center, Georgetown University Library, Washington, DC.

7. Throughout this chapter, I reference Carroll's letters as they are archived in the manuscript collections of the Georgetown University Special Collections Research Center. His papers have also been edited into three volumes by the American Catholic Historical Association and published by the University of Notre Dame Press. See Thomas O'Brien Hanley, ed. *The John Carroll Papers*, 3 vols. (Notre Dame: University of Notre Dame Press, 1976).

8. James Hennesey, "An Eighteenth-Century Bishop: John Carroll of Baltimore," in *Patterns of Episcopal Leadership*, ed. Gerald P. Fogarty (New York: Macmillan, 1989), 5–51.

9. On the suppression, see Geoffrey Cubitt, *The Jesuit Myth: Conspiracy Theory and Politics in Nineteenth-Century France* (Oxford, UK: Oxford University Press, 1993); William V. Bangert, *A History of the Society of Jesus* (St. Louis: Institute of Jesuit Sources, 1972); René Fülöp-Miller, *The Jesuits: A History of the Society of Jesus* (New York: Capricorn Books, 1963).

10. Quoted in Curran, *The Bicentennial History of Georgetown University*, 8.

11. Quoted in Curran, *The Bicentennial History of Georgetown University*, 9.

12. John M. Daley, *Georgetown University: Origin and Early Years* (Washington, DC: Georgetown University Press, 1957), 23–30; Hennesey, "An Eighteenth-Century Bishop," 9–16.

13. Letter from Charles Carroll to Charles Plowden, February 27, 1785, box 57, folder 4, Carroll-Plowden Correspondence (1) [202 B1–9], Archives, Maryland Province, Society of Jesus, Special Collections Research Center, Georgetown University Library, Washington, DC.

14. Curran, *The Bicentennial History of Georgetown University*, 12–13.

15. Philip Gleason, "The Main Sheet Anchor: John Carroll and Catholic Higher Education," *The Review of Politics* 38, no. 4 (1976): 584–85.

16. Letter from Charles Carroll to Charles Plowden, December 15, 1785, box 57, folder 5, Carroll-Plowden Correspondence (2) [202 B10–16], Archives, Maryland Province, Society of Jesus, Special Collections Research Center, Georgetown University Library, Washington, DC.

17. "Proposals for Establishing an Academy at George-Town, Patowmack-River, Maryland."

18. Curran, *The Bicentennial History of Georgetown University*, 9; Rachel L. Swarns, "Georgetown Confronts Its Role in Nation's Slave Trade," *New York Times*, April 17, 2016, A1.

19. Craig Steven Wilder, *Ebony & Ivy: Race, Slavery, and the Troubled History of America's Universities* (New York: Bloomsbury Press, 2013).

20. Swarns, "Georgetown Confronts Its Role."

21. Ibid.

22. Rachel L. Swarns, "Georgetown President Takes Step, Meeting with Descendant of Slaves," *New York Times*, June 15, 2016, A10; Rachel L. Swarns, "Georgetown Plans Steps to Atone for Slave Past," *New York Times*, September 2, 2016, A1.

23. Swarns, "Georgetown President Takes Step," A10.

24. Gleason, "The Main Sheet Anchor: John Carroll and Catholic Higher Education," 593–98.

25. Ibid., 593–94.

26. "College Prospectus—1798."

27. Daley, *Georgetown University*, 224.

28. *A Catalogue of the Officers and Students of Georgetown College, District of Columbia, for the Academic Year 1851–52* (Baltimore: Printed by John Murphy & Co., 1852), University Catalogues and Prospectuses, Georgetown University Archives, Special Collections Research Center, Georgetown University Library, Washington, DC.

29. Ibid.

30. Ibid.

31. "Address," letters, manuscripts, and notes from a diary by Bernard Maguire, box 1, folder 1, 1854–1886, Manuscripts Collections, Bernard A. Maguire, S.J. Papers, Special Collections Research Center, Georgetown University, Washington, DC.

32. *A Catalogue of the Officers and Students, 1851–52*.

33. John R. Friant, Thomas A. Rover, and Edwin M. Dahill, *Glimpses of Old Georgetown* (Washington, DC: The Hoya, 1939), 11.

34. "Expulsions and Dismissals: 1795–1914," box 1, folder: "College 1850s–1906," Archives Subject Files, Georgetown University Archives, Special Collections Research Center, Georgetown University Library, Washington, DC.

35. Eric M. George, "The Cultivation of Eloquence at Georgetown College: A History of the Philodemic Society from 1830–1890," in *Swift Potomac's Lovely Daughter: Two Centuries at Georgetown through Students' Eyes*, ed. Joseph Durkin (Washington, DC: Georgetown University Press, 1990), 110–12.

36. Joseph T. Durkin, *Georgetown University: First in the Nation's Capital* (Garden City, NY: Doubleday, 1964), 30–31; Curran, *The Bicentennial History*, 184–85.

37. Curran, *The Bicentennial History*, 25.

38. "1828 Prospectus," University Catalogues and Prospectuses, Georgetown University Archives, Special Collections Research Center, Georgetown University Library, Washington, DC.

39. "Reminiscences," folder: "Ray, Robert," Alumni Subject Series, University Records, Georgetown University Archives, Special Collections Research Center, Georgetown University Library, Washington, DC.

40. George M. Barringer, "They Came to Georgetown: The French Sulpicians," *Georgetown Magazine* July 1977, http://www.library.georgetown.edu/special-collections/archives/essays/french-sulpicians.

41. Curran, *The Bicentennial History*, 32–33.

42. J. Fairfax McLaughlin, *College Days at Georgetown and Other Papers* (Philadelphia: J. B. Lippincott, 1899), 117–18.

43. Entry by examiner from 1827, Academic Records, the Classical Journal of Georgetown College, page 104, Georgetown University Archives, Special Collections Research Center, Georgetown University Library, Washington, DC.

44. Middle Examination Report, February 1858, box 2, folder 1: "Examinations—1842, etc." Academic Records, Prefect of Schools, Georgetown University Archives, Special Collections Research Center, Georgetown University Library, Washington, DC.

45. Historian Robert Curran has produced a detailed analysis of student demographic data. See Curran, *The Bicentennial History of Georgetown University*, Appendix F.

46. Ibid., 162–63.

47. "Recollections: Georgetown College in 1820," *Woodstock Letters: A Record of Current Events and Historical Notes Connected with the Colleges and Missions of the Soc. of Jesus in North and South America*, Volume 13, Woodstock College, 1884, Special Collections & University Archives, Special Collections Research Center, Georgetown University Library, Washington, DC., 264–67.

48. Quoted in Durkin, *Georgetown University*, 14.

49. Curran, *The Bicentennial History*, 200–1.

50. "Debate: Philonomosian, 1845–1868," box 1, folder 2: June 10, 1845 – May 21, 1848 "Debating Societies," Archives Subject Files, Georgetown University Archives, Special Collections Research Center, Georgetown University Library, Washington, DC.

51. *The Annual Address of the Philodemic Society of Georgetown College, Delivered at Commencement on July 28, 1831 by Daniel J. Desmond, Esq.* (Philadelphia: Kay, Jun. & Co., 1832).

52. *An Address Delivered before the Philodemic Society of Georgetown College, D.C., at the Annual Commencement, July 8, 1856, by Alexander A. Allemong, of South Carolina* (Washington, DC: William H. Moore, 1856).

53. George, "The Cultivation of Eloquence," 106.

54. "Debate: Philonomosian, 1845–1868."

55. "Debate: Philodemic, –1837," box 1, folder 4: 1830–1837 proceedings, "Debating Societies," Archives Subject Files, Georgetown University Archives, Special Collections Research Center, Georgetown University Library, Washington, DC.

56. Ibid.

57. Ibid.

58. "Debate: Philodemic, 1849–1866," box 4, folder 7: January 8, 1860–June 24, 1866.

59. Quoted in Curran, *The Bicentennial History of Georgetown* University, 219.

60. Daley, *Georgetown University*, 163.

61. "Rules of the Sodality," box 1, folder 333: G.U. Sodality, Undated—1831, "Sodality— ca. 1831–1970," Archives Subject Files, Georgetown University Archives, Special Collections Research Center, Georgetown University Library, Washington, DC.

62. Easby-Smith, *Georgetown University in the District of Columbia*, 258–61.

63. Curran, *The Bicentennial History*, 408–9.

64. Ibid., 209.

65. Ibid., 416.

66. Ibid., 417.

67. "Dimitry, Alexander," *The National Cyclopedia of American Biography*, Volume 10 (New York: James T. White & Company, 1909), 176; Walter Lynwood Fleming, *The South in the Building of the Nation*, Volume 11 (Richmond: The Southern Historical Publication Society, 1909), 282–83.

68. The phrase is drawn from St. Paul's Letter to the Ephesians 2:14 in which Paul writes of the oneness of Jew and Gentile in Christ.

69. G. Ronald Murphy, "Georgetown's Shield: Utraque Unum," in *Splendor and Wonder: Jesuit Character, Georgetown Spirit, and Liberal Education*, ed. William J. O'Brien (Washington, DC: Georgetown University Press, 1988), 23–38.

70. *An Address Delivered before the Philodemic Society of Georgetown College, D.C., by John C. C. Hamilton, Esq., of Washington, D.C.* (Washington, DC: Henry Polkinhorn, 1862), 3–4.

71. Ibid., 4.

72. "A Bill Donating Public Lands to the Several States Which May Provide Colleges for the Benefit of Agriculture and the Mechanic Arts," *The Congressional Globe* 27 pt. 2 (April 20, 1858), 35th, 1st. session, 1609.

4. "TO SPREAD THROUGHOUT THE LAND, AN ARMY OF PRACTICAL MEN"

1. Theodore Roosevelt, "The Man Who Works with His Hands," in *Semi-Centennial Celebration of Michigan State Agricultural College*, ed. Thomas C. Blaisdell (Chicago: University of Chicago Press, 1908), 251–52.

2. Ibid., 239.

3. Scott M. Gelber, *The University and the People: Envisioning American Higher Education in an Era of Populist Protest* (Madison: University of Wisconsin Press, 2011), 18–34;

Roger L. Williams, *The Origins of Federal Support for Higher Education: George W. Atherton and the Land-Grant College Movement* (University Park: Pennsylvania State University Press, 1991), 22–26.

4. Stanley M. Guralnick, *Science and the Ante-Bellum American College* (Philadelphia: American Philosophical Society, 1975), chapter 7.

5. John R. Thelin, *A History of American Higher Education* (Baltimore: Johns Hopkins University Press, 2004), 76–77.

6. Roger Geiger, "The Rise and Fall of Useful Knowledge: Higher Education for Science, Agriculture & the Mechanic Arts, 1850–1875," *History of Higher Education Annual* 18 (1998): 51.

7. "A Bill Donating Public Lands to the Several States which May Provide Colleges for the Benefit of Agriculture and the Mechanic Arts," *The Congressional Globe*, April 20, 1858, Vol. 27, pt. 2, 35th, 1st. session, 1609.

8. Terry S. Reynolds, "The Education of Engineers in America before the Morrill Act of 1862," *History of Education Quarterly* 32, no. 4 (1992): 463–67; Julianna Chaszar, "Leading and Losing in the Agricultural Education Movement: Freeman G. Cary and Farmer's College, 1846–1884," *History of Higher Education Annual* 18 (1998): 27.

9. Quoted in J. Shearer, "Agriculture: Report of the Com. on Agriculture: A Bill for the Encouragement of Agriculture," *Michigan Farmer* 2 (1844): 3.

10. "Agricultural College," *Michigan Farmer* 11, no. 9 (1853): 263.

11. Gelber, *The University and the People*, 18.

12. Joseph F. Kett, *The Pursuit of Knowledge under Difficulties: From Self-Improvement to Adult Education in America, 1750–1990* (Stanford, CA: Stanford University Press, 1994), 104.

13. On agricultural societies specifically, see Alfred Charles True, *A History of Agricultural Education in the United States, 1785–1925* (Washington, DC: United States Government Printing Press, 1929), 7–17.

14. Williams, *The Origins of Federal Support*, 23.

15. A. J. Angulo, *William Barton Rogers and the Idea of MIT* (Baltimore: Johns Hopkins University Press, 2009), 58–59, 88–89, 179–80, and fn 7.

16. Quoted in Angulo, *William Barton Rogers*, 88–89.

17. Quoted in Williams, *The Origins of Federal Support*, 25.

18. Margaret W. Rossiter, *The Emergence of Agricultural Science: Justus Liebig and the Americans, 1840–1880* (New Haven, CT: Yale University Press, 1975), 10; Williams, *The Origins of Federal Support*, 29–31.

19. True, *A History of Agricultural Education*, 17–24.

20. Reproduced in "Instruction in Agriculture," *Michigan Farmer* 10, no. 1 (1852): 62.

21. Williamjames Hull Hoffer, *To Enlarge the Machinery of Government: Congressional Debates and the Growth of the American State, 1858–1891* (Baltimore: Johns Hopkins University Press, 2007), 11.

22. On the expansion of education in Michigan, see Willis F. Dunbar and George S. May, *Michigan: A History of the Wolverine State* (Grand Rapids: William B. Eerdmans Co., 1970), especially chapter 14.

23. Quoted in True, *A History of Agricultural Education*, 57–58.

24. Madison Kuhn, *Michigan State: The First Hundred Years* (East Lansing: Michigan State University Press, 1955), 1–2.

25. *Acts of the Legislature of the State of Michigan, Passed at the Annual Session of 1849, with an Appendix Containing the State Treasurer's Annual Report* (Lansing: Munger and Pattison, 1849), 157–61.

26. Clarence A. Sommer, "Agriculture at the University of Michigan," in *Studies in the History of Higher Education in Michigan*, ed. Claude Eggertsen (Ann Arbor: University of Michigan, 1950), 38.

27. Henry Coleman, "Plan of an Agricultural Institution," *Michigan Farmer* 3, no. 5 (1845): 77.

28. Hubbard, Bela. "Memorial for a State Agricultural College in Michigan," in J. C. Holmes, ed., *Transactions of the State Agricultural Society, with Reports of County Agricultural Societies, for 1850* (Lansing: The Society, 1851), 56.

29. Holmes, J. C., Secretary, "Minutes of the Meeting of the Executive Committee of the State Agricultural Society," in Holmes, *Transactions of the State Agricultural Society for 1850*, 12–14.

30. Ibid., 15.

31. Constitution of the State of Michigan of 1850, Article 13, Section 11; http://www.legislature.mi.gov/documents/historical/miconstitution1850.htm.

32. Kuhn, *Michigan State*, 6–7.

33. Ibid., 8.

34. W. J. Beal, *History of the Michigan Agricultural College and Biographical Sketches of Trustees and Professors* (East Lansing: Michigan Agricultural College, 1915), 13–14.

35. Letter from Samuel Crowther to the president of the Agricultural College at Lansing, dated June 13, 1857, Office of the President, Joseph R. Williams, Letter of Application—A,B,C,D,E,F, 1857, box 871, folder 26, collection UA 2.1.1, Michigan State University Archives and Historical Collections.

36. "An Act for the Establishment of a State Agricultural School," reproduced in Ira Mayhew, ed. *Reports of the Superintendent of Public Instruction of the State of Michigan for the Years 1855, '56, and '57* (Lansing: Hosmer & Kerr, 1858), 271–76.

37. Quoted in Beal, *History of the Michigan Agricultural College*, 16.

38. *Catalogue State Agricultural College: 1857–1870*. Michigan State University Archives and Historical Collections.

39. "Address of the Honorable Joseph R. Williams, President of the Institution, May 13, 1857," *The Agricultural College of the State of Michigan* (Lansing: Hosmer & Fitch, 1857), 39–40.

40. Ibid.

41. *Catalogue 1857–1870*.

42. Mayhew, *Reports of the Superintendent of Public Instruction*, 310.

43. *Catalogue of the Officers and Students of the State Agricultural College, Lansing, Michigan 1861* (Lansing: John A. Kerr & Co., 1861), 17, 22.

44. True, *A History of Agricultural Education*, 62.

45. Quoted in Beal, *History of the Michigan Agricultural College*, 28.

46. "Report of the President. Agricultural College, Lansing, Michigan, April 1, 1858," in Mayhew, *Reports of the Superintendent of Public Instruction*, 313.

47. Kuhn, *Michigan State*, 19.

48. Diary by Allan Benton Morse, dated 1859, microfilm reel 1, collection c419, Michigan State University Archives and Historical Collections.

49. Diary entry by Edward Granger, dated December 8, 1858, box F.D., folder 1, collection UA 10.3.56, Diary, 1858–1860, Edward Granger Papers, Michigan State University Archives and Historical Collections.

50. Diary entry by Edward Granger, dated December 14, 1858.

51. Diary entries by Allan Benton Morse, dated June 11 and 12, 1859, microfilm reel 1, collection c419, Michigan State University Archives and Historical Collections.

52. Diary entry by Edward Granger, dated December 8, 1858.

53. Diary entries by Edward Granger, dated December 2 and 20, 1858, and January 9, 1859.

54. Diary entry by Edward Granger, dated December 17, 1858.

55. Diary entry by Edward Granger, dated January 11, 1859.

56. Diary entry by Edward Granger, dated December 23, 1858.

57. Diary entry by Allan Benton Morse, dated May 30, 1859.

58. Diary entry by Allan Benton Morse, dated June 6, 1859.

59. Diary entry by Allan Benton Morse, dated June 10, 1859.

60. Diary entry by Theophilus Capen Abbott, dated October 28, 1861, box 861, volume 1, collection UA 2.1.3, Diary of President T. C. Abbott, 1855–1885, Theophilus Capen Abbott Papers, Michigan State University Archives and Historical Collections.

61. Letter from Charles A. Jewell to brother, dated October 27, 1861, box F.D., folder 1, collection UA 10.3.5, Correspondence, 1860–1862, Charles A. Jewell II Papers, Michigan State University Archives and Historical Collections.

62. Letter from Charles A. Jewell to brother, dated July 25 (no year given, probably 1860).

63. Quoted in Kuhn, *Michigan State*, 22.

64. "Report of the President: Agricultural College, Lansing, Michigan, April 1, 1858," in Mayhew, *Reports of the Superintendent of Public Instruction*, 319–20.

65. Michigan State Board of Education Meeting Minutes, May 14, 1857, 24–25, Offices of Board of Trustees and President, Michigan State University Archives and Historical Collections. http://onthebanks.msu.edu/Object/3-F-1D9/meeting-minutes-1857/

66. "Report of the President: Agricultural College, Lansing, Michigan, April 1, 1858," 321.

67. Kuhn, *Michigan State*, 26–27.

68. "First Annual Catalogue of the Agricultural College of the State of Michigan, 1860," in *Catalogue State Agricultural College: 1857–1870*; "Term Time and Course of Studies," *The Agricultural College of the State of Michigan* (Lansing: Hosmer & Fitch, 1857), 55–56.

69. Kuhn, *Michigan State*, 27.

70. "Address of the Honorable Joseph R. Williams, May 13, 1857," 33–34.

71. On Justin Morrill and the Land Grant movement, see Hoffer, *To Enlarge the Machinery of Government*, especially chapters 1 and 2; Coy F. Cross, *Justin Smith Morrill: Father of the Land-Grant Colleges* (East Lansing: Michigan State University Press, 1999); Eldon L. Johnson, "Misconceptions about the Early Land-Grant Colleges," in *The History of Higher Education*, ed. Lester F. Goodchild and Harold S. Wechsler (Needham Heights, MA: Simon & Schuster, 1997), 222–33; Williams, *The Origins of Federal Support for Higher Education*; J. B. Edmond, *The Magnificent Charter: The Origin and Role of the Morrill Land-Grant Colleges and Universities* (Hicksville, NY: Exposition Press, 1978); Allan Nevins, *The State Universities and Democracy* (Urbana: University of Illinois Press, 1962); Edward Danforth Eddy, *Colleges for Our Land and Time: The Land-Grant Idea in American Education* (New York: Harper & Brothers, 1956); Earle D. Ross, *Democracy's College: The Land-Grant Movement in the Formative Stage* (Ames: Iowa State College Press, 1942); William B. Parker, *The Life and Public Services of Justin Smith Morrill* (Boston: Houghton Mifflin, 1924).

72. Quoted in Eddy, *Colleges for Our Land and Time*, 30.

73. Cross, *Justin Smith Morrill*, 79.

74. "A Bill Donating Public Lands to the Several States," 1609.

75. Hoffer, *To Enlarge the Machinery of Government*, 14–36.

76. Quoted in Cross, *Justin Smith Morrill*, 82.

77. Ross, *Democracy's College*, 54–56.

78. Beal, *History of the Michigan Agricultural College*, 36–39; Kuhn, *Michigan State*, 50.

79. "Speech of the Honorable Justin S. Morrill of Vermont on the Bill Granting Lands for Agricultural Colleges; delivered in the House of Representatives, April 20, 1858," *The Congressional Globe*, April 20, 1858, Vol. 27, pt. 2, 35th, 1st. session, 1609.

80. Address on Agricultural Education Delivered at the State Fair, Syracuse, New York, October 8, 1858, box 871, folder 47, collection UA 2.1.1, Office of the President: Joseph R. Williams, Michigan State University Archives and Historical Collections.

81. Cross, *Justin Smith Morrill*, 83.

82. Michigan State Board of Education Meeting Minutes, March 7 & 8, 1859, 46, Offices of Board of Trustees and President, Michigan State University Archives and Historical Collections. http://onthebanks.msu.edu/Object/3-F-1DB/meeting-minutes-1859/

83. Cross, *Justin Smith Morrill*, 83.

84. Act of July 2, 1862 (Morrill Act), Public Law 37–108, which established land-grant colleges, 07/02/1862; Enrolled Acts and Resolutions of Congress, 1789–1996; Record Group 11; General Records of the United States Government; National Archives.

85. Eddy, *Colleges for Our Land and Time*, 32–35.

86. "Annual Report of the State Board of Education." *Twenty-Third Annual Report of the Superintendent of Public Instruction of the State of Michigan, with Accompanying Documents, for the Year 1859* (Lansing: Hosmer & Kerr, 1860), 125.

87. The curricular changes are detailed in the 1859 annual report, 126–31.

88. "Fourth Annual Catalogue of the Agricultural College of the State of Michigan, 1860," *Catalogue State Agricultural College: 1857–1870.*

89. Diary entry by Theophilus Capen Abbott, dated February 28, 1860.

90. Diary entry by Theophilus Capen Abbott, dated February 29, 1860.

91. Diary entry by Theophilus Capen Abbott, dated March 1, 1860.

92. "An Act to Reorganize the Agricultural College of the State of Michigan, and to Establish a State Board of Agriculture," 15 March 1861, in James S. Dewey, ed. *The Compiled Laws of the State of Michigan*, vol. 1 (Lansing: W.S. George & Co., 1872), 1183.

93. Kuhn, *Michigan State*, 57–65.

94. "Report of L. R. Fiske to the State Board of Agriculture, dated May 29 1861," box 862H, folder 5, collection UA 2.1.2, Office of the President, Lewis R. Fiske Papers, Michigan State University Archives and Historical Collections.

95. Keith R. Widder, *Michigan Agricultural College: The Evolution of a Land Grant Philosophy, 1855–1925* (East Lansing: Michigan State University Press, 2005), 48–49.

96. Michael David Cohen, *Reconstructing the Campus: Higher Education and the American Civil War* (Charlottesville: University of Virginia Press, 2012).

97. "Report of the Faculty of the State Agricultural College," *Third Annual Report of the Secretary of the State Board of Agriculture of the State of Michigan for the Year 1864* (Lansing: John A. Kerr & Co., 1864), 112.

98. Letter from T. C. Abbott to Charles A. Jewell Esq., dated December 1, 1862, box F.D., folder 1, collection UA 10.3.5, Correspondence, 1860–1862, Charles A. Jewell II Papers, Michigan State University Archives and Historical Collections.

99. Kuhn, *Michigan State*, 69.

100. Widder, *Michigan Agricultural College*, 51–55.

101. *Catalogue of the Officers and Students of the State Agricultural College: 1864. Lansing, Michigan* (Lansing: John A. Kerr & Co., 1864), 12–14.

102. Ibid., 14.

103. On coeducation in western land-grant colleges and universities, see Andrea G. Radke-Moss, *Bright Epoch: Women and Coeducation in the American West* (Lincoln: University of Nebraska Press, 2008).

104. Kuhn, *Michigan State*, 136–41.

105. Williams, *The Origins of Federal Support*, 33–34; Edmond, *The Magnificent Charter*, 7–14.

106. Paul L. Dressel, *College to University: The Hannah Years at Michigan State, 1935–1969* (East Lansing: Michigan State University Publications, 1987); David A. Thomas, *Michigan State College: John Hannah and the Creation of a World University, 1926–1969* (East Lansing: Michigan State University Press, 2008).

5. "THE INSTRUCTION NECESSARY TO THE PRACTICAL DUTIES OF THE PROFESSION"

1. Benjamin Franklin Gilbert, *Pioneers for One Hundred Years: San Jose State College, 1857–1957* (San Jose: San Jose State College, 1957); Benjamin Gilbert and Charles Burdick, *Washington Square, 1857–1979: The History of San Jose State University* (San José: San José State University, 1979); James P. Walsh, *San José State University: An Interpretive History, 1950–2000* (San José: San José State University, 2003); James P. Walsh, *One and the Same: The History of Continuing Education at San José State University, 1857–2007* (San José: San José State University, 2006).

2. On the history of teachers' institutes, see James W. Fraser, *Preparing America's Teachers: A History* (New York: Teachers College Press, 2007), chapter 4.

3. Ruth Royce, *Historical Sketch of the State Normal School at San José* (Sacramento: J. D. Young, Supt. State Printing, 1889), 8.

4. Report of the Committee on State Normal Schools, submitted to the Honorable A. J. Moulder, Superintendent of Public Instruction, San Francisco, California, January 2, 1862.

5. Ibid.

6. Martha M. Knapp, "Fallen Fetters," *The Class Paper*, May 20, 1880, 3.

7. "Choice of an Occupation," *The Normal Index* 1, no. 6 (1886): 69.

8. Christine A. Ogren, *The American State Normal School: "An Instrument of Great Good"* (New York: Palgrave Macmillan, 2005), 48.

9. Quoted in Nita Katharine Pyburn, *The History of the Development of a Single System of Education in Florida, 1822–1903* (Tallahassee: Florida State University, 1954), 208.

10. William Couper, *One Hundred Years at V.M.I.* (Richmond, VA: Garrett and Massie, 1939), 93.

11. Bradford Wineman, "J.T.L. Preston and the Origins of the Virginia Military Institute, 1834–42," *The Virginia Magazine of History and Biography* 114, no. 2 (2006): 253. See also Jennifer R. Green, "Networks of Military Educators: Middle-Class Stability and Professionalization in the Late Antebellum South," *The Journal of Southern History* 73, no. 1 (2007): 39–74.

12. As important as normal schools have been to the development of U.S. higher education, many historians have paid them little mind. Frederick Rudolph assigned just two out of five hundred pages of *The American College and University* to normal schools, while otherwise excellent historical studies by Barbara Solomon (*In the Company of Educated Women*) and John Thelin (*A History of American Higher Education*) provide relatively little analysis of normal schools' development. Laurence Veysey's celebrated work *The Emergence of the American University* fails completely to examine them. This is not to say that normal schools are understudied. Scholars such as James Fraser, Christine Ogren, Geraldine Jonçich Clifford, Richard J. Altenbaugh, Kathleen Underwood, Donald Warren, and Jurgen Herbst have all conducted investigations of these institutions. Rarely, however, have these studies been conducted in the context of broader histories of higher education. Fraser, *Preparing America's Teachers*; Ogren, *The American State Normal School*; Geraldine Jonçich Clifford, *"Equally in View": The University of California, Its Women, and the Schools* (Berkeley: Center for Studies in Higher Education and Institute of Governmental Studies Press, 1995); Richard J. Altenbaugh and Kathleen Underwood, "The Evolution of Normal Schools," in *Places Where Teachers Are Taught*, ed. John I. Goodlad, Roger Soder, and Kenneth A. Sirotnik (San Francisco: Jossey-Bass, 1990), 136–86; Donald Warren, ed. *American Teachers: Histories of a Profession at Work* (New York: Macmillan, 1989); Jurgen Herbst, *And Sadly Teach: Teacher Education and Professionalization in American Culture* (Madison: University of Wisconsin Press, 1989); Frederick Rudolph, *The American College and University: A History* (New York: Knopf, 1962); Barbara Miller Solomon, *In the Company of Educated Women: A History of Women and Higher Education in America* (New

Haven: Yale University Press, 1985); John R. Thelin, *A History of American Higher Education* (Baltimore: Johns Hopkins University Press, 2004); Laurence R. Veysey, *The Emergence of the American University* (Chicago: University of Chicago Press, 1965).

13. For a detailed explanation of this omission, see Christine Ogren, "The History and Historiography of Teacher Preparation in the United States: A Synthesis, Analysis, and Potential Contributions to Higher Education History," in *Higher Education: Handbook of Theory and Research*, ed. John C. Smart and Michael B. Paulsen (New York: Springer, 2013), 405–58.

14. Quoted in Patricia A. Palmieri, "From Republican Motherhood to Race Suicide: Arguments on the Higher Education of Women in the United States, 1820–1920," in *The History of Higher Education*, ed. Lester F. Goodchild and Harold S. Wechsler (Needham Heights, MA: Simon & Schuster, 1997), 177.

15. Although America's first publicly supported normal school was founded in Lexington in 1839, private efforts to provide teacher training, such as the Phillips Academy Teachers' Seminary in Andover, Massachusetts, were established earlier in the century. Fraser, *Preparing America's Teachers*, 14–20.

16. Robert W. Train, "Recovering Spanish-Language Education in Alta California: Ecologies, Ideologies and Intertexualities," in *Recovering the U.S. Hispanic Literary Heritage*, ed. Gabriela Baeza Ventura and Clara Lomas (Houston: Arte Público Press, 2011), 113–14.

17. Carl F. Kaestle, *Pillars of the Republic: Common Schools and American Society, 1780–1860* (New York: Hill and Wang, 1983), 81.

18. On women's education during the early national period, as well as a thorough examination of the arguments for women becoming teachers during the antebellum era, see Mary Kelley, *Learning to Stand and Speak: Women, Education, and Public Life in America's Republic* (Chapel Hill: University of North Carolina Press, 2006); Margaret A. Nash, *Women's Education in the United States, 1780–1840* (New York: Palgrave Macmillan, 2005), especially chapter 4; Andrea L. Turpin, "The Ideological Origins of the Women's College: Religion, Class, and Curriculum in the Educational Visions of Catharine Beecher and Mary Lyon," *History of Education Quarterly* 50, no. 2 (2010): 133–58.

19. Geraldine Jonçich Clifford, "Man/Woman/Teacher: Gender, Family, and Career in American Educational History," in *American Teachers: Histories of a Profession at Work*, ed. Donald Warren (New York: Macmillan, 1989), 293–343.

20. Nash, *Women's Education in the United States*, 60; Ogren, *The American State Normal School*, 12.

21. Mount Holyoke provided an important exception. Elizabeth Alden Green, *Mary Lyon and Mount Holyoke: Opening the Gates* (Hanover, NH: University Press of New England, 1979).

22. Ogren, *The American State Normal School*, 48.

23. John B. Freed, *Educating Illinois: Illinois State University, 1857–2007* (Virginia Beach: Donning Company Publishers, 2009), 47.

24. *The Annual Report of the Board of Education, to the Common Council of San Francisco, September 1, 1854* (San Francisco: Whitton, Towne & Co., 1854), 17.

25. Ibid., 17–18.

26. "San Francisco Public Schools," *Sacramento Daily Union*, May 21, 1855.

27. Gilbert and Burdick, *Washington Square*, 8–10.

28. Fraser, *Preparing America's Teachers*, 80–81.

29. *Eighth Annual Report of the Superintendent of Public Schools, of the City and County of San Francisco* (San Francisco: Whitton, Towne & Co., 1858), 18–19.

30. *Daily Alta California*, January 18, 1858, 2.

31. *Daily Alta California*, March 27, 1861, 3.

32. "Act to Establish and Maintain a State Normal School (May 2, 1862)," *The Statutes of California* (Sacramento: Benj. P. Avery, State Printer, 1862), 472–73.

33. Ibid.

34. Fraser, *Preparing America's Teachers*, 123.

35. "The State Normal School," *Daily Evening Bulletin*, May 22, 1862, 3.

36. Gilbert, *Pioneers for One Hundred Years*, 21–22. Holmes was one of a group of men historian Charles A. Harper characterized as "the sons of Bridgewater." Studying under Nicholas Tillinghast at the Massachusetts State Normal School in Bridgewater between 1840 and 1853, these men carried, according to Harper, "the flame of Bridgewater fire" to states throughout the nation where they served as normal school principals. Charles A. Harper, *A Century of Public Teacher Education: The Story of the State Teachers Colleges as They Evolved from the Normal Schools* (Washington, DC: American Association of Teachers Colleges, 1939), 28.

37. "Report of the Principal of the State Normal School." *Thirteenth Annual Report of the Superintendent of Public Instruction of the State of California for the Year 1863* (Sacramento: Department of Public Instruction, 1863), 192–93.

38. "Reminiscences by Martin V. Ashbrook, Class of May, 1864." Quoted in Royce, *Historical Sketch of the State Normal School at San José*, 22.

39. Diary entries by Ahira Holmes, dated October 31, 1862 and November 20, 1862, box 4, Ahira Holmes Diary 1862, series II: San José State Normal School Principals and Early Presidents Records, 1862–1915, San José State University Special Collections and Archives; Gilbert, *Pioneers for One Hundred Years*, 27.

40. Diary entry by Ahira Holmes, dated January 2, 1863.

41. Diary entry by Ahira Holmes, dated October 15, 1863.

42. Diary entry by Ahira Holmes, dated December 22, 1863.

43. Diary entry by Ahira Holmes, dated May 20, 1864.

44. Diary entry by Ahira Holmes, dated December 22, 1863.

45. Diary entry by Ahira Holmes, dated February 18, 1865.

46. John Aubrey Douglass, *The California Idea and American Higher Education* (Stanford: Stanford University Press, 2000), chapter 1.

47. "Reminiscences by Martin V. Ashbrook, Class of May, 1864." Quoted in Royce, *Historical Sketch of the State Normal School*, 23.

48. Gilbert, *Pioneers for One Hundred Years*, 37–38.

49. Quoted in Maxine Ollie Merlino, "A History of the California State Normal Schools: Their Origin, Growth, and Transformation into Teachers Colleges," Ed.D. Thesis, University of Southern California, 1962, 36.

50. Diary entry by Ahira Holmes, dated March 18, 1864.

51. Although it was in the State Normal School's early years that Ahira Holmes identified students' rush to graduate as a problem, Ruth Royce, writing more than twenty years later, claimed that this continued to pose "a great hindrance to the best success of the school." Royce, *Historical Sketch of the State Normal School*, 21.

52. Gilbert, *Pioneers for One Hundred Years*, chapter 5.

53. Ibid., 31; "Report of the Principal submitted by Charles H. Allen to the Board of Trustees," *Course Catalogue for California State Normal School 1874–1875*, 30; *Course Catalogue for California State Normal School from Academic Year Ending March 27, 1873* (Sacramento: T. A. Springer, State Printer, 1873), 21.

54. Royce, *Historical Sketch of the State Normal School*, 35–36.

55. Quoted in Gilbert, *Pioneers for One Hundred Years*, 48.

56. "Report of the Principal submitted by Charles H. Allen to the Board of Trustees," *Course Catalogue 1874–1875*, 27–28.

57. By the 1870s, this formulation had become common at normal schools throughout the United States. See Ogren, *The American State Normal School*, 87.

58. *Course Catalogue for California State Normal School 1877–1878* (Sacramento: F. P. Thompson, Supt. State Printing, 1878), 40–42.

59. Suzanne Bordelon, "Participating on an 'Equal Footing': The Rhetorical Significance of California State Normal School in the Late Nineteenth Century," *Rhetoric Society Quarterly* 41, no. 2 (2011): 175.

60. *Course Catalogue 1877–1878*, 40–42.

61. Gilbert, *Pioneers for One Hundred Years*, 94.

62. "Choice of an Occupation," 12.

63. Ogren, *The American State Normal School*, 151.

64. Ibid., 160.

65. Sarah A. J. Locke, "Is It Worth While?," *The Class Paper*, May 20, 1880, 2.

66. Quoted in Ogren, *The American State Normal School*, 168.

67. Journal entitled *Philomathian Society*, dated October 23, 1894, program for December 13, 1894, box 33, Normal School Societies Minutes and Records 1873–1918, series IV: Student, Faculty, and Alumni Records and Publications 1863–1927, San José State Normal School Records, 1869–1990, San José State University Special Collections and Archives.

68. Ogren, "The History and Historiography of Teacher Preparation."

69. "Co-Operation," *The Normal Index* 1, no. 7 (1886): 69; "The Text-Book," *The Normal Index* 2, no. 1 (1886): 9; "The Rod," *The Normal Index* 1, no. 5 (1886): 45; "The Progressive Teacher," *The Normal Index* 2, no. 1 (1886): 8.

70. See, for instance, Elise M. Asmus, "Single Women," *The Senior Journal*, December 18, 1884, 1; Emma Davis, "Girlhood and Womanhood," *The Class Paper*, May 20, 1880, 3.

71. Royce, *Historical Sketch of the State Normal School*, 65–66; Gilbert, *Pioneers for One Hundred Years*, 76–77.

72. Ogren, *The American State Normal School*, 57.

73. "Report of the Principal submitted by Charles H. Allen to the Board of Trustees," *Course Catalogue 1874–1875*, 30; Ogren, *The American State Normal School*, 58.

74. Fraser, *Preparing America's Teachers*, 146.

75. Ibid., 147.

76. Gilbert, *Pioneers for One Hundred Years*, 115.

77. Christopher Jencks and David Riesman, *The Academic Revolution* (Garden City, NY: Doubleday, 1968), 231–36; Fraser, *Preparing America's Teachers*, 125–30.

78. Douglass, *The California Idea and American Higher Education*, 137–40.

79. Gilbert, *Pioneers for One Hundred Years*, 135–39.

80. This change did not come without a price. As James Fraser has observed, "The new institutions had a level of academic quality and status that their predecessors did not. But it was a quality and status that came at a considerable cost in terms not only of institutional focus but also the breadth of the education offered to students and the commitment to teaching demanded of them." *Preparing America's Teachers*, 128.

81. The State Normal School of Manual Arts and Home Economics, established in Santa Barbara in 1910, was a notable exception. See Douglass, *The California Idea and American Higher Education*, especially chapters 5 and 6.

82. Jurgen Herbst, *And Sadly Teach*, 84.

83. Jurgen Herbst, "Nineteenth-Century Normal Schools in the United States: A Fresh Look," *History of Education Quarterly* 9, no. 3 (1980): 227.

84. For a statewide comparison, see Ogren, *The American State Normal School*, 66.

85. Madison Kuhn, *Michigan State: The First Hundred Years* (East Lansing: Michigan State University Press, 1955), 118–19.

86. Scott M. Gelber, *The University and the People: Envisioning American Higher Education in an Era of Populist Protest* (Madison: University of Wisconsin Press, 2011).

6. "TO QUALIFY ITS STUDENTS FOR PERSONAL SUCCESS"

1. Thorstein Veblen, *The Higher Learning in America: A Memorandum on the Conduct of Universities by Business Men* (New York: B. W. Huebsch, 1918), 194–96.

2. Ibid., 203.

3. See, for instance, Roger L. Geiger, "The Commercialization of the University," *American Journal of Education* 110, no. 4 (2004): 389–99; Marvin Lazerson, *Higher Education and the American Dream: Success and Its Discontents* (New York: Central European University Press, 2010).

4. Alan Trachtenberg, *The Incorporation of America: Culture and Society in the Gilded Age* (New York: Hill and Wang, 1982), 5.

5. Norman E. Tutorow, *The Governor: The Life and Legacy of Leland Stanford*, 2 vols. (Spokane: The Arthur C. Clark Company, 2004), 701–41; Hubert H. Bancroft, *History of the Life of Leland Stanford* (Oakland, CA: Biobooks, 1952), 89–124.

6. Laurence R. Veysey, *The Emergence of the American University* (Chicago: University of Chicago Press, 1965), 69; David Starr Jordan, *The Foundation Ideals of Stanford University* (Stanford: Stanford University, 1915), 7.

7. Frederick Rudolph, *The American College and University: A History* (New York: Knopf, 1962), 265–68; Roger L. Geiger, *To Advance Knowledge: The Growth of America's Research Universities, 1900–1940* (New York: Oxford University Press, 1986), 6–7; John R. Thelin, *A History of American Higher Education* (Baltimore: Johns Hopkins University Press, 2004), 117–18.

8. Ellen Coit Elliott, "The Cornell Colony at Palo Alto," in *The First Year at Stanford: Sketches of Pioneer Days at Leland Stanford Junior University*, ed. Alice Windsor Kimball (San Francisco: The Stanley-Taylor Company, 1905), 29–47.

9. "Stanford Interviewed," *Daily Palo Alto*, October 19, 1892, 2.

10. "Editorial," *The Sequoia* 2, no. 15 (1892): 177–78.

11. *Stanford University: The Founding Grant with Amendments, Legislation and Court Decrees* (Stanford: Stanford University Press, 1971).

12. David Starr Jordan, *The Days of a Man*, 2 vols., vol. 2 (New York: World Book Company, 1922), 690; John C. Scott, "The Mission of the University: Medieval to Postmodern Transformations," *The Journal of Higher Education* 77, no. 1 (2006): 25.

13. David Starr Jordan, "The Higher Sacrifice," *Daily Palo Alto*, May 27, 1896, 12.

14. Edward McNall Burns, *David Starr Jordan: Prophet of Freedom* (Stanford: Stanford University Press, 1953), 171–72.

15. Jordan, *The Foundation Ideals of Stanford University*, 16; Burns, *David Starr Jordan*, 155–57.

16. David Starr Jordan, "Over-Education," *The Sequoia* 3, no. 9 (1893): 112–13.

17. Ibid., 57–58.

18. J. David Hoeveler Jr., "The University and the Social Gospel: The Intellectual Origins of the 'Wisconsin Idea,'" in *The History of Higher Education*, ed. Lester F. Goodchild and Harold S. Wechsler (Needham Heights, MA: Simon & Schuster, 1997), 234. On the Wisconsin Idea, see Merle E. Curti and Vernon Carstensen, *The University of Wisconsin: A History 1848–1925*, vol. 2 of 2 (Madison: University of Wisconsin Press, 1949), chapter 3. On progressivism in higher education more broadly, see Rudolph, *The American College and University*, chapter 17.

19. Curti and Carstensen, *The University of Wisconsin*, 2 and 89 n3.

20. Nicholas Murray Butler, *Scholarship and Service: The Policies and Ideals of a National University in a Modern Democracy* (New York: Charles Scribner's Sons, 1921), 11.

21. Michael Dennis, *Lessons in Progress: State Universities and Progressivism in the New South, 1880–1920* (Urbana: University of Illinois Press, 2001).

22. John Aubrey Douglass, *The California Idea and American Higher Education* (Stanford: Stanford University Press, 2000), 96.

23. John Casper Branner served as Stanford president for just two years following Jordan's resignation. In 1915, Wilbur assumed the role, which he held for the next twenty-eight years. On Wilbur's tenure, see Edgar Eugene Robinson and Paul Carroll Edwards, eds., *The Memoirs of Ray Lyman Wilbur* (Stanford: Stanford University Press, 1960).

24. Ray Lyman Wilbur, *Human Hopes: Addresses & Papers on Education, Citizenship, & Social Problems* (Stanford: Stanford University Press, 1940), 15–16.

25. Ibid., 17.

26. "Commencement Exercises," *The Daily Palo Alto*, May 29, 1895, 3.

27. "Jenkins, O.P. Commencement Address (1910)," 14–16. Weymouth Family Papers, Box 3, Folder 4, Stanford University Archives.

28. By 1899, women's enrollment had increased so quickly that Jane Stanford, who had strongly supported women's admission, became anxious that the University was becoming a "girls' school." Stanford amended the institution's founding grant to impose a cap of five hundred women, or 40 percent of the student body. After reaching the cap just four years later, the percentage of women attending Stanford declined steadily until 1932, when the University Board of Trustees eliminated the cap and again set women's enrollment at 40 percent. The ratio remained university policy until 1973. Douglass, *The California Idea and American Higher Education*, 95; Orrin Leslie Elliott, *Stanford University: The First Twenty-Five Years* (Stanford: Stanford University Press, 1937), 132–36; David Starr Jordan, "The Policy of the Stanford Unversity," *Educational Review* 4 (1892): 1–5.

29. "Editorial," *Daily Palo Alto*, September 7, 1893, 2.

30. Geiger, *To Advance Knowledge*, 13.

31. "Editorial," *The Sequoia* 5, no. 7 (1895): 98.

32. "Letter to Mother dated February 4, 1900," Student Letters and Reminiscences, Box 2, Series 7, Frederick Jewel Perry Letters, 1896–1900, Folder 15, Letters 1899–1900, Stanford University Archives.

33. "Lecture Course," *The Daily Palo Alto*, September 21, 1892, 1.

34. Ibid., 1.

35. Grover Cleveland, "Does a College Education Pay?," *The Saturday Evening Post*, May 26, 1900, 1089.

36. Ibid.

37. Thelin, *A History of American Higher Education*, 129. Also see Hugh Hawkins, "American Universities and the Inclusion of Professional Schools," *History of Higher Education Annual* 13 (1993): 53–68; W. Bruce Leslie, *Gentlemen and Scholars: College and Community in the "Age of the University," 1865–1917* (University Park: Pennsylvania State University Press, 1992); Penina Migdal Glazer and Miriam Slater, *Unequal Colleagues: The Entrance of Women into the Professions, 1890–1940* (New Brunswick, NJ: Rutgers University Press, 1987); Burton J. Bledstein, *The Culture of Professionalism: The Middle Class and the Development of Higher Education in America* (New York: W. W. Norton & Company, 1976); Christopher Jencks and David Riesman, *The Academic Revolution* (Garden City, NY: Doubleday, 1968), chapter 5.

38. Rudolph, *The American College and University*, 343.

39. For a concise history of these schools, see J. Pearce Mitchell, *Stanford University, 1916–1941* (Stanford: The Board of Trustees of the Leland Stanford Junior University, 1958), 77–94. On the School of Education, also see Jesse B. Sears and Adin D. Henderson, *Cubberley of Stanford and His Contribution to American Education* (Stanford: Stanford University Press, 1957). On the Schools of Medicine and Nursing, also see John L. Wilson, *Stanford University School of Medicine and the Predecessor Schools: An Historical Perspective* (Stanford: Stanford University Lane Medical Library, 1999).

40. Howard Bromberg, "Our Professor, the President," *Stanford Lawyer*, Fall 1991, 10–15.

41. "Legal Legacies: A Brief History of the Stanford Law School," *Stanford Magazine*, September 1993, 43.

42. Marion R. Kirkwood and William B. Owens, "A Brief History of the Stanford Law School, 1893–1946," March 1961, http://www.law.stanford.edu/sites/default/files/landing-page/4952/doc/slspublic/historysls.pdf. Accessed September 2, 2016.

43. Quoted in Mitchell, *Stanford University*, 79.

44. Ibid., 80.

45. David O. Levine, *The American College and the Culture of Aspiration, 1915–1940* (Ithaca, NY: Cornell University Press, 1986), 19.

46. Ibid., 56.

47. Veblen, *The Higher Learning in America*, 204.

48. Thelin, *A History of American Higher Education*, 156.

49. Daniel A. Clarke, *Creating the College Man: American Mass Magazines and Middle-Class Manhood, 1890–1915* (Madison: University of Wisconsin Press, 2010), 14.

50. "Editorial," *The Sequoia* 2, no. 3 (1892): 38.

51. On the history of intercollegiate athletics, see John Thelin, *Games Colleges Play: Scandal and Reform in Intercollegiate Athletics* (Baltimore: Johns Hopkins University Press, 1996); Ronald Smith, *Sports and Freedom: The Rise of Big-Time College Athletics* (New York: Oxford University Press, 1988). On the development of athletics at Stanford, see Gary Cavalli, *Stanford Sports* (Stanford: Stanford Alumni Association, 1982); Don E. Liebendorfer, *The Color of Life Is Red: A History of Stanford Athletics, 1892–1972* (Stanford: Stanford University Department of Athletics, 1972); Emanuel B. McDonald, *Sam McDonald's Farm: Stanford Reminiscences by Emanuel B. "Sam" McDonald* (Stanford: Stanford University Press, 1954); Norris E. James, ed. *Fifty Years on the Quad* (Stanford: Stanford Alumni Association, 1938), 155–242; Frank Angell, "The Early History of Athletics at Stanford," in *The First Year at Stanford: Sketches of Pioneer Days at Leland Stanford Junior University*, ed. Alice Windsor Kimball (San Francisco: The Stanley-Taylor Company, 1905), 48–67.

52. "Annual Report of the President of Stanford University for the Thirty-Fourth Academic Year Ending August 31, 1925." *Stanford University Bulletin*, Fifth Series, No. 3 (January 1, 1926), 244–45.

53. As at a number of US colleges and universities, Stanford replaced football with rugby between 1906 and 1917 due to the increasing number of injuries and fatalities associated with the former game. On football's historic popularity in intercollegiate athletics, see John Sayle Watterson, *College Football: History, Spectacle, Controversy* (Baltimore: Johns Hopkins University Press, 2000); Michael Oriard, *Reading Football: How the Popular Press Created an American Spectacle* (Chapel Hill: University of North Carolina Press, 1993); Rudolph, *The American College and University*, chapter 18. On football's commercialization, see David L. Westby and Allen Sack, "The Commercialization and Functional Rationalization of College Football: Its Origins," *The Journal of Higher Education* 47, no. 6 (1976): 625–47.

54. "Editorial," *The Sequoia* 1, no. 12 (1892), 344–45.

55. "Annual Report of the President, 1925," 19.

56. Thelin, *A History of American Higher Education*, 178–79.

57. Ibid., 180.

58. For corporate influences on university management, see Christopher Newfield, *Ivy and Industry: Business and the Making of the American University, 1880–1980* (Durham, NC: Duke University Press, 2003), especially chapter 4.

59. Christopher J. Lucas, *American Higher Education: A History*, 2nd ed. (New York: Palgrave Macmillan, 2006), 199.

60. On changes in college and university governance during this period, see Clyde W. Barrow, *Universities and the Capitalist State: Corporate Liberalism and the Reconstruction of American Higher Education, 1894–1928* (Madison: University of Wisconsin Press, 1990).

61. Lucas, *American Higher Education*, 196.

62. Veblen, *The Higher Learning in America*, 63–70.

63. "The Point of View," *Scribner's Magazine*, July 1907, 123.

64. Veysey, *The Emergence of the American University*, 121–22.

65. John Marshall Barker, *Colleges in America* (Cleveland: Cleveland Printing and Publishing, 1894), 146–47.

66. Lucas, *American Higher Education*, 177–78.

67. See Anja Werner, *The Transatlantic World of Higher Education: Americans at German Universities, 1776–1914* (New York: Berghahn 2013).

68. Lucas, *American Higher Education*, 177–78.

69. On the history of Stanford University's motto, see http://www.stanford.edu/dept/pres-provost/president/speeches/951005dieluft.html. Accessed September 2, 2016.

70. Edwin E. Slosson, *Great American Universities* (New York: Macmillan, 1910), 114.

71. David Starr Jordan, *The Days of a Man*, 689.

72. "Fifth Annual Report of the President of the University for the Year Ending July 31, 1908." Leland Stanford Junior University Trustees' Series, No. 17 (Palo Alto: Stanford University, 1908), 24–31.

73. Bruce Kimball, *The "True Professional Ideal": A History in America* (Lanham, MD: Rowman & Littlefield, 1995), 200–4.

74. Ibid., 271.

75. Thelin, *A History of American Higher Education*, 128.

76. Rudolph, *The American College and University*, 410–16.

77. The most comprehensive work on the history of academic freedom continues to be Richard Hofstadter and Walter P. Metzger, *The Development of Academic Freedom in the United States* (New York: Columbia University Press, 1955). For a more recent examination, see Matthew W. Finkin and Robert C. Post, *For the Common Good: Principles of American Academic Freedom* (New Haven, CT: Yale University Press, 2009). For an extensive literature review, see Stephen H. Aby and James C. Kuhn, *Academic Freedom: A Guide to the Literature* (Westport, CT: Greenwood 2000).

78. Hofstadter and Metzger, *The Development of Academic Freedom in the United States*, 425–36.

79. Ibid., 330–32, 340–41.

80. The Ross case is examined in Elliott, *Stanford University*, 326–78; Hofstadter and Metzger, *The Development of Academic Freedom*, 438–45; Edith R. Mirrielees, *Stanford: The Story of a University* (New York: G.P. Putnam's Sons, 1959), 98–107; Veysey, *The Emergence of the American University*, 399–407.

81. Edward A. Ross, *Seventy Years of It: An Autobiography* (New York: D. Appleton–Century Company, 1936), 64–65.

82. Veysey, *The Emergence of the American University*, 400.

83. J. L. Stanford. "Address on the Right of Free Speech to the Board of Trustees of the Leland Stanford Junior University, April 25, 1903." Stanford University, 1903, 6–8.

84. Elliott, *Stanford University*, 340–41.

85. Ibid., 352–53.

86. Ross, *Seventy Years of It*, 69–72.

87. See, for instance, *San Francisco Chronicle*, November 15, 1900; *New York Evening Post*, February 23, 1901.

88. Quoted in Elliott, *Stanford University*, 442.

89. Hofstadter and Metzger, *The Development of Academic Freedom*, 442.

90. On the rise of the scientific spirit during this period, also see Andrew Jewett, *Science, Democracy, and the American University* (Cambridge, UK: Cambridge University Press, 2012), part one.

91. Julie A. Reuben, *The Making of the Modern University: Intellectual Transformation and the Marginalization of Morality* (Chicago: University of Chicago Press, 1996), 13.

92. *Stanford University: The Founding Grant*, 6.

93. "Memorial Church," *The Daily Palo Alto*, January 25, 1903, 2.

94. Reuben, *The Making of the Modern University*, 169.

95. Ibid., 168.

96. See, for instance, George M. Marsden, *The Soul of the American University: From Protestant Establishment to Established Nonbelief* (Oxford, UK: Oxford University Press, 1994); George M. Marsden and Bradley J. Longfield, eds., *The Secularization of the Academy* (New York: Oxford University Press, 1992), 9–45.

7. "THIS IS TO BE OUR PROFESSION—TO SERVE THE WORLD"

1. Letter from "Daisy" to Mother, dated November 1, 1881, Classification: 80, Students, Box #1395, "Brooks, Esther Herrick," Folder: "Brooks, Esther Herrick—Correspondence to Family (Sept.–Dec. 1881) and Frona Marie (1883)," Smith College Archives.

2. Letter from "Daisy" to Mother, dated October 21, 1879.

3. Sheila Rothman, *Woman's Proper Place: A History of Changing Ideals and Practices, 1870 to the Present* (New York: Basic Books, 1978).

4. "After College," *Smith College Weekly* 2, no. 6 (1911): 1–2.

5. For a contemporary overview of women's higher education published one year following Smith's opening, see "Education," *The Atlantic Monthly* Sept. 1876, 380–84. On the origins of women's colleges, specifically, see Andrea L. Turpin, "The Ideological Origins of the Women's College: Religion, Class, and Curriculum in the Educational Visions of Catharine Beecher and Mary Lyon," *History of Education Quarterly* 50, no. 2 (2010): 133–58. On the history of Smith College, see Laurenus Clark Seelye, *The Early History of Smith College, 1871–1910* (New York: Houghton Mifflin, 1923); Elizabeth Deering Hanscom, Helen French Greene, and John Morton Greene, *Sophia Smith and the Beginnings of Smith College* (Northampton, MA: Smith College, 1925); *Historical Handbook of Smith College*, (Northampton, MA: Smith College, 1932); Jacqueline Van Voris, *College: A Smith Mosaic* (West Springfield, MA: Smith College, 1975); William Allan Neilson. "Smith College: The First Seventy Years," unpublished typescript ca. 1949, Smith College Archives, http://clio.fivecolleges.edu/smith/pres-neilson/.

6. On the history of the "Seven Sisters," see Elaine Kendall, *"Peculiar Institutions": An Informal History of the Seven Sisters Colleges* (New York: Putnam, 1976).

7. Entry no. 9. Personal Journal of Sophia Smith: Transcript with annotation by John M. Greene, 1861–1870, Smith College: Key Founding Documents, http://clio.fivecolleges.edu/smith/ss-journal/text/?page=9.

8. Helen Lefkowitz Horowitz, *Alma Mater: Design and Experience in the Women's Colleges from Their Nineteenth-Century Beginnings to the 1930s* (New York: Alfred A. Knopf, 1984), 11.

9. "Last Will and Testament of Miss Sophia Smith, Late of Hatfield, Mass," http://clio.fivecolleges.edu/smith/ss-wills/1870/transcript.htm.

10. Paula Baker, "The Domestication of Politics: Women and Political Society, 1780–1920," *The American Historical Review* 89, no. 3 (1984): 620–47.

11. "Last Will and Testament of Miss Sophia Smith, Late of Hatfield, Mass."

12. Baker, "The Domestication of Politics," 625, 635.

13. Ibid., 625.

14. "Last Will and Testament of Miss Sophia Smith, Late of Hatfield, Mass."

15. *Addresses at the Inauguration of Rev. L. Clark Seelye as President of Smith College, and the Dedication of Its Academic Building, July 14, 1875* (Springfield, MA: Clark W. Bryan and Co., 1875), 32. The words for the seal were borrowed from the Second Epistle of Peter 1:5: "And beside this, giving all diligence, add to your faith virtue; and to virtue knowledge." For Seelye's biography, see Harriet Chapin Seelye Rhees, *Laurenus Clark Seelye: First President of Smith College* (New York: Houghton Mifflin, 1929).

16. "Last Will and Testament of Miss Sophia Smith, Late of Hatfield, Mass."

17. Barbara Miller Solomon, *In the Company of Educated Women: A History of Women and Higher Education in America* (New Haven, CT: Yale University Press, 1985), chapter 4.

18. Patricia A. Palmieri, "From Republican Motherhood to Race Suicide: Arguments on the Higher Education of Women in the United States, 1820–1920," in *The History of Higher Education*, ed. Lester F. Goodchild and Harold S. Wechsler (Needham Heights, MA: Simon & Schuster, 1997), 176.

19. Lynn D. Gordon, *Gender and Higher Education in the Progressive Era* (New Haven, CT: Yale University Press, 1990), 13–21.

20. Mabel Newcomer, *A Century of Higher Education for American Women* (New York: Harper & Brothers, 1959), 29–30.

21. Quoted in Gordon, *Gender and Higher Education in the Progressive Era*, 18–19.

22. Thomas Dyer, *Theodore Roosevelt and the Idea of Race* (Baton Rouge: Louisiana State University Press, 1992), chapter 7.

23. Seelye, *The Early History of Smith College*, 14.

24. Letter from John M. Greene to Sophia Smith, dated April 28, 1869, Key Founding Documents, Origins Collection, 1868–1933, Series 1: "Beginnings of Smith College: Original Documents Assembled by John M. Greene, 1868–1933," Smith College Archives.

25. Horowitz, *Alma Mater*, 77–78.

26. Seelye, *The Early History of Smith College*, 25–26.

27. Letter from John M. Greene to Sophia Smith, dated April 28, 1869.

28. John M. Greene. "Early History of Smith College." *Daily Hampshire Gazette*, April 5, 1893, http://clio.fivecolleges.edu/smith/greene/pubs/hist_sc/index.shtml?page=26.

29. Ibid.

30. Smith College President's Report, 1875–1876, 1–2, http://clio.fivecolleges.edu/smith/pres-reports/1875/.

31. Sarah H. Gordon, "Smith College Students: The First Ten Classes, 1879–1888," *History of Education Quarterly* 15, no. 2 (1975): 150–53.

32. Over time, the college enrolled students from Southern states as well. On these students' experiences at the Seven Sisters, see Joan Marie Johnson, *Southern Women at the Seven Sister Colleges: Feminist Values and Social Activism, 1875–1915* (Athens: University of Georgia Press, 2010).

33. Smith College President's Report, 1875–1876, 1.

34. The college did not graduate its first known black student, Otelia Cromwell, until 1900. Cromwell, whose father graduated from Howard University with a law degree in 1874, would go on to become the first black woman to receive a PhD from Yale University. On black women's experiences at the Seven Sisters broadly, see Linda M. Perkins, "The African American Female Elite: The Early History of African American Women in the Seven Sister Colleges, 1880–1960," *Harvard Educational Review* 67, no. 4 (1997): 718–57.

35. Smith College President's Report, 1875–1876, 7. For a contemporary comparison of college costs for women in the late 1800s, see Alice Hayes, "Can a Poor Girl Go to College?," *The North American Review* May 1891, 624–31.

36. Gordon, "Smith College Students," 151.

37. Seelye, *The Early History of Smith College*, 14.

38. Patricia Ann Palmieri, *In Adamless Eden: The Community of Women Faculty at Wellesley* (New Haven, CT: Yale University Press, 1995).

39. Greene, "Early History of Smith College."

40. Smith College President's Report, 1875–1876, 2.

41. Letter from "Daisy" to Mother, dated February 5, 1880, Classification: 80, Students, Box #1395, "Brooks, Esther Herrick," Folder: "Brooks, Esther Herrick—Correspondence to Family (Jan.–Mar. 1880) and Frona Marie (1883)," Smith College Archives.

42. Letter from "Daisy" to Mother, dated February 8, 1880.

43. "Scrapbook from 1881–1882," Classification: 80, Students, Box #1410, "1883, Lawrence, Elizabeth C., Journals, 1881–1885" (No Folder), Smith College Archives.

44. Smith College Circular, 1872, 1, http://clio.fivecolleges.edu/smith/catalogs/1872/index.shtml?page=1.

45. Seelye, *The Early History of Smith College*, 18.

46. Smith College President's Report, 1875–1876, 1.

47. Entry for May 5, 1876, Classification: 80, Students, Box #1395, "Brooks, Esther Herrick," Folder: "Class of 1882: Brooks, Esther Herrick—Student Notes," Smith College Archives.

48. Smith College Circular, 1874, 2, http://clio.fivecolleges.edu/smith/catalogs/1874/index.shtml?page=2.

49. Ibid.

50. Ibid.

51. Ibid., 1.

52. *Addresses at the Inauguration of Rev. L. Clark Seelye as President of Smith College*, 21.

53. Florence E. May, "Classics in the College Course," *The Alpha Quarterly* 1, no. 2 (1892): 7.

54. Ibid., 8–9.

55. "Smith College," *Scribner's Monthly*, May 1877, 16.

56. "A New Woman's College," *Scribner's Monthly*, October 1873, 748.

57. Horowitz, *Alma Mater*, 74.

58. "A New Woman's College," 748.

59. Ibid., 748.

60. See, for instance, Carroll Smith-Rosenberg, "The Female World of Love and Ritual: Relations between Women in Nineteenth-Century America," *Signs: Journal of Women in Culture and Society* 1, no. 1 (1975): 1–29; Nancy Sahli, "Smashing: Women's Relationships before the Fall," *Chrysalis* no. 8 (1979): 17–27; John D'Emilio and Estelle B. Freedman, *Intimate Matters: A History of Sexuality in America* (Chicago: University of Chicago Press, 1988); Christine Palumbo-DeSimone, *Sharing Secrets: Nineteenth-Century Women's Relations in the Short Story* (Cranbury, NJ: Associated University Press, 2000).

61. Entry for January 29, 1879, Classification: 30, Trustees, Box #16K5, "Tucker, Charlotte (Cheever)," Folder: "Tucker, Charlotte (Cheever), Journal 1879," Smith College Archives.

62. Entry for March 2, 1879.

63. Solomon, *In the Company of Educated Women*, 99.

64. Ibid.

65. Entry dated September 27, 1882, Classification: 80, Students, Box #1413, "1883, Mather, Mary Askew, General Journal," Folder: "Class of 1883, Mather, Mary H.—Journal: 1882–1883," Smith College Archives.

66. Ibid.

67. Entry dated September 28, 1882.

68. Entry dated October 9, 1882.

69. "Miss M.H.A. Mather, Club Woman, Dead." *Evening Journal*, May 9, 1925.

70. Barbara Walker Baumgartner, "The New Castle County Free Library, 1927–1933," *Delaware History* 13 (1968): 48–49.

71. Solomon, *In the Company of Educated Women*, 100.

72. Ibid.

73. L. Clark Seelye, "History of Smith College," in *Celebration of the Quarter Centenary of Smith College* (Cambridge, MA: The Riverside Press, 1900), 127–28.

74. Vita Dutton Scudder, "The College Woman and Social Reform," in *Celebration of the Quarter Centenary of Smith College* (Cambridge, MA: The Riverside Press, 1900), 42–48; Vida Dutton Scudder, *On Journey* (New York: E. P. Dutton & Co., 1937).

75. "About College," *The Smith College Monthly* 1, no. 5 (1894): 38.

76. "Lest We Forget," *Smith College Weekly* 1, no. 2 (1911): 1.

77. "Vocational Training for Women," Classification: 42, Faculty, Box #720, "Comstock, Ada Louise, 1897, Photographs and Speeches," Folder: "Speech—Smith College, Vocational Training for Women, 1915," Smith College Archives.

78. "Occupations for Women Suggested by Former Dean," April 1, 1918, Classification: 42. Faculty, Box #720, "Comstock, Ada Louise, 1897, Photographs and Speeches," Folder: "Publications, 1915–1945," Smith College Archives.

79. Newcomer, *A Century of Higher Education for American Women*, 210–12.

80. Ibid., 194–95.

81. Ten members of the class died prior to their thirtieth reunion. Statistics 1910, Classification: 80, Students, Box #1392, "1882 Records," Folder: "Class of 1882: Statistics," Smith College Archives.

82. See, for instance, Marion Talbot, *The Education of Women* (Chicago: University of Chicago Press, 1910); Lois Kimball Mathews, *The Dean of Women* (New York: Houghton Mifflin, 1915).

83. Alice Katharine Fallows, "Undergraduate Life at Smith College," *Scribner's Monthly* July 1898, 37–58.

84. Smith College President's Report, 1898–1899, 15, http://clio.fivecolleges.edu/smith/pres-reports/1898/index.shtml?page=15.

85. Fallows, "Undergraduate Life at Smith College," 38.

86. For a fictionalized account of this social life, see Josephine Dodge Daskam, *Smith College Stories* (New York: Charles Scribner's Sons, 1900).

87. Fallows, "Undergraduate Life at Smith College," 46.

88. "Department Clubs," Classification: 80, Students, Box #1409, "1883, Lawrence, Elizabeth Crocker, D-F," Folder: "Class of 1883, Lawrence, Elizabeth Crocker: Writings, *Early History of Smith College*—notes for 'Student Life' chapter D-G," Smith College Archives.

89. Fallows, "Undergraduate Life at Smith College," 57.

90. Gordon, *Gender and Higher Education in the Progressive Era*, 33.

91. "After College," *Smith College Weekly* 2, no. 6 (1911): 2.

8. "THE BURDEN OF HIS AMBITION IS TO ACHIEVE A DISTINGUISHED CAREER"

1. Quoted in *Du Bois on Education*, ed. Eugene F. Provenzo Jr. (Walnut Creek, CA: Altamira Press, 2002), 181–97.

2. Ibid., 185.

3. Ibid., 185–86.

4. Quoted in Raymond Wolters, *The New Negro on Campus: Black College Rebellions of the 1920s* (Princeton, NJ: Princeton University Press, 1975), 88–89.

5. Ibid., 89.

6. See, for instance, John R. Thelin, *A History of American Higher Education* (Baltimore: Johns Hopkins University Press, 2004), 187.

7. Lynn D. Gordon, *Gender and Higher Education in the Progressive Era* (New Haven, CT: Yale University Press, 1990), 33.

8. On Howard's history, see William W. Patton, *The History of Howard University, Washington, D.C.* (Washington, DC: Howard University, 1896); Walter Dyson, *Howard University: The Capstone of Negro Education* (Washington, DC: Howard University, 1941); Rayford W. Logan, *Howard University: The First Hundred Years, 1867–1967* (New York: New York University Press, 1969); Harry G. Robinson and Hazel Ruth Edwards, *The Long Walk: The Placemaking Legacy of Howard University* (Washington, DC: Howard University, 1996).

9. Oliver Otis Howard, *Autobiography of Oliver Otis Howard*, vol. 1 of 2 (New York: Baker and Taylor, 1907), 32.

10. Ibid., 32.

11. Ibid., 41.

12. Ibid., 81.

13. William S. McFeely, *Yankee Stepfather: General O. O. Howard and the Freedmen* (New Haven, CT: Yale University Press, 1968), 39.

14. John C. Carpenter, *Sword and Olive Branch: Oliver Otis Howard* (Pittsburgh: University of Pittsburgh Press, 1964), 86.

15. Williamjames Hull Hoffer, *To Enlarge the Machinery of Government: Congressional Debates and the Growth of the American State, 1858–1891* (Baltimore: Johns Hopkins University Press, 2007), 63–64.

16. Oliver Otis Howard, *Autobiography of Oliver Otis Howard*, vol. 2 of 2 (New York: Baker and Taylor, 1907), 221.

17. Logan, *Howard University*, 13.

18. Howard, *Autobiography of Oliver Otis Howard*, 396.

19. For an overview of the establishment of these institutions and others, see Bobby L. Lovett, *America's Historically Black Colleges and Universities: A Narrative History from the Nineteenth Century into the Twenty-First Century* (Macon, GA: Mercer University Press, 2011), 5–21.

20. Henry N. Drewry and Humphrey Doermann, *Stand and Prosper: Private Black Colleges and Their Students* (Princeton, NJ: Princeton University Press, 2001), 33.

21. Ibid., 36–39.

22. Eric Anderson and Alfred A. Moss Jr., *Dangerous Donations: Northern Philanthropy and Southern Black Education, 1902–1930* (Columbia: University of Missouri Press, 1999), 16–17.

23. For a complete list with data on racial composition of students, faculty, and administrators, see James M. McPherson, "White Liberals and Black Power in Negro Education, 1865–1915," *The American Historical Review* 75, no. 5 (1970): 1380–85.

24. W.E.B. DuBois, *The Souls of Black Folk* (New York: A. C. McClurg & Co., 1903), 100.

25. Dyson, *Howard University*, 442.

26. James D. Anderson, *The Education of Blacks in the South, 1860–1935* (Chapel Hill: University of North Carolina Press, 1988), 239.

27. Ibid., 240.

28. Ibid., 247.

29. *Catalogue of the Officers and Students of Howard University, District of Columbia. 1868-'69* (Washington, DC: Judd & Detweiler, Printers, 1869), 36–37.

30. Minutes of the Board of Trustees, December 4, 1866, Howard University Archives, Moorland-Spingarn Research Center, Howard University.

31. Minutes of the Board of Trustees, January 8, 1867.

32. Minutes of the Board of Trustees, January 16, 1867.

33. Minutes of the Board of Trustees, January 29, 1867; Charter reproduced in Dyson, *Howard University*, 448–51.

34. Constructing the University's physical plant occurred more slowly over time. For a visual history of the campus's development, see Robinson and Edwards, *The Long Walk*.

35. Minutes of the Board of Trustees, August 14, 1867.

36. *Annual Catalogue of the Normal and Preparatory Department of Howard University, 1867* (Washington, DC: Gibson Brothers, 1867), 3.

37. *Catalogue of the Officers and Students of Howard University, District of Columbia, 1868–'69*, 19.

38. *Annual Catalogue of the Normal and Preparatory Department of Howard University, 1867*, 9.

39. *Catalogue of the Officers and Students of Howard University, District of Columbia, 1868–'69*, 5.

40. Ibid., 19.

41. On Armstrong's life, see Robert Francis Engs, *Educating the Disfranchised and Disinherited: Samuel Chapman Armstrong and Hampton Institute, 1839–1893* (Knoxville: University of Tennessee Press, 1999).

42. Minutes of the Board of Trustees, January 16, 1868.

43. Dyson, *Howard University*, 109.

44. *Annual Report of Howard University for the Year 1868–'69* (Washington, DC: N.p., 1869), 8–9.

45. Minutes of the Board of Trustees, May 20, 1867.

46. Minutes of the Board of Trustees, September 10, 1867 and March 2, 1868.

47. *Annual Report of Howard University for the Year 1867–'68* (Washington, DC: Gibson Brothers, 1868), 9–10.

48. Logan, *Howard University: The First Hundred Years, 1867–1967*, 52.

49. Minutes of the Board of Trustees, March 7, 1870.

50. Minutes of the Board of Trustees, March 23, 1872.

51. *Annual Report of Howard University for the Year 1871–'72* (Washington, DC: N.p., 1872), 4.

52. *Catalogue of the Officers and Students of Howard University, District of Columbia. 1870–'71* (Washington, DC: Judd & Detweiler, 1871), 78.

53. Minutes of the Board of Trustees, October 12, 1868.

54. John Mercer Langston, *From the Virginia Plantation to the National Capitol or the First and Only Negro Representative in Congress from the Old Dominion* (Hartford, CT: American Publishing Company, 1894), 300.

55. Ibid.

56. Ibid.

57. Henry Louis Gates Jr., *Life upon These Shores: Looking at African American History, 1513–2008* (New York: Alfred A. Knopf, 2011), 173.

58. For a brief history of the Medical Department, see Daniel Smith Lamb, ed. *Howard University Medical Department* (Washington, DC: R. Beresford, 1900).

59. Logan, *Howard University*, 42.

60. Ibid., 41.

61. Lamb, *Howard University Medical Department*, ix.

62. On the persistence of gender discrimination at Howard, see Linda M. Perkins, "Merze Tate and the Quest for Gender Equity at Howard University: 1942–1977," *History of Education Quarterly* 54, no. 4 (2015): 516–51.

63. Logan, *Howard University*, 56–57.
64. Ibid., 51.
65. Dyson, *Howard University*, 402–6.
66. Logan, *Howard University*, 63.
67. Gordon L. Weil, *The Good Man: The Civil War's "Christian General" and His Fight for Racial Equality* (Harpswell, ME: Arthur McAllister Publishers, 2013), especially chapter 7.
68. Carpenter, *Sword and Olive Branch*, 203–8.
69. On Howard as peace envoy, see John A. Carpenter, "General Howard and the Nez Perce War of 1877," *Pacific Northwest Quarterly* 49, no. 4 (1958): 129–45.
70. Minutes of the Board of Trustees, June 29, 1872.
71. Logan, *Howard University*, 60.
72. Ibid.
73. Ibid., 74–75.
74. Minutes of the Board of Trustees, December 25, 1874.
75. Logan, *Howard University*, 76–77.
76. Langston, *From the Virginia Plantation to the National Capitol*, 321.
77. Logan, *Howard University*, 77.
78. Whipple's personal relationship with Langston, which dated back to when Whipple served as professor of mathematics at Oberlin and Langston, an Oberlin student, lived with Whipple's family, probably also played a role in his decision.
79. Dyson, *Howard* University, 55–69.
80. Zachery R. Williams, *In Search of the Talented Tenth: Howard University Public Intellectuals and the Dilemmas of Race, 1926–1970* (Columbia: University of Missouri Press, 2009), 11.
81. Jacqueline M. Moore, *Leading the Race: The Transformation of the Black Elite in the Nation's Capital, 1880–1920* (Charlottesville: University Press of Virginia, 1999), especially chapter 6.
82. Williams, *In Search of the Talented Tenth*, 15–16.
83. On Johnson, see Richard I. McKinney, *Mordecai: The Man and His Message* (Washington, DC: Howard University Press, 1997).
84. See, for instance, Anthony M. Platt, *E. Franklin Frazier Reconsidered* (New Brunswick, NJ: Rutgers University Press, 1991); Genna Rae McNeil, *Groundwork: Charles Hamilton Houston and the Struggle for Civil Rights* (Philadelphia: University of Pennsylvania Press, 1983); Mark V. Tushnet, *Thurgood Marshall and the Supreme Court, 1936–1961* (Oxford, UK: Oxford University Press, 1994); Charles P. Henry, *Ralph Bunche: Model Negro or American Other?* (New York: New York University Press, 1999); Beverly Jarrett, ed. *Tributes to John Hope Franklin: Scholar, Mentor, Father, Friend* (Columbia: University of Missouri Press, 2003).
85. Logan, *Howard University*, 206; For African American women's accomplishments at Howard in addition to Brown's, see Clifford L. Muse Jr., "Ethnic and Cultural Diversity in the Establishment and Development of Howard University, 1867–1910," http://www.huarchivesnet.howard.edu/9908huarnet/muse5.htm.
86. On Slowe's life and career, see Karen Anderson, "Brickbats and Roses: Lucy Diggs Slowe, 1883–1937," in *Lone Voyagers: Academic Women in Coeducational Universities, 1870–1937*, ed. Geraldine Jonçich Clifford (New York: The Feminist Press at The City University of New York, 1989), 283–307; Linda M. Perkins, "Lucy Diggs Slowe: Champion of the Self-Determination of African-American Women in Higher Education," *The Journal of Negro History* 81, no. 1/4 (1996): 89–104; Carroll L. L. Miller and Anne S. Pruitt-Logan, *Faithful to the Task at Hand: The Life of Lucy Diggs Slowe* (Albany: State University of New York Press, 2012), among others.

87. On the higher education of African American women, see, for instance, Jeanne Noble, "The Higher Education of Black Women in the Twentieth Century," in *Women and Higher Education in American History*, ed. John Mack Faragher and Florence Howe (New York: W.W. Norton & Company, 1988), 87–106; Elizabeth L. Ihle, ed. *Black Women in Higher Education: An Anthology of Essays, Studies, and Documents* (New York: Garland, 1992).

88. Miller and Pruitt-Logan, *Faithful to the Task at Hand*, 7–26.

89. "Report of the President of Howard University to the Secretary of the Interior for the Fiscal Year Ended June 30, 1909" (Washington, DC: Government Printing Office, 1909), 5.

90. Quoted in Dyson, *Howard University*, 37.

91. Miller and Pruitt-Logan, *Faithful to the Task at Hand*, 29–30.

92. *The Installation of Wilbur Patterson Thirkield, D.D., LL.D., as President of Howard University. Friday Afternoon, November the Fifteenth, at Two-Thirty o'Clock, Nineteen Hundred Seven* (Washington, DC: Howard University Board of Trustees, 1907).

93. On the movement, see Angela Jones, *African American Civil Rights: Early Activism and the Niagara Movement* (Santa Barbara, CA: ABC-CLIO, 2011); Raymond Wolters, *Du Bois and His Rivals* (Columbia: University of Missouri Press, 2003); among others.

94. On the historical development of black Greek letter societies, see Tamara L. Brown, Gregory S. Parks, and Clarenda M. Phillips, eds., *African American Fraternities and Sororities: The Legacy and the Vision* (Lexington: University Press of Kentucky, 2005). On Alpha Kappa Alpha specifically, see Deborah Elizabeth Whaley, *Disciplining Women: Alpha Kappa Alpha, Black Counterpublics, and the Cultural Politics of Black Sororities* (Albany: State University of New York Press, 2010).

95. Moore, *Leading the Race*, 115–18.

96. Michael H. Washington and Cheryl L. Nuñez, "Education, Racial Uplift, and the Rise of the Greek-Letter Tradition: The African-American Quest for Status in the Early Twentieth Century," in *African American Fraternities and Sororities: The Legacy and the Vision*, ed. Tamara L. Brown, Gregory S. Parks, and Clarenda M. Phillips (Lexington: University Press of Kentucky, 2005), 169.

97. Miller and Pruitt-Logan, *Faithful to the Task at Hand*, 72–75.

98. For a historical overview of the position of dean of women and the role of the National Association of Deans of Women, see Lynn M. Gangone, "The National Association for Women in Education: An Enduring Legacy," *Journal about Women in Higher Education* 1, no. 1 (2009): 3–24.

99. Christopher P. Loss, *Between Citizens and the State: The Politics of American Higher Education in the 20th Century* (Princeton, NJ: Princeton University Press, 2012), chapter 2.

100. Thomas D. Snyder, ed. *120 Years of American Education: A Statistical Portrait* (Washington, DC: US Department of Education National Center for Education Statistics, 1993), 76.

101. Loss, *Between Citizens and the State*, 21.

102. Miller and Pruitt-Logan, *Faithful to the Task at Hand*, 98–99.

103. On the changes to the University's federal appropriation over time, see Dyson, *Howard University*, chapter 20.

104. Wolters, *The New Negro on Campus*, 70.

105. Joanna H. Ransom, "Innovations Introduced into the Women's Program at Howard University by the Late Dean Lucy D. Slowe," *Journal of the National Association of College Women* 14 (1937): 51.

106. "Report of President Durkee to the Board of Trustees, Howard University, Washington, D.C. 1925–'26" (Washington, DC: Howard University Press, 1926), 20–21.

107. "1,500 Attend Opening of New Dorms," *The Hilltop*, December 10, 1931.

108. Perkins, "Lucy Diggs Slowe," 92–93.

109. Ibid.

110. Lucy D. Slowe, "Higher Education of Negro Women," *The Journal of Negro Education* 2, no. 3 (1933): 356–58.

111. Quoted in Perkins, "Lucy Diggs Slowe," 93.

112. Lucy Diggs Slowe, "The Colored Girl Enters College—What Shall She Expect?," *Opportunity: Journal of Negro Life* 15, no. 9 (1937): 278.

113. Slowe, "Higher Education of Negro Women," 353–54.

114. Ibid., 355. On the National Association of College Women, see Linda M. Perkins, "The National Association of College Women: Vanguard of Black Women's Leadership and Education, 1923–1954," *Journal of Education* 172, no. 3 (1990): 65–75.

115. Slowe, "The Colored Girl Enters College—What Shall She Expect?," 277.

116. "Woman Educator Foresees Great Future for Co-Eds," *Detroit People's News* March 1, 1931.

117. Lucy Diggs Slowe, "The College Woman and Her Community," Lucy Diggs Slowe Papers, Box 90–6, Folder: The College Woman and her Community, Howard University Archives, Moorland-Spingarn Research Center, Howard University.

118. Lucy Diggs Slowe, "The Dean of Women in a Modern University," Lucy Diggs Slowe Papers, Box 90–6, Folder: The Dean of Women in a Modern University, Howard University Archives, Moorland-Spingarn Research Center, Howard University.

119. Stephanie Y. Evans, *Black Women in the Ivory Tower: An Intellectual History* (Gainesville: University Press of Florida, 2007), 67; "Race Hatreds Will Destroy All, Says Dean Slowe over Air," *Washington Tribune*, May 1, 1937; "Washington in Disgrace," *The New York Age*, May 18, 1937.

120. Lucy Diggs Slowe, "The Business of Being a Dean of Women," Lucy Diggs Slowe Papers, Box 90–6, Folder: The Business of Being a Dean of Women, Howard University Archives, Moorland-Spingarn Research Center, Howard University.

121. Slowe, "The Colored Girl Enters College—What Shall She Expect?," 276.

122. For an examination of the impact of World War II on American education, see Charles Dorn, *American Education, Democracy, and the Second World War* (New York: Palgrave Macmillan, 2007).

123. See, for instance, Rebecca S. Lowen, *Creating the Cold War University: The Transformation of Stanford* (Berkeley: University of California Press, 1997); Stuart W. Leslie, *The Cold War and American Science: The Military-Industrial-Academic Complex at MIT and Stanford* (New York: Columbia University Press, 1993).

124. Charles Dorn, "Promoting the 'Public Welfare' in Wartime: Stanford University during World War II," *American Journal of Education* 112, no. 1 (2005): 122–23.

125. See, for instance, Arthur M. Cohen, *The Shaping of American Higher Education: Emergence and Growth of the Contemporary System* (San Francisco: Jossey-Bass, 1998), 175; Marvin Lazerson, "The Disappointments of Success: Higher Education after World War II," *Annals of the American Academy of Political and Social Science* 559 (1998), 68; Logan, *Howard University*, chapter 9.

126. Snyder, *120 Years of American Education*, 66, 78.

127. Linda Eisenmann, *Higher Education for Women in Postwar America, 1945–1965* (Baltimore: Johns Hopkins University Press, 2006); Charles Dorn, "'War Conditions Made It Impossible . . .': Historical Statistics and Women's Higher Education Enrollments, 1940–1952," *Studies in the Humanities* 36, no. 2 (2009): 108–15.

9. "A WEDDING CEREMONY BETWEEN INDUSTRY AND THE UNIVERSITY"

1. "Florida Needs Another 4-Year State University—Tampa is the Logical Site," Prepared by Greater Tampa Chamber of Commerce, The Papers of John S. Allen, Box 1, Folder: Groundbreaking, B1/F7, University Archives, Special Collections, University of South Florida.

2. "Office of Institutional Research, University of South Florida, May 15, 1960," 2–4, The Papers of John S. Allen, Box 1, Folder: Educational Program, B1/F32, University Archives, Special Collections, University of South Florida.

3. John S. Allen, "The University of South Florida," in *New Universities in the Modern World*, ed. Murray G. Ross (New York: St. Martin's Press, 1966), 153.

4. "Office of Institutional Research, University of South Florida, May 15, 1960," 3–4.

5. Ibid., 3.

6. Wilson Smith and Thomas Bender, eds. *American Higher Education Transformed, 1940–2005* (Baltimore: Johns Hopkins University Press, 2008), 14–15.

7. On the Truman Commission, see the special issue "History of Access to American Higher Education Commemorating the Sixtieth Anniversary of *Higher Education for American Democracy: The Report of the President's Commission on Higher Education*," *History of Education Quarterly* 47, no. 3 (2007).

8. Ibid., 268.

9. "Address to Charter Faculty, University of South Florida, September 6, 1960," 7–8, The Papers of John S. Allen, Box 1, Folder: Dr. John S. Allen Personal, University Archives, Special Collections, University of South Florida.

10. "University of South Florida, Opening Convocation, September 26, 1960, Remarks of Governor Collins," The Papers of John S. Allen, Box 1, Folder: Opening Convocation Program, University Archives, Special Collections, University of South Florida.

11. "The University of South Florida: An Invitation to Learn," The Papers of John S. Allen, Box 1, Folder: Groundbreaking, B1/F7, University Archives, Special Collections, University of South Florida.

12. *Accent on Learning* 1, no. 1 (1959): 32.

13. John Kenneth Galbraith, *The Affluent Society*, in *John Kenneth Galbraith: The Affluent Society and Other Writings, 1952–1967*, ed. James K. Galbraith (New York: Library of America, 2010).

14. Ibid., 475.

15. Ibid., 471.

16. Marvin Lazerson, *Higher Education and the American Dream: Success and Its Discontents* (New York: Central European University Press, 2010).

17. W. Norton Grubb and Marvin Lazerson, *The Education Gospel: The Economic Power of Schooling* (Cambridge, MA: Harvard University Press, 2004), 65.

18. Russell M. Cooper and Margaret B. Fisher, *The Vision of a Contemporary University: A Case Study of Expansion and Development in American Higher Education, 1950–1975* (Tampa: University of South Florida, 1982), 78.

19. The literature on these developments is extensive. See, for example, Kevin Phillips, *The Emerging Republican Majority* (New Rochelle, NY: Arlington House, 1969); Kirkpatrick Sale, *Power Shift: The Rise of the Southern Rim and Its Challenges to the Eastern Establishment* (New York: Random House, 1975); Robert B. Fairbanks and Kathleen Underwood, eds., *Essays on Sunbelt Cities and Recent Urban America* (College Station: Texas A&M University Press, 1990); Sean P. Cunningham, *American Politics in the Postwar Sunbelt: Conservative Growth in a Battleground Region* (New York: Cambridge University Press, 2014); Michelle Nickerson and Darren Dochuk, eds., *Sunbelt Rising: The Politics of Place, Space, and Region* (Philadelphia: University of Pennsylvania Press,

2011); Richard M. Bernard and Bradley R. Rice, eds., *Sunbelt Cities: Politics and Growth since World War II* (Austin: University of Texas Press, 1983); Margaret P. O'Mara, *Cities of Knowledge: Cold War Science and the Search for the Next Silicon Valley* (Princeton, NJ: Princeton University Press, 2005); Matthew D. Lassiter, *The Silent Majority: Suburban Politics in the Sunbelt South* (Princeton, NJ: Princeton University Press, 2006); Matthew D. Lassiter and Kevin M. Kruse, "The Bulldozer Revolution: Suburbs and Southern History since World War II," *The Journal of Southern History* 75, no. 3 (2009): 691–706; Raymond A. Mohl, ed. *Searching for the Sunbelt: Historical Perspectives on a Region* (Knoxville: University of Tennessee Press, 1990); Bruce J. Schulman, *From Cotton Belt to Sunbelt: Federal Policy, Economic Development, and the Transformation of the South, 1938–1980* (New York: Oxford University Press, 1994); Numan V. Bartley, *The New South, 1945–1980: The Story of the South's Modernization* (Baton Rouge: Louisiana State University Press, 1995).

20. Mark I. Greenberg, Andrew T. Huse, and Marilyn Keltz Stephens, *University of South Florida: The First Fifty Years, 1956–2006* (Tampa: University of South Florida, 2006), 6.

21. Russell M. Cooper, "Anatomy of a University: A Case Study in American Higher Education," 3–4, The Papers of Dean Russell M. Cooper, Box 105, Folder: Anatomy of a University, University Archives, Special Collections, University of South Florida.

22. "15 Statements of Fact on Florida's Higher Education Needs," The Papers of John S. Allen, Box 1, Folder: House Bill No. 1007—June 18, 1955, University Archives, Special Collections, University of South Florida.

23. On the history of the Tampa Bay region, see Karl H. Grismer, *Tampa: A History of the City of Tampa and the Tampa Bay Region of Florida* (St. Petersburg, FL: St. Petersburg Printing Company, 1950); Nancy A. Hewitt, *Southern Discomfort: Women's Activism in Tampa, Florida, 1880s–1920s* (Urbana: University of Illinois Press, 2001); Robert P. Ingalls, *Urban Vigilantes in the New South: Tampa, 1882–1936* (Knoxville: University of Tennessee Press, 1988); Nancy A. Hewitt, "Economic Crisis and Political Mobilization: Reshaping Cultures of Resistance in Tampa's Communities of Color, 1929–1939," in *Women's Labor in the Global Economy: Speaking in Multiple Voices*, ed. Sharon Harley (New Brunswick, NJ: Rutgers University Press, 2007), 62–81; and Steven F. Lawson, "From Sit-in to Race Riot: Businessmen, Blacks, and the Pursuit of Moderation in Tampa, 1960–1967," in *Southern Businessmen and Desegregation*, ed. Elizabeth Jacoway and David R. Colburn (Baton Rouge: Louisiana State University Press, 1982), 257–81, among others.

24. Gary R. Mormino, *Land of Sunshine, State of Dreams: A Social History of Modern Florida* (Gainesville: University Press of Florida, 2005), 19.

25. Bernard and Rice, "Introduction," in *Sunbelt Cities: Politics and Growth since World War II*, 8.

26. Gary R. Mormino and George E. Pozzetta, *The Immigrant World of Ybor City: Italians and Their Latin Neighbors in Tampa, 1885–1985* (Urbana: University of Illinois Press, 1990).

27. Elna C. Green, "Relief from Relief: The Tampa Sewing-Room Strike of 1937 and the Right to Welfare," *The Journal of American History* 95, no. 4 (2009): 1016; Walter T. Howard and Virginia M. Howard, "Family, Religion, and Education: A Profile of African-American Life in Tampa, Florida, 1900–1930," *The Journal of Negro History* 79, no. 1 (1994): 1–17.

28. Grismer, *Tampa*, 280–81.

29. Gary R. Mormino, "Tampa: From Hell Hole to the Good Life," in *Sunbelt Cities: Politics and Growth since World War II*, ed. Richard M. Bernard and Bradley R. Rice (Austin: University of Texas Press, 1983), 141.

30. Robert Kerstein, *Politics and Growth in Twentieth-Century Tampa* (Gainesville: University Press of Florida, 2001), 108.

31. Cunningham, *American Politics in the Postwar Sunbelt*, 11.

32. Ibid., 17.

33. Mormino, *Land of Sunshine, State of Dreams*, 12.

34. Ibid., 12–13.

35. Cooper and Fisher, *The Vision of a Contemporary University*, 3.

36. Ibid., 3–5.

37. Ibid., 5; Mormino, *Land of Sunshine, State of Dreams*, 108–9.

38. Cunningham, *American Politics in the Postwar Sunbelt*, 38.

39. John S. Allen, "The University of South Florida," in *New Universities in the Modern World*, ed. Murray G. Ross (New York: St. Martin's Press, 1966), 153.

40. Cooper and Fisher, *The Vision of a Contemporary University*, 6.

41. Andrew Huse, *USF Chronology* (Tampa: Florida Studies Center, 2002), 16; *Tampa Daily Times*, November 3, 1957.

42. *Accent on Learning* 1, no. 1 (1959), 60–61.

43. Ibid., 69–79.

44. "Planning a New State University" by John S. Allen, 24, The Papers of John S. Allen, Box 1, Folder: John S. Allen, Personal & Speeches, B1/F6, University Archives, Special Collections, University of South Florida.

45. *Accent on Learning* 1, no. 1, 62.

46. *Accent on Learning* 3, no. 2 (1961–1963), 33–43.

47. *Accent on Learning* 1, no. 1, 63.

48. Cooper, "Anatomy of a University," 10.

49. Thomas Sugrue, *The Origins of the Urban Crisis: Race and Inequality in Postwar Detroit* (Princeton, NJ: Princeton University Press, 1996).

50. Margaret P. O'Mara, "Beyond Town and Gown: University Economic Engagement and the Legacy of the Urban Crisis," *Journal of Technology Transfer* 37, no. 2 (2012): 234–50.

51. J. Martin Klotsche, *The Urban University and the Future of Our Cities* (New York: Harper & Row, 1966), especially chapter 2.

52. Lyndon B. Johnson, "Remarks of the President at the University of California, Irvine, June 20, 1964" (Washington, DC: Office of the White House Press Secretary, 1964).

53. For studies of these cases, see George Nash, Dan Waldorf, and Robert E. Price, *The University and the City* (New York: McGraw Hill, 1973).

54. Cooper and Fisher, *The Vision of a Contemporary University*, 10; Greenberg, Huse, and Stephens, *University of South Florida*, 36.

55. Cooper and Fisher, *The Vision of a Contemporary University*, 21.

56. "Role and Scope of the University of South Florida" by Lewis B. Mayhew, The Papers of John S. Allen, Box 2, Folder: USF Role and Scope Committee, Lewis B. Mayhew, B2/F6, University Archives, Special Collections, University of South Florida.

57. Huse, *USF Chronology*, 25; *Tampa Times University of South Florida Campus Edition*, February 4, 1963.

58. Huse, *USF Chronology*, 24; *The Tampa Times*, September 26, 1960.

59. "Report of Grade Point Averages Fall Term 1961," The Papers of John S. Allen, Box 3, Folder: Annual Reports 1961–1962, B3/F13, University Archives, Special Collections, University of South Florida.

60. Huse, *USF Chronology*, 24; *The Tampa Times*, September 26, 1960.

61. Greenberg, Huse, and Stephens, *University of South Florida*, 38–40.

62. Cooper and Fisher, *The Vision of a Contemporary University*, 78–79.

63. For an overview of these events, see Greenberg, Huse, and Stephens, *University of South Florida*, 66–78. On segregated education in Tampa, see Barbara J. Shircliffe, *The Best of That World: Historically Black High Schools and the Crisis of Desgregation in a Southern Metropolis* (Cresskill, NJ: Hampton Press, 2006).

64. Larry Johnson, Deirdre Cobb-Roberts, and Barbara Shircliffe, "African Americans and the Struggle for Opportunity in Florida Public Higher Education, 1947–1977," *History of Education Quarterly* 47, no. 3 (2007): 329.

65. Florida ex rel. Hawkins v. Board of Control, 350 U.S. 413 (1956).

66. Johnson, Cobb-Roberts, and Shircliffe, "African Americans and the Struggle for Opportunity in Florida Public Higher Education," 345.

67. Interview with Ernest Boger by Andrew Huse, December 2, 2003, USF Florida Studies Center, Oral History Program, USF 50th History Anniversary Project.

68. Interview with Sam Gibbons, USF Florida Studies Center, Oral History Program, 2001–2002. Quoted in Huse, *USF Chronology*, 2.

69. "White, Negro Undergraduates at Colleges Enrolling 500 or More, as Compiled from Reports to US Office for Civil Rights," *Chronicle of Higher Education*, April 22, 1968. At the time, USF enrolled 11,571 white students and 225 black students.

70. Otha L. Favors, "The Idea of One-to-One," *One-to-One Group Newsletter* 2, no. 2 (October 30, 1968), The Papers of Student Affairs, Box 124, Folder: One-to-One, University Archives, Special Collections, University of South Florida.

71. "Black Power," *One-to-One Group Newsletter* 2, no. 4 (November 27, 1968), The Papers of Student Affairs, Box 124, Folder: One-to-One, University Archives, Special Collections, University of South Florida.

72. "U. Senate OK's Bill for Negro Education," *The Oracle* 3, no. 1 (July 3, 1968): 1.

73. "Memo to participating faculty dated August 12, 1868, from Dean Edwin P. Martin," Papers of Dean Russell M. Cooper, Box 105, Folder: USF Programs: Disadvantaged Students, B105/F41, University Archives, Special Collections, University of South Florida.

74. "State of the University. An Address to the Faculty and Staff of the University of South Florida by John S. Allen, President. September 26, 1969," 19–21, The Papers of John S. Allen, Box 1, Folder: Dr. John S. Allen Personal, University Archives, Special Collections, University of South Florida.

75. Ibid., 19–21.

76. Ibid., 22.

77. "Letter from US Office for Civil Rights, Regional Civil Rights Director, Paul M. Rilling to Florida Board of Regents Chancellor Robert B. Mautz, dated February 26, 1970," Papers of Dean Russell M. Cooper, Box 105, Folder: USF Programs: Disadvantaged Students, B105/F41, University Archives, Special Collections, University of South Florida.

78. Quoted in Greenberg, Huse, and Stephens, *University of South Florida*, 119.

79. *The Tampa Times* November 15, 1974, 8-A.

80. Dongbin Kim and John L. Rury, "The Rise of the Commuter Student: Changing Patterns of College Attendance for Students Living at Home in the United States, 1960–1980," *Teachers College Record* 113, no. 5 (2011): 1058.

81. Cooper and Fisher, *The Vision of a Contemporary University*, 69; Greenberg, Huse, and Stephens, *University of South Florida*, 79.

82. Interview with M. Cecil Mackey by Andrew Huse, November 2, 2004, USF Florida Studies Center, Oral History Program, USF 50th History Anniversary Project.

83. Ibid.

84. "News Release, January 10, 1964," The Papers of John S. Allen, Box 10, University Folder: New Releases—USF News Bureau, University Archives, Special Collections, University of South Florida; "Annual Report, The Natural Sciences and Mathematics Division,

1961–1962," The Papers of John S. Allen, Box 3, Folder: Annual Reports—1961–1962, B3/F13, University Archives, Special Collections, University of South Florida.

85. "Sponsored Research and Projects, University of South Florida, Tampa, Florida, Prepared by Office of Sponsored Research, July 1, 1964," The Papers of John S. Allen, Box 10, Folder: Annual Reports, B10/F31, University Archives, Special Collections, University of South Florida.

86. "Annual Report of the State University System of Florida, 1969–1970," The Papers of John S. Allen, Box 1, Folder: Dr. John S. Allen Personal, University Archives, Special Collections, University of South Florida.

87. Richard C. Atkinson and William A. Blanpied, "Research Universities: Core of the US Science and Technology System," *Technology in Society* 30 (2008): 34.

88. One the best known of these policymakers was Vannevar Bush, former Dean of Engineering at the Massachusetts Institute of Technology, president of the Carnegie Institution of Washington, DC, and author of the influential 1945 report *Science: The Endless Frontier*, whom President Franklin Roosevelt appointed head of the Office of Scientific Research and Development, precursor to the National Science Foundation. See G. Pascal Zachary, *Endless Frontier: Vannevar Bush, Engineer of the American Century* (New York: Free Press, 1997).

89. For a detailed analysis of federal research support during this period, see Roger L. Geiger, *Research and Relevant Knowledge: American Research Universities since World War II* (New York: Oxford University Press, 1993), chapter 6.

90. Atkinson and Blanpied, "Research Universities," 36; Kristjan T. Sigurdson, "Clark Kerr's Multiversity and Technology Transfer in the Modern American Research University," *College Quarterly* 16, no. 2 (2013), http://www.collegequarterly.ca/2013-vol16-num02-spring/sigurdson.html.

91. O'Mara, "Beyond Town and Gown," 241.

92. Interview with M. Cecil Mackey.

93. Quoted in *Building a Research University: A USF Retrospective*, Annual Report, 1994–1995, 23, University Archives, Special Collections, University of South Florida.

94. Clark Kerr, *The Uses of the University*, 4th ed. (Cambridge, MA: Harvard University Press, 1995).

95. Interview with M. Cecil Mackey.

96. Quoted in "USF Professors Exploring Research Frontiers," *The Tampa Tribune*, October 18, 1986.

97. Hugh Davis Graham and Nancy Diamond, *The Rise of American Research Universities: Elites and Challengers in the Postwar Era* (Baltimore: Johns Hopkins University Press, 1997), 55.

98. Ibid., 56.

99. Cooper and Fisher, *The Vision of a Contemporary University*, 78.

100. Ibid., 78–80.

101. Geiger, *Research and Relevant Knowledge*, 266.

102. Greenberg, Huse, and Stephens, *University of South Florida*, 137–42.

103. Geiger, *Research and Relevant Knowledge*, 312.

104. Greenberg, Huse, and Stephens, *University of South Florida*, 142, 156.

105. Burton Clark has been credited with coining the term "entrepreneurial university." Burton R. Clark, *Creating Entrepreneurial Universities* (New York: IAU Press, 1998). For an overview of university entrepreneurialism, see Nathan Rosenberg, "America's Entrepreneurial Universities," in *The Emergence of Entrepreneurship Policy: Governance, Start-Ups, and Growth in the U.S. Knowledge Economy*, ed. David M. Hart (Cambridge, UK: Cambridge University Press, 2003): 113–37.

106. Rebecca S. Lowen, *Creating the Cold War University: The Transformation of Stanford* (Berkeley: University of California Press, 1997); Stuart W. Leslie, *The Cold War and*

American Science: The Military-Industrial-Academic Complex at MIT and Stanford (New York: Columbia University Press, 1993); O'Mara, *Cities of Knowledge.*

107. On the process leading up to the passage of the Bayh-Dole Act, see Elizabeth Popp Berman, "Institution-Building and the Road to the Bayh-Dole Act," *Social Studies of Science* 38, no. 6 (2008): 835–71.

108. Geiger, *Research and Relevant Knowledge*, 320.

109. The center was later renamed "Center for Engineering Development and Research."

110. Quoted in Mark Chesney, "Cedar: High Tech, Higher Education Join Forces," *USF Magazine*, June 1983, 8.

111. Ibid., 9.

112. Ibid., 8.

113. In 1984, biologist Richard Mansell received USF's first patent royalties resulting from his development of a process that sweetened grapefruit. Greenberg, Huse, and Stephens, *University of South Florida*, 98.

114. On the development of technology transfer in higher education, see Roger L. Geiger and Creso M. Sá, *Tapping the Riches of Science: Universities and the Promise of Economic Growth* (Cambridge, MA: Harvard University Press, 2008), chapter 1; Maryann P. Feldman, "Entrepreneurship and American Research Universities: Evolution in Technology Transfer," in *The Emergence of Entrepreneurship Policy: Governance, Start-Ups, and Growth in the U.S. Knowledge Economy*, ed. David M. Hart (Cambridge, UK: Cambridge University Press, 2003), 92–112; Sigurdson, "Clark Kerr's Multiversity and Technology Transfer in the Modern American Research University." On the development of the patenting and licensing of university technologies, see Geiger and Sá, *Tapping the Riches of Science*, chapter 4; Sheila Slaughter and Gary Rhoades, *Academic Capitalism and the New Economy: Markets, State, and Higher Education* (Baltimore: Johns Hopkins University Press, 2004), chapter 3. On the challenges to the university resulting from these practices, particularly in the field of biomedical research, see Sheldon Krimsky, *Science in the Private Interest: Has the Lure of Profits Corrupted Biomedical Research?* (Lanham, MD: Rowman & Littlefield, 2003).

115. Geiger and Sá, *Tapping the Riches of Science*, 118.

116. Derek Bok, *Universities in the Marketplace: The Commercialization of Higher Education* (Princeton, NJ: Princeton University Press, 2004), 12.

117. Ann Carney, "Valuable Connections," *USF Magazine*, Fall/Winter 2004, 12.

118. Ibid., 12.

119. http://www.research.usf.edu/rf/usf-connect.asp.

120. Roger L. Geiger, *Knowledge and Money: Research Universities and the Paradox of the Marketplace* (Stanford, CA: Stanford University Press, 2004), 205.

121. Michael I. Luger and Harvey A. Goldstein, *Technology in the Garden: Research Parks and Regional Economic Development* (Chapel Hill: University of North Carolina Press, 1991), 5.

122. Geiger, *Knowledge and Money*, 205.

123. Huse, *USF Chronology*, 347; *The Oracle*, January 23, 1979.

124. "University Technology Center," Office of the President: Francis T. Borkowski, Box 884, Folder: F24 Research and Development Park, University Archives, Special Collections, University of South Florida.

125. Ibid.

126. Interview of USF President Judy Genshaft by Mark I. Greenberg, April 23, 2004, USF Florida Studies Center, Oral History Project, USF 50th History Anniversary Project.

127. Huse, *USF Chronology*, 347; *The Oracle*, January 28, 2004.

128. Greenberg, Huse, and Stephens, *University of South Florida*, 218–19.

129. Huse, *USF Chronology*, 347; *The Oracle*, January 28, 2004.

130. Malcolm G. Scully, "Student Focus on Practicality Hits Humanities," *The Chronicle of Higher Education* 8, no. 18 (1974): 1.

131. Ibid.

132. Verne A. Stadtman, "Happenings on the Way to the 1980s," in *Higher Education in American Society*, ed. Philip G. Altbach and Robert O. Berdahl (Buffalo: Prometheus Books, 1981), 105–6.

133. Klotsche, *The Urban University and the Future of Our Cities*, 93–94.

134. Ibid.

135. "State of the University. An Address to the Faculty and Staff of the University of South Florida by John S. Allen, President. September 26, 1969," 19–21.

136. Irma Rubin, "A Foot in the Door and More: Co-Op Program Is a Triple Winner," *USF Magazine*, January 1983, 12–13.

137. USF established its campuses in St. Petersburg in 1965, Fort Meyers in 1974, and Sarasota-Manatee in 1975. Greenberg, Huse, and Stephens, *University of South Florida*, 55–58, 128–30, 26–31.

138. Interview of Jack E. Fernandez by Yael V. Greenberg, March 4, 2003, USF Florida Studies Center, Oral History Project, USF 50th History Anniversary Project.

139. Greenberg, Huse, and Stephens, *University of South Florida*, 176.

140. Ibid., 212–13.

141. Quoted ibid., 215.

142. Interview of USF President Judy Genshaft by Mark I. Greenberg, April 23, 2004.

143. Cooper and Fisher, *The Vision of a Contemporary University*, 4.

10. "TO MEET THE TRAINING AND RETRAINING NEEDS OF ESTABLISHED BUSINESS"

1. http://www.aacc.nche.edu/AboutCC/Pages/fastfactsfactsheet.aspx.

2. http://www.ed.gov/edblogs/whiaiane/tribes-tcus/tribal-colleges-and-universities/.

3. See http://ccrc.tc.columbia.edu/Community-College-FAQs.html.

4. Although the scholarly literature on community colleges is vast, histories of the institution are comparatively few. For a comprehensive list of historical studies as well as unpublished dissertations, see Matthew Delmont, "Working toward a Working-Class College: The Long Campaign to Build a Community College in Philadelphia," *History of Education Quarterly* 54, no. 4 (2014): 432–34, n10 and 11; David F. Labaree, *How to Succeed in School without Really Learning: The Credentials Race in American Education* (New Haven, CT: Yale University Press, 1997), 284–85, n5.

5. Kevin James Dougherty, *The Contradictory College: The Conflicting Origins, Impacts, and Futures of the Community College* (Albany: State University of New York Press, 1994), 197–98.

6. Ibid., 191.

7. Roger L. Geiger, *To Advance Knowledge: The Growth of America's Research Universities, 1900–1940* (New York: Oxford University Press, 1986), 13.

8. Thomas D. Snyder, ed. *120 Years of American Education: A Statistical Portrait* (Washington, DC: US Department of Education National Center for Education Statistics, 1993), Table 8, 34.

9. David O. Levine, *The American College and the Culture of Aspiration, 1915–1940* (Ithaca, NY: Cornell University Press, 1986), 167.

10. Snyder, *120 Years of American Education*, Table 19, 55.

11. Ibid., Table 23, 75.

12. At some four-year institutions, this effort began even earlier, as at the University of Georgia in 1859 and the University of Michigan in 1852. Arthur M. Cohen and Florence B. Brawer, *The American Community College* (San Francisco: Jossey-Bass, 1982), 7.

13. Hugh Ross, "University Influence in the Genesis and Growth of Junior Colleges in California," *History of Education Quarterly* 3, no. 3 (1963): 144–46.

14. Dougherty, *The Contradictory College*, 127–28.

15. Levine, *The American College and the Culture of Aspiration*, 175. On the development of junior colleges in California, specifically, see John Aubrey Douglass, *The California Idea and American Higher Education* (Stanford, CA: Stanford University Press, 2000), chapter 4.

16. Steven Brint and Jerome Karabel, *The Diverted Dream: Community Colleges and the Promise of Educational Opportunity in America, 1900–1985* (New York: Oxford University Press, 1989), 28–29.

17. Levine, *The American College and the Culture of Aspiration*, 173.

18. On community colleges' "democratic" character, see Jesse P. Bogue, *The Community College* (New York: McGraw-Hill, 1950), chapter 1; Edmund J. Gleazer, *This Is the Community College* (Boston: Houghton Mifflin, 1968), 4–21; Levine, *The American College and the Culture of Aspiration, 1915–1940*, 163; among others.

19. Brint and Karabel, *The Diverted Dream*, 31–32.

20. Levine, *The American College and the Culture of Aspiration*, 179–83.

21. Labaree, *How to Succeed in School without Really Learning*, 200.

22. Quoted in J. M. Beach, *Gateway to Opportunity?: A History of the Community College in the United States* (Sterling, VA: Stylus Publishing, 2011), 7–8.

23. Quoted in Gregory L. Goodwin, *A Social Panacea: A History of the Community-Junior College Ideology.* (ERIC Document: ED 093–427, 1973), 157.

24. *State Higher Education in California*, The Suzzallo Report, Carnegie Foundation for the Advancement of Teaching (Sacramento: California State Printing Office, 1932); Douglass, *The California Idea and American Higher Education*, 146–55.

25. Quoted in Levine, *The American College and the Culture of Aspiration*, 172.

26. Levine, *The American College and the Culture of Aspiration*, 174.

27. Brint and Karabel, *The Diverted Dream*, 43.

28. Labaree, *How to Succeed in School without Really Learning*, 202–206.

29. On the Truman Commission, see the special issue "History of Access to American Higher Education: Commemorating the Sixtieth Anniversary of *Higher Education for American Democracy: The Report of the President's Commission on Higher Education*," *History of Education Quarterly* 47, no. 3 (2007).

30. Brint and Karabel, *The Diverted Dream*, 70.

31. Burton R. Clark, "The 'Cooling Out' Function in Higher Education," *The American Journal of Sociology* 65, no. 6 (1960): 569–76.

32. See, for instance, Samuel Bowles and Herbert Gintis, *Schooling in Capitalist America: Educational Reform and the Contradictions of Economic Life* (New York: Basic Books, 1976).

33. L. Steven Zwerling, *Second Best: The Crisis of the Community College* (New York: McGraw-Hill, 1976), xix; K. Patricia Cross, *Beyond the Open Door* (San Francisco: Jossey-Bass, 1974); David Nasaw, *Schooled to Order: A Social History of Public Schooling in the United States* (New York: Oxford University Press, 1979).

34. Brint and Karabel, *The Diverted Dream*, 91.

35. Ibid., 226.

36. Quoted in Dougherty, *The Contradictory College*, 214.

37. Brint and Karabel, *The Diverted Dream*, 121.

38. W. Norton Grubb, "The Bandwagon Once More: Vocational Preparation for High-Tech Occupations," *Harvard Educational Review* 54, no. 4 (1984): 449–51.

39. John G. Melville and Thomas J. Chmura, "Strategic Alignment of Community Colleges and State Economic Policy," in *Economic and Workforce Development*, ed. Geneva Waddell (San Francisco: Jossey-Bass, 1991), 7–8.

40. Ibid., 8–9. For examples from additional states, see Janice B. Carmichael, "Meeting Small Business Needs through Small Business Development Centers," in *Economic and Workforce Development*, ed. Geneva Waddell (San Francisco: Jossey-Bass, 1991), 25–30.

41. Melville and Chmura, "Strategic Alignment of Community Colleges and State Economic Policy," 10.

42. Robert L. Breuder, "Technology Transfer and Training," *AACJC Journal* 59 (1988): 32–33.

43. Robert E. Bailey, Linda E. Cooper, and Karen L. Kramer, "The Ohio Technology Transfer Organization—Otto: An Experiment in Academia Assisting Business," *The Journal of Technology Transfer* 9, no. 2 (1985): 9–10.

44. Elizabeth Brient Smith, "Responding to Industry Demands: Advanced Technology Centers," *AACJC Journal* 61 (1991): 20; Melville and Chmura, "Strategic Alignment of Community Colleges and State Economic Policy," 11.

45. Lawrence A. Nespoli, "Investing in Human Capital: State Strategies for Economic Development," in *Economic and Workforce Development*, ed. Geneva Waddell (San Francisco: Jossey-Bass, 1991), 21–22. For a detailed examination of Massachusetts's experience, see Brint and Karabel, *The Diverted Dream*, chapter 7.

46. *The Diverted Dream*, 131.

47. Ibid., 133.

48. Dougherty, *The Contradictory College*, 197.

49. John S. Levin, "The Revised Institution: The Community College Mission at the End of the Twentieth Century," *Community College Review* 28, no. 2 (2000): 20–21.

50. Brint and Karabel, *The Diverted Dream*, 116.

51. Snyder, *120 Years of American Education*, Table 24, 77.

52. Brint and Karabel, *The Diverted Dream*, 83–86.

53. Public Laws of the State of Rhode Island and Providence Plantations Relating to Rhode Island Junior College. "An Act to Establish Two-Year Community Colleges, in Amendment of and in Addition to Title 16 of the General Laws, Entitled 'Education.'" Chapter 44, "Community Colleges."

54. Edward J. Liston, *Recollections of a Pioneer President: The Evolution of the Community College of Rhode Island* (Warwick, RI: Community College of Rhode Island, 2000), 18–19.

55. *Report of the President—1964–1965*, pamphlet, Rhode Island Junior College, 3, Community College of Rhode Island Archives, Community College of Rhode Island, Knight Campus.

56. Ibid., 4.

57. Ibid., 4–5.

58. *Rhode Island Junior College Student Handbook, 1967–1968*, 4, Box: RIJC Student Handbook, 1967–1979, Folder: RIJC Student Handbook, 1967–1968, Community College of Rhode Island Archives, Community College of Rhode Island, Knight Campus.

59. Ibid.

60. *Rhode Island Junior College, 1965 Catalogue*, 26–41, Community College of Rhode Island Archives, Community College of Rhode Island, Knight Campus.

61. *Your Future in Technology*, brochure, Rhode Island Junior College, 1968. Community College of Rhode Island Archives, Community College of Rhode Island, Knight Campus.

62. "Rhode Island Junior College Annual Curriculum Comparisons—September Enrollments, dated October 2, 1973," Box: RIJC Institutional Statistics—1969–1975,

Folder: Statistical Reports. Community College of Rhode Island Archives, Community College of Rhode Island, Knight Campus.

63. *Report of the President—1965–1966*, pamphlet, Rhode Island Junior College, 12–13, Community College of Rhode Island Archives, Community College of Rhode Island, Knight Campus.

64. "Rhode Island Junior College Annual Curriculum Comparisons—September Enrollments, dated October 2, 1973."

65. *Report of the President—1968–1969*, pamphlet, Rhode Island Junior College, 44–45; *Report of the President—1969–1970*, pamphlet, Rhode Island Junior College, 39. Community College of Rhode Island Archives, Community College of Rhode Island, Knight Campus.

66. *Primus 1966*, First Edition, Rhode Island Junior College, Providence, Rhode Island.

67. Ibid.

68. "Knight Campus—Warwick, Rhode Island. Recommended Master Plan. The Perkins & Will Partnership," Box 2: Knight Campus, Folder: First RIJC Proposed Master Plan for Knight Campus—Circa 1965, Community College of Rhode Island Archives, Community College of Rhode Island, Knight Campus.

69. "Rhode Island Junior College Enrollment Statistics," Box: RIJC Institutional Statistics—1965–1975, Folder: Statistical Reports. Community College of Rhode Island Archives, Community College of Rhode Island, Knight Campus.

70. Liston, *Recollections of a Pioneer President*, 38.

71. Ibid., 48–49.

72. *Miracle on Promenade: A Documentary about the History of Rhode Island's Only Community College: RIJC/CCRI 1964–1980*. Produced by the Community College of Rhode Island, 2015.

73. Liston, *Recollections of a Pioneer President*, 44–49.

74. "From the President." *Knightly News: Community College of Rhode Island* 2, no. 4 (January 1981): 1. Box 1: Knightly News 1979–1986. Community College of Rhode Island Archives, Community College of Rhode Island, Knight Campus.

75. "NTMA Apprentices Enroll in Machine Processes Program," *Knightly News: Community College of Rhode Island* 3, no. 8 (June 1982): 4.

76. Ibid.

77. "CCRI Established Business and Industry Advisory Council," *Knightly News: Community College of Rhode Island* 4, no. 3 (December 1982): 4.

78. "Community College of Rhode Island Business and Industry Partnership," Box: CCRI Career Services, Folder: CCRI Career Services: Business and Industry Partnership—1985, Community College of Rhode Island Archives, Community College of Rhode Island, Knight Campus.

79. "Business and Industry Program Renamed," *Knightly News: Community College of Rhode Island* 7, no. 6 (April 1986): 1.

80. "CCRI Offers Customized Programs at Raytheon and Electric Boat," *Knightly News: Community College of Rhode Island* 4, no. 6 (May 1983): 1.

81. Ibid.

82. *Community College of Rhode Island Annual Report, 1989–1990*, 9, Box: CCRI Annual Reports, Community College of Rhode Island Archives, Community College of Rhode Island, Knight Campus.

83. Liston, *Recollections of a Pioneer President*, 75.

84. Ibid., 57.

85. "CCRI Receives Grant to Promote Computer Literacy," *Knightly News: Community College of Rhode Island* 4, no. 2 (October 1982): 1.

86. "Governor's High Technology Grant Will Increase Computer Capabilities," *Knightly News: Community College of Rhode Island* 5, no. 2 (October 1983): 1.

87. "From the President," *Knightly News: Community College of Rhode Island* 1, no. 7 (March 1980): 1.

88. "Mentor Program Instituted and Coordinator Named," *Knightly News: Community College of Rhode Island* 8, no. 1 (September 1988): 4.

89. "Minority Enrollment Reaches 10 Percent," *Knightly News: Community College of Rhode Island* 8, no. 5 (March/April 1990): 1.

90. Liston, *Recollections of a Pioneer President*, 66.

91. "Urban Educational Center Transferred to CCRI," *Knightly News: Community College of Rhode Island* 7, no. 5 (March 1987): 4; "UEC Dedicated to Community Service," *Knightly News: Community College of Rhode Island* 8, no. 1 (August 1987): 4.

92. "Community College Establishes Permanent Campus in Providence," *Knightly News: Community College of Rhode Island* 8, no. 5 (May 1990): 1; "CCRI Opens Providence Campus." *Knightly News: Community College of Rhode Island* 9, no. 1 (September 1990): 1–2.

93. "CCRI Appoints EOC Director," *Knightly News: Community College of Rhode Island* 8, no. 5 (February 1988): 3; *Community College of Rhode Island Annual Report, 1989–1990*, 4–5.

94. "Community College Establishes Permanent Campus in Providence," *Knightly News: Community College of Rhode Island* 8, no. 5 (May 1990): 1–2.

95. *Community College of Rhode Island Annual Report, 1990–1991*, 20–21, 28–29.

96. Ibid., 14.

97. Ibid., 34.

98. Liston, *Recollections of a Pioneer President*, 66.

99. Antonio Esquibel, "A Review of Public Two-Year Institutions of Higher Education in New Mexico" (Albuquerque: New Mexico University Press, 1974), 19–20; Frank J. Renz and Marjorie Black, *Position Paper for Community Colleges in New Mexico*, New Mexican Association of Community and Junior Colleges, Santa Fe, September 1985, 16–20.

100. Henry J. Tobias and Charles E. Woodhouse, *Santa Fe: A Modern History, 1880–1990* (Albuquerque: University of New Mexico Press, 2001), 209–10; 1980 Census of Population, Volume 1: Characteristics of the Population, Chapter A: Number of Inhabitants, Part 33: New Mexico, U.S Department of Commerce, Bureau of the Census, Issued January 1982, 33–38; "Santa Fe County Community Profile," Folder CA PR 115 1982, Santa Fe Community College Library.

101. "Report of a Survey on the Feasibility of Creating a Junior College District in Santa Fe, New Mexico. Prepared for the Santa Fe Public School District for presentation to the State Board of Educational Finance and the New Mexico Legislature by Dr. Bill J. Priest, Consultant in Community/Junior College Education, September 1982," 18–19, Folder: CA PR 203 1982, Santa Fe Community College Library.

102. "Santa Fe Community College Recommendation, Board of Educational Finance, dated June 1982" and "Santa Fe Community College," document produced by the Santa Fe School Board and Superintendent of Schools James P. Miller describing the proposed community college, dated December 1, 1982, Folder CA PR 115 1982, Santa Fe Community College Library.

103. "Report of a Survey on the Feasibility of Creating a Junior College District in Santa Fe, New Mexico," 18–19.

104. "Memo to All School Employees from Dr. James P. Miller, Superintendent of Schools regarding Election Issues, dated January 19, 1983," Folder CA PR 115 1982, Santa Fe Community College Library.

105. New Mexico State Legislature, House Bill 2, Laws 1983, Chapter 46.

106. New Mexico State Legislature, House Bill 113, Laws 1983, Chapter 149.

107. "Report of a Survey on the Feasibility of Creating a Junior College District," 16.

108. Tobias and Woodhouse, *Santa Fe*, 196–204.

109. "Santa Fe Community College Self Study Report, 1984," 32–39, Box CA 21, Santa Fe Community College Library.

110. "Santa Fe Community College: The President's Annual Report, 1983–1984," 11, Box: CA AR7/SFCC President's Annual Reports, 1983–2002, Santa Fe Community College Library.

111. For a comparison of New Mexico community college tuition and fees with those of other states at the time, see Renz and Black, *Position Paper for Community Colleges in New Mexico*, 39.

112. *Santa Fe Community College Student Handbook, 1983–84*, 19, Box: CA Box 15 Student Handbooks, 1983-present, Santa Fe Community College Library.

113. *Santa Fe Community College Catalog, 1983–1984*, i, Box: CA Box 15 SFCC Catalogs, 1983–2000, Santa Fe Community College Library.

114. Ibid., 1.

115. *Santa Fe Community College, Fact Book 2001–2002*, 1, Office of Institutional Research, Santa Fe Community College Library; "Santa Fe Community College: The President's Annual Report, 1983–1984," 12–13.

116. "Santa Fe Community College Self Study Report, 1984," 39–40.

117. "Santa Fe Community College: The President's Annual Report, 1983–1984," 4.

118. *Santa Fe Community College Student Handbook, 1983–84*, 1.

119. "Santa Fe Community College's Divisional Annual Reports, 1985–86," Box: CA Box 22 Division Annual Reports, Santa Fe Community College Library.

120. "Santa Fe Community College's Divisional Annual Reports, 1985–86."

121. "Santa Fe Community College: The President's Annual Report, 1983–1984," 9.

122. "Santa Fe Community College's Divisional Annual Reports, 1985–86."

123. "Santa Fe Community College: The President's Annual Report, 1983–1984," 22.

124. "Santa Fe Community College Self-Study Report, 1985–86," 1, Box CA 21, Santa Fe Community College Library.

125. "Santa Fe Community College: The President's Annual Report, 1987–1988," 24.

126. Ibid., 3.

127. "Student Services Annual Report for 1985–1986," Folder CA SS 33 1985, Santa Fe Community College Library.

128. Ibid.

129. "Santa Fe Community College: The President's Annual Report, 1983–1984," 18.

130. "SFCC Operating Budget 2000–2001," Santa Fe Community College Self-Study Report for Accreditation by the North Central Association of Colleges and Schools, 2002, 4.15, Box CA 21, Santa Fe Community College Library.

131. Ibid.

132. http://www.sfcc.edu/about_SFCC/training_center_corporation.

133. http://hec.sfcc.edu/about_the_sfhec/.

134. Ibid.

135. Ibid.

136. Jason Song, "Fifteen Community Colleges in California to Offer Four-Year Degrees," *Los Angeles Times*, January 20, 2015, http://www.latimes.com/local/lanow/la-me-ln-community-colleges-degrees-20150120-story.html.

137. Alene Russell, "Update on the Community College Baccalaureate: Evolving Trends and Issues," American Association of State Colleges and Universities, Higher Education Policy Brief, October 2010, 1.

138. Ashley A. Smith, "Challenges Remain for Community Colleges Offering Bachelor's Degrees," *Inside Higher Ed*, April 20, 2015, https://www.insidehighered.com/news/2015/04/20/challenges-remain-community-colleges-offering-bachelors-degrees.

139. Stephen J. Handle, "2-Year Students Have Long Had 4-Year Dreams," *The Chronicle of Higher Education*, September 23, 2013, http://chronicle.com/article/2-Year-Students-Have-Long-Had/141787/.

140. Doug Shapiro, et al., *Completing College: A National View of Student Attainment Rates* (Herndon, VA: National Student Clearinghouse Research Center, 2012).

141. Quoted in Julie Hirschfeld Davis and Tamar Lewin, "Obama Plan Would Help Many Go to Community College Free," *New York Times*, January 8, 2015, http://www.nytimes.com/2015/01/09/us/politics/obama-proposes-free-community-college-education-for-some-students.html?_r=0.

142. Richard D. Kahlenberg, "Community of Equals?," *Democracy: A Journal of Ideas* 32 (2014). http://democracyjournal.org/magazine/32/community-of-equals/.

143. Mark Bauerlein, "What's the Point of a Professor?," *The New York Times Sunday Review*, May 9, 2015, http://www.nytimes.com/2015/05/10/opinion/sunday/whats-the-point-of-a-professor.html?_r=0.

EPILOGUE

1. Marvin Lazerson, *Higher Education and the American Dream: Success and Its Discontents* (New York: Central European University Press, 2010), 189.

2. W. Norton Grubb and Marvin Lazerson, *The Education Gospel: The Economic Power of Schooling* (Cambridge, MA: Harvard University Press, 2004), 15.

3. Rebekah Nathan, *My Freshman Year: What a Professor Learned by Becoming a Student* (New York: Penguin Books, 2005), 155.

4. Jennifer Washburn, *University, Inc.: The Corporate Corruption of American Higher Education* (New York: Basic Books, 2005); Eric Gould, *The University in a Corporate Culture* (New Haven, CT: Yale University Press, 2003); Derek Bok, *Universities in the Marketplace: The Commercialization of Higher Education* (Princeton, NJ: Princeton University Press, 2004); James E. Côté and Anton L. Allahar, *Lowering Higher Education: The Rise of Corporate Universities and the Fall of Liberal Education* (Toronto: University of Toronto Press, 2011).

5. See, for instance, Martha C. Nussbaum, *Not for Profit: Why Democracy Needs the Humanities* (Princeton, NJ: Princeton University Press, 2012); Christopher Newfield, *Unmaking the Public University: The Forty-Year Assault on the Middle Class* (Cambridge, MA: Harvard University Press, 2011).

6. Nicolaus Mills, "The Corporatization of Higher Education," *Dissent: A Quarterly Journal of Politics and Culture* 59, no. 4 (2012): 6.

7. Ibid., 6.

8. http://www.nytimes.com/aponline/2015/03/04/us/ap-us-sweet-briar-college-closure.html.

9. http://www.pbs.org/newshour/rundown/women-sweet-briar-college-decides-close-114-years/.

10. Anemona Hartocollis, "At Small Colleges, Harsh Lessons about Cash Flow," *The New York Times*, April 29, 2016.

11. James Engell and Anthony Dangerfield, *Saving Higher Education in the Age of Money* (Charlottesville: University of Virginia Press, 2005), 4.

12. William Deresiewicz, *Excellent Sheep: The Miseducation of the American Elite and the Way to a Meaningful Life* (New York: Free Press, 2014), 69.

13. Ibid., 69.

14. Sheila Slaughter and Gary Rhoades, *Academic Capitalism and the New Economy: Markets, State, and Higher Education* (Baltimore: Johns Hopkins University Press, 2004), 1–2.

15. Frank Donoghue, *The Last Professors: The Corporate University and the Fate of the Humanities* (New York: Fordham University Press, 2008), 56.

16. Ibid., 102.

17. John R. Thelin, *A History of American Higher Education* (Baltimore: Johns Hopkins University Press, 2004), 56–58.

18. Allen Ezell and John Bear, *Degree Mills: The Billion-Dollar Industry That Has Sold over a Million Fake Diplomas* (Amherst, NY: Prometheus Books, 2012).

19. For a history of the for-profit sector, see A. J. Angulo, *Diploma Mills: How For-Profit Colleges Stiffed Students, Taxpayers, and the American Dream* (Baltimore: Johns Hopkins University Press, 2016).

20. Paul Fain and Doug Lederman, "Boom, Regulate, Cleanse, Repeat: For-Profit Colleges' Slow but Inevitable Drive toward Acceptability," in *Remaking College: The Changing Ecology of Higher Education*, ed. Michael W. Kirst and Mitchell L. Stevens (Stanford, CA: Stanford University Press, 2015), 61.

21. Suzanne Mettler, *Degrees of Inequality: How the Politics of Higher Education Sabotaged the American Dream* (New York: Basic Books, 2014), 34.

22. Ibid., 2–3, 35–37.

23. Ibid., 36.

24. On possible approaches to better understanding the strengths and weaknesses of for-profit colleges, see William G. Tierney, "The Conundrum of Profit-Making Institutions of Higher Education," in *Preparing Today's Students for Tomorrow's Jobs in Metropolitan America*, ed. Laura W. Perna (Philadelphia: University of Pennsylvania Press, 2013), 149–74.

25. http://www.nytimes.com/2014/07/05/education/corinthian-colleges-to-largely-shut-down.html.

26. See http://www.nytimes.com/2016/09/08/business/downfall-of-itt-technical-institutes-was-a-long-time-in-the-making.html?_r=0.

27. Ibid.

28. Paul Fain and Doug Lederman, "Boom, Regulate, Cleanse, Repeat," 63.

29. Clayton M. Christensen, Michael B. Horn, and Curtis W. Johnson, *Disrupting Class: How Disruptive Innovation Will Change the Way the World Learns* (New York: McGraw-Hill, 2011).

30. "Role and Scope of the University of South Florida by Lewis B. Mayhew," The Papers of John S. Allen, Box 2, Folder: USF Role and Scope Committee, Lewis B. Mayhew, B2/F6, University Archives, Special Collections, University of South Florida.

31. Ray Lyman Wilbur, *Human Hopes: Addresses & Papers on Education, Citizenship, & Social Problems* (Stanford, CA: Stanford University Press, 1940), 15–16.

32. Julie Bosman, "2016 Ambitions Seen in Walker's Push for University Cuts in Wisconsin," *The New York Times*, February 16, 2015.

33. Paul Fain, "Closing Doors No More," *Inside Higher Ed*, March 28, 2013. http://www.insidehighered.com/news/2013/03/28/pima-community-colleges-deep-accreditation-crisis#sthash.4k5xwQ0V.dpbs.

34. See, for instance, Frank Bruni, "Rethinking College Admissions," *The New York Times*, January 20, 2016, A25.

35. *The Children We Mean to Raise: The Real Messages Adults Are Sending about Values*, Making Caring Common Project, Harvard Graduate School of Education, 2014, 6, http://mcc.gse.harvard.edu/files/gse-mcc/files/mcc-research-report.pdf?m=1448057487.

36. *Turning the Tide: Inspiring Concern for Others and the Common Good through College Admissions*, Making Caring Common Project, Harvard Graduate School of Education, 2016, 1, http://mcc.gse.harvard.edu/files/gse-mcc/files/20160120_mcc_ttt_report_interactive.pdf?m=1453303517.

37. "The Inaugural Address, delivered in Brunswick, September 2, 1802, by the Rev. Joseph McKeen, A.M. & A.S.S.," Department of Special Collections, Bowdoin College Archives.

Selected Bibliography

Aby, Stephen H., and James C. Kuhn. *Academic Freedom: A Guide to the Literature.* Westport, CT: Greenwood, 2000.

Allen, John S. "The University of South Florida." In *New Universities in the Modern World,* edited by Murray G. Ross, 152–69. New York: St. Martin's Press, 1966.

Allmendinger, David F. *Paupers and Scholars: The Transformation of Student Life in Nineteenth-Century New England.* New York: St. Martin's Press, 1975.

Altenbaugh, Richard J., and Kathleen Underwood. "The Evolution of Normal Schools." In *Places Where Teachers Are Taught,* edited by John I. Goodlad, Roger Soder, and Kenneth A. Sirotnik, 136–86. San Francisco: Jossey-Bass, 1990.

Anderson, Eric, and Alfred A. Moss Jr. *Dangerous Donations: Northern Philanthropy and Southern Black Education, 1902–1930.* Columbia: University of Missouri Press, 1999.

Anderson, James D. *The Education of Blacks in the South, 1860–1935.* Chapel Hill: University of North Carolina Press, 1988.

Anderson, Karen. "Brickbats and Roses: Lucy Diggs Slowe, 1883–1937." In *Lone Voyagers: Academic Women in Coeducational Universities, 1870–1937,* edited by Geraldine Jonçich Clifford, 283–307. New York: The Feminist Press at The City University of New York, 1989.

Angell, Frank. "The Early History of Athletics at Stanford." In Kimball, *The First Year at Stanford,* 48–67.

Angulo, A. J. *Diploma Mills: How For-Profit Colleges Stiffed Students, Taxpayers, and the American Dream.* Baltimore: Johns Hopkins University Press, 2016.

——. *William Barton Rogers and the Idea of MIT.* Baltimore: Johns Hopkins University Press, 2009.

Appleton, Jesse. *The Works of Rev. Jesse Appleton, D.D., Late President of Bowdoin College: Embracing His Course of Theological Lectures, His Academic Addresses, and a Selection from His Sermons.* 2 vols. Andover, MA: Gould and Newman, 1836.

Arum, Richard, and Josipa Roksa. *Academically Adrift: Limited Learning on College Campuses.* Chicago: University of Chicago Press, 2010.

——. *Aspiring Adults Adrift: Tentative Transitions of College Graduates.* Chicago: University of Chicago Press, 2014.

Atkinson, Richard C., and William A. Blanpied. "Research Universities: Core of the US Science and Technology System." *Technology in Society* 30 (2008): 30–48.

Bailey, Robert E., Linda E. Cooper, and Karen L. Kramer. "The Ohio Technology Transfer Organization—Otto: An Experiment in Academia Assisting Business." *The Journal of Technology Transfer* 9, no. 2 (Spring 1985): 9–26.

Baker, Paula. "The Domestication of Politics: Women and Political Society, 1780–1920." *The American Historical Review* 89, no. 3 (June 1984): 620–47.

Bancroft, Hubert H. *History of the Life of Leland Stanford.* Oakland, CA: Biobooks, 1952.

Bangert, William V. *A History of the Society of Jesus.* St. Louis: Institute of Jesuit Sources, 1972.

Barker, John Marshall. *Colleges in America.* Cleveland: Cleveland Printing and Publishing, 1894.

Barringer, George M. "They Came to Georgetown: The French Sulpicians." *Georgetown Magazine*, July 1977.

Barrow, Clyde W. *Universities and the Capitalist State: Corporate Liberalism and the Reconstruction of American Higher Education, 1894–1928*. Madison: University of Wisconsin Press, 1990.

Bartley, Numan V. *The New South, 1945–1980: The Story of the South's Modernization*. Baton Rouge: Louisiana State University Press, 1995.

Baumgartner, Barbara Walker. "The New Castle County Free Library, 1927–1933." *Delaware History* 13 (1968): 45–56.

Beach, J. M. *Gateway to Opportunity? A History of the Community College in the United States*. Sterling, VA: Stylus Publishing, 2011.

Beal, W. J. *History of the Michigan Agricultural College and Biographical Sketches of Trustees and Professors*. East Lansing: Michigan Agricultural College, 1915.

Beatty, Richard Croom, ed. *Journal of a Southern Student, 1846–1848*. Nashville: Vanderbilt University Press, 1944.

Belz, Herman, ed. *The Webster-Hayne Debate on the Nature of the Union*. Indianapolis: Liberty Fund, Inc., 2000.

Bennett, Colin. "Compacts and Compromises: Thomas S. Twiss and West Point Influence in the Antebellum South Carolina College." *The South Carolina Historical Magazine* 109, no. 1 (2008): 7–37.

Berman, Elizabeth Popp. "Institution-Building and the Road to the Bayh-Dole Act." *Social Studies of Science* 38, no. 6 (December 2008): 835–71.

Bernard, Richard M., and Bradley R. Rice, eds. *Sunbelt Cities: Politics and Growth since World War II*. Austin: University of Texas Press, 1983.

Bledstein, Burton J. *The Culture of Professionalism: The Middle Class and the Development of Higher Education in America*. New York: W. W. Norton & Company, 1976.

Bogue, Jesse P. *The Community College*. New York: McGraw-Hill, 1950.

Bok, Derek. *Universities in the Marketplace: The Commercialization of Higher Education*. Princeton, NJ: Princeton University Press, 2004.

Bordelon, Suzanne. "Participating on an 'Equal Footing': The Rhetorical Significance of California State Normal School in the Late Nineteenth Century." *Rhetoric Society Quarterly* 41, no. 2 (2011): 168–90.

Bowen, William G., Martin A. Kurzweil, and Eugene M. Tobin. *Equity and Excellence in American Higher Education*. Charlottesville: University of Virginia Press, 2005.

Bowles, Samuel, and Herbert Gintis. *Schooling in Capitalist America: Educational Reform and the Contradictions of Economic Life*. New York: Basic Books, 1976.

Breuder, Robert L. "Technology Transfer and Training." *AACJC Journal* 59 (October/ November 1988): 30–33.

Brint, Steven, and Jerome Karabel. *The Diverted Dream: Community Colleges and the Promise of Educational Opportunity in America, 1900–1985*. New York: Oxford University Press, 1989.

Bromberg, Howard. "Legal Legacies: A Brief History of the Stanford Law School." *Stanford Magazine*, September 1993, 42–45.

——. "Our Professor, the President." *Stanford Lawyer*, Fall 1991, 10–15.

Brown, Tamara L., Gregory S. Parks, and Clarenda M. Phillips, eds. *African American Fraternities and Sororities: The Legacy and the Vision*. Lexington: University Press of Kentucky, 2005.

Brown, Victoria Bissell. *The Education of Jane Addams*. Philadelphia: University of Pennsylvania Press, 2007.

Burns, Edward McNall. *David Starr Jordan: Prophet of Freedom*. Stanford, CA: Stanford University Press, 1953.

Butler, Nicholas Murray. *Scholarship and Service: The Policies and Ideals of a National University in a Modern Democracy*. New York: Charles Scribner's Sons, 1921.

Calhoun, Charles C. *A Small College in Maine: Two Hundred Years of Bowdoin*. Brunswick, ME: Bowdoin College, 1993.

Calhoun, Richard J., ed. *Witness to Sorrow: The Antebellum Autobiography of William J. Grayson*. Columbia: University of South Carolina Press, 1990.

Carey, Kevin. *The End of College: Creating the Future of Learning and the University of Everywhere*. New York: Riverhead Books, 2015.

——. "Meet the Man Who Wrote the Greatest Book about American Higher Ed." *The Chronicle of Higher Education*, October 29, 2015.

Carmichael, Janice B. "Meeting Small Business Needs through Small Business Development Centers." In Waddell, *Economic and Workforce Development*, 25–30.

Carney, Ann. "Valuable Connections." *USF Magazine*, Fall/Winter 2004, 12.

Carpenter, John A. "General Howard and the Nez Perce War of 1877." *Pacific Northwest Quarterly* 49, no. 4 (1958): 129–45.

——. *Sword and Olive Branch: Oliver Otis Howard*. Pittsburgh: University of Pittsburgh Press, 1964.

Cavalli, Gary. *Stanford Sports*. Stanford, CA: Stanford Alumni Association, 1982.

Chaszar, Julianna. "Leading and Losing in the Agricultural Education Movement: Freeman G. Cary and Farmer's College, 1846–1884." *History of Higher Education Annual* 18 (1998): 25–46.

Chesney, Mark. "Cedar: High Tech, Higher Education Join Forces." *USF Magazine*, June 1983, 8–9.

Christensen, Clayton M., Michael B. Horn, and Curtis W. Johnson. *Disrupting Class: How Disruptive Innovation Will Change the Way the World Learns*. New York: McGraw-Hill, 2011.

Church, Robert. "Conversation: Renegotiating the Historical Narrative: The Case of American Higher Education." *History of Education Quarterly* 44, no. 4 (Winter 2004): 585–89.

Cisco, Walter Brian. *States Rights Gist: A South Carolina General of the Civil War*. Shippensburg, PA: White Maine Publishing Co., 1991.

Clark, Burton R. "The 'Cooling Out' Function in Higher Education." *The American Journal of Sociology* 65, no. 6 (1960): 569–76.

——. *Creating Entrepreneurial Universities*. New York: IAU Press, 1998.

Clarke, Daniel A. *Creating the College Man: American Mass Magazines and Middle-Class Manhood, 1890–1915*. Madison: University of Wisconsin Press, 2010.

Cleaveland, Nehemiah. *An Address, Delivered at Bowdoin College, before the Peucinian Society, at Their Annual Meeting, September 3, 1821*. Brunswick, ME: Joseph Griffin, 1821.

——. *History of Bowdoin College*. Boston: J. R. Osgood & Co., 1882.

Cleveland, Grover. "Does a College Education Pay?" *The Saturday Evening Post*, May 26, 1900, 1089–90.

Clifford, Geraldine Jonçich. *"Equally in View": The University of California, Its Women, and the Schools*. Berkeley: Center for Studies in Higher Education and Institute of Governmental Studies Press, 1995.

——. "Man/Woman/Teacher: Gender, Family, and Career in American Educational History." In Warren, *American Teachers: Histories of a Profession at Work*, 293–343.

Cohen, Arthur M. *The Shaping of American Higher Education: Emergence and Growth of the Contemporary System*. San Francisco: Jossey-Bass, 1998.

Cohen, Arthur M., and Florence B. Brawer. *The American Community College*. San Francisco: Jossey-Bass, 1982.

Cohen, Joshua. "Taking People as They Are?" *Philosophy and Public Affairs* 30, no. 4 (2002): 363–86.

Cohen, Michael David. *Reconstructing the Campus: Higher Education and the American Civil War*. Charlottesville: University of Virginia Press, 2012.

Coleman, Henry. "Plan of an Agricultural Institution." *Michigan Farmer* 3, no. 5 (1845): 77–79.

Cooper, Russell M., and Margaret B. Fisher. *The Vision of a Contemporary University: A Case Study of Expansion and Development in American Higher Education, 1950–1975*. Tampa: University of South Florida Press, 1982.

Cooper, Thomas. "Letters of Dr. Thomas Cooper." *American Historical Review* 6, no. 4 (1901): 725–36.

Côté, James E., and Anton L. Allahar. *Lowering Higher Education: The Rise of Corporate Universities and the Fall of Liberal Education*. Toronto: University of Toronto Press, 2011.

Couper, William. *One Hundred Years at V.M.I.* Richmond, VA: Garrett and Massie, 1939.

Cross, Coy F. *Justin Smith Morrill: Father of the Land-Grant Colleges*. East Lansing: Michigan State University Press, 1999.

Cross, K. Patricia. *Beyond the Open Door*. San Francisco: Jossey-Bass, 1974.

Cubitt, Geoffrey. *The Jesuit Myth: Conspiracy Theory and Politics in Nineteenth-Century France*. Oxford, UK: Oxford University Press, 1993.

Cunningham, Sean P. *American Politics in the Postwar Sunbelt: Conservative Growth in a Battleground Region*. New York: Cambridge University Press, 2014.

Curran, Robert Emmett. *The Bicentennial History of Georgetown University: From Academy to University, 1798–1889*. 2 vols. Washington, DC: Georgetown University Press, 1993.

Curti, Merle E., and Vernon Carstensen. *The University of Wisconsin, A History: 1848–1925*. 2 vols. Madison: University of Wisconsin Press, 1949.

Daley, John M. *Georgetown University: Origin and Early Years*. Washington, DC: Georgetown University Press, 1957.

Daskam, Josephine Dodge. *Smith College Stories*. New York: Charles Scribner's Sons, 1900.

Davidson, Chalmers G. *The Last Foray: The South Carolina Planters of 1860*. Columbia: University of South Carolina Press, 1971.

Davis, Emma. "Girlhood and Womanhood." *The Class Paper*, May 20 1880, 3.

Delmont, Matthew. "Working toward a Working-Class College: The Long Campaign to Build a Community College in Philadelphia." *History of Education Quarterly* 54, no. 4 (2014): 429–64.

D'Emilio, John, and Estelle B. Freedman. *Intimate Matters: A History of Sexuality in America*. Chicago: University of Chicago Press, 1988.

Dennis, Michael. *Lessons in Progress: State Universities and Progressivism in the New South, 1880–1920*. Urbana: University of Illinois Press, 2001.

Deresiewicz, William. *Excellent Sheep: The Miseducation of the American Elite and the Way to a Meaningful Life*. New York: Free Press, 2014.

Donoghue, Frank. *The Last Professors: The Corporate University and the Fate of the Humanities*. New York: Fordham University Press, 2008.

Dorn, Charles. *American Education, Democracy, and the Second World War*. New York: Palgrave Macmillan, 2007.

———. "Promoting the 'Public Welfare' in Wartime: Stanford University during World War II." *American Journal of Education* 112, no. 1 (2005): 103–28.

——. "'War Conditions Made It Impossible . . .': Historical Statistics and Women's Higher Education Enrollments, 1940–1952." *Studies in the Humanities* 36, no. 2 (2009): 108–15.

Dougherty, Kevin James. *The Contradictory College: The Conflicting Origins, Impacts, and Futures of the Community College.* Albany: State University of New York Press, 1994.

Douglass, John Aubrey. *The California Idea and American Higher Education.* Stanford, CA: Stanford University Press, 2000.

Dressel, Paul L. *College to University: The Hannah Years at Michigan State, 1935–1969.* East Lansing: Michigan State University Publications, 1987.

Drewry, Henry N., and Humphrey Doermann. *Stand and Prosper: Private Black Colleges and Their Students.* Princeton, NJ: Princeton University Press, 2001.

DuBois, W.E.B. *Dubois on Education,* edited by Eugene F. Provenzo Jr. Walnut Creek, CA: Altamira Press, 2002.

——. *The Souls of Black Folk.* New York: A. C. McClurg & Co., 1903.

Dunbar, Willis F., and George S. May. *Michigan: A History of the Wolverine State.* 2nd ed. Grand Rapids, MI: William B. Eerdmans Co., 1970.

Durkin, Joseph T. *Georgetown University: First in the Nation's Capital.* Garden City, NY: Doubleday, 1964.

Dyer, Thomas. *Theodore Roosevelt and the Idea of Race.* Baton Rouge: Louisiana State University Press, 1992.

Dyson, Walter. *Howard University: The Capstone of Negro Education.* Washington, DC: Howard University, 1941.

Easby-Smith, James Sanislaus. *Georgetown University in the District of Columbia, 1789–1907.* 2 vols. New York: Lewis Publishing Company, 1907.

Eddy, Edward Danforth. *Colleges for Our Land and Time: The Land-Grant Idea in American Education.* New York: Harper & Brothers, 1956.

Edgar, Walter B. *South Carolina: A History.* Columbia: University of South Carolina Press, 1998.

Edmond, J. B. *The Magnificent Charter: The Origin and Role of the Morrill Land-Grant Colleges and Universities.* Hicksville, NY: Exposition Press, 1978.

Eisenmann, Linda. *Higher Education for Women in Postwar America, 1945–1965.* Baltimore: Johns Hopkins University Press, 2006.

Elliott, Ellen Coit. "The Cornell Colony at Palo Alto." In Kimball, *The First Year at Stanford,* 29–47.

Elliott, Orrin Leslie. *Stanford University: The First Twenty-Five Years.* Stanford, CA: Stanford University Press, 1937.

Ellis, H. M. "Thomas Cooper: A Survey of His Life." *South Atlantic Quarterly* 19, no. 1 (1920): 24–42.

Engell, James, and Anthony Dangerfield. *Saving Higher Education in the Age of Money.* Charlottesville: University of Virginia Press, 2005.

Engs, Robert Francis. *Educating the Disfranchised and Disinherited: Samuel Chapman Armstrong and Hampton Institute, 1839–1893.* Knoxville: University of Tennessee Press, 1999.

Evans, Stephanie Y. *Black Women in the Ivory Tower: An Intellectual History.* Gainesville: University Press of Florida, 2007.

Ezell, Allen, and John Bear. *Degree Mills: The Billion-Dollar Industry That Has Sold over a Million Fake Diplomas* Amherst, NY: Prometheus Books, 2012.

Fain, Paul, and Doug Lederman. "Boom, Regulate, Cleanse, Repeat: For-Profit Colleges' Slow but Inevitable Drive toward Acceptability." Chap. 3 In *Remaking College: The Changing Ecology of Higher Education,* edited by Michael W. Kirst and Mitchell L. Stevens, 61–83. Stanford, CA: Stanford University Press, 2015.

Fairbanks, Robert B., and Kathleen Underwood, eds. *Essays on Sunbelt Cities and Recent Urban America*. College Station: Texas A&M University Press, 1990.

Fallows, Alice Katharine. "Undergraduate Life at Smith College." *Scribner's Monthly*, July 1898, 37–58.

Faust, Drew Gilpin. *James Henry Hammond and the Old South: A Design for Mastery*. Baton Rouge: Louisiana State University Press, 1982.

Feldman, Maryann P. "Entrepreneurship and American Research Universities: Evolution in Technology Transfer." In Hart, *The Emergence of Entrepreneurship Policy*, 92–112.

Finkin, Matthew W., and Robert C. Post. *For the Common Good: Principles of American Academic Freedom*. New Haven, CT: Yale University Press, 2009.

Fraser, James W. *Preparing America's Teachers: A History*. New York: Teachers College Press, 2007.

Freed, John B. *Educating Illinois: Illinois State University, 1857–2007*. Virginia Beach: Donning Company, 2009.

Friant, John R., Thomas A. Rover, and Edwin M. Dahill. *Glimpses of Old Georgetown*. Washington, DC: The Hoya, 1939.

Fülöp-Miller, René. *The Jesuits: A History of the Society of Jesus*. New York: Capricorn Books, 1963.

Galbraith, John Kenneth. "The Affluent Society." In *John Kenneth Galbraith: The Affluent Society and Other Writings, 1952–1967*, edited by James K. Galbraith, 345–605. New York: Library of America, 2010.

Gangone, Lynn M. "The National Association for Women in Education: An Enduring Legacy." *Journal about Women in Higher Education* 1, no. 1 (2009): 3–24.

Gates, Henry Louis Jr. *Life upon These Shores: Looking at African American History, 1513–2008*. New York: Alfred A. Knopf, 2011.

Geiger, Roger L. "The Commercialization of the University." *American Journal of Education* 110, no. 4 (2004): 389–99.

——. *The History of American Higher Education: Learning and Culture from the Founding to World War II*. Princeton, NJ: Princeton University Press, 2015.

——. *Knowledge and Money: Research Universities and the Paradox of the Marketplace*. Stanford, CA: Stanford University Press, 2004.

——. *Research and Relevant Knowledge: American Research Universities since World War II*. New York: Oxford University Press, 1993.

——. "The Rise and Fall of Useful Knowledge: Higher Education for Science, Agriculture & the Mechanic Arts, 1850–1875." *History of Higher Education Annual* 18 (1998): 47–65.

——. *To Advance Knowledge: The Growth of America's Research Universities, 1900–1940*. New York: Oxford University Press, 1986.

Geiger, Roger L., and Creso M. Sá. *Tapping the Riches of Science: Universities and the Promise of Economic Growth*. Cambridge, MA: Harvard University Press, 2008.

Gelber, Scott M. *The University and the People: Envisioning American Higher Education in an Era of Populist Protest*. Madison: University of Wisconsin Press, 2011.

George, Eric M. "The Cultivation of Eloquence at Georgetown College: A History of the Philodemic Society from 1830–1890." In *Swift Potomac's Lovely Daughter: Two Centuries at Georgetown through Students' Eyes*, edited by Joseph Durkin, 103–19. Washington, DC: Georgetown University Press, 1990.

Gilbert, Benjamin Franklin. *Pioneers for One Hundred Years: San Jose State College, 1857–1957*. San Jose: San Jose State College, 1957.

Gilbert, Benjamin, and Charles Burdick. *Washington Square, 1857–1979: The History of San Jose State University*. San Jose: San Jose State University, 1979.

Glazer, Penina Migdal, and Miriam Slater. *Unequal Colleagues: The Entrance of Women into the Professions, 1890–1940*. New Brunswick, NJ: Rutgers University Press, 1987.

Gleason, Philip. "The Main Sheet Anchor: John Carroll and Catholic Higher Education." *The Review of Politics* 38, no. 4 (1976): 576–613.

Gleazer, Edmund J. *This Is the Community College*. Boston: Houghton Mifflin, 1968.

Glover, Lorri. "An Education in Southern Masculinity: The Ball Family of South Carolina in the New Republic." *The Journal of Southern History* 69, no. 1 (2003): 39–70.

Goodchild, Lester F., and Harold S. Wechsler. *The History of Higher Education*. Needham Heights, MA: Simon & Schuster, 1997.

Goodwin, Gregory L. *A Social Panacea: A History of the Community-Junior College Ideology*. ERIC Document: ED 093–427., 1973.

Gordon, Lynn D. *Gender and Higher Education in the Progressive Era*. New Haven, CT: Yale University Press, 1990.

Gordon, Sarah H. "Smith College Students: The First Ten Classes, 1879–1888." *History of Education Quarterly* 15, no. 2 (Summer 1975): 147–67.

Gould, Eric. *The University in a Corporate Culture*. New Haven, CT: Yale University Press, 2003.

Graham, Hugh Davis, and Nancy Diamond. *The Rise of American Research Universities: Elites and Challengers in the Postwar Era*. Baltimore: Johns Hopkins University Press, 1997.

Green, Edwin L. *A History of the University of South Carolina*. Columbia, SC: The State Company, 1916.

Green, Elizabeth Alden. *Mary Lyon and Mount Holyoke: Opening the Gates*. Hanover, NH: University Press of New England, 1979.

Green, Elna C. "Relief from Relief: The Tampa Sewing-Room Strike of 1937 and the Right to Welfare." *The Journal of American History* 95, no. 4 (2009): 1012–37.

Green, Jennifer R. "Networks of Military Educators: Middle-Class Stability and Professionalization in the Late Antebellum South." *The Journal of Southern History* 73, no. 1 (February 2007): 39–74.

Greenberg, Mark I., Andrew T. Huse, and Marilyn Keltz Stephens. *University of South Florida: The First Fifty Years, 1956–2006*. Tampa: University of South Florida, 2006.

Grismer, Karl H. *Tampa: A History of the City of Tampa and the Tampa Bay Region of Florida*. St. Petersburg, FL: St. Petersburg Printing Company, 1950.

Grubb, W. Norton. "The Bandwagon Once More: Vocational Preparation for High-Tech Occupations." *Harvard Educational Review* 54, no. 4 (November 1984): 429–51.

Grubb, W. Norton, and Marvin Lazerson. *The Education Gospel: The Economic Power of Schooling*. Cambridge, MA: Harvard University Press, 2004.

Guralnick, Stanley M. *Science and the Ante-Bellum American College*. Philadelphia: The American Philosophical Society, 1975.

Hamlin, Cyrus. *My Life and Times*. Boston: Congregational Sunday School and Publishing Society, 1893.

Hanley, Thomas O'Brien, ed. *The John Carroll Papers*. 3 vols. Notre Dame, IN: University of Notre Dame Press, 1976.

Hanscom, Elizabeth Deering, Helen French Greene, and John Morton Greene. *Sophia Smith and the Beginnings of Smith College*. Northampton, MA: Smith College, 1925.

Harper, Charles A. *A Century of Public Teacher Education: The Story of the State Teachers Colleges as They Evolved from the Normal Schools*. Washington, DC: American Association of Teachers Colleges, 1939.

Hart, David M., ed. *The Emergence of Entrepreneurship Policy: Governance, Start-Ups, and Growth in the US Knowledge Economy*. Cambridge, UK: Cambridge University Press, 2003.

Hatch, Louis C. *The History of Bowdoin College*. Portland, ME: Loring, Short & Harmon, 1927.

Hawkins, Hugh. "American Universities and the Inclusion of Professional Schools." *History of Higher Education Annual* 13 (1993): 53–68.

——. "The Making of the Liberal Arts College Identity." *Daedalus* 128, no. 1 (1999): 1–25.

Hayes, Alice. "Can a Poor Girl Go to College?" *The North American Review* 152, no. 414 (1891): 624–31.

Helmreich, Ernst Christian. *Religion at Bowdoin College: A History*. Brunswick, ME: Bowdoin College, 1982.

Hennesey, James. "An Eighteenth-Century Bishop: John Carroll of Baltimore." In *Patterns of Episcopal Leadership*, edited by Gerald P. Fogarty, 5–51. New York: Macmillan, 1989.

Henry, Charles P. *Ralph Bunche: Model Negro or American Other?* New York: New York University Press, 1999.

Herbst, Jurgen. *And Sadly Teach: Teacher Education and Professionalization in American Culture*. Madison: University of Wisconsin Press, 1989.

——. *From Crisis to Crisis: American College Government, 1636–1819*. Cambridge, MA: Harvard University Press, 1982.

——. "Nineteenth-Century Normal Schools in the United States: A Fresh Look." *History of Education Quarterly* 9, no. 3 (1980): 219–27.

——. "The Yale Report of 1828." *International Journal of the Classical Tradition* 11, no. 2 (2004): 213–31.

Hewitt, Nancy A. "Economic Crisis and Political Mobilization: Reshaping Cultures of Resistance in Tampa's Communities of Color, 1929–1939." In *Women's Labor in the Global Economy: Speaking in Multiple Voices*, edited by Sharon Harley. New Brunswick, NJ: Rutgers University Press, 2007.

——. *Southern Discomfort: Women's Activism in Tampa, Florida, 1880s–1920s*. Urbana: University of Illinois Press, 2001.

Hoeveler, J. David Jr. "The University and the Social Gospel: The Intellectual Origins of the 'Wisconsin Idea.'" In Goodchild and Wechsler, *The History of Higher Education*, 234–46.

Hoffer, Williamjames Hull. *To Enlarge the Machinery of Government: Congressional Debates and the Growth of the American State, 1858–1891*. Baltimore: Johns Hopkins University Press, 2007.

Hofstadter, Richard, and Walter P. Metzger. *The Development of Academic Freedom in the United States*. New York: Columbia Univeristy Press, 1955.

Hollis, Daniel Walker. *University of South Carolina*. 2 vols. Columbia: University of South Carolina Press, 1951.

Horowitz, Helen Lefkowitz. *Alma Mater: Design and Experience in the Women's Colleges from Their Nineteenth-Century Beginnings to the 1930s*. New York: Alfred A. Knopf, 1984.

Howard, Oliver Otis. *Autobiography of Oliver Otis Howard*. 2 vols. New York: Baker and Taylor, 1907.

Howard, Walter T., and Virginia M. Howard. "Family, Religion, and Education: A Profile of African-American Life in Tampa, Florida, 1900–1930." *The Journal of Negro History* 79, no. 1 (1994): 1–17.

Ihle, Elizabth L., ed. *Black Women in Higher Education: An Anthology of Essays, Studies, and Documents*. New York: Garland, 1992.

Ingalls, Robert P. *Urban Vigilantes in the New South: Tampa, 1882–1936*. Knoxville: University of Tennessee Press, 1988.

James, Norris E., ed. *Fifty Years on the Quad*. Stanford, CA: Stanford Alumni Association, 1938.

Jarrett, Beverly, ed. *Tributes to John Hope Franklin: Schlolar, Mentor, Father, Friend*. Columbia: University of Missouri Press, 2003.

Jencks, Christopher, and David Riesman. *The Academic Revolution*. Garden City, NY: Doubleday, 1968.

Jewett, Andrew. *Science, Democracy, and the American University*. Cambridge, UK: Cambridge University Press, 2012.

Johnson, Eldon L. "Misconceptions about the Early Land-Grant Colleges." In Goodchild and Wechsler, *The History of Higher Education*, 222–33.

Johnson, Joan Marie. *Southern Women at the Seven Sister Colleges: Feminist Values and Social Activism, 1875–1915*. Athens: University of Georgia Press, 2010.

Johnson, Larry, Deirdre Cobb-Roberts, and Barbara Shircliffe. "African Americans and the Struggle for Opportunity in Florida Public Higher Education, 1947–1977." *History of Education Quarterly* 47, no. 3 (August 2007): 328–58.

Jones, Angela. *African American Civil Rights: Early Activism and the Niagara Movement*. Santa Barbara, CA: ABC-CLIO, 2011.

Jones, Ida E. *The Heart of the Race Problem: The Life of Kelly Miller*. Littleton, MA: Tapestry Press, 2011.

Jordan, David Starr. *The Days of a Man*. 2 vols. New York: World Book Company, 1922.

——. *The Foundation Ideals of Stanford University*. Stanford, CA: Stanford University, 1915.

——. "The Higher Sacrifice." *Daily Palo Alto*, May 27 1896, 1–12.

——. "Over Education." *The Sequoia* 3, no. 9 (November 1, 1893): 112–13.

——. "The Policy of the Stanford University." *Educational Review* 4 (June–December 1892): 1–5.

Kaestle, Carl F. *Pillars of the Republic: Common Schools and American Society, 1780–1860*. New York: Hill and Wang, 1983.

Kelley, Mary. *Learning to Stand and Speak: Women, Education, and Public Life in America's Republic*. Chapel Hill: University of North Carolina Press, 2006.

Kendall, Elaine. *"Peculiar Institutions": An Informal History of the Seven Sisters Colleges*. New York: Putnam, 1976.

Kerr, Clark. *The Uses of the University*. 4th ed. Cambridge, MA: Harvard University Press, 1995.

Kerstein, Robert. *Politics and Growth in Twentieth-Century Tampa*. Gainesville: University Press of Florida, 2001.

Kett, Joseph F. *The Pursuit of Knowledge under Difficulties: From Self-Improvement to Adult Education in America, 1750–1990*. Stanford, CA: Stanford University Press, 1994.

Kilbride, Daniel. "Slavery and Utilitarianism: Thomas Cooper and the Mind of the Old South." *The Journal of Southern History* 59, no. 3 (1993): 479–86.

Kim, Dongbin, and John L. Rury. "The Rise of the Commuter Student: Changing Patterns of College Attendance for Students Living at Home in the United States, 1960–1980." *Teachers College Record* 113, no. 5 (2011): 1031–66.

Kimball, Alice Windsor, ed. *The First Year at Stanford: Sketches of Pioneer Days at Leland Stanford Junior University*. San Francisco: The Stanley-Taylor Company, 1905.

Kimball, Bruce. *The "True Professional Ideal": A History in America*. Lanham MD: Rowman & Littlefield, 1995.

Klotsche, J. Martin. *The Urban University and the Future of Our Cities*. New York: Harper & Row, 1966.

Knight, Edgar W., ed. *A Documentary History of Education in the South before 1860*. 5 vols. Chapel Hill: University of North Carolina Press, 1952.

Krimsky, Sheldon. *Science in the Private Interest: Has the Lure of Profits Corrupted Biomedical Research?* Lanham, MD: Rowman & Littlefield, 2003.

Kuhn, Madison. *Michigan State: The First Hundred Years*. East Lansing: Michigan State University Press, 1955.

Labaree, David F. *How to Succeed in School without Really Learning: The Credentials Race in American Education*. New Haven, CT: Yale University Press, 1997.

LaBorde, Maximilian. *The History of the South Carolina College*. Charleston, SC: Walker, Evans & Cogswell, 1874.

Lamb, Daniel Smith, ed. *Howard University Medical Department*. Washington, DC: R. Beresford, 1900.

Lane, Jack C. "The Yale Report of 1828 and Liberal Education: A Neorepublican Manifesto." *History of Education Quarterly* 27, no. 3 (1987): 325–38.

Langston, John Mercer. *From the Virginia Plantation to the National Capitol or the First and Only Negro Representative in Congress from the Old Dominion*. Hartford, CT: American Publishing Company, 1894.

Lassiter, Matthew D. *The Silent Majority: Suburban Politics in the Sunbelt South*. Princeton, NJ: Princeton University Press, 2006.

Lassiter, Matthew D., and Kevin M. Kruse. "The Bulldozer Revolution: Suburbs and Southern History since World War II." *The Journal of Southern History* 75, no. 3 (2009): 691–706.

Lawson, Steven F. "From Sit-in to Race Riot: Businessmen, Blacks, and the Pursuit of Moderation in Tampa, 1960–1967." In *Southern Businessmen and Desegregation*, edited by Elizabeth Jacoway and David R. Colburn, 257–81. Baton Rouge: Louisiana State University Press, 1982.

Lazerson, Marvin. "The Disappointments of Success: Higher Education after World War II." *Annals of the American Academy of Political and Social Science* 559 (September 1998): 64–76.

———. *Higher Education and the American Dream: Success and Its Discontents*. New York: Central European University Press, 2010.

Leslie, Stuart W. *The Cold War and American Science: The Military-Industrial-Academic Complex at MIT and Stanford*. New York: Columbia University Press, 1993.

Leslie, W. Bruce. *Gentlemen and Scholars: College and Community in the "Age of the University," 1865–1917*. University Park: Pennsylvania State University Press, 1992.

Levin, Henry M. "Educating for a Commonwealth." *Educational Researcher* 30, no. 6 (2001): 30–33.

Levin, John S. "The Revised Institution: The Community College Mission at the End of the Twentieth Century." *Community College Review* 28, no. 2 (Fall 2000): 1–25.

Levine, David O. *The American College and the Culture of Aspiration, 1915–1940*. Ithaca, NY: Cornell University Press, 1986.

Liebendorfer, Don E. *The Color of Life Is Red: A History of Stanford Athletics, 1892–1972*. Stanford, CA: Stanford University Department of Athletics, 1972.

Logan, Rayford W. *Howard University: The First Hundred Years, 1867–1967*. New York: New York University Press, 1969.

Loss, Christopher P. *Between Citizens and the State: The Politics of American Higher Education in the 20th Century*. Princeton, NJ: Princeton University Press, 2012.

Lovett, Bobby L. *America's Historically Black Colleges and Universities: A Narrative History from the Nineteenth Century into the Twenty-First Century*. Macon, GA: Mercer University Press, 2011.

Lowen, Rebecca S. *Creating the Cold War University: The Transformation of Stanford*. Berkeley: University of California Press, 1997.

Lucas, Christopher J. *American Higher Education: A History*. 2nd ed. New York: Palgrave Macmillan, 2006.

Luger, Michael I., and Harvey A. Goldstein. *Technology in the Garden: Research Parks and Regional Economic Development*. Chapel Hill: University of North Carolina Press, 1991.

Malone, Dumas. *The Public Life of Thomas Cooper, 1787–1839*. New Haven, CT: Yale University Press, 1926.

Marsden, George M. *The Soul of the American University: From Protestant Establishment to Established Nonbelief*. Oxford, UK: Oxford University Press, 1994.

Marsden, George M., and Bradley J. Longfield, eds. *The Secularization of the Academy*. New York: Oxford University Press, 1992.

Mathews, Lois Kimball. *The Dean of Women*. New York: Houghton Mifflin, 1915.

May, Florence E. "Classics in the College Course." *The Alpha Quarterly* 1, no. 2 (June 1892): 6–13.

Mayhew, Ira, ed. *Reports of the Superintendent of Public Instruction of the State of Michigan for the Year 1855, '56, and '57*. Lansing, MI: Hosmer & Kerr, 1858.

McDonald, Emanuel B. *Sam McDonald's Farm: Stanford Reminiscences by Emanuel B. "Sam" McDonald*. Stanford, CA: Stanford University Press, 1954.

McFeely, William S. *Yankee Stepfather: General O. O. Howard and the Freedmen*. New Haven, CT: Yale University Press, 1968.

McKinney, Richard I. *Mordecai: The Man and His Message*. Washington, DC: Howard University Press, 1997.

McLaughlin, J. Fairfax. *College Days at Georgetown and Other Papers*. Philadelphia: J. B. Lippincott, 1899.

McNeil, Genna Rae. *Groundwork: Charles Hamilton Houston and the Struggle for Civil Rights*. Philadelphia: University of Pennsylvania Press, 1983.

McPherson, James M. "White Liberals and Black Power in Negro Education, 1865–1915." *The American Historical Review* 75, no. 5 (June 1970): 1357–86.

Melville, John G., and Thomas J. Chmura. "Strategic Alignment of Community Colleges and State Economic Policy." In Waddell, *Economic and Workforce Development*, 7–15.

Merlino, Maxine Ollie. "A History of the California State Normal Schools: Their Origin, Growth, and Transformation into Teachers Colleges." Ed.D. Thesis, University of Southern California, 1962.

Mettler, Suzanne. *Degrees of Inequality: How the Politics of Higher Education Sabotaged the American Dream*. New York: Basic Books, 2014.

Miller, Carroll L. L., and Anne S. Pruitt-Logan. *Faithful to the Task at Hand: The Life of Lucy Diggs Slowe*. Albany: State University of New York Press, 2012.

Mills, Nicolaus. "The Corporatization of Higher Education." *Dissent: A Quarterly Journal of Politics and Culture* 59, no. 4 (Fall 2012): 6–9.

Mirrielees, Edith R. *Stanford: The Story of a University*. New York: G. P. Putnam's Sons, 1959.

Mitchell, J. Pearce. *Stanford University, 1916–1941*. Stanford, CA: The Board of Trustees of the Leland Stanford Junior University, 1958.

Mohl, Raymond A., ed. *Searching for the Sunbelt: Historical Perspectives on a Region.* Knoxville: University of Tennessee Press, 1990.

Moore, Jacqueline M. *Leading the Race: The Transformation of the Black Elite in the Nation's Capital, 1880–1920.* Charlottesville: University Press of Virginia, 1999.

Mormino, Gary R. *Land of Sunshine, State of Dreams: A Social History of Modern Florida.* Gainesville: University Press of Florida, 2005.

——. "Tampa: From Hell Hole to the Good Life." In Bernard and Rice, *Sunbelt Cities: Politics and Growth since World War II,* 138–61.

Mormino, Gary R., and Goerge E. Pozzetta. *The Immigrant World of Ybor City: Italians and Their Latin Neighbors in Tampa, 1885–1985.* Urbana: University of Illinois Press, 1990.

Munroe, John A. *The University of Delaware: A History.* Newark: The University of Delaware, 1986.

Murphy, G. Ronald. "Georgetown's Shield: Utraque Unum." In *Splendor and Wonder: Jesuit Character, Georgetown Spirit, and Liberal Education,* edited by William J. O'Brien, 23–38. Washington, DC: Georgetown University Press, 1988.

Murphy, Marjorie, *Blackboard Unions: The AFT and the NEA, 1900–1980.* Ithaca: Cornell University Press, 1990.

Nasaw, David. *Schooled to Order: A Social History of Public Schooling in the United States.* New York: Oxford University Press, 1979.

Nash, George, Dan Waldorf, and Robert E. Price. *The University and the City.* New York: McGraw Hill, 1973.

Nash, Margaret A. *Women's Education in the United States, 1780–1840.* New York: Palgrave Macmillan, 2005.

Nathan, Rebekah. *My Freshman Year: What a Professor Learned by Becoming a Student.* New York: Penguin Books, 2005.

Nespoli, Lawrence A. "Investing in Human Capital: State Strategies for Economic Development." In Waddell, *Economic and Workforce Development,* 17–24.

Nevins, Allan. *The State Universities and Democracy.* Urbana: University of Illinois Press, 1962.

Newcomer, Mabel. *A Century of Higher Education for American Women.* New York: Harper & Brothers, 1959.

Newfield, Christopher. *Ivy and Industry: Business and the Making of the American University, 1880–1980.* Durham, NC: Duke University Press, 2003.

——. *Unmaking the Public University: The Forty-Year Assault on the Middle Class.* Cambridge, MA: Harvard University Press, 2011.

Newman, Stephen L. "Thomas Cooper, 1759–1839: The Political Odyssey of a Bourgeois Ideologue." *Southern Studies* 24, no. 3 (1985): 295–305.

Nickerson, Michelle, and Darren Dochuk, eds. *Sunbelt Rising: The Politics of Place, Space, and Region.* Philadelphia: University of Pennsylvania Press, 2011.

Nivison, Kenneth. "'But a Step from College to the Judicial Bench': College and Curriculum in New England's 'Age of Improvement.'" *History of Education Quarterly* 50, no. 4 (2010): 460–87.

Noble, Jeanne. "The Higher Education of Black Women in the Twentieth Century." In *Women and Higher Education in American History,* edited by John Mack Faragher and Florence Howe, 87–106. New York: W. W. Norton & Company, 1988.

Nussbaum, Martha C. *Not for Profit: Why Democracy Needs the Humanities.* Princeton, NJ: Princeton University Press, 2012.

Ogren, Christine A. *The American State Normal School: "An Instrument of Great Good."* New York: Palgrave Macmillan, 2005.

——. "The History and Historiography of Teacher Preparation in the United States: A Synthesis, Analysis, and Potential Contributions to Higher Education History." In *Higher Education: Handbook of Theory and Research*, edited by John C. Smart and Michael B. Paulsen. New York: Springer, 2013.

O'Mara, Margaret P. "Beyond Town and Gown: University Economic Engagement and the Legacy of the Urban Crisis." *Journal of Technology Transfer* 37, no. 2 (2012): 234–50.

——. *Cities of Knowledge: Cold War Science and the Search for the Next Silicon Valley.* Princeton, NJ: Princeton University Press, 2005.

Oriard, Michael. *Reading Football: How the Popular Press Created an American Spectacle.* Cultural Studies of the United States. Chapel Hill: University of North Carolina Press, 1993.

Pace, Robert F., and Christopher A. Bjornsen. "Adolescent Honor and College Student Behavior in the Old South." *Southern Cultures* 6, no. 3 (2000): 9–28.

Palmieri, Patricia A. "From Republican Motherhood to Race Suicide: Arguments on the Higher Education of Women in the United States, 1820–1920." In Goodchild and Wechsler, *The History of Higher Education*, 173–82.

——. *In Adamless Eden: The Community of Women Faculty at Wellesley.* New Haven, CT: Yale University Press, 1995.

Palumbo-DeSimone, Christine. *Sharing Secrets: Nineteenth-Century Women's Relations in the Short Story.* Cranbury: Associated University Press, 2000.

Parker, William B. *The Life and Public Services of Justin Smith Morrill.* Boston: Houghton Mifflin Company, 1924.

Patton, William W. *The History of Howard University, Washington, DC.* Washington, DC: Howard University, 1896.

Perkins, Linda M. "The African American Female Elite: The Early History of African American Women in the Seven Sister Colleges, 1880–1960." *Harvard Educational Review* 67, no. 4 (1997): 718–57.

——. "Lucy Diggs Slowe: Champion of the Self-Determination of African-American Women in Higher Education." *The Journal of Negro History* 81, no. 1/4 (1996): 89–104.

——. "Merze Tate and the Quest for Gender Equity at Howard University: 1942–1977." *History of Education Quarterly*, 54, no. 4 (2015): 516–51.

——. "The National Association of College Women: Vanguard of Black Women's Leadership and Education, 1923–1954." *Journal of Education* 172, no. 3 (1990): 65–75.

Phillips, Kevin. *The Emerging Republican Majority.* New Rochelle, NY: Arlington House, 1969.

Platt, Anthony M. *E. Franklin Frazier Reconsidered.* New Brunswick: Rutgers University Press, 1991.

Potts, David B. "American Colleges in the Nineteenth Century: From Localism to Denominationalism." *History of Education Quarterly* 11, no. 4 (1971): 363–80.

Pyburn, Nita Katharine. *The History of the Development of a Single System of Education in Florida, 1822–1903.* Tallahassee: Florida State University, 1954.

Radke-Moss, Andrea G. *Bright Epoch: Women and Coeducation in the American West.* Lincoln: University of Nebraska Press, 2008.

Ransom, Joanna H. "Innovations Introduced into the Women's Program at Howard University by the Late Dean Lucy D. Slowe." *Journal of the National Association of College Women*, no. 14 (1937): 51–52.

Reesman, John A. "A School for Honor: South Carolina College and the Guard House Riot of 1856." *The South Carolina Historical Magazine* 84, no. 4 (1983): 195–213.

Reuben, Julie A. *The Making of the Modern University: Intellectual Transformation and the Marginalization of Morality*. Chicago: University of Chicago Press, 1996.

———. "Patriotic Purposes: Public Schools and the Education of Citizens." In *The Public Schools*, edited by Susan Fuhrman and Marvin Lazerson, 1–24. Oxford, UK: Oxford University Press, 2005.

Reynolds, Terry S. "The Education of Engineers in America before the Morrill Act of 1862." *History of Education Quarterly* 32, no. 4 (1992): 459–82.

Rhees, Harriet Chapin Seelye. *Laurenus Clark Seelye: First President of Smith College*. New York: Houghton Mifflin Company, 1929.

Robinson, Edgar Eugene, and Paul Carroll Edwards, eds. *The Memoirs of Ray Lyman Wilbur*. Stanford, CA: Stanford University Press, 1960.

Robinson, Harry G., and Hazel Ruth Edwards. *The Long Walk: The Placemaking Legacy of Howard University*. Washington, DC: Howard University, 1996.

Roosevelt, Theodore. "The Man Who Works with His Hands." In *Semi-Centennial Celebration of Michigan State Agricultural College*, edited by Thomas C. Blaisdell, 239–55. Chicago: University of Chicago Press, 1908.

Rosenberg, Nathan. "America's Entrepreneurial Universities." In Hart, *The Emergence of Entrepreneurship Policy*, 113–37.

Ross, Edward A. *Seventy Years of It: An Autobiography*. New York: D. Appleton-Century Company, 1936.

Ross, Hugh. "University Influence in the Genesis and Growth of Junior Colleges in California." *History of Education Quarterly* 3, no. 3 (1963): 143–52.

Rossiter, Margaret W. *The Emergence of Agricultural Science: Justus Liebig and the Americans, 1840–1880*. New Haven, CT: Yale University Press, 1975.

Rothman, Sheila. *Woman's Proper Place: A History of Changing Ideals and Practices, 1870 to the Present*. New York: Basic Books, 1978.

Royce, Ruth. *Historical Sketch of the State Normal School at San José*. Sacramento: J. D. Young, Supt. State Printing, 1889.

Rubin, Irma. "A Foot in the Door and More: Co-Op Program Is a Triple Winner." *USF Magazine*, January 1983, 12–13.

Rudolph, Frederick. *The American College and University: A History*. 2nd ed. Athens: University of Georgia Press, 1990.

Sahli, Nancy. "Smashing: Women's Relationships before the Fall." *Chrysalis*, 1979, 17–27.

Sale, Kirkpatrick. *Power Shift: The Rise of the Southern Rim and Its Challenges to the Eastern Establishment*. New York: Random House, 1975.

Schmidt, George Paul. *The Old Time College President*. New York: Columbia University Press, 1930.

Schulman, Bruce J. *From Cotton Belt to Sunbelt: Federal Policy, Economic Development, and the Transformation of the South, 1938–1980*. New York: Oxford University Press, 1994.

Scott, John C. "The Mission of the University: Medieval to Postmodern Transformations." *The Journal of Higher Education* 77, no. 1 (2006): 1–39.

Scott, Patrick. "From Rhetoric to English: Nineteenth Century English Teaching at South Carolina College." *The South Carolina Historical Magazine* 85, no. 3 (1984): 233–43.

Scudder, Vida Dutton. "The College Woman and Social Reform." In *Celebration of the Quarter Centenary of Smith College*, 42–48. Cambridge, MA: The Riverside Press, 1900.

———. *On Journey*. New York: E. P. Dutton & Co., 1937.

Scully, Malcolm G. "Student Focus on Practicality Hits Humanities." *The Chronicle of Higher Education* 8, no. 18 (1974): 1, 3.

Sears, Jesse B., and Adin D. Henderson. *Cubberley of Stanford and His Contribution to American Education.* Stanford, CA: Stanford University Press, 1957.

Seelye, Laurenus Clark. *The Early History of Smith College, 1871–1910.* New York: Houghton Mifflin, 1923.

———. "History of Smith College." In *Celebration of the Quarter Centenary of Smith College,* 95–131. Cambridge, MA: The Riverside Press, 1900.

Shain, Barry Alan. *The Myth of American Individualism: The Protestant Origins of American Political Thought* Princeton, NJ: Princeton University Press, 1994.

Shalhope, Robert E. "Republicanism and Early American Historiography." *The William and Mary Quarterly* 39, no. 2 (1982): 334–56.

Shea, John Gilmary. *Memorial of the First Centenary of Georgetown College, D.C., Comprising a History of Georgetown University.* Washington, DC: Published for the College by P. F. Collier, 1891.

Shearer, J. "Agriculture: Report of the Com. On Agriculture. A Bill for the Encouragement of Agriculture." *Michigan Farmer* 2 (February 15 1844): 3.

Shircliffe, Barbara J. *The Best of That World: Historically Black High Schools and the Crisis of Desgregation in a Southern Metropolis.* Cresskill, NJ: Hampton Press, Inc., 2006.

Sigurdson, Kristjan T. "Clark Kerr's Multiversity and Technology Transfer in the Modern American Research University." *College Quarterly* 16, no. 2 (2013).

Sklar, Kathryn Kish. *Catharine Beecher: A Study in American Domesticity.* New York: W. W. Norton, 1973.

Slaughter, Sheila, and Gary Rhoades. *Academic Capitalism and the New Economy: Markets, State, and Higher Education.* Baltimore: Johns Hopkins University Press, 2004.

Slosson, Edwin E. *Great American Universities.* New York: The Macmillan Company, 1910.

Slowe, Lucy Diggs. "The Colored Girl Enters College—What Shall She Expect?" *Opportunity: Journal of Negro Life* 15, no. 9 (September 1937): 276–79.

———. "Higher Education of Negro Women." *The Journal of Negro Education* 2, no. 3 (July 1933): 352–58.

Smith, Elizabeth Brient. "Responding to Industry Demands: Advanced Technology Centers." *AACJC Journal* 61 (1991): 18–21.

Smith, Ronald. *Sports and Freedom: The Rise of Big-Time College Athletics.* New York: Oxford University Press, 1988.

Smith, Wilson and Thomas Bender, eds. *American Higher Education Transformed, 1940–2005.* Baltimore: Johns Hopkins University Press, 2008.

Smith-Rosenberg, Carroll. "The Female World of Love and Ritual: Relations between Women in Nineteenth-Century America." *Signs: Journal of Women in Culture and Society* 1, no. 1 (1975): 1–29.

Snyder, Thomas D., ed. *120 Years of American Education: A Statistical Portrait.* Washington, DC: US Department of Education National Center for Education Statistics, 1993.

Solomon, Barbara Miller. *In the Company of Educated Women: A History of Women and Higher Education in America.* New Haven, CT: Yale University Press, 1985.

Sommer, Clarence A. "Agriculture at the University of Michigan." In *Studies in the History of Higher Education in Michigan,* edited by Claude Eggertsen, 36–38. Ann Arbor: University of Michigan, 1950.

Sprague, William B. *Annals of the American Pulpit.* 9 vols. New York: Robert Carter and Brothers, 1857.

Stadtman, Verne A. "Happenings on the Way to the 1980s." In *Higher Education in American Society*, edited by Philip G. Altbach and Robert O. Berdahl, 101–10. Buffalo: Prometheus Books, 1981.

Stanford University: The Founding Grant with Amendments, Legislation and Court Decrees. Stanford, CA: Stanford University Press, 1971.

Stowe, Steven M. *Intimacy and Power in the Old South: Ritual in the Lives of the Planters.* Baltimore: Johns Hopkins University Press, 1987.

Sugrue, Michael. "'We Desired Our Future Rulers to Be Educated Men': South Carolina College, the Defense of Slavery, and the Development of Secessionist Politics." In *The American College in the Nineteenth Century*, edited by Roger Geiger. Nashville: Vanderbilt University Press, 2000.

Sugrue, Thomas. *The Origins of the Urban Crisis: Race and Inequality in Postwar Detroit.* Princeton, NJ: Princeton University Press, 1996.

Sumner, Margaret. *Collegiate Republic: Cultivating an Ideal Society in Early America.* Charlottesville: University of Virginia Press, 2014.

Talbot, Marion. *The Education of Women.* Chicago: University of Chicago Press, 1910.

Thelin, John R. *Games Colleges Play: Scandal and Reform in Intercollegiate Athletics.* Baltimore: Johns Hopkins University Press, 1996.

———. *A History of American Higher Education.* Baltimore: Johns Hopkins University Press, 2004.

Tierney, William G. "The Conundrum of Profit-Making Institutions of Higher Education." In *Preparing Today's Students for Tomorrow's Jobs in Metropolitan America*, edited by Laura W. Perna, 149–74. Philadelphia: University of Pennsylvania Press, 2013.

Tobias, Henry J., and Charles E. Woodhouse. *Santa Fe: A Modern History, 1880–1990.* Albuquerque: University of New Mexico Press, 2001.

Towles, Louis P. "A Matter of Honor at South Carolina College, 1822." *The South Carolina Historical Magazine* 94, no. 1 (1993): 6–18.

Trachtenberg, Alan. *The Incorporation of America: Culture and Society in the Gilded Age.* New York: Hill and Wang, 1982.

Train, Robert W. "Recovering Spanish-Language Education in Alta California: Ecologies, Ideologies and Intertexualities." In *Recovering the US Hispanic Literacy Heritage*, edited by Gabriela Baeza Ventura and Clara Lomas. Houston: Arte Público Press, 2011.

True, Alfred Charles. *A History of Agricultural Education in the United States, 1785–1925.* Washington, DC: United States Government Printing Press, 1929.

Turpin, Andrea L. "The Ideological Origins of the Women's College: Religion, Class, and Curriculum in the Educational Visions of Catharine Beecher and Mary Lyon." *History of Education Quarterly* 50, no. 2 (May 2010): 133–58.

Tushnet, Mark V. *Thurgood Marshall and the Supreme Court, 1936–1961.* Oxford, UK: Oxford University Press, 1994.

Tutorow, Norman E. *The Governor: The Life and Legacy of Leland Stanford.* 2 vols. Spokane: Arthur C. Clark Company, 2004.

Veblen, Thorstein. *The Higher Learning in America: A Memorandum on the Conduct of Universities by Business Men.* New York: B. W. Huebsch, 1918.

Veysey, Laurence R. *The Emergence of the American University.* Chicago: University of Chicago Press, 1965.

Voris, Jacqueline Van. *College: A Smith Mosaic.* West Springfield, MA: Smith College, 1975.

Waddell, Geneva, ed. *Economic and Workforce Development*. San Francisco: Jossey-Bass, 1991.

Wakelyn, Jon L. "Antebellum College Life and the Relations between Fathers and Sons." In *The Web of Southern Social Relations: Women, Family, & Education*, edited by Walter J. Fraser, R. Frank Saunders, and Jon L. Wakelyn, 107–26. Athens: University of Georgia Press, 1985.

Walsh, James P. *One and the Same: The History of Continuing Education at San José State University, 1857–2007*. San José: San José State University, 2006.

——. *San José State University: An Interpretive History, 1950–2000*. San José: San José State University, 2003.

Walther, Eric H. *The Fire-Eaters*. Baton Rouge: Louisiana State University Press, 1992.

Warren, Donald, ed. *American Teachers: Histories of a Profession at Work*. New York: Macmillan, 1989.

Washburn, Jennifer. *University, Inc.: The Corporate Corruption of American Higher Education*. New York: Basic Books, 2005.

Washington, Michael H., and Cheryl L. Nuñez. "Education, Racial Uplift, and the Rise of the Greek-Letter Tradition: The African-American Quest for Status in the Early Twentieth Century." In *African American Fraternities and Sororities: The Legacy and the Vision*, edited by Tamara L. Brown, Gregory S. Parks, and Clarenda M. Phillips. Lexington: University Press of Kentucky, 2005.

Watterson, John Sayle. *College Football: History, Spectacle, Controversy*. Baltimore: Johns Hopkins University Press, 2000.

Weil, Gordon L. *The Good Man: The Civil War's "Christian General" and His Fight for Racial Equality*. Harpswell, ME: Arthur McAllister Publishers, 2013.

Werner, Anja. *The Transatlantic World of Higher Education: Americans at German Universities, 1776–1914*. New York: Berghahn 2013.

Westby, David L., and Allen Sack. "The Commercialization and Functional Rationalization of College Football: Its Origins." *The Journal of Higher Education* 47, no. 6 (1976): 625–47.

Whaley, Deborah Elizabeth. *Disciplining Women: Alpha Kappa Alpha, Black Counterpublics, and the Cultural Politics of Black Sororities*. Albany: State University of New York Press, 2010.

Whiteside, William B. *The Will to Learn: Education and Community at Bowdoin College*. Brunswick, ME: Bowdoin College, 1970.

Widder, Keith R. *Michigan Agricultural College: The Evolution of a Land Grant Philosophy, 1855–1925*. East Lansing: Michigan State University Press, 2005.

Wilbur, Ray Lyman. *Human Hopes: Addresses & Papers on Education, Citizenship, & Social Problems*. Stanford, CA: Stanford University Press, 1940.

Williams, Roger L. *The Origins of Federal Support for Higher Education: George W. Atherton and the Land-Grant College Movement*. University Park: Pennsylvania State University Press, 1991.

Williams, Zachery R. *In Search of the Talented Tenth: Howard University Public Intellectuals and the Dilemmas of Race, 1926–1970*. Columbia: University of Missouri Press, 2009.

Wilson, John L. *Stanford University School of Medicine and the Predecessor Schools: An Historical Perspective*. Stanford, CA: Stanford University Lane Medical Library, 1999.

Wineman, Bradford. "J.T.L. Preston and the Origins of the Virginia Military Institue, 1834–42." *The Virginia Magazine of History and Biography* 114, no. 2 (2006): 226–61.

Winterer, Caroline. *The Culture of Classicism: Ancient Greece and Rome in American Intellectual Life*. Baltimore: Johns Hopkins University Press, 2002.

Wolters, Raymond. *Du Bois and His Rivals*. Columbia: University of Missouri Press, 2003.

——. *The New Negro on Campus: Black College Rebellions of the 1920s*. Princeton, NJ: Princeton University Press, 1975.

Wood, Gordon S. *The Creation of the American Republic, 1776–1787*. Chapel Hill: University of North Carolina Press, 1969.

Wyatt-Brown, Bertram. *Southern Honor: Ethics and Behavior in the Old South*. New York: Oxford University Press, 1982.

Zachary, G. Pascal. *Endless Frontier: Vannevar Bush, Engineer of the American Century*. New York: Free Press, 1997.

Zwerling, L. Steven. *Second Best: The Crisis of the Community College*. New York: McGraw-Hill, 1976.

Index

community colleges, 6, 10, 171–72, 199, 200–
209, 212, 223–25; corporate partnerships,
207–8, 211, 213–14, 222; criticisms of,
205–7; enrollment rates, 200, 203, 209, 211,
224; histories of, 202–9, 274n4; statistics,
209, 224; tuition rates, 231
Comstock, Ada Louise, 147
Cook, George William, 165
Cooper, Russell M., 184, 192
Cooper, Thomas, 44–46, 242n62
Corinthian Colleges, 231–32
Cornell, Ezra, 116
Cornell University, 166
Côté, James E., 228
Cromwell, Mary, 164
Cromwell, Otelia, 260n34
Cross, K. Patricia, 206
Crummel, Alexander, 164
Cunningham, Sean, 180
Curran, Robert, 59, 65, 245n45

Dangerfield, Anthony, 229
Dartmouth College, 155
Davidson, Chalmers, 34–35
Davis, William, 38
debating societies. See literary societies
Debs, Eugene V., 129
DeGioia, John J., 56
Delaware College, 145
Deresiewicz, William, 230
DeSaussure, Henry W., 32
Desmond, Daniel J., 62–63
Development of Academic Freedom in the
United States, The (Hofstadter/Metzger),
258n77
Dimitry, Alexander, 65–66
diploma mills, 230–31
Diverted Dream, The (Brint/Karabel), 206
Donoghue, Frank, 230
Dougherty, Kevin, 201
Douglass, Frederick, 162
Douglass, John Aubrey, 119
Drayton, John, 30–31, 32, 33, 34
DuBois, W. E. B., 151–52, 153, 156, 165
dueling, 40–42
Durkee, James Stanley, 166
Dyson, Walter, 163

Ebony & Ivy (Wilder), 55–56
elementary education, 96; California, 97–98,
99, 100
Elementary Treatise on Mineralogy and Geology
(Cleaveland), 20

Elements of the Philosophy of the Human Mind
(Stewart), 18
Eliot, Charles W., 116
Ely, Richard T., 128
Emergence of the American University, The
(Veysey) 4–6, 251n12
Engell, James, 229
enrollment figures. See under colleges and
universities
equal opportunity, 187–89, 214
Essay Concerning Human Understanding, An
(Locke), 18
Ethical Works (Cicero), 43
ethos, US social, 3, 6, 234, 237n7; affluence,
9–11, 170, 172, 178, 189–90, 192–93,
197–98, 201, 210, 227–28, 232, 234, 235–36;
civic-mindedness, 3, 7, 9, 10, 11, 17–18,
21, 23, 24–28, 30–32, 35–37, 42, 49–50, 52,
57–59, 62–63, 66–69, 74–75, 80, 82, 90, 94,
96, 111, 115–20, 125, 130–32, 134–37, 140–43,
146–47, 153, 164, 175–77, 183–84, 210,
232–36; commercialism, 9, 17–18, 26–27,
68, 83–84, 98, 102, 111–12, 115–26, 130–32,
142, 146–53, 160, 168, 193–98, 201, 228,
234–35; practicality, 8, 11, 19–20, 43, 67–69,
74–80, 83–86, 90–91, 93–95, 98, 99, 101–2,
111, 116–18, 126, 134, 142, 146–47, 156, 234
Euphradian Society (USC), 47
Evidences of Christianity (Paley), 18, 47, 136

faculty, 126, 127–28; adjunct, 230; community
college, 230; institutional conflicts with,
126, 128–30, 185; in research institutions,
192, 194
Fain, Paul, 232
Fallows, Alice Katharine, 148–49
Farmer's College, 75
Fernandez, Jack E., 197–98
Field, Marshall, 116
financial aid, student, 26–27, 189, 229, 232,
240n48
Fisher, Margaret E., 187
Fiske, Lewis R., 82–83, 87, 88
Fitzhugh, George, 47
Flanagan, William F., 209–11, 212
Flexner, Abraham, 234
Florida, 95, 179–81, 186
Florida A&M University, 186
football. See athletics
for-profit institutions. See colleges and
universities, for-profit
Franklin, John Hope, 164
Fraser, James, 98, 99, 251n12, 254n80

Universities in the Marketplace (Bok), 228
University in a Corporate Culture, The (Gould), 228
University, Inc. (Washburn), 228
University of California, Berkeley, 109, 125, 205
University of California, Los Angeles, 109
University of Chicago, 116, 184
University of Florida, 186
University of Georgia, 33, 119, 275n12
University of Michigan, 77, 275n12
University of New Mexico, 223
University of North Carolina, 33, 34
University of Phoenix, 231
University of South Carolina, 2, 7, 30–50, 35, 119; alumni of, 35; curriculum, 42–43, 45; purpose of, 30–32, 37; regulations, 36–39, 40; secession/states' rights and, 44–47, 48–49; slavery and, 47, 48–49; student characteristics, 34–35, 37; student life at, 35–36; student organizations, 47–48, 63–64. See also dueling; gentlemanliness
University of South Florida, 10, 175–99, 181; corporate partnerships, 193, 197; curriculum, 182–83; faculty, 184–85, 192, 233; purpose of, 175, 176–78, 183–84, 189–90, 191; racial makeup of, 186–89, 271n71; research at, 190–96, 198, 273n113; student activism at, 186–87; student characteristics, 175–76, 185, 186–89, 196, 197–98; student organizations, 185, 198
University of Tampa, 186
University of Virginia, 30, 44, 119
US Agricultural Society, 76–77
US News and World Report, 229
USC. See University of South Carolina
useful arts. See practical studies
USF. See University of South Florida

Van Hise, Charles, 119, 235
Vassar College, 134, 140, 143, 148
Veblen, Thorstein, 115–16, 124, 126, 228
veterans, as students, 171
Veysey, Laurence, 4–6, 131, 251n12
Vinton, Maria, 133–34, 148
Virginia Military Institute, 95

vocational education. See community colleges; practical studies

Walker, Francis A., 116
Walker, Scott, 235
Ward, Francis, 60–61
Warren, Donald, 251n12
Washburn, Jennifer, 228
Washington, Booker T., 159, 165
Washington, George, 61
Washington, Michael H., 166
Webster, Daniel, 45–46, 59
Wellesley College, 95, 134, 139–40
West Point, 75, 87
Whipple, George, 163, 265n78
White, Andrew, 116
White, John, 214
Wigfall, Louis, 41
Wilberforce University, 155
Wilbur, Ray Lyman, 119–20, 234–35, 256n23
Willard, Emma, 96
Williams, Edward F., 157, 159
Williams, Joseph R., 79–80, 84, 85, 86–87, 88–89, 111
Williams, Roger L., 76
Williams, Zachery R., 163–64
Wilson, John Lynde, 41
Winchell, Alexander, 128
Wineman, Bradford, 95
Winterer, Caroline, 19
Wisconsin Idea, 119, 235
Witherspoon, John, 17
Witter, William C., 220, 221
women, 135; as administrators, 147, 164, 166, 169; as board members, 164; education and health of, 137; as faculty, 140, 161, 162; lower wages of, 94, 96–97; in nonteaching work, 134, 147, 149–50, 161, 168–69, 170; as schoolteachers, 94, 96–97, 98–99, 102, 168; as students, 90, 95, 97, 106–7, 108, 111, 133–34, 136–37, 148, 149, 157, 161, 167–69, 171, 260n34
Wood, Gordon S., 3
Woodson, Carter G., 164
Wyatt-Brown, Bertram, 36

Yale University, 17–18, 19, 74

Zwerling, L. Steven, 206

CPSIA information can be obtained
at www.ICGtesting.com
Printed in the USA
LVOW11*2041010817

543428LV00005B/80/P

11

CHAD PENNINGTON

NO ONE REALLY KNEW for sure what Chad Pennington was going to turn out to be.

Sure, he was a first-round draft pick, one of the four the Jets had in the first round of the 2000 draft thanks to trading Keyshawn Johnson. But was Pennington, who played for a smaller school, Marshall University, going to be a big fish in a small pond in college and then a small fish in a big ocean in the NFL?

The blond-haired boywonder, who sat quietly and obediently behind veteran Vinny Testaverde until he got his chance at the start of the 2002 season, never really showed who he was until he got a chance to play.

That's when the fun began.

"STICK A FORK IN THEM"

Chad Pennington never seemed like the trash-talking type. He never came off as the I-told-you-so type. He was, after all, a young backup quarterback who

The golden boy of the future, Chad Pennington, celebrates on the field.

hadn't even thrown a pass in anger in the NFL at the time.

However, Pennington's ire—and his competitive side—came out in full force the night the Jets defeated the Raiders to advance to the 2001 playoffs.

The Jets had just come off an uninspiring 14-9 home loss to the 2-12 Buffalo Bills in a game that could have clinched a playoff berth for them, and during the week that followed, *The New York Post* had doubted the Jets' chances of going to Oakland with the pressure of an entire season on them and beating the Raiders to get into the playoffs.

The Post's back-page headline blared: "Stick a Fork in Them."

Inside, the headline with the story read: "Dead Team Walking: The Jets Are Doomed to Miss Playoffs."

Those words irritated the Jets, particularly Pennington.

And so when the Jets prevailed in a dramatic 24-22 victory, propelled by a 53-yard John Hall field goal in the final seconds of the game, Pennington made his presence felt amidst the euphoria of the winning locker room.

Pennington marched right out of the shower, approached the reporter who wrote the story that raised his ire and yelled at the top of his lungs, "Stick a fork in them! Stick a fork in them. What do you have to say about that now?"

PLANE TRUTH

The Jets were at about 30,000 feet when Vinny Testaverde felt this feeling in his gut and decided to tell some teammates about it.

"It's going to happen," Testaverde started telling some of the guys he was closest to.

What he meant was, following a 1-3 start, punctuated by a 28-3 loss in Jacksonville only two hours earlier, Testaverde knew he was going to be benched in favor of Chad Pennington.

At 11:52 a.m. two days later, Herman Edwards confirmed it, announcing Pennington as the starter and doing his best to not hang Testaverde out to dry.

After telling Testaverde and Pennington privately and separately, Edwards called a team meeting and told the players he wasn't blaming Testaverde, but that he had no choice but to make Testaverde the fall guy.

"We're all held accountable, but I think the quarterback is the guy that always takes the hit first, and Vinny understood that," Edwards said. "It's not on Vinny at all. I think it's just the way we've performed."

Testaverde, always the good soldier, bit his tongue hard.

"I'm not going to sit here and tell you I'm getting a raw deal, because that will be the headline," he said. "Anybody in my position isn't happy about it. Understand that I don't want to be a distraction for this football team. I understand how the process works ...

"As you get older, you tend to understand why certain things happen, but that doesn't mean I like it any more. It still bothers me. I feel like if I couldn't help this team win games, it would be OK. But that's not the case."

Pennington, the 18th overall pick in the 2000 draft, tried to act as tough as he could under the difficult circumstance.

"Talk is cheap," he said. "We're going to get the ball into the end zone. I'm not focused on how pretty it looks, how many completions I have, how many touchdown passes I throw. It's about putting points on the board and helping the Jets win."

And so he did. After losing his first game as the starter, Pennington led the Jets to nine wins in their last 12 games and into the playoffs and entrenched himself as "The Franchise."

A SEASON RUINED IN AUGUST

It would have been a devastating blow regardless of when it happened, but that it happened in a meaningless preseason game made it all the more galling.

Quarterback Chad Pennington, the Jets' "franchise," was rolling to his right and taken down by Giants linebacker Brandon Short. Pennington tried to break his fall with his left arm, and as his wrist planted in the grass turf, it all but shattered, leaving the Jets' 2003 season in tatters.

"All of our hearts stopped," Jets running back Curtis Martin recalled. "Chad is an integral part of this team, and for him to go down scared everyone."

Short recalled coming in on a "read" blitz and after running in untouched, grabbing Pennington's legs just as he threw the ball. Pennington fell awkwardly on his left arm.

"He was just lying there," Short said. "I asked him if he was all right, and he just kept lying there until the trainers came out. It's unfortunate to see someone go down like that."

Pennington, who was the catalyst to the 2002 season in his first starting duty by throwing 22 touchdown passes and only six interceptions, was rushed to Lenox Hill Hospital in Manhattan, where he was operated on by Jets orthopedists Dr. Elliott Hershman and Dr. Ken Montgomery.

Adding to the stress of the moment was the fact that as Pennington lay in recovery at Lenox Hill, his father-in-law died following complications from his battle with leukemia.

"I told him, 'We'll be fine. Don't feel bad for us; we feel bad for you,'" Jets head coach Herman Edwards said.

Pennington missed the first six games of the season, and the Jets, who went 2-4 in his absence, never recovered.

12

HERMAN EDWARDS

WHEN HERMAN EDWARDS WAS HIRED on January 18, 2001, he brought with him to New York a sense of passion, enthusiasm, and calm.

Calm is what the Jets needed most based on the fact that Edwards was, technically speaking, the fourth Jets head coach of the millennium. Four head coaches (including Bill Belichick's short tenure) in three years is not the kind of stability and continuity any team is seeking.

In Edwards, the Jets were hiring a man with no NFL head coaching experience. In fact, they were hiring a man with no head coaching experience at all—pro, college, or high school. They were, however, hiring a lifetime NFL man, who had played at the highest level in the NFL as a cornerback, and who had worked as a scout, in personnel, and as an assistant coach.

They landed someone with an immense sense of pride and integrity. They got a good man who would work himself, through experience, into a good head coach.

Edwards, who would be as open and accessible as anyone in the league, provided an interesting opposite to Bill Parcells and his dictatorial style. The hiring of Edwards got immediate approval from those around the league who've known him for years and have helped mold his career.

"He has a personality that I think will play very well in New York," ESPN's Ron Jaworski, a former teammate of Edwards when they were with the Eagles, said. "People want a guy that's dynamic. Herman is dynamic. Herm is the kind of guy New Yorkers are really going to enjoy. What you see is what you get."

FIRED-UP CHREBET

Jets receiver Wayne Chrebet recalled driving in his car in New Jersey and listening to Herman Edwards speak on the live broadcast of the press conference announcing his hiring and finding himself fired up to play—even though it was the off-season.

"I was listening to it on the radio in my car, and he made me want to strap on my helmet, stop the car, get out, and start hitting things," Chrebet said. "He's definitely motivational."

WE WON'T PLAY

Vinny Testaverde was as resolute as he'd ever been behind center or conducting a volatile locker room team meeting.

Vinny Testaverde (16) was a leader on and off the field.

The question, in the wake of the September 11 terrorist acts, was about whether the NFL should play on the following weekend. And a pioneering Testaverde spoke out powerfully for himself and his Jet teammates.

"I think all the games should be canceled this week; I don't think anyone wants to play this week," Testaverde said. "We've never, in our lifetimes, seen anything like this in this country. What happened is a threat to everybody in America. We've been violated. For me being a New Yorker, I'm still waiting on calls that I know I'm going to get that family of friends were in those buildings. Playing football is not what you want to be doing. You want to be mourning the loss of those people and be with your family."

"It's hard to say we should be playing," center Kevin Mawae said. "People in this locker room have neighbors missing. Our children's friends don't have moms and dads any more. As far as this locker room is concerned it's going to be hard to have us play. It's hard to concentrate. Football is probably the least important thing in the world right now."

The mood in that locker room meeting was solemn, yet as serious as it had ever been. The players, to a man, were in support of Testaverde's bold words.

Head coach Herman Edwards was asked his reaction to those who thought the games should have been played to offer Americans a diversion.

"If they want to get some diversion, you know what the country should do? Go to church, go pray. Pray for those that are dead."

SUPPORT

The Jets had no intention of playing even if the games were to remain on the schedule.

Following a conference call with NFL Players Association union chief Gene Upshaw, a handful of Jets veterans, led by Vinny Testaverde, walked into Herman Edwards' office and informed him that, if the NFL planned to go ahead with the games on September 16, the players were prepared to boycott the game. The Jets, Testaverde said, would not board a plane to Oakland, where the team was scheduled to play just five days after the attacks.

"I took it to heart," Edwards recalled. "I told him it was OK to feel that way."

Fortunately, the league reacted to the opinions of the players and the public and canceled the games.

"This is America," Testaverde said. "We mourn, we comfort, and we come together. After a period of time, we get back to a normal way of life. It would be hard for us to fly out of LaGuardia and look at that smoke and rubble as we take off, knowing there's people buried in there and people dead in there."

Jets running back Curtis Martin, who had a close friend barely escape one of the collapsed buildings in the financial district, echoed Testaverde's thoughts.

"I would've lost respect for anyone who tried to force us to play," Martin said. "It would've been disrespectful. There's nothing they could've said to me that would've legitimized it. That would've been one time you saw Curtis Martin rebel."

Another shaken player was Wayne Chrebet, who lost a friend who was working on the 104th floor of the North Tower.

Offensive guard Kerry Jenkins witnessed the horror up close, from the roof of his girlfriend's East Village apartment building in Manhattan.

"I saw more than I needed to see," Jenkins said.

The emotional Edwards, his eyes moistening, said, "We're not robots. You can't plug us in and say, 'Go play.' These players are human beings just like everybody else."

The Jets visit a local fire station in the wake of September 11.

PAYING HOMAGE

Vinny Testaverde's late father, Al, was a mason who helped construct the World Trade Centers.

That's a big part of why he felt compelled to visit the site where the buildings lay crumbled. Testaverde visited Ground Zero and spoke to firefighters and rescue workers who were still trying to dig out possible survivors.

"I felt their pain," Testaverde recalled. "It was just amazing to see a group of people, men and women come together from across the country, but mostly from our area right here, and see how committed they were trying to save lives. You could see their heads were hanging, their morale was low. They hadn't saved anybody, and that was their purpose for going down there. I just wanted to go down and tell them, 'Thanks for all your efforts and thanks for being so brave and stay healthy, stay strong, and keep hope alive.'"

In Testaverde's locker was a section of concrete, about five inches by five inches and two pounds. It had what appeared to be a granite/marble finish. He said he wanted it to symbolize a commitment to what the players do in the locker room in terms of fighting for each other and making a commitment to being stronger together.

JETS VISIT

The Jets visited Ground Zero as a team three days after Vinny Testaverde went there. They did some volunteer work, helping the Red Cross unload tons of bottled water and other beverages to help those in need.

It was a memorable sight—40 huge football players, working like an assembly line, unloading cases and cases of drinks from trucks on the street and into a building for storage.

"After witnessing some of the things I saw, you can't understand or get a feel for the magnitude of the destruction down there and what it's done, not only to the buildings, but to the people and their way of living," Testaverde said.

Testaverde told a story of a man coming up to him in church and informing him that his brother had died in the building. "He asked me if I could get him an autographed football from the team because his

Coach Herman Edwards presents the game ball to the city of New York.

brother was a big Jets fan, and he wanted to leave something to his daughter in memory of him," Testaverde said. "It's just chilling."

RETURN TO WORK

The moment was one that every Jets player will never forget.

Each of them had just filed jubilantly into the cramped Foxboro Stadium visitors locker room after a 10-3 win over the Patriots, greeted with hugs, high-fives, and low-fives from team owner Woody Johnson. Once the entire Jets family was together in the locker room and the doors were closed, head coach Herman Edwards emerged with the game ball in his hands.

"We needed this for a lot of different reasons," Edwards said of the win. "We needed a win like this, one that was in doubt, that was a struggle. This tests your will and belief. This team accepted the challenge."

Edwards then looked at the football he was clutching in the air and said with emotion, "This is going to the city of New York, for all of those people that have worked to try to save lives and all of those who lost their lives. It's only fitting that this ball goes to them."

"It was pretty quiet, and there were some pretty teary eyes," Jets linebacker James Darling recalled. "Everyone was just sitting there thinking about what that meant. It was pretty deep."

The Jets knew they would have to play football again, after a week of games was postponed because of the September 11 attacks. Their win over the Patriots in New England wasn't pretty; both teams were a bit off for obvious reasons. But it was a triumphant return to work.

"This is the first step in getting back to our normal lives," Jets receiver Wayne Chrebet said. "This touches a lot of people. If you don't feel it, you don't have a heart."

FINALLY, A WIN

There would be a blip on the Oakland radar screen in 2001, Herman Edwards' first year as head coach. The Jets went to Oakland for the final game of the regular season in a win-and-they're-in game against the Raiders.

Expectations in the press were low after a home loss to the struggling Buffalo Bills the previous week. The press expected the Jets to let them down with the season on the line.

With the score 22-21, the Jets got within a prayer of a field goal—53 yards. Edwards called to his side kicker John Hall, who had missed a key kick at the end of the 2000 season under Al Groh and had been saved from unemployment by Groh's leaving and Edwards' hiring. Edwards looked him in the eye.

"Can you make it?" he asked bluntly.

"I can make it," Hall answered back.

Edwards sent him out on the field. The ball was snapped, and the kick was straight, but Hall, for whom it was his longest outdoor attempt, waited to see if it had the distance. When Hall's field goal split the uprights, it secured a playoff spot, the first since 1998.

"When he hit it, he hit it," Edwards said. "That thing looked like it was going to go out of the stadium when he hit it."

In the locker room, the Jets were euphoric. Players were so proud of themselves, yelling and screaming in that visiting locker room, where they had felt so much disappointment in the past.

"We shocked the world today," Jets right guard Randy Thomas yelled throughout the locker room.

Kicker John Hall redeemed himself for his 2000 miss against the Detroit Lions when, a year later, he hit the game-winning field goal against the Oakland Raiders.

The Jets were headed to the playoffs with a 10-6 record, and guess who they faced on the road?

Oakland.

"What this football team does is we try to exterminate ghosts," said Edwards, who lead the Jets to three victories in the final four games to earn a postseason berth. "Every time we play there's another ghost. This was another one and we've got a lot more ghosts ahead. We understand that."

PLAYOFF ANGST

A mere six days after one of the most momentous wins in franchise history, that 24-22 win to end the 2001 regular season, the Jets were back in Oakland to play the Raiders in a wild-card playoff showdown. Unfortunately for the Jets, their euphoria would be short lived.

The Raiders' aged receiving corps, led by Jerry Rice, riddled a clueless Jets defense that saw Pro Bowl defensive end John Abraham never make it out of the halftime locker room with what was described as a virus. Abraham was throwing up at halftime, and the Jets couldn't get him right.

The end result was the end of the Jets' season in the form of a 38-24 loss to the Raiders after Rice made the Jets' secondary look silly, catching nine passes for 183 yards and a touchdown.

"It was like volleyball—back and forth, back and forth—and we couldn't stop them," Herman Edwards said, particularly referring to Rice, who seemed all day to be streaking behind the Jets' secondary as though their cornerbacks and safeties were statues back there.

"This is the worst way to end the season," Jets running back Curtis Martin said. "You don't come to the playoffs just to come to the playoffs. You come to get to the Super Bowl. And when it doesn't happen you have to deal with the bitter end. That's what we're dealing with now."

QUITTERS? BITE YOUR TONGUE

This was 2002, and the Jets were 2-5 and on the verge of dumping their second season under Herman Edwards into the Hudson River. Coming off a home loss to the lowly Cleveland Browns in which they blew an 18-point lead, the Jets were readying for a trip to San Diego to play the Chargers, who were 6-1 at the time. The season was, indeed, on the brink.

So several reporters posed a seemingly innocent question to Edwards about whether he was worried about "human nature" taking over the locker room with a sixth loss, one that would surely end the team's already scant playoff hopes, if the possibility of a playoff berth became out of reach.

Edwards took the questions to mean that they were suggesting the team was poised to quit and that he had quitters in his locker room. The tension in the room escalated as Edwards went on a rant that would land him on sports highlight shows across the nation.

As he spoke from the podium inside the press room at Weeb Ewbank Hall, Edwards' face became redder, the veins in his neck began to bulge, and his voice got louder with each sentence.

"Oh no, they're not going to do that," Edwards said. "Not on my watch. It's inexcusable. Don't even think about it. It's called being a professional. They're going to do that. You don't quit in sports; you retire. You don't get to quit. It's not an option, see?

"Someone told me a long time ago that ain't even an option," Edwards went on, referring to his late father, Herman Sr.

"You play to win the game," Edwards continued, his words measured and getting louder by the moment. "Hello ... you play to win the game. You don't play just to play it. I don't care if you don't have any wins, you play to win. When you start telling me it doesn't matter, then retire, get out. Because it matters ...

"This whole conversation bothers me big-time. It really does. You know what? That's what you practice for this week, to get it back up. You get your game plan, you say, 'I'm going to try to win a game, man. I get to go compete.' That's why you're a pro. That's what makes you different than everybody else.

"See, the problem is this is what happens when you lose, people start assuming they quit. Well, this team ain't doing that. It's not an option. Retirement, yeah. Quitting, no. You don't do that in sports. It's ridiculous. That's crazy."

His players, led by quarterback Chad Pennington, backed Edwards up with defiance.

Pennington, speaking in front of his locker less than 30 minutes after Edwards' speech, said, "There's no way on the face of this earth this team is going to quit. There's no doubt in my mind that we're going to keep fighting. Like I've said all year long, it's not over by any stretch of the imagination. I'm aware of the Jets' history, but that's what it is, history. We have to make our own history. I am really focused on putting our name on something and to do whatever it takes to make people remember this team and how we turned it around. Until the door is totally slammed on us, doubt will never creep in. This is a free ticket for us to go out and have fun and play to the best of our abilities."

Added defensive end John Abraham: "I'm not flushing the season down the toilet."

Indeed, the Jets did not flush their season. They used Edwards' words as a rallying cry, smoked the Chargers 44-13 in San Diego, and won seven of their last nine regular-season games.

BAD CHAD

The nightmares in Oakland were hardly over. They came back in the 2002 season for more aggravation. With a chance to seize first place in the AFC East with a win, the Jets lost 26-20 to the Raiders in a game defined by punt returner Chad Morton's fumble of a punt in the second half. Morton, usually a very reliable returner, made a poor decision even trying to field the punt, which was short. He lunged forward, never really secured the catch, and was hit as he tried, losing the ball—and the game for the Jets.

The loss snapped the Jets' four-game winning streak and forced them to make a serious late-season move to make the playoffs again.

"It gets to the point where we really can't breathe," Jets tight end Anthony Becht said. "We're in a do-or-die situation every week. It's to the point of the year where we've got to win every game. We've got to overcome everything."

LAV LASHES OUT

Laveranues Coles was informally named by Herman Edwards as the Jets' Most Valuable Player in the 2002 season. A year later, he was a member of the Washington Redskins because the Jets wouldn't fork over the $13 million signing bonus Washington gave him as a restricted free agent.

Coles, instead of being happy about his new millionaire status, could not keep himself from lashing out at Edwards and the Jets. Coles always did thrive on playing the angry young man, and this case was no different.

"Coach [Edwards] was saying that as long as he's there, I would be," an angry Coles said. "So there was no doubt in my mind. But it never happened."

Laveranues Coles was a valuable receiver for the Jets—but apparently not valuable enough. He left after the Washington Redskins offered him a $13 million signing bonus.

Coles claimed that Edwards promised him during the season that a new contract would be done before the end of the 2002 season.

"I show up early, I'm one of the last ones to leave, you don't read about me in the paper," he said. "Heck, last year my coach named me the MVP before there was a vote. And this is how you say thanks? By making me doubt myself again? When I signed [with the Redskins], I thought everyone would be happy for me. Instead, everyone just said Washington paid too much."

As usual, Edwards took the high road.

"He has the right to feel how he feels," Edwards said. "I like Laveranues as a player. He's a young man who's growing up and maturing, and I think there's a lot more maturing he has to go through. It's a part of the process of him growing, and I'll leave it at that."

GATEGATE

One rainy morning in September 2003, Herman Edwards felt an annoying pinch from the over-the-top security Bill Parcells had brought in to keep the outside world from the Jets' facility.

Parcells had fences and locked gates built all around the facility, precluding anyone from accessing the team parking lot through the press room or from the outside unless they were let in by his security personnel.

He also brought with him a director of security named Steve Yarnell, a former FBI agent with a 24-hour scowl scrawled on his face. Yarnell was in charge of locking the world out.

Edwards, an early riser who's often inside the team facility around 4 a.m. to work out and begin his day, arrived one early rainy morning in September 2003, the opening week of that regular season, to start his day. He punched his personal code into the keypad that controls the front gate, and nothing happened. The gate did not move. He tried again and found himself still locked out.

Edwards, annoyed, got out of his car and climbed the six-foot fence with barbed wire on top.

"Came to work and I thought, 'That's odd; did they fire me already? They didn't let me get to the season yet,'" Edwards joked. "It's the first place I ever came to that they didn't want me to come to work. That's how the day started."

Afterward, he decided he was going to boycott the reserved lot for the coaches, players, and team personnel and park several hundred yards away in one of the Hofstra University student lots.

Edwards immediately had one of the maintenance people remove the "Reserved, Head Coach" sign that stands in the parking space right in front of the players' and coaches' entrance and told his players that spot was open for whomever arrives first each day. He joked that they never personalized that parking sign because the Jets have had so many head coaches over the years.

WEST MEETS EAST

The Jets had arrived in Tokyo for the unorthodox opening of their 2003 preseason schedule, and it didn't take long for the bizarre to take over.

Funny scene No. 1: It was 9:45 a.m. Tokyo time and the elevator in the Tokyo Dome Hotel, occupied by a Japanese family of four, stopped at the 26th floor. The door opened and in sauntered the Jets' mammoth defensive tackle Dwayne Robertson, all 6-foot-1 and 320 pounds of him. That didn't include the fully padded uniform and helmet he was wearing.

It was truly as if Godzilla had entered the elevator as the family of four ceased their conversation, pressed their bodies against the back of the elevator, and gawked as the elevator sank 26 floors down to the ground.

Funny scene No. 2: A gaggle of Japanese onlookers stood slackjawed as Tampa Bay defensive players Warren Sapp and Simeon Rice folded themselves into a tiny taxicab. The President of the United States gathers less attention.

Funny scene No. 3: The Jets' enormous center Kevin Mawae represented the Jets at a noon tea party. Mawae and several teammates later would eschew the authentic Japanese cuisine and eat at a Sizzler steakhouse located in the Americanized team hotel.

"Hey," Mawae quipped, "go with what you know."

Funny scene No. 4: It was 11:15 p.m. local time on a Thursday and the elevator door at the Tokyo Dome Hotel opened. Inside were Jets defensive tackle James

Reed and long snapper James Dearth. Both looked a bit beleaguered.

"How many times have you been to the McDonald's today?" a reporter asked Reed.

"We were trying to go there right now, but it's closed," a downtrodden Dearth interrupted. "We're trying to find something to eat right now."

When another reporter told Dearth that there was a Denny's around the corner, Dearth's face lit up as if he'd just seen Santa Claus and he said, "There's a Denny's? Where? Are they still open?"

ACCOUNTABILITY

In all sports and on all teams, there are accountable players, those who stand up after a loss and explain what happened and why, and there are those who run and hide.

On the Jets, one of the players most notorious over the years for avoiding reporters by hiding in the trainer's room or somewhere else off-limits to reporters was linebacker Mo Lewis.

One day early in the 2003 season, after a loss to the Miami Dolphins, Lewis, as much a part of the Jets' defensive problems as anyone, was merrily on his way into the locker room after a defensive meeting when he saw several reporters in the room, and he stopped dead in his tracks, grumbled about their presence, and took a right-hand turn into the bathroom, which is fortunately off-limits for reporters.

A moment later, fellow linebacker Marvin Jones entered the locker room and stood patiently before reporters answering question after question about the team's problems and 0-2 start.

While Jones answered questions, a young locker room attendant quietly collected sweat pants, a T-shirt, and sneakers out of Lewis' locker so he could deliver them to Lewis where he could get dressed away from reporters.

Even later still, Jets defensive end John Abraham walked into the room and not only answered a litany of questions, but blamed himself for the loss, taking it on his shoulders.

"I'm supposed to be a prime-time player on this team, and I've got to make more plays," Abraham said. "That was probably my worst game since I've been an NFL player. I put that on me. I had a pretty bad game. I didn't play to my potential, my Pro Bowl stature, and I put this loss on me. I was one of the reasons we lost. I didn't have any big plays. People look for me to make big plays. That's what I've got to do."

NICE CALL

No one on Herman Edwards' coaching staff hears and feels more heat than his offensive coordinator Paul Hackett, who seems to receive the wrath for every team offensive failure.

On this one particular morning in 2003 following the injury of Chad Pennington, which necessitated the elevation of Vinny Testaverde to starter, Hackett was greeted by the following telephone message on his voicemail.

"Hey Hackett, I hope you learned something last year," the caller ranted. "Testaverde can't run the West Coast offense. Get yourself a new offense."

"Then the guy hung up," Hackett recalled. "That was my morning."

PRIVATE RELATIONS

The Jets have often had as many problems getting things right off the field as on the field.

One recent gaffe came during the 2003 season after the Jets had spent the entire season promoting their "Four Decades Team," which features players fans voted on with a top player at each position. When the team was announced, you'd have thought the organization would want to promote it and make a big splash of it.

Instead, a mere one-page release was handed out to reporters and some of the facts on that one sheet were incorrect, such as the years some the players had played with the organization.

Two of the players were on the Jets' active roster, linebacker Mo Lewis and defensive end John Abraham, neither of whom were talking to reporters at the time for whatever reason. The Jets' public relations department not only didn't make any of the legendary players, such as Joe Namath, available via conference call, but they could not even get Lewis or Abraham to speak to the press.

So, after their season-long promotion of this thing, the only thing that anyone will remember about the campaign is Joe Namath's nationally televised on-air flirtation with ESPN reporter Suzy Kolber.

REDEMPTION

Even in a year with no playoff berth, the Jets got a slight measure of revenge against the Raiders in Oakland in 2003, beating them 27-24 on a 38-yard overtime field goal by kicker Doug Brien, who was a culprit in a botched overtime field goal situation the week before against the Giants.

"I was up at 5 a.m. almost every morning thinking about what I could have gone differently," Brien said of his previous week's botched attempt. "It was tough to put behind me and tough for the team because it was the Giants. I was tormented by it. I was able to block out all the things that don't matter. When you have something bad happen to you like last week, you want something good to erase it. I'm just glad to be called on again when my teammates needed me."

Quarterback Chad Pennington said, "I'm happiest for Doug, because we win as a team and lose as a team and for him to take all the blame is ludicrous. He stood up like a man, answered the questions, and didn't hide, and he came into a hostile environment and won the game."

For a change, the Jets won in Oakland, albeit against a downtrodden Raiders team.

BILL BETS HERMAN

During the 2003 season Herman Edwards was asked if he could envision himself coaching into his 60s, like Dallas Cowboys coach Bill Parcells has done.

"No ... no way," Edwards, 49, said emphatically. "No. I promise you. That's a promise. I won't do it to myself. I won't, because I literally couldn't do it. I don't have enough energy to last that long. I put too much energy into it. I sleep three, four hours a day. I give everything I can give to this football team, to these players.

"Sixty years old? No way. Ain't no way, ever. If I dream [about coaching beyond 60], I wake up and slap myself. When I wake up my wife and she asks, 'Why did you slap yourself?' and I tell her, then she slaps me and says, 'Are you crazy?' There is no way. No. No. No.

"I like it, but I don't like it that much. In New York it is like dog years, where one year is three. I've been here two years already, which is six. And, when you start off like we've started off, it seems like it's been 10. I'm 49 years old going into my third season. You won't see me at 60, I promise you."

When Parcells, 62 at the time, heard of Edwards' colorful response, he was amused. "Herman said there's no way he'll be coaching when he's 60?" Parcells asked. "Well, you tell Herman I made that statement, only it was 50 [years old]. I think Bill Belichick referred to that one in his departure speech. It's true. You get into where the game beats you down and eats you alive and then you find out [you feel differently later]."

"Here's the best way to describe it: At some point in time the game ceases to be a job and it becomes your life. At some point in time you no longer are ashamed of that. Tell Herman that I have the advantage of a retrospective view, and if he keeps winning like he's been doing, there's a good chance he might keep doing it."

Parcells, explaining for the umpteenth time why he went back into coaching for the umpteenth time, said, "I know some cynics will laugh, but I really didn't think I was ever going to coach again. But then all of a sudden something happens that gets you going and wakes you up and it rekindles what you think and then you don't remember all the crap and the times you're beat down and how this game kills you. It's like your body not remembering pain. Well, your mind doesn't remember the pain either and you say, 'I can do that.' Then you go and you do it.

"I just wanted to try it once more," Parcells went on. "I can't explain to you why. I'll know if it's not going to work and I'll be the first one to know."

Edwards insisted that he understood why Parcells came back after promising everyone when he left the Jets that he'd coached his last game.

"Competitive," Edwards said of Parcells. "He's very, very competitive. That's why guys get out and come back. There's nothing that fulfills that void. Whether you're a player or a coach, that's the void you lose. Some guys can do it when they get out. Some guys do it for a while. Dick Vermeil is the same way. He came back.

You don't get the same adrenaline rush as you do [when you're out of the game].

"The best is when you're playing, to be quite honest, because you can control what's happening. When you're a coach, you live through your players. That's what keeps you in the game."

13

ERIC MANGINI

WHEN ERIC MANGINI WAS HIRED TO replace Herman Edwards in January of 2006, he was immediately hailed as a young genius.

He was replacing Edwards following a dismal 4-12 season and was a direct disciple of the decorated Bill Belichick-Bill Parcells coaching tree.

The Jets and Patriots are bitter rivals, but the reality is the Jets—and most other teams around the league—emulate the Patriots and their winning tradition. That tradition can be directly traced to Belichick's arrival to Foxborough, Massachussets—though the accidental discovery of Tom Brady surely didn't hurt.

As the ever-revolving NFL coaching cycle goes, the Mangini hiring was somewhat predictable in that he was the direct opposite of Edwards.

When an NFL team doesn't find the success it wants from a "players' coach" it goes with the disciplinarian and vice versa. Edwards, a former NFL cornerback, was the quintessential "players' coach."

Mangini represented everything Edwards wasn't—a close-the-ranks, coach-by-paranoia head coach. Edwards was all about openness. Mangini was all about giving out no information and hiding everything.

Belichick used to joke to his assistant coaches about how much information about the Jets he would glean by simply reading about the glut of information Edwards doled out to reporters. Mangini was determined not to be the butt of any Belichick jokes in New England.

While Edwards worked a room full of reporters with the aplomb of a trained professional public speaker, Mangini never looked comfortable in front of the press.

His strengths, though, came not from his sound bites but in his preparation.

"I think the 'wow' is in his work," Terry Bradway, the general manager at the time Mangini was hired, said. "He's a good teacher. He wants smart, hardworking players. He's very detailed, very confident. He knows what he wants to do."

BORDER WAR HEATS UP

When Mangini, who had never been a head coach on any level, interviewed with the Jets and was offered the position, Belichick implored him not to take the job.

Belichick, who holds a famous disdain for the Jets, told Mangini a better opportunity would come his way. Mangini, whose father died too young, wasn't so sure of that and wanted to pounce on the chance while it was before him.

That created a significant rift between the two and heated up the famous "border war" between the Jets and Patriots.

Just hours after Mangini accepted the Jets job, his security card-key to get into the Patriots' building—and his office—had been deactivated, so he was locked out. His office belongings were even withheld for weeks before they were finally sent to him in boxes.

It was a disappointing end to a relationship Mangini cherished with Belichick who had become not only his mentor but a close friend. Mangini and his wife Julie would travel with Belichick and his wife to Bruce Springsteen concerts and socialize together.

Mangini began his NFL career as a public relations assistant and then a ball boy and a go-fer with the Cleveland Browns when Belichick was the head coach there.

Belichick, recognizing Mangini's smarts hunger, started to give him some football assignments. He went from ordering pizza for the Browns beat writers to delivering valuable coaching information to Belichick.

Now, years later, the apprentice accepting the Jets job against Belichick's will was unacceptable to the mentor, who would now have to coach against his former student.

This, of course, would lead to some fascinating subplots in the Jets-Patriots rivalry.

Mangini, upon his hiring, insisted he would be his own man. The reality is he tried too much to be Belichick initially, but grew more and more comfortable with his methods as he progressed on the job.

"I've got tremendous mentors," Mangini said. "I worked with some of the greatest coaching minds in the NFL. I am not Bill Belichick and I am not Bill Parcells. I am Eric Mangini and I'm going to approach it my way."

Mangini spent 10 of his 11 NFL seasons working under Belichick with the Browns (1995), Jets (1997-99), and Patriots (2000-2005).

IGNITING A FLAME

Mangini's presence became an instant lit match to the Belichick gasoline. What had already been a heated rivalry was now stoked to a different level because of Belichick's hatred for the Jets and disdain for Mangini.

Mangini's Jets split the regular-season series with New England in Mangini's rookie year, and then the two teams met in a wildcard playoff game in which the Patriots beat the Jets 37-16.

This was only the beginning, though.

The teams' first meeting, September 17, 2006 in Mangini's second game as head coach, the Patriots won, 24-17, but the lead-up to the game was even more entertaining.

In a mid-week conference call with New York reporters, Belichick refused to acknowledge Mangini. In an embarrassing, petty display, Belichick refused to even use Mangini's name while speaking to reporters.

When asked if he'll root for Mangini to do well in his career, Belichick said, "I'm more concerned about us doing well. Really, I don't sit around, cheering for everybody else."

When the Jets and Patriots met again that year, on November 12 in Foxborough, Massachusetts, the Jets won 17-14.

In the pregame conference call that week, Belichick was again icy to the point of disrespectful toward Mangini.

When asked what kind of job Mangini had done with the Jets, Belichick blandly droned on, saying, "I think the

Jets are a very good football team. They're a very talented team, and they're a very explosive team in all three phases of the game. They play that way on a weekly basis."

Through it all, Mangini remained resolute in his admiration for his mentor.

"My feelings on Bill haven't changed," Mangini said. "I talked quite a bit last time [before the teams' September 17 meeting at Giants Stadium] how important he was to my career, and how much I appreciate that. So nothing has changed for me in that sense."

HANDSHAKE DISAGREEMENT

Some of the highlight moments from the three games the Jets and Patriots played in 2006 centered around the postgame handshakes between Mangini and Belichick.

Following the Jets Week Two loss to the Patriots, Belichick barely acknowledged Mangini when Mangini approached him to give him the customary congratulatory handshake at midfield.

After the Jets won the second meeting, Belichick didn't even look at Mangini and gave him the wet fish handshake.

Because Belichick had created so much attention on the handshake ceremony from the first two games, the playoff game provided the best theater of all.

After the wildcard game the Patriots won, Belichick, surrounded by photographers, angrily shoved a snapper away from him as he made it a point to meet Mangini like a man at midfield for the handshake.

After the game, when asked about it, Belichick reacted with his usual indifference.

"Do you want to talk about the game?" he said tersely. ``I'm not going to get into a postgame handshake analysis here. Really, I've had enough of that."

Mangini said after the game that Belichick told him, "Good luck."

Despite the calamity, Mangini's appreciation for what Belichick did for him remained unwavering.

"I can't say enough about what I learned from Bill Belichick," Mangini said. "Bill has always been very support-ive of the things I've done, and has helped me throughout my career. I can't thank him enough for the opportunities he's given me.

"There are so many things you can learn from him. He's incredibly smart, he's extremely hard-working, and it doesn't matter how much success he's had, he approaches things the same way week in and week out. His focus is amazing."

In the seven games they coached against each other, Mangini went 2-5 against Belichick as the Jets head coach.

MANGENIUS IS IN THE HOUSE

Mangini's first year as Jets head coach not only pro-duced a 10-6 record and a playoff berth, but it propelled him into pop culture.

He became such a success so quickly, the New York tabloids gave him the back page nickname "Mangenius."

It stuck so well that the hit HBO series, The Sopranos asked him onto the set for a cameo.

In his scene, Mangini is dining with his wife at the New Jersey restaurant owned by Artie Bucco, who says to Tony Soprano, eating at a nearby table, "Hey, Tone. You know who's in tonight? Mangenius."

Three years after his tenure, though, "Mangenius" wasn't perceived that way anymore.

BRETT FAVRE

Little did anyone know it at the time, but Brett Favre's arrival to the Jets in 2008 marked the beginning of the end for Mangini's tenure as the Jets head coach.

After Mangini had worked with quarterbacks Chad Pennington and Kellen Clemens for the entire offseason, Jets owner Woody Johnson and general manager Mike Tannenbaum got a sniff of Favre's availability and they jumped at the opportunity.

The Jets traded for Favre in August of 2008 and so began a whirlwind ride that would not end well for the Jets and particularly Mangini.

All the offseason work Mangini and offensive coordinator Brian Schottenheimer had put in with Pennington and Clemens was moot and they were suddenly thrust into getting Favre ready with precious little time before the season would start.

Mangini, who warned Johnson and Tannenbaum of the potential pitfalls of the ballyhooed transaction, played the good soldier and even helped recruit Favre to New Jersey by researching places for him to hunt in his free time.

But make no mistake—Mangini knew this was a mistake all along. Favre was at the end of his career and had almost no time to learn the system.

"The goal was to build an organization for the long term, not the short-term," Mangini said.

Mangini said all of a sudden with Favre available, "the plan wasn't the plan anymore."

There was so much more to the Favre trade than merely winning football games. The Jets and Giants were about to open a new stadium and they were force-feeding high-priced public seat licenses (PSLs) on their fans. That created a desperation to create a buzz around the team.

Johnson would never admit it publicly, but Favre was as much brought in as a draw for excitement to sell PSLs.

Mangini understood the powerful forces at play were larger than his needs, so he tried to make the best of his owner's fascination with Favre.

"There were going to be some exciting plays and there were going to be some interceptions and we were going to win some games and lose some games based on that," Mangini said. "Brett was great for a lot of reasons and there are other things that happen that aren't always great. You're not going to change him. He's not going to be different wearing our uniform than he was wearing another uniform.

"With all the good there comes some downside, and you've got to live with both. You've got to be honest about what it is. That's where I thought things were."

The Favre experiment looked good for awhile, as the Jets opened the 2008 season with an 8-3 record and they looked like one of the best teams in the league.

Favre's performance suddenly dropped off the face of the planet and he went from being the toast of the NFL to looking like a guy twice his age. He suddenly couldn't complete the simplest of passes and instead became an interception machine.

The final indignity for Mangini and the Jets came on the last day of the regular season, when they played the Dolphins, who'd signed Pennington after the Jets released him when they traded for Favre. With a win that day, the Jets had a chance to make the playoffs, but Pennington beat them.

So Pennington took the Dolphins to the playoffs while Favre and the Jets went home.

FRIGHTFUL FINISH

The Jets staggered home to a 9-7 record and missed the playoffs and Mangini was fired before the tears dried on the cheeks of the devastated fans.

It all unfolded badly for the Jets after the 8-3 start and talk around New York about a Super Bowl. The Jets lose their mojo after the 8-3 start, losing four of their last five games.

The ugly stretch included excruciating losses to the Denver Broncos at home (34-17), the San Francisco 49ers on the road (24-14), the Seattle Seahawks on the road (13-3) and finally the Dolphins at home (24-17).

One week after the Jets beat the league-best Tennessee Titans to get to 8-3, they let Broncos quarterback Jay Cutler throw for 357 yards and two touchdowns on them.

"We realize we're not as good as we thought we were," Jets running back Leon Washington said after the game.

While Cutler flourished in the cold, wet and windy conditions, Favre struggled, finishing 23-of-43 for 247 yards and an interception.

The Jets began to spiral with the loss against a 49ers team that had little to play for and was nowhere near playoff contention.

For the second consecutive week, the Jets struggled on offense, managing only 182 total yards. Favre (20-for-31, 137 yards) was unable to take advantage of a mediocre defense.

The loss in Seattle was a low point for the Jets. Favre was awful, throwing two more interceptions while the Jets scored a season-low three points against one of the league's lowest-ranked defenses.

"We knew what was at stake and we didn't take advantage of it," Favre said afterward. "It's not good enough. That's the bottom line."

The loss left the Jets at (9-6) and needing to beat AFC East co-leading Miami at home the next week along with either New England or Baltimore losing to get in the playoffs.

You know the rest: Dolphins 24, Jets 17.

This was the end for Mangini and Favre and delicious revenge for Pennington.

When it was all over—when Mangini's three-year ride was finished—he didn't sidestep his hand in all of it.

"I'm not by any means saying I couldn't have done better that stretch run," Mangini said. "I'm not absolving myself from accountability. But when you throw a lot of touchdowns you throw a lot of picks (interceptions). Sometimes that leads to wins, sometimes it leads to losses.

"The plan was the plan and we were all together and everybody was in, and at the end of the day the plan changed and someone had to pay."

14

REX RYAN

THE NFL HEAD COACHING CYCLES WERE AT IT AGAIN after Mangini was let go.

The rigid Mangini was predictably replaced by a man who's so loose it made you wonder if he was chosen by team owner Woody Johnson after winning some sort of fan contest.

It didn't take long, however, for Rex Ryan to show the league that he was no "coach for a day" contest winner. Ryan, despite his swashbuckling, shoot-from-the-hip style, showed he was the real deal by quickly backing up his words of bravado.

Building the best defense in the NFL—almost overnight—and reaching the AFC Championship Game with a rookie starting at quarterback (Mark Sanchez) will do that.

With each day and each bold prediction, Ryan continued to build his legend. The Jets, under Ryan's watch, would get to the AFC Championship game in his second season, 2010, as well.

Suddenly for all the good things Mangini built in his three seasons, and despite what was unquestionably an unfair dismissal, all of that was forgotten, because the present and the future under Ryan seemed limitless—not to mention sure to be a fun ride.

• • •

Ryan immediately began to forge his legend with his introductory press conference.

It was there, in front of a roomful of reporters, that Ryan told everyone that he planned to make a visit to the White House with his team as Super Bowl champions within the next few years.

"With all the cameras and all that, I was looking for our new president back there," Ryan said to the full house. You know, I think we'll get to meet him in the next couple years anyway."

Later, explaining his uncommon bravado, Ryan said matter-of-factly, "I'm not afraid of expectations. My goal is to win a Super Bowl. It's not to just win X number of games."

Ryan, who came to the Jets after four years as the Baltimore Ravens defensive coordinator, added, "We want to be known as the most physical football team in the NFL. The players will have each other's backs, and if you take a swipe at one of ours, we'll take a swipe at two of yours.

"We expect to win," Ryan said. "We have a lot of talent here that's already in place."

Ryan, who was the last remaining defensive assistant from the Baltimore Ravens' 2000 Super Bowl team, had interviewed for head coaching jobs with the San Diego Chargers, Atlanta Falcons, Miami Dolphins, St. Louis Rams, and Ravens in the two years before the Jets hired him.

"I'm not a one-hit wonder," Ryan said. "When you look at my background, I think I've been successful at all stops along the way. I know the kind of responsibility it takes to be a head football coach."

One of Ryan's most famous lines came before his rookie season began when he said, "I didn't come here to kiss Bill Belichick's rings," referring to the three Super Bowl rings Belichick won with the Patriots.

Those words would forever be brought back up every time the rivals would play against each other.

VIVA SANCHEZ

Once the Jets got through free agency, they made a big move in the draft—Ryan's first with the team.

Enter Mark Sanchez, who the Jets traded up 12 spots in the 2009 NFL Draft to pick. The Jets' trading partner? The Cleveland Browns, who were coached by Mangini.

The Jets traded their No. 17 overall pick in the first round along with their second-round pick (No. 52 overall), and defensive end Kenyon Coleman, safety Abram Elam and quarterback Brett Ratliff.

The acquisition of Sanchez quickly answered the question everyone already knew the answer to: The Favre era was over.

Sanchez would be the new face of the franchise—other than Ryan, of course.

This move did not come without risk, however. Sanchez, who came out a year early with one more year of eligibility remaining at USC, started only 16 games in college, raising questions about how ready he'd be for the NFL as a starter right away.

In fact, his college coach, Pete Carroll, made some controversial public comments, saying that he thought Sanchez was making a mistake by coming out when he did and that he needed another year of college ball to develop.

Though his first year wasn't without a good dose of unwanted and drama, Sanchez would take little time proving Carroll wrong. Helping take his team to the AFC Championship as a rookie will do that.

CALAMITY RULES

Along the way to helping the Jets get to the AFC title game, Sanchez endured his share of forgettable moments on his eventful rookie season.

He won his first game as a pro, completing 18-of-31 passes for 272 yards and a touchdown in a 24-7 win over the Texans in Houston.

Sanchez made it 2-0 when the Jets beat the Patriots 16-9 and then led the Jets to 3-0 with a win over the Tennessee Titans.

The bubble, however, burst in a rather magnificent way in Week 4, however, as Sanchez literally threw the Jets' game against the Saints, who were also 3-0, in New Orleans.

After looking so poised the first three games, Sanchez looked like the wide-eyed rookie he was in the New Orleans Superdome, turning the ball over four times—three interceptions (one returned for a touchdown) and one fumble in the Jets end zone that was recovered by the Saints for a touchdown.

So Sanchez gave the Saints 14 points in a 24-10 loss.

"The kid, Sanchez, at times he looked like a rookie today," Ryan said.

"My mistakes absolutely killed us," Sanchez said.

Two weeks later Sanchez looked even worse in a 16-13 home loss to the Buffalo Bills, throwing five interceptions in the game. Those five interceptions, including one in overtime, led directly to 13 of Buffalo's 16 points.

"Just an embarrassing day," Sanchez said afterward. "I've never played like this. Ever. Not even close. This is bad. To be perfectly honest, I don't know if I can play any worse."

Sanchez was 10-of-29 for 119 yards, five interceptions and a staggering 8.3 rating. He completed half as many passes (five) to the Bills as he did to his own receivers (10).

Sanchez, too, had some issues with the way he scrambled, sometimes refusing to slide feet-first.

That bad habit led to some injury issues and it led Ryan to call New York Yankees manager Joe Girardi, who came to the Jets training facility in New Jersey and tutored Sanchez on the proper sliding techniques.

There, too, were issues with Sanchez' decision making in games. Offensive coordinator Brian Schottenheimer became so exasperated at Sanchez trying to force passes into receivers that would be picked off, that he devised a color code system for his rookie quarterback.

If the coaches on the sideline flashed a yellow card it meant for Sanchez to act with added caution and just throw the ball away if no one was open.

The whole thing was met with some humor and cynicism, but Sanchez handled it like a professional and did what the coaches asked.

In the end, it made him a better quarterback as the playoffs approached.

DID I SAY THAT?

One of the most memorable and bizarre sequences of the Ryan first season came after the Jets lost to the Atlanta Falcons 10-7 at home to fall to 7-7.

Ryan was so upset following the game that he declared the Jets' playoff chances dead.

"This is tough, because we're obviously out of the playoffs," he said. "We thought we had a great chance to make it to the playoffs. This is hugely disappointing."

The next day, though, Ryan was informed that the Jets weren't mathematically eliminated from contention quite yet and he stood before reporters and spoke about his embarrassing gaffe.

"First off, I was dead wrong in the playoff scenario," Ryan said. "You would think that the head coach of the team would know the (playoff) situations. I thought we had to win out. We had a single focus that we were going to have to win six straight games (after the 4-6 start).

"We don't (just) have a possibility; we have a huge possibility—if we'll win out—that we can be in the playoffs. We're actually in a better situation right now, this week, than we were last week at this time. That's unbelievable. We're there. We've got a chance. To make the playoffs and, hey, we're going for it.

The scenario for which the Jets to get into the playoffs was complicated and a long shot but was presented in a power point presentation to the players by Ryan on the Monday after the Atlanta loss.

Ryan showed the players the way how they could control their own destiny entering the final week of the season.

Incredibly, every scenario the Jets needed happened and they got into the playoffs.

Making the entire episode even more surreal was the Jets second-to-last game against the Colts, who were 14-0 at the time and decided to pull their starters in the third quarter to rest for the postseason.

The controversial decision by the Colts helped the Jets win 29-15 and keep their playoff hopes alive.

In the regular-season finale against the Bengals, Cincinnati didn't need the win because it had already clinched its division title, was going to hold a playoff game and wouldn't change its postseason seeding.

The Jets routed the Bengals 37-0 and made the playoffs.

That earned them a wildcard playoff game against the Bengals the following week in Cincinnati, where they'd win 24-14 to earn a trip to San Diego to play the favored Chargers.

"This was just the first step in what we think is going to be a great journey," Ryan said.

Indeed, the journey would continue.

The Jets beat the Chargers 17-14 to advance to the AFC Championship game for the first time since 1998. Their opponent: The Colts.

"I don't think anybody could have drawn it up any better

than this," Jets linebacker Calvin Pace said.

The Jets, who hadn't won a Super Bowl (or even gotten to one) since 1968, were 60 minutes away.

"We definitely feel like this is our year," Jets right guard Brandon Moore said.

THE AFC CHAMPIONSHIP

The AFC Championship game turned out to be a horrible tease for the Jets. After leading 17-13 at halftime, they lost 30-17 because their secondary couldn't contain Peyton Manning and the Colts' passing game.

"We expected to go to the Super Bowl," right tackle Damien Woody said. "And to come so far ... it was right there sitting in front of us and yet so far away. We were 30 minutes way."

Safety Jim Leonhard said, "This will eat us up all offseason. When you come up short there are a lot of thoughts that go through your head. You could see all across this locker room, guys are like, 'Where do we go from here? What do we do now?'

"We feel like we're ready to take that next step. We felt like we were ready this year. Maybe we weren't. But we'll prepare next season to take that next step."

2010: THE NEXT STEP

The Jets, indeed, looked like a better, more organized team in 2010, and they would again reach the AFC Championship game. But the result would be the same. They finished one win short of the Super Bowl.

The Jets craftily added key talent to the 2010 team, including enigmatic cornerback Antonio Cromartie, a physical freak of nature whose play was up and down in his career. They, too, made a trade for receiver Santonio Holmes, a big playmaker who was facing a four-game suspension to start the season for violating failing the NFL's substance abuse policy.

They also released workhorse running back Thomas Jones and signed LaDainian Tomlinson, a better pass receiver out of the backfield than Jones and considered a better fit in a two-back rotation with Shonn Greene.

Oh yes, and the flashy Jets also signed on to be the stars of the HBO series Hard Knocks, which would chronicle their every move in training camp.

WHERE'S DARRELLE?

That HBO thing all sounded great except for the fact that Darrelle Revis, the Jets' All-Pro cornerback, held out of camp for a new contract in a dispute that became bitter.

So the Revis holdout dominated training camp.

When he finally reached an agreement with the team and joined them in a practice at their New Jersey facility, Revis got a special greeting from his teammates.

As he walked slowly to the practice field, players bowed to their knees and chanted "Revis Christ" and then broke into a slow and steady "Rudy" clap.

"I had butterflies," Revis said. "I didn't know how my teammates were going to accept be because I hadn't been here for a month. But after they started chanting my name and it was a good feeling to see the guys and wanting to be around them."

The Revis saga would continue into the regular season when he pulled a hamstring unsuccessfully trying to stop a Randy Moss touchdown catch in the second week of the season. For a player who missed an entire summer of training camp, it was a cliché injury and it cost Revis a couple of weeks of games.

ROUGH START

The summer of Hard Knocks fame, the key offseason acquisitions and the second year of Sanchez development and more Ryan bluster created an incredible buzz for the beginning of the 2010 season, which would begin against Ryan's former team, the Ravens, under the glare of the first Monday Night Football game telecast of the season.

The Jets committed 14 penalties for 125 yards and their offense was putrid in the game (six first downs) and they lost 10-9, also losing starting nose tackle Kris Jenkins for the season to a knee injury early in the game.

After the game, the Ravens chirped about all the Jets' pregame talk.

"Rex put a bull's eye on them," Ravens running back Ray Rice said.

"That's not who we are; that's not how we play," Ryan insisted after the game. "That was a joke."

RIGHTED SHIP AGAINST HATED RIVAL

The disappointment of the season-opener loss was quickly quelled when the Jets whipped the Patriots 28-14 by outscoring them 18-0 in the second half. "We're back to being who we think we are," Rex Ryan said after the game.

"To hear everyone say we were pretenders not contenders, that pissed us off," receiver Braylon Edwards said. "Today showed who we really are."

Sanchez outplayed Tom Brady, throwing for three touchdowns.

"This is just the beginning for us," Sanchez said.

WILD RIDE

The Jets propelled themselves to a 5-1 record entering their bye week and expectations were as lofty as they'd been in years.

After Ryan gave the players the better part of a week off, they responded by sleepwalking through a 9-0 home loss to the Green Bay Packers—the first time they'd been shut out in four years. The disappointing loss to the Packers, however, wouldn't turn into a prolonged losing streak the way it did the year before.

They rebounded with an overtime win against the Lions in Detroit, where after the Jets offense struggled for the first 55 minutes, Sanchez led the Jets back from a 10-point fourth-quarter deficit for a 23-20 overtime win.

Nick Folk's winning field goal in overtime was set up by a 52-yard catch-and-run by Holmes.

After going his entire rookie year without a fourth quarter comeback victory on his resume, the Detroit game was the second such comeback in three games Sanchez helped engineer—a 24-20 win at Denver the game before the bye week being the first.

A week later, the script would be similar. This time it was a 26-20 overtime win over the Browns in Cleveland. That made the Jets the first team in NFL history to win back-to-back overtime games on the road.

There were two intriguing subplots to the week and the game—Mangini coaching the Browns against his former team and Rex coaching against his twin brother, Rob, who was Mangini's defensive coordinator.

"Clearly, (the game) wasn't just personal for me, it was personal for a lot of guys," Rex said after the game. "But like I told the guys, at 1 o'clock, (the Browns) are nameless, faceless objects and that's what you have to treat it as. Whether it's your twin brother, your friend or whomever, you've got a job to do."

The cardiac Jets won another thriller the next week, beating the Houston Texans in a remarkable late comeback after blowing 23-7 fourth-quarter lead. Holmes caught the game-winning TD with seconds remaining.

It was the third consecutive game that Holmes made the decisive play the win the game, and the fourth in five games.

"Santonio's been the home run hitter we thought he was going to be," Jets linebacker Calvin Pace said.

"The guy is a gamer," Sanchez said. The win gave the Jets an 8-2 record, tying them for the best record in the NFL and with the Patriots for first place in the AFC East.

JETS-PATRIOTS, PART DEUX

A win over the Bengals on Thanksgiving set the fascinating stage for the 9-2 Jets to play the 9-2 Patriots at Gillette Stadium.After arriving to Foxborough, Massachussets. with hopes of seizing control of the AFC East, the Jets staggered out stunned by a 45-3 loss.

"The biggest butt whipping I've ever taken as a coach," Ryan said. "We were outplayed and outcoached."

Before the game, Ryan ranted about how he was going to take it to Belichick. "I came in to kick his butt and he kicked mine," Ryan said. "We knew this was a big division game and we thought we would put a stranglehold on it. We could have been up one game on them and the tiebreaker. Now they've won one and we've won one."

NO DIVISION TITLE, NO PROBLEM

The loss to New England derailed the Jets' chances of winning the division, but it hardly dampened their spirits.

Three days after the loss, the always creative Ryan gathered his players together at one end of the practice fields, dug a hole in the ground with a shovel and buried the game ball from the Patriots loss.

The Jets would lose to the Dolphins 10-6 at home the following week, but righted themselves with a tough 22-17 win over the Steelers in Pittsburgh to get to 10 wins.Based on the way the Jets limped into the game playing and how tough the Steelers are at home, it was a significant upset.

"We said we were going to come in here and weren't going to leave without a win," Jets receiver Jerricho Cotchery said.

The victory gave the Jets a two-game lead for wildcard berth with two to play. It was their first win in Pittsburgh in eight tries.

The night before the game Ryan delivered a Saturday night speech to his players that got so intense it had tears in Ryan's eyes.

"His passion fueled us as a team," Jets right tackle Wayne Hunter said. " "He welled up, he got emotional and we took it as a personal challenge. Rex is very emotional guy and just seeing that passion in his heart and seeing the passion in his eyes fired us up. The game could not come any sooner."

THE POSTSEASON

It wouldn't be Ryan and the Jets if there wasn't some delicious drama and irony added to the mix.

So the Jets first playoff opponent would be the same Colts team that ended their Super Bowl dreams the year before.

Colts quarterback Peyton Manning had become a nemesis for Ryan, having beaten him in five of six games against him. The only Ryan win over Manning's Colts came in that 2009 regular-season game in which the Colts pulled their starters in the second half to rest for the playoffs.

In the five Manning-led wins over Ryan the Colts had outscored the Ryan-coached teams 144-53 with Manning going 94-of-150 for 1,321 yards, 12 TDs and two INTs. Two of those five wins came in the postseason, ending Ryan's season.

Because of that, Ryan began the week leading up to the game saying this time it was going to be "personal" against Manning.

"Is it personal? Yes, it's personal," Ryan said, unprovoked. "It's personal against him, Reggie Wayne, all those guys, yeah. (Dwight) Freeney and (Robert) Mathis and those other dudes? Absolutely. Peyton Manning has beaten me twice in the playoffs. That's well-documented. You've got all the stats. But this is about this year, and I've waited a whole year for this."

The Jets finally overcame the Colts, winning 17-16 on a 32-yard game-winning field goal by Nick Folk as time expired in Indianapolis. That propelled the Jets to a third showdown of the year against the Patriots.

JETS-PATRIOTS III

Ryan, in his unique, aggressive motivational ways, this time called this game "personal" between him and Belichick, setting the tone for yet more dramatics.

"This week is about Bill Belichick against Rex Ryan," Ryan told reporters at the start the hype week. "It's personal. It's about him against me and that's what it's going to come down to. This is going to be about me raising my level against Bill Belichick. I recognize he's the best, but I'm just trying to be the best on Sunday. I plan on being the best coach on Sunday. I recognize that my level has to come up and he's going to get my best shot. He's going to get everything I have on Sunday. If he slips at all, we're going to beat him."

Belichick and the Patriots did slip a bit and the Jets pounced, winning 28-21 to earn a second trip to Pittsburgh to play the Steelers—this time in the AFC Championship game with a Super Bowl berth on the line.

Before the game, Ryan was at his motivational genius best, bringing in former Jets defensive end Dennis Byrd as a surprise speaker at the Saturday night team meeting. Byrd stood before the Jets players with the actual jersey that was cut away from his paralyzed body after a collision ended his career in 1992.

After the game, players spoke about how moved they were at Byrd's powerful message, which was that he would do it all over again, give everything he had in his life away to play in one more game like the one the Jets were about to play the next day.

Entering the game, the Patriots had been 8-0 at home and Brady had won an NFL-record 28 consecutive games at home.

Ryan's defense was the star of this show, stifling a Patriots offense that entered the game having scored 30 or more points in their last eight games and was averaging 32.4 points per game.

Jets defensive tackle Trevor Pryce reveled in the confused look in Brady's eyes in the game.

"He was terrified," Pryce said. "It's shocking because you don't see it very often. The game plan was out of sight. We did some stuff I've never seen a pro football coach do. It was craziest thing I ever saw.

"Tom Brady is going to look at the film tomorrow and say, 'Oh, that's what they were doing.' Well, too late mother (bleeper). We confused a Hall of Fame quarterback, but we think we have a Hall of Fame coach."

PITTSBURGH, PART DEUX

The Jets hadn't been to the Super Bowl since the 1968-69 season when Joe Namath made history.

They felt this was their time—a year removed from the disappointing end in Indianapolis.

The Jets, who'd been to three AFC Championship games in the 42 years since their lone Super Bowl victory and lost all three, felt like the fourth would be a charm.

It wasn't.

They trailed 24-3 at the half and a furious second-half rally fell short in a 24-19 loss."This was our year," Cotchery said after the loss. "Last year hurt, but this hurts even more because this was our year and the Steelers took it from us."Jets veteran linebacker Jason Taylor, finishing his 14th season, called it "the toughest loss I've ever been a part of."

"We were so close you could see it, you could smell it, feel it," Taylor said.

"There's no tomorrow now," Jets defensive tackle Sione Pouha said. "We go home now."Ryan was crestfallen, his eyes reddened from crying in the locker room as he stood before reporters after the loss.

"Of course it's emotional," Ryan said. "We came up short. One game short again. It cuts your heart out. It's supposed to hurt. Our goal for next year won't change and it'll never change. We're going to chase that Super Bowl and chase it until we get it. And then we'll chase it again after that."